D0921023

Fundamentalism, Sectarianism, and Revolution is a major comparative analysis of fundamentalist movements in cultural and political context, with an emphasis on the contemporary scene. Leading sociologist S. N. Eisenstadt examines the meaning of the global rise of fundamentalism as one very forceful contemporary response to tensions in modernity and the dynamics of civilizations. He compares modern fundamentalist movements with the protofundamentalist movements which arose in the great "Axial Civilizations" in pre-modern times; he shows how the great revolutions in Europe which arose in connection with these movements shaped the political and cultural programs of modernity; and he contrasts post-World War II Muslim, Jewish, and Protestant fundamentalist movements with communal national movements, notably in Asia. The central theme of the book is the distinctively Jacobin features of fundamentalist movements and their ambivalent attitude to tradition: above all their attempts to essentialize tradition in an ideologically totalistic way.

S. N. Eisenstadt is Rose Isaacs Professor Emeritus of Sociology at the Hebrew University of Jerusalem and Senior Fellow, The Van Leer Jerusalem Institute. He has served as a visiting professor at numerous universities, including Harvard, Stanford, MIT, Chicago, Michigan, Washington, Oslo, Zurich, and Vienna. He is the recipient of a number of awards, among them the International Balzan Prize in Sociology and the McIver award of the American Sociological Association. He is the author of numerous books and articles; his recent publications include *Power, Trust and Meaning* (1995) and *Japanese Civilization* (1996).

Fundamentalism, Sectarianism, and Revolution

Cambridge Cultural Social Studies

Series editors: JEFFREY C. ALEXANDER, *Department of Sociology, University of California, Los Angeles, and* STEVEN SEIDMAN, *Department of Sociology, University at Albany, State University of New York.*

Titles in the series

ILANA FRIEDRICH SILBER, *Virtuosity, charisma, and social order*
0 521 41397 4 hardback

LINDA NICHOLSON AND STEVEN SEIDMAN (eds.), *Social postmodernism* 0 521 47516 3 hardback 0 521 47571 6 paperback

WILLIAM BOGARD, *The simulation of surveillance* 0 521 55081 5 hardback 0 521 55561 2 paperback

SUZANNE R. KIRSCHNER, *The religious and Romantic origins of psychoanalysis* 0 521 44401 2 hardback 0 521 55560 4 paperback

PAUL LICHTERMAN, *The search for political community* 0 521 48286 0 hardback 0 521 48343 3 paperback

ROGER FRIEDLAND AND RICHARD HECHT, *To rule Jerusalem* 0 521 44046 7 paperback

KENNETH H. TUCKER, *French revolutionary syndicalism and the public sphere* 0 521 56359 3 hardback

ERIK RINGMAR, *Identity, interest and action* 0 521 56314 3 hardback

ALBERTO MELUCCI, *The playing self* 0 521 56401 8 hardback 0 521 56482 4 paperback

ALBERTO MELUCCI, *Challenging codes* 0 521 57051 4 hardback 0 521 57843 4 paperback

SARAH M. CORSE, *Nationalism and literature* 0 521 57002 6 hardback 0 521 57912 0 paperback

DARNELL M. HUNT, *Screening the Los Angeles "riots"* 0 521 57087 5 hardback 0 521 57814 0 paperback

LYNETTE P. SPILLMAN, *Nation and commemoration* 0 521 57404 8 hardback 0 521 57432 3 paperback

MICHAEL MULKAY, *The embryo research debate*, 0 521 57180 4 hardback 0 521 57683 0 paperback

LYNN RAPAPORT, *Jews in Germany after the Holocaust* 0 521 58219 9 hardback 0 521 58809 X paperback

CHANDRA MUKERJI, *Territorial ambitions and the gardens of Versailles*
0 521 49674 6 hardback 0 521 59959 8 paperback

LEON H. MAYHEW, *The New Public* 0 521 48146 5 hardback 0 521 48493 6
paperback

VERA L. ZOLBERG and JONI M. CHERBO (eds.), *Outsider art*
0 521 58111 7 hardback 0 521 58921 5 paperback

SCOTT BRAVMANN, *Queer fictions of the past* 0 521 59101 5 hardback
0 521 59907 5 paperback

STEVEN SEIDMAN, *Difference troubles* 0 521 59043 4 hardback 0 521 59970 9
paperback

RON EYERMAN and ANDREW JAMISON, *Music and social movements*
0 521 62045 7 hardback 0 521 62966 7 paperback

MEYDA YEGENOGLU, *Colonial fantasies* 0 521 48233 X hardback
0 521 62648 7 paperback

LAURA DESFOR EDLES, *Symbol and ritual in the new Spain* 0 521 62140 2
hardback 0 521 62885 7 paperback

NINA ELIASOPH, *Avoiding politics* 0 521 58293 8 hardback 0 521 58759 X
paperback

BERNHARD GIESEN, *Intellectuals and the German nation* 0 521 62161 5
hardback 0 521 63996 4 paperback

PHILIP SMITH (ed.), *The New American Cultural Sociology* 0 521 58415 9
hardback 0 521 58634 8 paperback

To the memory of
Myron Weiner
1931–1999

Fundamentalism, Sectarianism, and Revolution

The Jacobin Dimension of Modernity

S. N. Eisenstadt

CAMBRIDGE
UNIVERSITY PRESS

PUBLISHED BY THE PRESS SYNDICATE OF THE UNIVERSITY OF CAMBRIDGE
The Pitt Building, Trumpington Street, Cambridge CB2 1RP, United Kingdom

CAMBRIDGE UNIVERSITY PRESS
The Edinburgh Building, Cambridge, CB2 2RU, United Kingdom
http://www.cup.cam.ac.uk
40 West 20th Street, New York, NY 10011–4211, USA http://www.cup.org
10 Stamford Road, Oakleigh, Melbourne 3166, Australia

S. N. Eisenstadt 1999

This book is in copyright. Subject to statutory exception and to the provisions of
relevant collective licensing agreements, no reproduction of any part may take
place without the written permission of Cambridge University Press.

First published 1999

Printed in the United Kingdom at the University Press, Cambridge

Typeset in 10/12.5 pt Times New Roman in QuarkXPress™   [SE]

A catalogue record for this book is available from the British Library

ISBN 0 521 64184 5 hardback
ISBN 0 521 64586 7 paperback

Contents

Preface   *page* xiii

1 Heterodoxies, sectarianism, and utopianism in the constitution
   of proto-fundamentalist movements   1

   Introduction   1
   Heterodoxies and utopianism in Axial-Age Civilizations   3
   The basic antinomies in the cultural programs of Axial
   Civilizations   7
   Alternative visions; sectarianism and utopianism in different
   Axial civilizations: "otherworldly civilizations"   13
   This-worldly civilizations – Confucianism   16
   The monotheistic civilizations   19
   Proto-fundamentalist movements in different Axial Civilizations   25

2 The Great Revolutions and the transformation of sectarian
   utopianism in the cultural and political program of modernity   39

   The distinctive characteristics of the Great Revolutions – the
   modern transformation of sectarian utopianism   39
   The cultural and political program of modernity: basic premises   51
   The cultural program of modernity: antinomies, tensions, and
   criticisms   62
   The tensions in the political program of modernity – pluralistic
   and Jacobin tendencies   68
   Social movements as bearers of the major antinomies of the
   cultural and political programs of modernity   75

ix

Social movements: the political process and the continual
reconstruction of the realm of the political in modern societies   78

3   Fundamentalism as a modern Jacobin anti-modern utopia
and heterodoxy – the totalistic reconstruction of tradition   82

Introduction: the historical settings   82

The distinct sectarian utopian characteristics of modern
fundamentalist movements   89

The Jacobin components and characteristics of the modern
fundamentalist movements   94

The paradoxical attitude of modern fundamentalist movements to
tradition; essentialized traditions as modern totalistic ideologies   98

The power of the Jacobin component of the fundamentalist
movements   105

The fundamentalist and the Communist regimes – a comparison
of two modern Jacobin movements and regimes   106

Fundamentalist, fascist and national-socialist and contemporary
communal national movements   112

A brief analytical-typological summary: proto-fundamentalist,
fundamentalist, and communal-national movements   115

4   Historical setting and variability of fundamentalist movements   119

The intercivilizational setting of fundamentalist movements –
the hegemony of the West and the premises of the Western
program of modernity   119

National and communist movements and regimes: the
incorporation of socialist symbols and the crystallization of
different programs of modernity   125

Changing intercivilizational settings, globalization, the weakening
of Western hegemony and new challenges to it – the development
of communal-religious and fundamentalist movements   135

Ontological conceptions and the development of fundamentalist
and communal-religious movements – some comparative
indications   149

The puzzle of the weak development of fundamentalist
movements in Japan   155

Collective identity, institutional formations, and the development
and impact of fundamentalist and communal-religious
movements – the USA   163

Collective identity, institutional formations, and the development
and impact of fundamentalist and communal-religious
movements: Asian societies, with a comparative look at Europe   173

Collective identity, institutional formations and the development
and impact of fundamentalist and communal-religious
movements: the historical and contemporary experience of India   179

The fundamentalist and communal-religious challenge to
modern pluralistic regimes   184

5   Some considerations on modernity   196

Notes   208
Select bibliography   244
Index   270

Preface

This book has many origins. Its remote origins lie in my interest in the place of sectarianism in the dynamics of great civilizations – an interest that arose from my reexamination of the Protestant ethic and my attempts to put it in a broader comparative perspective.[1]

This interest became interwoven with my study of the Axial Civilizations, first in a series of conferences, organized by a core group headed by Prof. W. Schluchter reexamining Weber's analysis of the major civilizations,[2] and later in the conferences on the Axial Age organized by me.[3] An interim step was the analysis of Revolutions which I presented in my book on revolutions and transformation.[4]

All these have been connected with a continual reexamination of the theories of modernization and of the major characteristics of modernity,[5] of modern civilization.

The more immediate origins of this book as related to fundamentalism have been the conferences organized in the framework of the Project on Fundamentalism sponsored by the American Academy of Arts and

---

[1] See S. N. Eisenstadt, "The Protestant Ethic in Analytical and Comparative Framework," in Eisenstadt, *The Protestant Ethic and Modernization*. New York, Basic Books, 1968, pp. 3–46.

[2] W. Schluchter: *Max Webers Studie uber Konfuzianismus und Taoismus*. Frankfurt, Suhrkamp Verlag, 1983; *Max Webers Studie uber Induismus und Buddhismus*. Ed. Wolfgang Schluchter. Frankfurt, Suhrkamp Verlag, 1984; *Max Webers Sicht des Antiken Christentum*. Webers Analyse des Islams und die Gestalt der Islamischen Zivilization. Frankfurt, Suhrkamp Taschenbuch Wissenschaft, 1985; *Max Webers Sicht des Islams*. Frankfurt, Suhrkamp Verlag, 1987; and S. N. Eisenstadt, "The Axial Age: The Emergence of Transcendental Visions and the Rise of Clerics," *European Journal of Sociology* 23, 2, 1982, 294–314.

[3] S. N. Eisenstadt (ed.): *The Origins and Diversity of Axial Age Civilizations*. Albany, State University of New York Press, 1986; *Kulturen der Achsenzeit*, I, 2 volumes, 1987; and *Kulturen der Achsenzeit*, II, 3 volumes, 1992.

[4] S. N. Eisenstadt, *Revolutions and Transformation of Societies*. New York, Free Press, 1978. Hebrew, Portuguese and German translations.

[5] S. N. Eisenstadt, *Tradition, Change and Modernity*. New York, John Wiley & Sons, 1973. German and Italian translations.

Sciences and organized by Martin Monty and Scott Appleby in some of which I participated,[6] and in one of the volumes of which I published a chapter which constituted the kernel of several papers ultimately leading to the present book.

During the preparation of this book, I have engaged in conversations about the problems of fundamentalism with many colleagues – Nehemia Levtzion and Hava Lazarus Jaffe in Jerusalem; Nikki Keddie in Los Angeles who also was kind enough to send me a draft of her very interesting paper on the subject; Bjorn Wittrock and Ulf Hannez of SCASSS (the Swedish Collegium for Advanced Studies in the Social Sciences) in Uppsala; with Jeffrey C. Alexander during our common stay at SCASSS; Nilufer Güle during a preparatory workshop on Multiple Modernities convened in September 1997 in Cambridge under the auspices of *Daedalus*.

A crucial stage in the preparation of the manuscript occurred during my stay as a Fellow at the Woodrow Wilson Center for Scholars in Washington D.C. in the fall of 1996 where I had many conversations with Henry Munson Jr. who was then studying in depth different fundamentalist movements; and with Dale Eickelman, and with Seymour Martin Lipset. During that period Raymond Grew gave me very detailed comments on an earlier draft of the manuscript.

During the spring and summer of 1997 I served as the Max Weber Visiting Professor at the University of Heidelberg, and one of the lectures I gave in the Max Weber lectures was devoted to fundamentalism. I greatly enjoyed the discussions with my host and friend Prof. W. Schluchter as well as the discussions after the lectures – and indeed those in all the seminars and lectures I gave on these topics in various universities in America and Europe.

I am also very grateful to two anonymous readers from Cambridge University, and Catherine Max and Elizabeth Howard at Cambridge University Press, who were helpful in the preparation of the manuscript, and above all to Jason Mast for his excellent editorial work.

Last, I would like to thank my secretary in Jerusalem, Batia Slonim, for her continual help; to Marjo Schejtman for his research assistance throughout the preparation of this book, and above all for the help in the arduous preparation of the bibliography; and to Esther Rosenfeld who has faithfully typed and retyped the many – too many – drafts of the manuscript.

The Hebrew University of Jerusalem
and the Van Leer Jerusalem Institute, Jerusalem

---

[6] S. N. Eisenstadt, "Fundamentalism, Phenomenology and Comparative Dimensions," in Martin E. Marty and R. Scott Appleby eds., *Fundamentalisms Comprehended*. Chicago, University of Chicago Press, 1995, pp. 259–276.

1

Heterodoxies, sectarianism, and utopianism in the constitution of proto-fundamentalist movements

Introduction

I

The major aim of this chapter is to explore the relations between modern fundamentalist movements and modernity, and its major claim is that contemporary fundamentalist movements are thoroughly modern movements, albeit promulgating anti-modern or anti-Enlightenment ideologies. This chapter also intends to demonstrate the importance of heterodox sectarian movements in influencing both the dynamics of civilizations as well as the expansion and crystallization of modern civilization.

By modern fundamentalist movements I am referring particularly to those that emerged in the twentieth century. However, some of these movements do have earlier origins that led to further development through the twentieth century, such as Protestant groups in the United States, while others emerged more recently, first in Islam, and later in Judaism. Beyond the original Protestant ones, these latter movements did not usually refer to themselves as fundamentalists (with perhaps the partial exception of some Islamic movements in Egypt) but were rather so dubbed by Western scholarly and more general discourse.[1] We place all of these movements under the rubric fundamentalist because, despite all their great differences and disparities, it seems to us that some of the characteristics that they do have in common are indeed crucial to our attempts at understanding their dynamics. This chapter will explore both the commonalities and the differences between these fundamentalist movements, noting also the seemingly similar, yet quite distinct religious ones – communal or national – which have developed especially in India and in Buddhist societies of South and Southeast Asia.[2]

It is the major thesis of our analysis that all these fundamentalist movements do not constitute, as has often been portrayed, an eruption of traditional or traditionalistic "pre-modern" forces which were repressed, as it were, by modern regimes and by the cultural program of modernity, nor are they simply cases of reactionary anti-modern movements. Rather, it is here contended that modern fundamentalist movements constitute a distinctive form of modern political movement, namely a special type that demonstrates strong Jacobin tendencies. In other words, modern fundamentalist movements contain a very strong Jacobin component which constitutes one of their distinctive characteristics.

The general affinity between fundamentalist movements and varying aspects of modernity has been touched upon in the literature: many tend towards a very tight, even party-like, discipline; they tend to use modern communication technologies and propaganda techniques; and they have appropriated of many modern tropes and modes of discourse. Despite the growing recognition of such affinities, the distinct features of these movements as modern ones have not been adequately or thoroughly delineated. My central argument here is that the crucial aspect that renders these movements products of modernity is the appropriation by them, to varying degrees per movement and at different times in their histories, of one central component of the political program of modernity, which crystallized in the so-called Great Revolutions – namely the Jacobin, totalistic, participatory, and later totalitarian ones. As we shall see later in greater detail, in some ways, even if paradoxically at times, the fundamentalist groups and regimes share some crucial characteristics with most extreme, secular, left Jacobin movements and regimes – namely the communist ones.

It is above all with respect to some of the features of their ideologies, to the mode of construction of their ideologies, that the close relations between the fundamentalist movements and the modern world, modernity, are most conspicuous. Indeed, one of the major manifestations of such Jacobin tendencies within these movements is the construction by them of highly elaborate ideologies which are part and parcel of the modern political agenda, even if their basic ideological orientations and symbols are in many ways anti-modern, especially anti-Enlightenment. From the point of view of the construction of their ideologies, they constitute thoroughly modern movements, which promulgate an anti-modern traditionalistic ideology – an ideology which is, however, couched very much in modern, especially Jacobin, terms just as their organization evinces some distinct Jacobin tendencies. Moreover, their very strong anti-modern, or rather anti-Enlightenment ideology constitutes a part of the more general cultural and political discourse of modernity from the eighteenth century into the nineteenth, and above all as it developed in the twentieth century, with the continual expansion of modernity. The crucial importance of the modern dimensions of these movements is also evident in the strong emphases to be found in most of them on the importance of conscious moral choice in their continual confrontation with the outside world, in joining them, in continual adherence to them, in the promulgation of their ideologies, and in the belief that such choice may affect the course of history.

More than simply containing some traditional elements, modern fundamentalist movements build on earlier religious traditions and historical experiences, and indeed are deeply rooted in their respective religious traditions. Significantly enough, however, they are rooted not in the hegemonic orthodoxies of their respective traditions but rather in the traditions of their heterodoxies. They evince above all close relation or parallels to some specific, especially utopian, sectarian heterodox tendencies and movements, some of which can be designated as proto-fundamentalist, which developed in their respective religions or civilizations.

The common core of the proto-fundamentalist and modern fundamentalist movements alike is a special type of renovative utopian sectarianism. Such sectarian ideologies and organization developed in all so-called Axial Civilizations. It is such sectarian heterodox movements that constituted also, as we shall see yet in greater detail later, a central component of the crystallization of modernity in Europe, above all in the Great Revolutions. The sectarian utopian orientations prevalent in these movements became, in a highly transformed way, through the impact of these revolutions a central component of modernity – a component that became manifest in many modern movements including the fundamentalist ones. Concomitantly, the composition of these movements also greatly differs from that of the proto-fundamentalist movements of earlier periods, very much in line with the composition of many of the more militant modern movements. Accordingly, fundamentalist movements have to be analyzed in the context of both the historical experience of their civilizations and their various religious traditions, as well as the cultural and political program of modernity.

We shall start this analysis with an examination of sectarian and heterodox tendencies in so-called Axial Civilization – the Weberian Great Religions – as it is within the framework of some of these civilizations that the proto-fundamentalist and fundamentalist movements arose.

Heterodoxies and utopianism in Axial-Age Civilizations

II

By Axial-Age Civilizations (to use Karl Jaspers' nomenclature)[3] we mean those civilizations that crystallized during the 1,000 years from 500 BC to the first century of the Christian era, within which new types of ontological visions, of conceptions of a basic tension between the transcendental and mundane orders emerged and were institutionalized in many parts of the world. Examples of this process of crystallization include ancient Israel, later in Second-Commonwealth Judaism and Christianity; Ancient Greece; possibly Zoroastrianism in Iran; early imperial China; Hinduism and Buddhism; and, beyond the Axial Age proper, Islam.

The crystallization of such civilizations can be seen as a series of some of the greatest revolutionary breakthroughs in human history, which changed its course. The central aspect of these revolutions was the emergence and institutionalization of the new basic ontological conceptions of a chasm between the transcendental and mundane orders referred to above. These conceptions, which first developed among small groups of autonomous, relatively unattached "intellectuals" (a new social element at the time), particularly among the carriers of models of cultural and social order, were ultimately transformed into the basic "hegemonic" premises of their respective civilizations, and were subsequently institutionalized. That is, they became the predominant orientations of both the ruling elites as well as of many secondary elites, fully embodied in the centers or sub-centers of their respective societies.

The development and institutionalization of such conceptions of a basic tension between the transcendental and the mundane order entailed the perception of the given mundane order as incomplete, inferior – oftentimes as evil or polluted, and as in need of reconstruction. Such reconstruction was to be effected according to the basic transcendental ontological conceptions prevalent in these societies; especially according to the conception of bridging the chasm between the transcendental and the mundane orders, according to the precepts of a higher ethical or metaphysical order or vision. In Weberian terms, this reconstruction suggests a movement toward "salvation," basically a Christian term for which equivalents can be found in all the Axial Civilizations.[4] Accordingly, the institutionalization of such conceptions in these civilizations was closely related to attempts to reconstruct their major institutional contours. It gave rise in all these civilizations to attempts to reconstruct the mundane world, from the human personality to the socio-political and economic order, according to the appropriate transcendental vision, to the principles of the higher ontological or ethical order.

Thus, in these civilizations there developed a strong tendency to define certain collectivities and institutional arenas as most appropriate for resolving these tensions, as arenas of "salvation" for the implementation of their respective transcendental visions. This act created new types of collectivities or endowed seemingly natural and primordial groups with special meaning in terms of the tensions and their resolution. The most important transformation of this sort was the construction of unneeded "cultural" or "religious," as distinct from "ethnic" or "political," collectivities.

Alongside these major collectivities, there developed within these civilizations strong tendencies to construct a societal center or centers to serve as the major autonomous and symbolically distinct embodiments of the respective transcendental ontological visions, that is, the major loci of the charismatic dimension of human existence. The center's symbolic distinctiveness from the periphery received a relatively strong emphasis, yet at the same time the center tended to permeate the periphery and restructure it according to its own autonomous visions, conceptions, and rules. Sometimes this tendency was accompanied by a parallel impingement by the periphery on the center.[5]

These processes of center formation and reconstruction of collectivities were connected to the construction of great traditions as autonomous and distinct symbolic frameworks, and to the transformation of the relations between the great and little traditions. Hence there developed in all these civilizations attempts by the carriers of the Great Traditions to permeate the peripheries and to absorb the Little Traditions into their realm of influence and control. Consequently, the carriers of the Little Traditions attempted to profane the Great ones, to dissociate themselves from them, and to generate a distinct ideology of their own that also included and incorporated the peripheries.[6]

Thus, in these civilizations, the center (or centers) emerged as a distinct symbolic organizational arena, one whose "givenness" could not necessarily be taken for granted. The construction and characteristics of the center, characterized for instance as either strong and guiding or weak, tended to become central issues under the gaze of the increasing reflexivity that was developing in these civilizations.

The different modes of reflexivity that developed in these civilizations focused above all on the relations between the transcendental and mundane orders. The political dimension of such reflexivity was rooted in the transformed conceptions of the political arena and of the accountability of rulers.[7] The political order as one of the central loci of the mundane order was usually conceived as lower than the transcendental ideal and therefore had to be restructured according to the precepts of the latter. It had to be reconstructed above all according to what was perceived as the proper mode of overcoming the tension between the transcendental and mundane orders, and with special regard to the basic premises of their respective transcendental visions of "salvation." It was the rulers who were usually held responsible for organizing the political order according to such precepts.

At the same time the nature of the rulers became greatly transformed. The king-god, the embodiment of the cosmic and earthly order alike, disappeared, and a secular ruler appeared, even if with strong sacral attributes, which was, in principle, accountable to some higher order. Thus there emerged the conception of the accountability of rulers and community to a higher authority, God, Divine Law, and the like. Accordingly, the possibility of calling a ruler to judgment appeared. One such dramatic appearance of this conception appeared in ancient Israel, in the priestly and prophetic pronunciations. "Secular" conceptions of such accountability, an accountability to the community and its laws, appeared in both the northern shores of the eastern Mediterranean, in ancient Greece, as well as in the Chinese conception of the Mandate of Heaven. In varying forms this conception of accountability appeared in all these civilizations.[8]

Concomitantly with the emergence of conceptions of accountability of rulers there began to develop autonomous spheres of law as somewhat distinct from ascriptively bound custom and from purely customary law. Such developments could also entail some beginnings of a conception of rights even if the scope of these spheres of law and rights varied greatly.

The basic premise of these civilizations, and the closely related accountability of rulers to some higher law or principles, were closely connected with the crystallization of distinct new roles and groups. In all these civilizations the development and institutionalization of a perceived tension between the transcendental and the mundane orders, the perceived importance of this tension, as well as the subsequent attempts to overcome it via the implementation of a transcendental vision, were closely connected to the emergence of a new social element. Autonomous intellectuals emerged as a new type of elite who acted as carriers of models of cultural and social order such as the ancient Israeli prophets and priests and the later Jewish sages, the Greek philosophers and sophists, the Chinese literati, the Hindu Brahmins, the Buddhist Sangha, and the Islamic Ulema. The small nuclei of such intellectuals and elites that developed these new ontologies, these new transcendental visions and conceptions, saw themselves as representatives and promulgators of such visions of the higher law, and thus further considered themselves entitled to call rulers to accountability.[9]

III

The new type of elites that arose with the processes of institutionalization of such transcendental visions differed greatly from the ritual, magical, and sacral specialist in the pre-Axial Age Civilizations. New elites, intellectuals, and clerics were recruited and legitimized according to distinct, autonomous criteria, and were organized in autonomous settings distinct from those of the basic ascriptive political units of the society. They acquired a conscious, potentially countrywide status of their own. They also tended to become potentially independent of other categories of elites, social groups, and sectors. The new cultural groups became transformed into relatively autonomous partners in the major ruling coalitions and protest movements.

At the same time there took place a far-reaching transformation of other elites, such as political elites, or the articulators of the solidarity of different collectivities. All these elites tended to develop claims to an autonomous place in the construction of the cultural and social order. They saw themselves not only as performing specific technical, functional activities – be they those of scribes, ritual specialists, and the like – but also as potentially autonomous carriers of a distinct cultural and social order related to the transcendental vision prevalent in their respective societies. All of these elites saw themselves as the autonomous articulators of the new order and rival elites as both accountable to them and as essentially inferior.

Moreover, each of these groups of elites was not homogeneous (in these civilizations even more than in others), and within each of them as well as within the broader sectors of the society there developed a multiplicity of secondary cultural, political, or educational groups and influentials, each very often carrying different conceptions of the cultural and social order. Accordingly these various groups, elites, and influentials often competed strongly with each other, especially over the production and control of symbols and media of communication.

It is these elites and influentials that were the most active in the restructuring of the world and in contributing to the institutional creativity that developed in these societies. Above all – and this is crucial for our analysis – these different elites in general and the intellectuals in particular also constituted the most active proponents of various alternative conceptions of the social and cultural order that have developed in all these civilizations.

The basic antinomies in the cultural programs of Axial Civilizations

IV

It was indeed one of the distinct characteristics of these civilizations that there continually developed within them alternative, competing transcendental visions. These alternative conceptions or visions crystallized around three basic antinomies inherent in the very premises of these civilizations and in the process of their institutionalization – namely, first, around the awareness of a great range of possibilities of transcendental visions and of the range of methods of their possible implementation; secondly, around the tension between reason and revelation or faith (or their equivalents in the non-monotheistic Axial Civilizations); and thirdly, around the problematique of the desirability of attempts at full institutionalization of these visions in their pristine form.[10]

The awareness of a great range of possibilities of transcendental visions, of the very definition of the tensions between the transcendental and the mundane order and of the quest to overcome these tensions by implementation of such visions, constituted an inherent part of their institutionalization in the Axial Civilizations. Historically such a process of institutionalization was never a simple, peaceful one. Any such institutionalization usually contained strong heterogeneous and even contradictory elements. It was usually connected with a continuous struggle and competition between many groups and between their respective visions. Because of this multiplicity of visions, no single one could be taken as given or complete. Once the conception of a basic tension between the transcendental and the mundane order was institutionalized in a society, or at least within its center, it became in itself very problematic. The elaboration of any such vision attendant on such institutionalization generated the possibility of different emphases, directions, and interpretations, all of which were reinforced by the existence in any historical setting of such institutionalization of multiple visions carried by different groups.

The second basic antinomy inherent in these civilizations has been between reason and revelation or faith in the monotheistic tradition, or commitment to some equivalent transcendental principle in the Confucian, Hinduistic, and Buddhist ones. The premises of these civilizations and their institutionalization entailed a high level of reflexivity, including a second order reflexivity suggesting a critical awareness of these very premises. Such reflexivity has been, of course, reinforced by the awareness of the possibility – and existence – of alternative visions. It necessarily entailed the exercise of human judgment and reason, not only as a pragmatic tool but as at least one arbiter or guide of such reflexivity. Such exercise often gave rise to the construction of "reason" as a distinct category in the discourse that developed in these civilizations. Hence, it may have easily endowed reason with a metaphysical or transcendental dimension and autonomy which did not exist in pre-Axial Civilizations – and could generate confrontations between its autonomous exercise on the one hand and revelation or faith (or their non-monotheistic equivalents) on the other. Such confrontation was historically central in the monotheistic civilizations as they confronted the only Axial Civilization that did indeed define reason, or "logos," as the ultimate transcendental value, namely the Greek civilization. But parallel confrontations, even if couched in other terms and in less confrontational ways, developed in the Axial Civilizations.

The above antinomy is closely related to the third one inherent in the Axial Civilizations which concerns the desirability of full attempts at institutionalizing these visions in their pristine forms. In most of these civilizations it was strongly emphasized that there exists a sharp discrepancy between the ideal order, as prescribed or envisaged by the transcendental visions prevalent in them (by the commandments of God, by the ideals of cosmic harmony or the like), and the mundane order as constructed by the exigencies of social and political life or by the vagaries of human nature (often conceived as guided by purely utilitarian conditions, by strict considerations of power, or as *raison d'état*).

At issue here is the development within the reflexive traditions of these civilizations, given the at least implicit assumption of human imperfectability, of doubts about the possibility, or even the feasibility of full implementation of such a vision. Such views were not inherently exogenous to the basic conceptions and premises of these civilizations, rather they were a fundamental, even if controversial, component of these premises. The very emphasis on a chasm between these two orders entailed the notion of the inherent imperfectibility of humanity. It was thus often emphasized in the discourse of these civilizations that attempts to completely overcome the chasm between these two orders could be very dangerous and perhaps lead to attempts by fragile humans to claim for themselves divine power. Accordingly there developed within these civilizations strong emphases on the necessity to regulate mundane affairs with reference to the transcendental vision without full, extreme attempts at totalistic implementation of the pristine version of the vision. The proper limits of such implementation, or the scope of the arenas and aspects of life that should be regulated according to such vision, as opposed to arenas possibly better left to regulation by more mundane means such as economic and political processes, constituted one of the major concerns of the reflexive discourse in all these civilizations.

Augustine's famous distinction between the City of God and the City of Man is one of the best-known illustrations of this concern – as is the resolution of this problem in the direction of the separation of the two cities – which was challenged by many heterodox, among them gnostic, groups. Similar discourses can also be found in other Axial Civilizations.

These concerns were closely related to yet another problem that was central in the discourse of all these civilizations, namely that of the evaluation of hedonistic and anarchic impulses, as well as of the general mundane interests of people. That is, there was a strong preoccupation with the relationship or tension between, on the one hand, the impulses and interests of potentially egoistical, hedonistic, and anarchic individuals and groups in society, and on the other, the maintenance of a proper social order. In close relation to these considerations, there developed in many of these civilizations some notions of the concept of a social contract, that the actual mundane, especially the political order, is constituted through some implicit contract between the members of a society, one to another, and especially between them and the ruler. Variations of such notions as social contract can be found in some of the great writings on political and social matters of the Asian civilizations, as for instance the Artashartra of Katulya, in the work of Ibn Khaldoun, and in some of the work of such Chinese thinkers as Motzu or Hsunt-su. Most of these discussions emphasized that such contracts with rulers were based on some utilitarian considerations as well as on fear. Such considerations were usually seen as being natural parts of the mundane order as the anarchic potentials of human nature had to be regulated and hemmed in by laws, customs, and potentially by the power of the rulers. The recognition of this necessity was often connected with the legitimation of the political order as grounded in considerations of power and fear of anarchy. Contracts based on such considerations could be seen as legitimate, but certainly not as adhering to the full implementation of a pristine transcendental vision. Their legitimation could likewise be connected with the fear of attempts to totalistically implement a pristine transcendental vision.

At the same time, however, the possibility was raised in this discourse that the regulation of such impulses could be best assured by the exercise of human judgment, by reason rather than by attempts to fully implement transcendental visions in some pristine form.

V

The various alternative visions of the transcendental and mundane orders that developed in these civilizations focused above all on these basic antinomies inherent in their premises. These alternative visions, with their strong antinomian possibilities, usually entailed some reconstruction of the basic ontological conceptions of reality, of the conception of the transcendental order and its relations to the mundane order – especially to the political order and the basic social formations that were institutionalized in these civilizations.

Some such visions often denied the validity of the very definitions of ontological reality upheld in the respective civilizations. One direction of such denial was the reformulation of the tension between the transcendental and mundane orders, as was the case with both the Buddhist reformulation of the premises of Hinduism and the Christian reformulation of the premises of Judaism. Such alternative visions could also promulgate the ideological denial of the very stress on the tension between transcendental and mundane orders and proffer a return to a "pagan" conception of a pre-transcendental, pre-Axial stage. Such alternative visions suggested a mutual reembedment of the transcendental and the mundane, sometimes suggesting a chtonic conception of the world. Another very strong trend connected to the quest for the "return" to such reembedment was the gnostic vision which attempted to imbue the world with a deep but hidden meaning. This quest could also become connected with the emphasis on the autonomy of reason and the legitimacy of mundane efforts. Such different alternative visions could become connected with the elaboration of a great variety of religious and intellectual orientations, especially those with mystical and esoteric ideologies which went beyond the established, routinized, orthodox version of implementation of the transcendental vision.[11]

All these visions with their very strong antinomian potentialities were usually articulated by special actors, especially cultural and religious elites, who presented themselves as the bearer of the pristine religious and/or civilizational visions of their times. Illustrations of such carriers include the holy men of antiquity, the Indian or Buddhist renouncers, Christian monks, and the like – in other words, religious virtuosi. These religious virtuosi often held ambivalent or dialectic relationships with the existing ways of institutionalizing the transcendental visions, often acted from within liminal situations, and tended to coalesce into distinct groups, sectors, or orders which could become heterodoxies with schismatic tendencies.

These actors often sought to connect the attempts to implement such visions with wider social movements, especially with movements of protest.[12] Accordingly, such alternative visions very often became combined with perennial themes of social protest, particularly those concerned with the tension and predicaments inherent in the institutionalization of the social order such as: the tension between equality and hierarchy; the tension between complexity and fragmentation of human relations inherent in any institutional division of labor and the possibility of some total, unconditional, unmediated participation in social and cultural orders; the tension between the quest for meaningful participation in central symbolic and institutional arenas by various groups in the society and the limitations on the access to these arenas; and finally, with attempts to overcome and supersede the predicaments and limitations of human existence in general and of death in particular.

One of the most important outcomes of the combinations of such alternative visions with both the implementation of the respective transcendental visions and the universal themes of protest was the emergence of utopian visions of an alternative cultural and social order in these Axial Civilizations.[13] Such utopian conceptions or visions often contained strong millenarian and revivalist elements which can be also found in pre-Axial-Age or non-Axial Civilizations such as Japan. However, these utopian visions go beyond millenarian ones by combining them with the search for an alternative "better" order beyond the given one, a new social and cultural order that will be constructed according to the precepts of the higher transcendental order and which will negate and transcend the given one. Such utopian visions also often contained very strong gnostic and eschatological components or dimensions.[14]

VI

These alternative visions, with their strong antinomian potentialities, were not confined to the purely intellectual realm. Rather they could, and often did have broader institutional and political implications. Such implications were rooted in the fact that these visions usually entailed strong orientations to the construction of the mundane world and thus gave rise to a strong potential for dissent. Beyond this potential for dissent, such visions borne by sects, potential heterodoxies, broader social movements, and especially by religious virtuosi, had more specific and direct institutional and political implications. The promulgation of the various alternative visions was closely connected to struggles between elites, influentials, and popular leaders, struggles that helped to transform these elites into "political demagogues" (to follow Weber's designation of the ancient Israelite prophets) who could develop distinct political programs of their own.[15] Such programs could in principle, and under appropriate conditions, become forceful challenges to existing regimes as well as to political and religious establishments.

The political potential of these actors and their alternative visions was rooted in the problems arising out of any concrete institutionalization of the Axial Civilizations, above all out of the connection of such institutionalization to conceptions of the accountability of rulers to some higher order. This potential for political dissent was particularly closely connected with the relations of the accountability of rulers to the realistic possibilities and limitations of the implementation of pristine transcendental visions. Any institutionalization of such visions naturally entailed some compromise of the pristine vision with mundane social and political realities; the acceptance of the impossibility of a total bridging of the chasm between the transcendental and mundane orders; the close interweaving of such partial implementation with the political order; and the concomitant emphasis on the maintenance and stability of a political order needed to bring about even the partial implementation of a transcendental vision. At the same time, however, it was exactly such "compromise" that could constitute the butt of criticism from different, particularly sectarian utopian movements that promulgated the full bridging of the visionary chasm as well as the construction of a political order that would ensure such full implementation.

Alternative visions; sectarianism and utopianism in different Axial Civilizations: "otherworldly civilizations"

VII

Although such alternative visions, sectarianism, and tendencies to heterodoxy crystallized in all these civilizations, there developed great differences between them with respect to the extent of the development of such utopias and heterodoxies and of their impact on the political scene. That is, differences developed above all with regard to the extent to which the existing institutional and political order constituted a central focus of such sectarian heterodox orientations and activities, especially of utopian and eschatological visions. Such differences were closely related to the conceptions and criteria of accountability of rulers, especially to the extent to which the rulers were seen as responsible for the implementation in their respective societies of the predominant transcendental visions, as well as to the specification of the institutional loci and processes through which such accountability could be effected.[16]

The different ways in which the conceptions of accountability of rulers were conceived in these civilizations were closely related first of all to the different transcendental visions that were prevalent in these civilizations, i.e. to the basic ontological conceptions of the nature of the chasm between the transcendental and the mundane spheres and of the ways of bridging this chasm. Second, conceptions of accountability were connected with and influenced by the conception of the political arena and its place in the implementation of the transcendental visions. Third, they were related to the extent of acceptance and possible legitimization of the utilitarian, egoistic dimensions of human nature.

The specific impacts of these sects and the conceptions borne by them on the institutional formations and dynamics of their respective civilizations could be most clearly seen in the ways in which major heterodoxies became interwoven with broader socio-political movements. In this context, of special importance were the models of alternative social and cultural order that developed within them, as was the nature of their linkages with different types of political struggle and rebellion – i.e., the nature of the coalitions into which they entered, their place in the central ruling coalitions, and their impact on them.

VIII

In most general terms, within the other-worldly civilizations such as Buddhism and, as Gabriella Eichinger Ferro-Luzzi put it, that polythetic prototypical conglomerate which could be designated as Hinduism,[17] the political arena was not viewed as a major soteriological arena, that is, as the primary arena for the implementation of the major transcendental vision. Most of the alternative visions which developed in the major other worldly civilizations, again Hinduism and Buddhism, such as for instance Bhakti, and Jainism, were oriented against those institutional solutions that seemed to compromise both the renunciation of the mundane world and emphasis on the reconstruction of the inner experience of the believer.

Most of these alternative visions were closely connected with the traditions and orientations of the renouncer, and promulgated different pristine otherworldly orientations. They developed, however, not only as intellectual or ascetic exercises, as elaborations of esoteric doctrines, but as potentially fully-fledged sect-like, if not schismatic groups that offered their own interpretation of the proper way to salvation and gave rise to far-reaching innovations in different social arenas. These various sect-like movements, Buddhism itself originally just such a movement within Hinduism, had far reaching impacts not only on the religious sphere (if one can distinguish such a sphere in these civilizations), but on the entire institutional framework of this civilization.[18] However, this impact developed in rather specific directions.

These dynamics led to the restructuring and continuous expansion of the civilizational, political, and religious frameworks and collectivities, and they were often connected with far-reaching changes in the scope and concrete organization of political and economic units.[19] They were not, however, oriented to the reconstruction of political centers or of the basic premises of the political regimes.

These civilizations' basic definition of ontological reality and their strong other-worldly components, as well as their forms of implementation of their transcendental visions, did not generate strong alternative conceptions of the social and, in particular, the political orders. Accordingly the dynamics generated by these sect-like groups in coalition with other social groups differed greatly from those of other Axial-Age Civilizations, whether from China, in which this-worldly orientations were predominant, or from the monotheistic ones where this-worldly orientations were closely interwoven with otherworldly ones.

Within these "otherworldly" civilizations there have but rarely developed attempts, articulated by various secondary elites and sect-like movements, to reconstruct the political centers, their symbols, and the general criteria of access to them, although many of these movements did participate in political struggles attempting to structure a wider space for themselves and to influence the policies. Many of these movements often focused on attempts to promulgate universalistic definitions of the religious communities, and on attainment within them of greater equality rooted in a pure unmediated devotion to the Absolute, taking them beyond any ascriptive communal and above all caste settings.[20]

Concomitantly in many of these visions and movements a strong emphasis on equality tended to develop – especially in the religious and cultural arenas, and to some extent also in the definition of membership in the various collectivities. Similarly, some of these movements that developed in these civilizations, and which sometimes became connected with rebellions and political struggle, articulated millenarian orientations. But these were not characterized by strongly articulated political goals, nor linked with attempts to restructure the political regimes. It was mostly in popular uprisings against alien or "bad" rulers that such goals crystallized briefly.

The socio-political demands voiced in these movements were focused on attempts to change the concrete application of existing rules and to persuade the rulers to implement more benevolent policies. Such demands were not, however, usually seen as entailing new principles of political action or of accountability of rulers to different sectors of the population, but rather as an articulation of the latent moral premises of legitimization inherent in the existing regimes.[21]

The impact of these sects on the dynamics of Hinduistic or Buddhist civilizations was closely related to the fact that, while the various sectarian "religious" groups, organizations, and conglomerations were continually autonomous in the cultural-religious arena, in the more "mundane" sphere they were mostly embedded in various ascriptive and political groups. Hence, while the leaders of these sect-like movements were able to form many new coalitions with different social groups and movements, these coalitions were very similar to those existing in the major arenas of their respective societies. These coalitions therefore rarely generated markedly different principles of political organizations.[22]

This-worldly civilizations – Confucianism

IX

Confucianism, or the combined Confucian-legal conceptions that became predominate even if in different ways in China, Vietnam, and Korea, provides an interesting case between other-worldly and monotheistic civilizations. In a way, Confucianism provides a mirror image of other-worldly civilizations, and yet in many other ways it comes nearer to the monotheistic than to the other-worldly social forms. Ultimately in some regards it differs significantly from both of them. Comparisons are particularly relevant with respect to the nature of Confucianism's conceptions of ontological reality and the conception's relation to the definition and regulation of the major arenas of social life, to its conception of accountability of rulers, and to the characteristics of sectarian activities that developed within it. Its major difference from the monotheistic civilizations has been the fact that in the Confucian realm it was only, and particularly, the this-worldly political order that constituted the major arena of the implementation of a transcendental vision, while in this central institutional arena there developed but very little or only very weak other-worldly orientations.

Truly enough, powerful utopian visions and orientations did develop in China, especially among the neo-Confucian from the time of the Sung on. These visions were also oriented – as was the case in other Axial Civilizations – against specific aspects of the institutionalization of what was conceived as the major metaphysical and ethical messages of the Confucian vision.[23]

And yet in China, unlike in the monotheistic civilizations, these utopian and sectarian movements did not lead to far-reaching institutional reconstruction of the political centers of the society. "Heterodox" tendencies developed not only from within the Buddhist (or Taoist) groups but also from – and probably most forcefully – within the Confucian ones. Their orientations were seemingly similar to those of the monotheistic civilizations in that they were in principle oriented to the reconstruction of the mundane, particularly the political arena. However, their overall institutional impact differed greatly from that of their counterparts in the monotheistic civilizations.[24]

Here the interpretation of neo-Confucianism is of great importance and it has often constituted a focus of scholarly controversy. There can be no doubt that neo-Confucian groups were intensively concerned with the reconstruction of the imperial order in accordance with the metaphysical and moral visions they articulated, and that they had a far-reaching impact on some aspects of policy – such as land allotment, taxation, and to some extent some of the details of the examination system. Moreover, they continually veered between the acceptance of the legitimacy of mundane utilitarian activities, an acceptance which entailed a rather limited scope of moral regulation by the government, and the semi-utopian call for the crystallization of a moral vision in society which significantly enough was, according to most of these thinkers, to be effected by the government.

Confucian thinkers of different generations, and especially neo-Confucians from the Sung period on, were very concerned with the imperfections of the political system, of the emperor, of the examination system, and of the bureaucracy, and attempted to find some fulfillment beyond them.[25] They continuously called for government based on the golden rule. Moreover, many important attempts at reform grounded in Confucian and neo-Confucian visions abounded in China, especially from the Sung period onward, however they rarely challenged the basic premises of the regimes or of the political order. In none of these attempts do we find those tendencies to the reconstruction of the premises and centers of the regimes that can be found in the monotheistic civilizations. Even when they advocated that the political order had to conform to the moral one, they never challenged the very foundation of the imperial order or, above all, the view that the political, or political-cultural arenas, were the main possible institutional (as distinct from the more private contemplative one) arenas for implementing the Confucian transcendental vision. Given this basic adherence to the identification of the political-cultural center, of the political arena, as the major arena of implementation of the Confucian vision, they did not go beyond concrete attempts at reforms, and did not entail strong attempts at the reconstruction of the basic premises of the center itself. The major thrust of their critical, potentially heterodox orientations was in the direction of cultural, and to some extent educational, activities, of greater moral sensibility and responsibility, and even of critical appraisal of the political arena yet not to the extent of calling for its transformation. The strong emphasis on individual responsibility and on the moral cultivation of the individual – which was highly developed especially among the neo-Confucians – was oriented either toward perfecting the philosophical premises of their respective systems or toward the development of private intellectual or even mystic religious tendencies and reflexivity. These could become connected with otherworldly tendencies, but mostly on the private level.

True, the various neo-Confucian schools incorporated some Buddhist or Taoist thematics and tropes into their intellectual universe and attempted to provide more explicit rules for defining the basic ontology. The very development of these neo-Confucian schools can be seen as a reaction to the strong attraction of Buddhism and Taoism for many strata – including the literati – in times of trouble and division. But the incorporation of some Buddhist or Taoist themes into neo-Confucianism was effected within the basic framework of the neo-Confucian this-worldly orientations; the cultivation of otherworldly orientations was left to the various sects in their relatively segregated arenas, or to the private arenas of the literati.[26]

The uniqueness of the Chinese case lay in the ability of the ruling elites in China to regulate the numerous internal and external impingements on its symbolic premises and institutional frameworks, without these impingements being able to change or restructure the basic premises of these frameworks – although the different neo-Confucian schools did generate far-reaching reinterpretations of such premises.

This ability of the ruling elites to regulate change in China was closely related to very weak ideological and structural linkage between the different movements and processes of change and the central political struggle. This weak linkage was closely connected to the lack of predilection – especially among the literati – to generate enduring organizational and ideological linkages between their own activities and those of the different secondary institutional elites, thus minimizing the development of full-fledged confrontation between orthodoxy and heterodoxy in China. This tendency to such weak linkages and the consequent ability of the ruling groups to regulate the movements of change without their direct impingement on the center was connected with the basic characteristics of the literati. This tendency was especially connected with the fact that the literati constituted both an autonomous intellectual stratum and the sector from which the combined intellectual, cultural, political, and administrative elite developed. This relationship did not allow for the development of a distinction equivalent to that between church and state, and therefore they did not organize any continuous and strong independent resources or power bases which could serve as bases of action and linkages with broader groups, sects, or movements. The tendency to such weak linkages and to the weak development of orientations toward political action and organization which went beyond the existing order, was indeed closely related to the continual reinforcing feedback with major cultural orientations that developed in the realm of Confucian civilizations. This further entailed the assumption that the political and cultural center and arena was the major arena of the implementation of the hegemonic transcendental vision.[27]

The monotheistic civilizations

X

The mode of utopias, of eschatological visions, of conceptions of accountability of rulers, and the characteristics of the different sectarian movements which were the bearers of these visions developed in the monotheistic civilizations in a distinct direction. In all the monotheistic religions, with the strong interweaving of this- and other-worldly orientations that was prevalent in them, the reconstruction of the mundane world was seen – even if in different degrees – as one, but only one, focus or arena of the implementations of transcendental visions with strong otherworldly or "out-worldly" components. In these civilizations the mundane, above all the political arena, was conceived as but one arena of the implementation of such transcendental visions even if its impotence probably varied between these civilizations and in the different historical periods of each one. Additionally, at the same time there developed within these civilizations continuous tensions between the emphasis on different mundane arenas as well as between them and transmundane arenas as the proper foci of implementation of the transcendental visions prevalent within them. Hence, the proper designation of the reconstruction of such arenas became a focus of central concern and of contention between the ruling orthodoxies and the numerous heterodoxies and of the utopian vision that developed within them.

Accordingly, common to the monotheistic – Jewish, Christian, and Islamic – civilizations have been strong tendencies to the development of some visions of different political and, to some extent, social orders based on the reconstruction of the basic ontologies prevalent in them.

In the Jewish tradition, the discrepancy between the ideal, transcendental, and the given mundane order and attempts to reconstruct such order according to utopian soteriological visions was quite strongly emphasized in the periods of political independence – especially in the period of the Second Commonwealth,[28] after the experience of the destruction of the First Temple and the Babylonian exile, and later during the encounter with Hellenistic civilization and kingdoms. The Maccabean revolt and the establishment of the Hasmonean kingdom was probably rooted in such a vision. After the destruction of the Second Temple, given the special historical circumstances of the Jewish people – their dispersion and lack of political independence – the concrete, actual political dimension of the transcendental and utopian visions with their strong antinomian potentiality became subdued but it never disappeared.[29]

In the long period of exile the attempts to bridge the tension between the given, mundane order and the ideal continued to be transposed into the future stressing the difference between the existing reality in exile, devoid in itself of any ultimate meaning, and the messianic future. Throughout the long medieval period heterodox tendencies in general, and those with potential political, above all messianic and antinomian potentials in particular, were successfully hemmed in by the rabbinical and communal authorities, by the very facts of dispersion, and by being conceived as a distinct, subjugated minority. But such messianic political and antinomian orientations have never fully disappeared, instead reemerging in different guises after the expulsion from Spain, and attempts to bridge such tensions in the present would erupt from time to time in messianic movements – above all in the last and greatest of them, the Sabbatean movement of the seventeenth century.[30]

In the modern era, with the crystallization of more open attitudes to the Jews, first in seventeenth-to-eighteenth-century Holland, later on after the French Revolution and the Emancipation in Europe, and still later in America, the different heterodox tendencies with varying, often conflicting, political orientations started to bloom gathering special momentum in the state of Israel and in the contemporary Diaspora.

XI

The pattern of political dynamics and sectarianism in Islam was closely related to Islam's basic drive to create a civilization with its own specific premises with one crucial aspect being the conflation of the political and religious communities (in which military conquests constitute an important element) as expressed in the ideal of the *ummah*.[31] Such a conception was probably only implicit in the early formative period of Islam. The possibility of attaining the pristine vision of Islam, of the ideal fusion between the political and the religious community (or of constructing the *ummah*), was actually given up during relatively early periods in the formation and expansion of Islam. But although it was never fully attained it was continually promulgated, as Aziz Al Azmeh has shown,[32] by different scholars and religious leaders and connected with a very strong utopian orientation in the later periods. Given the continual perceptions of the perfect age of the Prophet as an ideal, even utopian model, the idea of renovation constituted a continual component of Islamic civilization and religion. Muhammad's state in Medina became, as Henry Munson, Jr. has aptly put it, the Islamic "primordial utopia."[33]

In fact there developed in Muslim civilization the separation between the caliph and the actual ruler, the Sultan, a separation that crystallized in the late Abbasid period heralding *de facto* separation between the rulers and the religious establishment (ulema).[34] The caliph, who became in effect powerless, did yet continue to serve as an ideal figure insofar as he appeared to be the presumed embodiment of the pristine Islamic vision of the *ummah*. He further served as the major source of legitimization of the sultan, even if usually he had no way to refuse this role.

In close relation to this separation and to the continual quest for the "true" ruler there developed in Muslim societies two major types of legitimization of rulers. One type, most prevalent in mainstream Islamic (Sunni) religious thought, stressed the legitimacy of any ruler who assures the peaceful existence of the Muslim community and the upholding of the Islamic law (the sharia), while simultaneously emphasizing the coercive nature of such rulers, of the political order, and its basic distance from the pristine ideal. This type of legitimization and accountability of rulers was also closely connected, as was the case in other Axial Civilizations, with the acceptance of the legitimacy of the mundane concerns of the ruler or of many given sectors of the population, be they of utilitarian or power related origins. Whatever the extent of the acceptance of such legitimization, it usually entailed the duty of the rulers to implement justice, and hence further entailed also the scrutinization of their behavior by the ulema even if such scrutiny did not usually have direct and clear institutional political effects. It was indeed the ulema, however weak their organization, that constituted the guardians of the pristine Islamic vision, of the normative dimensions of the *ummah*, and it was from these latter sources that they derived the strength of their moral force.

The second type of legitimization and accountability promulgated the vision of the ruler as the upholder of the pristine, transcendental vision. However weak the caliphs were, the continuity of their existence epitomized the continuity of the ideal of the pristine Islamic vision. Many later rulers (such as the Abbasids and Fatimids) came to power on the crest of religious movements that upheld this ideal and legitimized themselves in such religious-political terms. They further sought to retain popular support by stressing the religious aspect of their authority and by courting the religious leaders and religious sentiments of the community. Concomitantly, political problems were the central problem of Islamic theology.[35]

Many rulers, for instance the Moroccan sultans Sidi Muhammed and Mowlay Suleiman, attempted (especially if they could claim to be descendants of the Prophet) to portray themselves as such caliphs, often to be challenged by the different sectors of the ulema and various popular sect-like movements. Such challenges could be reinforced by the strong messianic or eschatological orientations with which the visions borne by these movements often became imbued.[36]

Such a conception of the legitimization of rulers, especially when combined with messianic or eschatological orientations, could become promulgated, and embodied, in the figures of Mahdis, Messiah-like renovators who appeared throughout history in many Muslim societies.

It was especially within Shi'ite Islam that a stronger potential for the implementation of such visions of the ruler continually existed in the image of the hidden imam, even if in a subterranean fashion,[37] but it also constituted a strong component of various sects in mainstream, Sunni, Islam.[38]

The impact of the continuity of this utopian vision of the original Islamic period and ideal, of the fact that this ideal was both never fully implemented and never fully given up, became evident in some specific characteristics of the political dynamism of Islamic regimes and of Islamic sects, or rather movements with sectarian tendencies. One has, of course, to be very careful in using the term "sect" with respect to Islam and, as we have seen above, with respect to Hinduism, considering the term's Jewish and especially Christian roots. One of the distinct characteristics of Christian sectarianism – the tendency to schism – has been, after the great break between the Shi'ites and the Sunnis, barely applicable to Islam. However, sectarian-like tendencies did exist in the continual social movements that developed in Muslim societies.

The visions promulgated by many of these movements were never given up, be they of political or renovative orientations, or commonly some combination of the two aimed at the renovation of a pristine vision of Islam. Such renovative visions or orientations were embodied in the different versions of the Mujaddid tradition – the tradition of reform – and possibly even innovative reforms.[39]

This renovative component could be oriented toward active participation in the center, its destruction or transformation, or toward a conscious withdrawal from it. But even such withdrawal, which developed both in Shi'ism and Sufism, often harbored tendencies toward renovation of the pristine vision. Such withdrawal could also often entail, as was the case with the Sufi orders in the eighteenth century, the reconstitution of the public sphere with many implicit, sometimes even explicit, political implications.

Truly enough, there never developed within Islam, as Bernard Lewis has shown, a concept of revolution. Indeed, despite the potential autonomous standing of members of the ulema, within no single Muslim policy did there develop a continual institutional mechanism for ensuring the accountability of rulers, much less one capable of deposing them, beyond any possible impact of rebellion. But at the same time, as Ernest Gellner indicated in his interpretation of Ibn Khaldoun's work, a less direct yet *very* forceful pattern of indirect accountability of rulers arose in the combination of social movements with the resurgence of tribal revival against "corrupt" or weak regimes,[40] rooted in the mode of expansion of Islam.

This tendency was closely related to the famous cycle of tribal conquest depicted by Ibn Khaldoun, whereby internal solidarity and religious devotion gave rise to the conquest of cities and the subsequent settlement of them. This conquest was followed by the degeneration of the ruling elite (stemming from the former tribe) and its possible subsequent regeneration or replacement out of new tribal elements from the vast, be it old or new, tribal reservoirs.

A very important characteristic of Islamic societies was that the political impact of such movements with their sectarian tendencies was often connected with processes attendant on the expansion of Islam and especially with the continuous impingement on the core of Islamic politics by tribal elements who presented themselves as the carriers of the original ideal Islamic vision and of the pristine Islamic polity. Significantly enough, many tribes (e.g. the Mongols or Pathans), after being converted to Islam, transformed their own "typical" tribal structures to accord with Islamic religious-political visions and presented themselves as the symbol of pristine Islam, with strong renovative tendencies oriented to the restoration of pristine Islam.

Such new "converts" – along with the seemingly dormant tribes of the Arabian peninsula, of which the Wahabites constitute probably the latest and most forceful illustration – become dynamic political forces in Islamic civilization, with the constitution of its international system or framework.[41]

It was because of these distinct characteristics of Islam's expansion that it was probably the only Axial Civilization within which sect-like movements, frequently in combination with tribal leaders or councils, often led to the establishment of new political regimes oriented, at least initially, at the implementation of the original pristine primordial Islamic utopia.

XII

The pattern of sectarianism that developed in the Christian civilizations, especially in medieval Catholicism, shared some characteristics with the other monotheistic civilizations, yet also developed some distinctive traits of its own. Christianity, from its very beginnings, contained a very strong this-worldly orientation which was reinforced when it became the dominant religion of the empire. Thus, a major characteristic of many, if not all heterodoxies and sects in Christianity, particularly those of the West, was that their alternative visions usually comprised a very strong this-worldly component, a very strong orientation to the restructuring and control of the political and cognitive arenas, and a strong predilection to enter into coalition with movements of social and political protest. The strong utopian this-worldly orientation became to some degree reinforced from the later Middle Ages on possibly by – as Eric Voegelin indicated,[42] probably in an exaggerated manner – the growing permeation of gnostic orientations into the mainstream of Christian thought against the predominant Augustinian vision. This permeation gave rise to continuous, intensive attempts at bridging the chasm between the ideal and existing realities, with many of these attempts based on belief in the possibility of infusing the existing community with the ideal vision and transforming it into the epitome of the full realization of the ideal order. The view promulgated by St. Augustine which stressed the separation between the City of God and the City of Man was, for a long period of time, the dominant one.

The basic characteristics of the heterodoxies and sects that developed in Western and Eastern Christianity were closely related to the characteristics of the respective orthodoxies. Such close relations included first, the existence of an organized church which attempted to monopolize at least the religious sphere and usually also the relations of this sphere to the political powers, and second, attempts by the church to promulgate and regulate doctrines according to clear, cognitive criteria and to construct boundaries of the realm of cognitive discourse.[43]

This tendency to the promulgation and regulation of doctrine was rooted in the prevalence within the monotheistic civilizations, especially Christianity with its strong connections to the Greek philosophical heritage, of strong orientations to the cognitive elaboration of the relations between God, man, and the world.

Throughout the Middle Ages, and even later in the Catholic tradition of the Counter-Reformation, heterodox anti-Augustinian tendencies often imbued with strong gnostic orientations were hemmed in by official, mainstream recognition of the basic discrepancy between the ideal order as envisaged by the transcendental vision and the actual, existing, social and political order or orders.[44] This view was espoused by the church and also by most political authorities – both attempting very strongly to bracket out the utopian and eschatological orientations with strong political components from the central political arena.

The Reformation constituted the crucial point of transformation of "Catholic" sectarianism in a this-worldly direction: Luther's famous saying concerning making the whole world into a monastery – while overtly oriented against the existing monastic orders – denoted a radical transformation of the hitherto prevalent hegemonic tendencies towards sectarian activities in Christianity. Such transformation was taken up even more forcibly both by the radical Reformation and by Calvinism – in which strong emphasis on the bringing together of the City of God and the City of Man developed. But Lutheranism did not on the whole give rise to dynamic autonomous political activities, and the radical Reformation and Calvinism were successful – and only for relatively short periods in relatively small communities – as for instance in Geneva, in some Dutch and Scottish sects, and in some of the early American colonies.

But all these developments did indeed provide a crucial background for the development of the Great Revolutions. But it was only in the revolutions that such sectarian activities were taken out, as it were, into the broader society and into the centers thereof. It was only with the Great Revolutions of modernity – possibly by the time of the revolt of the Netherlands, and certainly with the great rebellion (or civil war) in England and the American and French revolutions – that the central political arena became imbued with very strongly utopian, eschatological, and millennarian orientations which later became transformed in a more secular way in the Enlightenment and French Revolution.[45]

Proto-fundamentalist movements in different Axial Civilizations

XIII

Proto-fundamentalist movements constituted one of the utopian heterodoxies that developed in these civilizations, especially in the monotheistic civilizations. They usually developed side by side with many other types of religious movements, particularly with different types of reformist and other heterodox movements, as well as a multiplicity of different types of popular religiosity. Indeed, the basic characteristic of proto-fundamentalist, and later of fundamentalist movements, is that they continually crystallized through their, especially confrontational, relations with such other movements as well as with the existing religious establishments of their respective societies and the ways of life thereof.

These movements promulgated eschatological visions which emphasized the totalistic reconstruction of the mundane world according to sharply articulated transcendental visions. Such visions emphasized the necessity of constructing the mundane order according to the precepts of the higher transcendental one, with the search for an alternative "better" order beyond the existing one. These visions aimed at the utopian reconstruction of the existing order according to what had been promulgated by them as the pristine "original" vision of the given religion, a vision most fully realized in the past. They were oriented against the existing situation into which religion had degenerated, and promulgated the necessity to purify the existing social and political reality in name of their pristine vision. Such a vision could be perhaps most easily presented in terms of a sacred text or book as was the case with Judaism, Islam, and in a much more complicated way, in Christianity (especially Protestantism). But it could in principle also be presented in some "original" exemplary act or exemplary period often seen as depicted in a sacred text, as was the case in Islam, although not every emphasis on such return to a pristine model or on literal interpretation of a text necessarily entailed the development of such totalistic tendencies.

As do other utopian sectarian groups, proto-fundamentalist (and later fundamentalist) movements emphasized the construction of sharp symbolic and institutional boundaries; they stressed the distinction between purity and pollution, or the purity of the internal fundamentalist community as against the pollution of the outside world.[46] They evinced strong ideological totalistic tendencies, attempting to construct a self-enclosed universe which demarcates and organizes clearly all arenas of life with very weak tolerance of ambiguity and a closely related tendency to ritualization of patterns of behavior. They tended also to promulgate visions of the enemy outside or inside their own society, the two being, as for instance in the case of the Pharisees' struggle against the Hellenized Jews, often intermixed but certainly outside their own sect, an enemy who is the epitome of pollution, and against whom they have to battle.

The proto-fundamentalist groups were distinguished from other sectarian groups, movements, and heterodoxies, be they esoteric, mystical, reformist, or popular religious and the like (that is, however much they could be interwoven with these movements in concrete situations), by several basic characteristics which were rooted in their distinct attitudes to the basic antinomies inherent in the Axial Civilizations. While fully recognizing the existence of an egoistical, anarchic dimension of human nature, they not only refused to accept these dimensions as legitimate, but saw them as manifestations of depravity and pollution which had to be suppressed. The bearers of these visions emphasized the corruption and pollution of this world, of the mundane institutional reality, the people living in these conditions, and above all, the rulers and the existing religious establishment whom they held responsible for the full implementation of such vision. These movements denied also the autonomy of reason as against revelation and faith, and strongly opposed those philosophical schools that promulgated the possibility of such autonomy as their major enemies. Concomitantly they denied any vision differing from their own, often confronting the varying visions of other groups or sects.

As indicated above, in all these civilizations the proto-fundamentalist movements constituted only one of many different sectarian, potentially heterodox, movements. While some components of their sectarian-utopian vision could be found in many other movements or in popular culture, it was only in very few that all these components came together – the importance of their presence varied between different civilizations and in different periods of their respective histories. As in the case of all social movements the lines between these and other movements could become, in many instances, blurred, and the distinct characteristics of these movements diluted. But under appropriate circumstances these characteristics could forcefully crystallize again, thus highlighting their distinct dynamics.

XIV

The kernels of such movements existed in all the Axial Civilizations, yet they developed more in some than in others. The contents, intensity, and impact of different heterodoxies, and especially of proto-fundamentalist movements, varied greatly between these civilizations, as did the general impact of sectarian movements within them. The various features of these proto-fundamentalist movements have differed in extent of presence and intensity in the various civilizations and in the different periods of each of their histories. This is particularly so with regard to such features as the extent to which they have been totalistic or attempted to shape all arenas of life; their rigidity, especially with respect to the differentiation between internal and external, pure and polluted forces; and in the nature of their impact, particularly their political impact, on the societies in which they developed.

These differences in the proto-fundamentalist movements and their impacts on their respective societies were influenced by some of the basic characteristics of the Axial Civilizations and by their particular historical experiences. First, these differences were influenced by the concrete definitions of the chasm or tension between the transcendental and mundane orders, especially whether this tension was couched in secular terms (as in Confucianism and the classical Chinese belief systems, and in a somewhat different way in the Greek and Roman worlds), or conceived in terms of a religious hiatus (as in the great monotheistic religions, in Hinduism, and in Buddhism). In the latter cases, an important distinction exists between the monotheistic religions, in which a concept of God standing outside the universe and potentially guiding it was promulgated, and those systems such as Hinduism and Buddhism, in which the transcendental cosmic system was conceived in impersonal, almost metaphysical terms, in a state of continuous existential tension with the mundane system.

Secondly, such differences were influenced by the nature of the arenas that were perceived as appropriate for the implementation of the transcendental vision or visions. It is probably no accident that the "secular" conception of this tension was connected, as in China, Greece, and Rome, with an almost wholly this-worldly conception of the mode of implementation of the transcendental vision or that the metaphysical non-deistic conception of this tension, as in Hinduism and Buddhism, tended toward other-worldly conceptions of such implementation. The monotheistic religions, by contrast, tended to stress combinations of this- and other-worldly conceptions of such implementation.[47]

The fullest development of the various characteristics of proto-fundamentalist movements and ideologies has taken place, first, in those religions and civilizations in which there developed a non-secular definition of the chasm between the transcendental and mundane orders, and in which the mundane world, in particular its political realm, has constituted one – but only one – major arena for the implementation of a transcendental vision with strong other-worldly components. Or, to put it somewhat differently, such tendency has been manifest above all in those civilizations in which there is a strong emphasis on the reconstruction of the mundane world according to a transcendental vision and in which the mundane world constitutes at least one – but only one – arena for the implementation of such visions. It is in such religions or civilizations that the political dimensions of proto-fundamentalist movements become most fully articulated.

But under some, probably rather exceptional circumstances, even within civilizations in which these characteristics are not fully developed, sects or groups with strong proto-fundamentalist tendencies may develop. The case of the Sikh, albeit a monotheistic sect, is one such exception.[48] In Theravada Buddhist countries, in which already in medieval times a strong tendency had developed to conflate Buddhism with specific countries, like medieval Sri-Lanka planting proto-fundamentalist seeds to flourish at least partially in modern times.[49]

XV

The concrete contents and intensity of sectarian and heterodox movements in different Axial Civilizations were influenced not only by the basic ontological conceptions prevalent in them and by the conceptions of what constitutes the locus of implementation of the pristine transcendental visions, but also by the mode of distinction and confrontation between orthodoxy and heterodoxy that developed in these civilizations.[50]

From the point of view of such distinction, the most crucial difference is between those civilizations to which it is legitimate to apply the term "heterodoxy" and those in which it is more appropriate to talk "only" about sects and sectarianism. The term "heterodoxy" is fully applicable only to cases in which one can talk about orthodoxy, and this term in turn refers to both certain types of organizational and cognitive doctrinal structures. Organizationally the crucial aspect is, of course, the existence of some type of highly structured religious organizations – a church – which attempts to monopolize at least the religious arena and usually also the relations to political powers. But of no lesser importance is the organization of doctrine, that is, the structuring of clear, cognitive, and symbolic boundaries of systems of belief. Thus indeed, tendencies to the development of proto-fundamentalist characteristics have also been stronger in those civilizations in which there has been a relatively heavy emphasis on doctrine and on logocentric exposition thereof, and in which it is relatively easy to identify a clear version of such a doctrine.

With respect to both the organizational and doctrinal aspects, the major difference among the Axial-Age Civilizations is between the monotheistic civilizations in general and Christianity in particular on the one hand, and between Hinduism and Buddhism, with Confucian China constituting a sort of median representation, on the other.

It is within Christianity, within the Christian civilization or civilizations, that these organizational and doctrinal aspects of orthodoxy developed in the fullest way. This clear demarcation of doctrine tendency was rooted in the prevalence, within the monotheistic civilizations in general and within Christianity with its stronger connections to the Greek philosophical heritage in particular, of strong orientations to the cognitive elaboration of the relations between God, man, and the world. While the confrontation with the Greek philosophical heritage was also central in the case of Judaism and Islam, the institutional picture differed from that of Christianity. Christianity developed fully-fledged churches which constituted potentially active and autonomous partners of the ruling coalitions. In Judaism and Islam these developments were weaker. In these civilizations, there developed rather powerful, but not always as fully organized and autonomous organizations of clerics.

The importance of the structuring of such cognitive boundaries for the struggle between orthodoxies and heterodoxies is best seen, in a seemingly negative way, in the case of Hinduism and Buddhism.[51] In both these cases (as well as in Confucianism) we find that the structuring of cognitive doctrines (as distinct from ritual), and above all of their applicability to mundane matters, did not constitute as central an aspect or premise of these religions or civilizations as in the monotheistic ones. Thus even when, as in Buddhism, it is not entirely wrong to talk about something akin to church – albeit a much more loosely organized one – it is very difficult to talk about heterodoxy. At the same time non-schismatic sectarianism abounded, Buddhism itself being in a sense a sect that developed out of Hinduism. Buddhism also introduced new elements into the political scene – notably that special way in which Sangha, usually politically a very compliant group, could in some cases, as Paul Mus has shown,[52] become a sort of moral conscience of the community, calling the rulers to some accountability.

But this impact of these "sects" was, as we have seen, of a different nature from that of the struggles between the reigning orthodoxies and the numerous heterodoxies that developed within the monotheistic civilizations. In the latter cases a central aspect of such struggles was the attempt to reconstruct the political and cultural centers of their respective societies whereby these struggles became a central component of the central political processes in these civilizations – processes that often led to or were connected with wars of religion. While vicious and violent struggles often took place between different "Hindu" religious sects these did not entail the major characteristics of the wars of religion that developed within the monolithic civilizations – namely the attempts to impose by political means their respective religion and to construct a religiously pure and homogeneous political community.

The third aspect of Axial Civilization that was important in influencing the extent of development of proto-fundamentalist ideologies and movements was the extent of monopolization of the access to the sacred and to the proper interpretation thereof by any institution or group. The lack of such monopolization increases the range of possible interpretations, and facilitates the possibility of any group to present itself not just as opposing the existing religious authorities and their interpretation of religion, but as embodying the true vision of the religion – thus paradoxically also facilitating the development of multiple proto-fundamentalist groups. It is not accidental that it was within Protestantism, especially sectarian Protestantism, that fundamentalism developed in some of its most crystallized ways – while such developments were always much weaker in Catholic Christianity. In the latter case, such movements' fullest crystallization was always confronted by the mediating functions of the pope and the church, by its regulation of different monastic orders, and by Catholic establishment's ability to hem in fundamentalist tendencies.[53] Truly enough, even in those civilizations with strong other-worldly orientations in which there developed a strong emphasis on mediation of the access to the sacred, proto-fundamentalist tendencies may develop. However, these developments in such instances were generally weak, the contents of their utopian vision remained less fully articulated or structured, their internal organization and their orientation to the political arena were looser, and above all, the scope and intensity of their impacts were much weaker.

XVI

Influencing what was constituted in the eyes of the proto-fundamentalist movements as the embodiment of the pristine vision of their civilizations was a combination of the basic ontological visions, the conceptions of the proper loci for the implementation of the transcendental visions and the structuring of cognitive boundaries, and the conceptions of access to the sacred that predominated in them.[54]

The first "original" modern fundamentalism, which developed within the fold of American Protestantism, focused on a book, the Bible, particularly the Old Testament, as the embodiment of the original pristine vision as the guide for the reconstruction of the world. But it was not in all the Axial Civilizations that a book was seen as such an embodiment. Apart from Protestantism, this was probably also to a large extent the case in Islam. In both these cases, one book was seen as the direct source of ultimate authority, unmediated by any institution such as church or pope, and hence accessible to all believers.

While the New Testament did of course play a very important role in Catholic (as well as Eastern) Christianity, it did not attain the same position as the Old Testament in Protestant Christianity or the Koran in Islam. This was probably due to two interconnected facts. First, it was due to strong emphasis on mediation through the pope and church in Catholic Christianity and of the church in Eastern Christianity. Secondly, it was due to the fact that, unlike the Old Testament and Koran, the prescriptive legal dimension is not very strong in the New Testament.

In Judaism the situation was more complex. The Jewish Bible – the "Old Testament" – did not enjoy such authority in the Jewish tradition as the Koran in Islam or the Bible in Protestantism. In Rabbinical Judaism at least, it was open even in principle to many interpretations. The struggle over the relative supremacy of Oral as against the Written Law – the original Torah, the Pentateuch – constituted one of the major bones of contention among different Jewish groups from the beginning of the Second Temple period. Indeed, the Karaite movement which denied the validity of the Oral Law and harked back only to the Old Testament probably constituted the first full proto-fundamentalist movement to develop within the fold of rabbinical Judaism – or rather, to be more accurate, in conjunction with the full institutionalism of the halakhic mold. Later on, different interpretations of the Oral Law, sometimes in combination with different references to the Bible, could serve as the foci of the different proto-fundamentalist visions if these did not develop into fully fledged movements.

But such a pristine vision need not necessarily be embodied in a book or in some literal interpretation of it. It may be embodied by an exemplary personality or exemplary time period, or even a combination of these potential sources. It is thus not some particular emphasis on a specific attitude to a text or event, be it a literal interpretation of the text or some sanctification of the event, that distinguished "proto-fundamentalist" from other sectarian orientations. It is rather the utopian orientation to a pristine vision, whatever its concrete embodiment (text or exemplary period), with its specific sectarian orientations, that is the distinguishing characteristic of such movements.

XVII

Therefore, the most important factors shaping the contours of various proto-fundamentalist movements and explaining the differences between them have been these civilizations' basic ontological conceptions, their conceptions of the proper loci of implementation of the transcendental visions of the structuring of cognitive boundaries, and their prevalent conception of access to the sacred. Thus, it was the combination of these factors, albeit as they were interwoven with the particular institutional formations that developed in each society and civilization, that most influenced the shape and form of the various proto-fundamentalist movements.

In Jewish history, the problem of the range of feasible interpretations of the law constituted a central focus of controversy as early as the Second Temple period when the Sadducees upheld the sanctity of the biblical text against the Pharisees' far-ranging attempts at interpretation promulgated in the Oral Law. The more totalistic tendencies, focused on the proper interpretation and above all upholding of the law, were probably at the root of the Maccabean revolt and had developed among many of the "Dead Sea" sects. Significantly enough, there may have developed many differences between them as to the proper interpretation of the texts and over the relevance and importance of various texts. The first fully crystallized such movement was, as indicated above, probably the Karaite movement which probably built, to some extent at least, on those earlier developments during the Second Commonwealth. This heterodoxy developed in the sixth and seventh centuries in close connection with, and probably in reaction against, the crystallization of the hegemony of the Halakhah.[55]

The central focus of the Karaite vision was the principled negation of the primacy and hegemony of the Halakhah, not simply of the various details thereof, but of its ultimate legitimation. The Karaites denied the validity of the Oral Law and upheld – to a high degree in continuity with and with reference to earlier, especially Sadducean approaches – a sort of proto-fundamentalist view of the Written (as against the Oral) law, of a "realistic" as opposed to "nominalistic" view of the law.[56] At the same time at least some of the Karaites espoused a strong political orientation and negation of exilic existence, as the attitude to Eretz Israel and to *Galut* is very indicative.[57]

The emphasis on return to scripture could be found in many Jewish sects in the Middle Ages,[58] and it constituted a continual component in the Jewish historical experience. Such emphases could become connected with strong antinomial tendencies with respect to the upholding of law and with utopian and messianic orientations. Different combinations of such orientations could also be found in some of the sectarian, especially medieval (as distinct from early modern) "Hasidim"-pietist, and in many of the messianic movements.

A rather similar combination of the reexamination of the place of the Oral Law and its bases of legitimacy in connection with broader cultural themes and the possible redefinition of the political and collective Jewish identity, was to reappear, albeit naturally in an already new guise, with the beginning of the disintegration of the halakhic mold – first of all among some groups of returned Marranos. Later on proto-fundamentalist tendencies moving in the direction of modern fundamentalism developed to some extent in the reaction of neo-orthodoxy to the Enlightenment and to "Liberal" or Reformed Judaism.

XVIII

In Islam, proto-fundamentalist orientations developed above all in the various movements of renovation and reform. These movements could be focused on a "mahdi" and/or be promulgated by a Sufi order or tribal groups, such as the Wahabites,[59] as well as fostered in some of the schools of law. As Emanuel Sivan has pointed out:

Islamic Sunni radicalism was born out of the anti-accommodative attitude towards political power which had always existed within this tradition as a vigilante-type, legitimate, albeit secondary strand. Its most consistent and powerful paragon over the last seven centuries was the neo-Hanbalite school of Islamic law. When modern Sunni radicals looked in the 1920s and 1960s for a tradition to build upon, they turned quite naturally, like their predecessors in the late eighteenth century (the founders of Saudi Arabia) to neo-Hanbalism.[60]

The problem of authoritative scripture was also quite central in early Shi'ite civilization.[61]

Such fundamentalist tendencies were often connected with strong utopian eschatological orientations. As Aziz Al Azmeh has put it:

The Medinan Caliphate can thus be regarded, with Laroui, as a utopia. What Laroui omits is an important complement without which consideration of this matter would remain incomplete: this is eschatology. Unlike activist, fundamentalist utopia, this finalist state of felicity and rectitude associated with the future reigns of the Mahdi (the Messiah) and of 'Isab. Maryam (Jesus Christ) is not the result of voluntaristic action. Like the medinan regime and the prophetic example, it is a miraculous irruption by divine command onto the face of history, although it will be announced for the believers by many cosmic and other signs. Not only is the End a recovery of the Muslim prophetic experience, it is also the recovery of the primordial Adamic order, of the line of Abel, of every divine mission like those of Noah, Abraham, Moses, David, Solomon, Jesus and Muhammad, who incorporates, transcends and consummates them all in the most definitive form of primeval religiosity, Islam. The End, like the beginning and like the periodic irruptions of prophecy, is really against nature; it is the calque of the beginning so often repeated in history, and is the ultimate primitivism.[62]

It was indeed the Wahabites who probably constituted the last – and very forceful – case of a "traditional" Islamic proto-fundamentalist movement.

To follow John Voll in his analysis of their distinct characteristics:

The vision of creating a society in which the Qur'an is implemented means that Abd al-Wahhab's mission would inevitably entail political consequences. It was the local rulers who forced him to leave the town where he began teaching, and it was another local ruler, Ibn Sa'ud, who provided necessary support. The political system shared by the Wahhabis did not place the inspirational teacher in a position of political rule. Instead, the Wahhabi state was based on the close cooperation of a learned ruler (shayleh) and an able commander (*emir*). The combination reflected a long-standing perception of the proper relations between the institutions of the scholars and those of the commanders. Such a system of institutionalization reflected a reduced emphasis on charismatic leadership among Sunni fundamentalists and was also an important aspect of the great Sunni sultanates of the medieval era.

"Wahhabism" is thus a term used today to indicate the type of reformism elucidated in Ibn 'Abd al-Wahhab's opposition to popular religious superstitions and institutions, his insistence on informed independent judgment over against the rote reliance on medieval authorities, and his call for the Islamization of society and the creation of a political order which gives appropriate recognition of Islam. Wahhabism represents an important type of fundamentalism that continues to operate within the modern world but was not initiated as a result of conflict with the modernized West. The Wahhabis succeeded in establishing a state which, while imperfect, has nonetheless been recognized by many in the Islamic world as consonant with the fundamentalist vision to create an Islamic society. It is the most enduring experiment within the broader mission and as such has provided a standard against which other movements and states could be measured.[63]

XIX

Medieval Western Christianity was replete with sectarian, including proto-fundamentalist, movements. The various monastic movements and orders contained many proto-fundamentalist components as did many of the numerous heterodox sects.

At the same time, there developed many gnostic and eschatological trends – the best known probably being the Joachimite ones. Many of these movements were from time to time connected with peasant or urban uprisings. On the whole, they were – as those that developed in Eastern Byzantine Christianity were, as we have seen – successfully suppressed, or more often hemmed in, bracketed out as it were, by the religious and secular authorities, above all segregated and regulated in specific spaces. It was only with the Reformation that, as we have indicated above, a far-reaching, momentous change with respect to the place of sectarian, utopian fundamentalist-like movements in the social and political orders took place.

Extreme sectarian Protestantism can perhaps itself be seen as such proto-fundamentalism, or perhaps as the transitory phenomenon between proto-fundamentalist and modern fundamentalist tendencies. Such sectarian groups emerged in Europe with the first stage of institutionalization of Protestantism in such movements as the Anabaptists and other sectors of the radical reformation.[64] Later on they developed in combination with millennial and eschatological orientations in the American colonies.

Here, of course, of special importance from the point of view of our analysis is the fact that these sectarian heterodox tendencies became very influential in the crystallization of modernity. In a highly transformed way, they have become a central component of modern civilization manifest in different modern, political movements, among which are the fundamentalist movements. These tendencies constituted a central component in the crystallization of modern civilization and in modernity as it took shape in the Enlightenment and in the Great Revolutions. Contrary to some simplistic interpretations of Weber's Protestant Ethic thesis, these sectarian orientations did not directly give rise, as it were, to capitalism or to modern civilization in general. Rather, in addition to and when interwoven with very specific and distinctive institutional and geo-political conditions such as institutional pluralism, autonomy of cities, and developed legal institutions, these sectarian heterodox tendencies constituted a very important component in the crystallization of this civilization.[65]

The crystallization of this civilization gave rise to a new type of cultural and political dynamics in which social movements played a crucial part – a part that entailed both a continuation and a radical transformation of the place of sectarianism and proto-fundamentalist movements in the dynamics of Axial Civilizations.

XX

The prevalence of the "appropriate" ontological and doctrinal conceptions as well as the lack of mediatory constitutions greatly influence the propensity of development, in different civilizations, of proto-fundamentalist movements. But the actualization of these propensities greatly depends on concrete historical contexts and institutional settings. Although there are many studies of various specific proto-fundamentalist movements there have been but few systematic studies of the social and historical conditions and contexts in which these movements – especially as distinct from other sectarian movements – tend to develop, and the systematic comparative research on these problems is, if at all, only in its beginnings. Some very general and preliminary indications, which should be viewed mainly as possible starting points for such research, deserve further attention and elaboration.

Such movements tend to develop in situations that are seen or interpreted by some active sectors of their societies – especially some sectors of their intellectual or religious elites, as an onslaught, challenge, or threat – be it military, political, and/or cultural on their respective civilizations. Additionally, such situations are characterized by a diversity of ways and styles of life that developed together with a crystallization of what is seen as compromising, too-flexible orthodoxy with potentially degenerative tendencies, usually in situations when the existing regime became weaker through internal strife or external pressure.

In these situations such developments have been perceived by some influential religious elite groups as being closely interconnected with the potential undermining of the basic premises of their religion by an emphasis on what seem to be extra-religious criteria, above all by "reason"; often in combination with the acceptance, even legitimization of utilitarian, mundane concerns. In many such situations the combined impact of internal change and impingement of external forces is seen by some groups as undermining, in the name of autonomous reason and/or purely egoistical hedonistic constitution, however defined, their ultimate religious premises and their tradition.

Proto-fundamentalist groups' central focus in the perception of such a threat and attack is not simply the feeling that many groups and sectors of society, and especially the religious establishment, deviate from what is perceived as the proper traditional life and give in to the temptation of power and wealth. Rather, it is above all the seemingly willing adaptation of the religious establishment, of the predominant orthodoxy to these changes, of what is seen as its inherent compromise with these developments, that is seen by the proto-fundamentalist groups – and some wider sectors of the society – as providing the threat to their civilizations.

Sometimes this perception of a threat may be connected in a rather paradoxical way with the successful expansion of their respective religions. Such expansion, which is usually connected with the intensification of encounters with other religions or societies, often entails an almost inevitable compromise of the pristine vision with political realities which may be seen by some groups as pollution of this pristine vision and, as portrayed for instance by Ibn Khaldoun, as the degeneration and pollution of the rulers. It is the combination of all these tendencies that may give to the development of proto-fundamentalist movements the most central focus of their critique.

The social groups that promulgate the various proto-fundamentalist visions and those that are responsive to these visions vary greatly in different civilizations, but they seem to share several common characteristics. The major bearers of the proto-fundamentalist vision were usually sectors of the traditional religious leaders and communities, especially those that were dispossessed and dislocated from the old cultural and political centers. Concomitantly, in situations of expansion of civilizations, as for instance in the case of Islam, it is various groups in the periphery that may rebel against what may be seen by them as the polluted center. The most common characteristic of these groups is indeed dislocation and dispossession from the more central political or religious, and not solely economic, centers. Such dislocations did, of course, develop in many historical situations. It was, however, above all when such dislocations were combined with the weakening of existing regimes under external and internal pressures alike that the propensities to strong proto-fundamentalist tendencies developed. Such weakening of the existing – usually patrimonial or patri-monial-imperial – regimes was usually closely connected with the weaken-ing of the components of civility, from being predominant in the crystallization of the collective identities of these regimes and of the closely related tendency to bracket the primordial and transcendental sacred relig-ious or ideological dimensions thereof and of some concomitant pluralis-tic institutional arrangements. It entailed also the weakening of the structure and autonomy of the major elites; of the autonomy, cohesiveness, and accessibility of the center; of the inter-elite relations; of the mutual openings and trust between various elites, and between the different elites and broader social strata in the structuring of the center of these societies.

It was these conditions, especially the growing rigidity of the centers and the weakening of the solidarity relations between the center and the various elites and broader social strata that generated the displacement of the more active fundamentalist leaders, their concomitant feeling of dispossession or dislocation from the respective centers of their societies, and the resonance of broader (potentially or actually) dispossessed groups to the messages of threat to their respective civilizations that were being promulgated by these leaders.

The preceding observations are, however, only very preliminary indica-tions which hopefully can be helpful in the development of systematic research on conditions that facilitate the development of proto-fundamen-talist movements.

2

The Great Revolutions and the transformation of sectarian utopianism in the cultural and political program of modernity

The distinctive characteristics of the Great Revolutions – the modern transformation of sectarian utopianism

I

In the preceding discussion we have seen that while the kernels of proto-fundamentalist movements existed in all the Axial Civilizations, in some they developed more and had greater influence. Their influence became very important, possibly central, in the crystallization of modernity, and they have generated, in a highly transformed way, a central component of the cultural and political program of the discourse of modernity, as well as of different modern social and political movements, including that of the modern fundamentalist movements.

Modern fundamentalist movements, despite their seemingly traditional flavor and their affinity to proto-fundamentalist movements, can – perhaps paradoxically – best be understood against the background of the development of modernity and within the framework of this development. These movements and ideologies constitute one of the social movements in modern societies as movements of protest that developed with modernity. They constitute one possible development within, or component of, the cultural and political program and discourse of modernity, as it crystallized above all with the Enlightenment and with the Great Revolutions, as it expanded throughout the world and has continually developed with its different potentialities, contradictions, and antinomies.

By the Great Revolutions we mean, following general usage, the English Civil War and Great Rebellion; the first Great Revolutions – the American and French Revolutions; and the later ones – the Russian, Chinese and Vietnamese Revolutions. The Revolt of the Netherlands has been sometimes designated, and justly so in my mind, as the precursor of the first Great Revolutions.

This seemingly paradoxical situation is rooted in two basic facts. The first fact is that these revolutions have been in a way the culmination of the sectarian heterodox potentialities that developed in the Axial Civilizations – especially in those in which the political arena was seen as at least one of the arenas of implementation of their transcendental vision, including other-worldly components or orientations thereof. Such transformation entailed the turning upside down – even if ultimately, in the French and subsequent revolutions, in secular terms – of the hegemony of Augustinian vision, and the concomitant attempt to implement both the heterodox "gnostic" visions and the sectarian visions that wanted to bring the City of God to the City of Man. Secondly, and in close relation to the first fact, is that these modern fundamentalist movements share with other modern social movements some crucial characteristics which have crystallized in the Great Revolutions and in the cultural and political program of modernity.

The Great Revolutions can indeed be seen as the first or at least the most dramatic, and possibly the most successful, attempt in the history of mankind to implement on a macro-societal scale utopian visions with strong gnostic components. Such visions shared many characteristics with the proto-fundamentalist movements, except that in these revolutions it was above all future-oriented visions that have become predominant and have become a central component of the cultural program of modernity. It was indeed Eric Voegelin's great insight – even if he possibly presented it in a rather exaggerated way – to point out those deep roots of the modern political program in the heterodox-gnostic traditions of medieval Europe.[1] The modern cultural and political program, the cultural and political program as it crystallized with the Renaissance, Reformation, Enlightenment, and above all in the Great Revolutions, was indeed greatly influenced by the sectarian proto-fundamentalist movements of the late medieval and early modern era. It is the attempts in these revolutions to implement in the central political arena these utopian sectarian often gnostic conceptions that provide the crucial (even if indeed paradoxical) link between modernity, the modern cultural and political program, and the modern fundamentalist movements.

II

The historical roots of the Great Revolutions and the transformation of these roots in the modern setting are closely related to some of the revolutions' particular characteristics which distinguish them from other movements of rebellion, protest, or change of ruler that can be found in most societies. And it is these historical roots that are also very important for understanding the political processes that crystallized after these revolutions, and above all, the various modern social movements, including the modern fundamentalist movements.

Revolutions, especially the "Great Revolutions," denote of course radical changes of political regime far beyond the deposition of rulers or even the changing of ruling groups. They denote a situation in which such deposition and change, often connected with the execution or assassination of the rulers or sometimes "just" with their dethronement and banishment, results in some radical change in the rules of the political game and in the symbols and bases of legitimization of the regime. Such changes have usually been violent – but the violence that develops in these revolutions is not just of the type found in many riots, uprisings, court intrigues, and in the position of rules that can be found in most political regimes. Rather, what characterizes such violence is its ideological justification, amounting to near sanctification. Such justification is often rooted in the attempt to combine the change in symbols, bases of legitimization, and the basic institutional framework of a regime with new visions of political and social order. It is this combination that is distinctive in these revolutions. In other words, such revolutions tend, with the unfolding of the revolutionary process, to spawn, to use Said Arjomand's term, some distinct cosmologies, some very distinct cultural and political programs.[2]

The combination of violent change of regime with the promulgation of a very strong ontological and political vision is not exclusive to these revolutions. The crystallization of the Abbasid caliphate, often called the Abbasid revolution, is a very important illustration, if possibly only a partial one, of such a combination in earlier historical periods.[3]

What is distinct in these modern revolutions is the nature of their ontologies and cosmologies; their concomitant political-ideological visions and the relationship of such visions to both the mode of deposition of the rulers, and the development of new conceptions of accountability of rulers. However great the differences between these revolutions, they all shared from this point of view some basic characteristics. Within all of them there developed an attempt to reconstruct the polity – to topple the old and create new political institutions on the basis of a new vision in which themes of equality, justice, freedom, and participation of the community in the political center and process were promulgated. The promulgation of these themes was not, of course, limited to these revolutions; they can be found in many movements of protest throughout human history. What was new in these revolutions was, first, the combination of these perennial themes of protest with new "modern" themes such as the belief in progress, and with the demands for full access to the central political arenas and participation in it; secondly, the combination of all these themes not just with millenarian visions of protest but with an overall utopian vision of the reconstruction of society and of the political order. It was the transposition of the strong utopian component, which indeed built on the utopian traditions of the societies or civilizations in which these revolutions developed into the centers of their respective societies, that was central in these revolutions.

The distinctiveness of the utopian visions that constituted the central core of the cosmologies or ontologies of these revolutions is evidenced, in addition, in the conception of society as an object which can be remolded above all by political action according to such vision. That is, it is this view of society as an object of active construction by human beings – above all by future-oriented political action – that constitutes one of the distinct characteristics of the cosmologies of these revolutions. They proclaimed the primacy of the political in the process of reconstruction of society accordingly to such visions.[4]

Closely related to these future-oriented visions was the strong emphasis in most sectors of these revolutionary groups on dissociation from the preceding historical background of the respective societies, a denial of the past, an emphasis on a new beginning, and the combination of such discontinuity with violence. This orientation was rather muted in the Revolt of the Netherlands and even in the English Civil War, in which the references to the (basically utopian) English past were very strong; it was already much stronger – despite the frequent references to the English tradition – in the American Revolution and became a major theme in the French and the subsequent – especially Russian, Chinese, and Vietnamese Revolutions.[5]

These revolutionary visions also entailed very strong missionary orientations. Although each such revolution set up a new regime in a particular country, and although these regimes promulgated, especially in the later stages of their institutionalization, strong patriotic themes, always bearing the ineradicable stamp of the countries in which they developed, the revolutionary visions were nevertheless presented and promulgated, even if in different degrees, as universal – applicable in principle to the entire humanity.

The English Puritans were part of a wide international network of different radical reformatory groups, and although their activities were oriented mostly and quite consciously to the English scene, and often presented as English, they were at the same time promulgated as being of universal validity.

The declarations of the American Revolution, whether the Declaration of Independence, the Preamble to the Constitution, or the Bill of Rights, were couched in universalistic terms. Although the American Revolution, possibly because of the relative geo-political isolation of the colonies and of the United States, did not tend to "export" itself beyond the continent, the American revolutionary vision nevertheless implied the universal validity of its message, of what would later be defined as the "American way of life."[6] Such a universalistic message was of course even more pronounced in the French and later in the Russian Revolution.

The importance of the universal and missionary aspects of the ideologies of these revolutions can also be seen in the relative weakness or secondary importance, within their symbolic repertoire, of primordial symbols. The primordial component in the revolutionary construction of the symbols of collective identity or consciousness of the societies in which these revolutions occurred was of secondary, even if not necessarily negligible, importance.

True enough, all these revolutions in fact occurred within the framework of their respective political societies and were greatly influenced by their distinctive political traditions. In all these revolutions, some emphasis on primordial elements, as for instance the emphasis on the rights of Englishmen in the English Civil War, or on "La Patrie" in the French Revolution, and even more on strong patriotic themes was promulgated by the revolutionary regimes.[7] In all these revolutions there took place a far-reaching patriotic mobilization and cultural construction of the modern nation state. These themes were promulgated in all these revolutions and in the post-revolutionary regimes through the initiation of festivals, establishment of citizens' armies, and in the kernels of a modern school system. But the specific "national" primordial themes were usually, in the more official promulgations of the revolutionary vision presented, secondary to the more general, universalistic ones that constituted the core of the revolutionary vision. The various patriotic themes were promulgated in universalistic terms and the respective nations presented as bearers of universalistic visions.

III

It was not only with respect to their ontologies or cosmologies, or in terms of their results, that the Great Revolutions evinced some very distinct characteristics. Of no less importance were the distinct characteristics of political process that developed in them.

This process shared some very important characteristics with several types of processes of social and political struggle to be found in many societies, to some extent in all of them. Rebellions and movements of protest are closely related to liminal situations that develop in all human societies, and they themselves evince liminal characteristics – as was also the case in these revolutions. Another crucial component of the political process that developed in the Great Revolutions which can be found in all societies is that of political struggle between different groups in the center. In the case of the revolutions, such struggle in the center tends to be, as Charles Tilly has pointed out, a struggle about competing sovereignties,[8] a struggle between different groups who attempt to dislodge the existing "sovereigns" (those groups that monopolize sovereignty and the exercise of power in a given society at a given period of time) and to transfer sovereignty to themselves.

All these types of social and political struggle are to be found in the Great Revolutions – but these revolutions exhibit some distinct core characteristics which go beyond these types of struggle and distinguish them from movements of protest and central political struggle in other societies. These common characteristics are to be found in all of them, even if their relative importance naturally varies between different revolutions, and they have been crucial in the shaping of some of the distinct characteristics of modern political processes and regimes.

The first such characteristic has been the great intensity and continuity of these rebellions, movements of protest and struggle in the center over relatively long periods of time. The second such distinctive characteristic is the fact that these different types of processes of change and movements of political struggle have here become interwoven in relatively continuous and common organizational frameworks. Temporary alliances between rebelling lords and peripheral rebellions or movements of protest could be found in many societies. Struggles at the center did in many societies weaken them and hence facilitate the outbreak of rebellion, and vice versa. Continuous, protracted rebellions could also often set the stage for struggles at the center.

Yet another distinct characteristic of these revolutions was, as Eric Hobsbawm has shown, the crucial importance of the direct impact on the central political struggle of popular uprisings, that is, the movement of popular uprisings into the center.[9] Additionally unique to the political process that developed in these revolutions was the continuous interweaving of these different political processes into some common, however fragile and intermittent, frameworks of political action. In other words, in these revolutions, new forms of political organization and ideology developed which brought together sectors of each of these types of political activity and processes into common frameworks, even if, especially in the first revolutions, in an intermittent way. The model army in the English

Revolution, the various clubs and political groupings of the American one, and the many clubs and cliques of the French Revolution are among the most important illustrations of such new types of frameworks or organizations. Even when no continual new political organizations developed, the impact of revolutionary activity transformed the nature of the electoral process[10] from a sort of status competition between different sectors of the higher social echelon into radical political competition.

The development of such new types of organization was contingent, of course, on a new type of leadership, one that appealed to various sectors of the population and which was not embedded in any of them or seen as representing only one or a few such sectors. In the Russian, Chinese, and Vietnamese revolutions, organized groups which existed already as parties or at least proto-parties before the revolutions constituted the vanguards of the revolutions.

But the most central component of such leadership, the most central component in these revolutionary processes – and one that probably constitutes their most distinct characteristic – is the place of distinct cultural, religious, or secular groups, and above all, of intellectuals and political activists. Especially prominent among them were the bearers of the "gnostic" vision of bringing the Kingdom of God, or some secularized vision thereof, to earth. The English and to a different extent the American Puritans; the members of the French clubs so brilliantly described by Albert Cochin and later on by François Furet, Mona Ozouf,[11] and others; and the various groups of Russian intelligentsia[12] are the best-known illustrations of this social type. It was usually these groups that provided the distinctive element that transformed rebellions into revolutions.

It was not only that these groups promulgated and articulated the distinct ideologies of these revolutions. It was also, usually above all from the members of these groups, that the new leadership and the organizational skills that were so central for the crystallization of the new political activities discussed above were recruited. It was also these groups that promulgated the visions and articulated the ideologies and propaganda that was crucial in bringing together the disparate social forces that joined in the revolutionary process. It was, in other words, these groups that provided the crucial link between the distinct revolutionary cosmologies and the revolutionary process.

IV

The Great Revolutions were characterized not only by each of these distinct features, i.e. the development of revolutionary cosmologies and political programs, of the political processes that developed within them, and of their far-reaching results, but also and above all by their combination.

Needless to say, the relative importance of these different components varied greatly among the various revolutions. Some of these components – as for instance the full elaboration of the distinct modern cosmologies and the break with the past – were weaker in the English Revolution. It was indeed in the French Revolution that all these components came together in the most dramatic way, and hence it is the French Revolution that has been seen as the first pristine model of modern revolutions. Moreover, the interweaving between different social and political actors in the revolutionary process was not continuous, nor were such organizations stable or homogeneous. It often developed quite haltingly – being rather weak in the first stages of the revolutionary process, when the older types of rebellions were predominant. Such interweaving became stronger when various rebellious or reformist groups faced "counter-revolutionary" forces and usually gathered momentum thereafter.

Concomitantly, in each phase of the revolutionary process there developed not just one but several common frameworks of political activity. Throughout the revolutionary process there developed also numerous conflicts and cleavages between different political and social groups which participated in these processes. Two such cleavages and conflicts were of special importance in shaping the process and outcomes of the revolutions. The first cleavage was the "class" composition of these groups, whether it was aristocracy, gentry, middle and lower urban or peasant groups, and the relations between these classes that provided the social basis of these groups and the relative predominance of each of these different elements. The second instance was the sectarian cleavage between different groups of intellectuals, of religious sects and the like, each of which was the bearer of a distinct revolutionary vision. It was the combination of these two types of cleavage – class and political sectarian – that provided the specific dynamics, and to no small degree shaped the outcomes of the various revolutions. It was the relation between these cleavages, between the different political classes and ideological groups, that shaped the coalitions that were most active in different phases of the revolutionary process and greatly influenced the nature of the different post-revolutionary regimes. But whatever the difference between the Great Revolutions, they were characterized by some combination of the various components developed above and the central role of the intellectuals and autonomous political activists in them.[13]

V

Such participation by intellectuals in the political process entailed a rather far-reaching change, indeed transformation, of their role in the Axial Civilizations in their political activities, and in their relation to power – a transformation which is of central importance for the understanding of modern political dynamics.

Intellectuals and clerics have played, as we have seen, a crucial role in the institutionalization and dynamics of these civilizations. At the same time the institutionalization of Axial civilizations often transformed the nature of the political elites and converted the new intellectual elites into relatively autonomous partners in the major ruling coalitions and movements of protest. The process of such institutionalization entirely changed the basic characteristics of intellectuals in comparison with the specialists in ritual, magical, and sacral activities of the pre-Axial Civilizations. Such specialized technical activities became components of the relatively autonomous construction of the cultural and social order, and their carriers constituted special elites – intellectuals and clerics – who were recruited and legitimized according to distinct, autonomous criteria, and organized in autonomous settings distinct from those of the basic ascriptive units. Accordingly, intellectuals and clerics tended to become potentially independent of other elites and of other social groups and categories. At the same time they were necessarily in strong competition with the other elites in particular, above all over the monopoly of the production and spread of symbols and media of communication.

Closely related to the place of such intellectuals in the construction of these civilizations, two types of tension developed between them and other, especially the political, elites. The first such tension, which has often been analyzed in the literature, was that between the intellectuals and the rulers. The focus of such tension was usually the scope of the relative autonomy of the intellectuals in their specialized activities.

The second, and perhaps more intensive, tension focused on the attempts of the intellectuals to impose their own distinct conceptions of the cultural and social order on other elites (including other intellectual elites) and on broader groups and strata, and also on the contradiction between the attempts to exercise such power and influence and the need to maintain the conditions that ensured maximum autonomy in the different areas of intellectual specialization and creativity.

These tensions became intensified with the Great Revolutions and with the crystallization of the modern cultural political order. In all these Great

Revolutions, it was, as we have seen, religious and secular intellectuals who promoted the basic cultural and ideological visions that were promulgated in the crystallization of these revolutions and which shaped the premises of modern societies. Hence, all these tensions and problems were intensified with the crystallization of modern civilization in the wake of the Great Revolutions.

These revolutionary origins of modernity and the place of intellectuals in them had many repercussions on the relationship between intellectuals and political elites and in the place of intellectuals in the political process. The basic symbolic, as opposed to organizational distinction between intellectuals and political elites becomes even more blurred than before. Some sectors of the more institutionalized intellectuals performing various functions in universities, in legal institutions and the more "marginal" heterodox, were at least for short periods brought together into the center attempting to reconstruct it.[14] Hence, paradoxically, the tensions between them could become exacerbated, at the same time intensifying the internal contradictions and antinomies in the cultural program of modernity.

VI

The central role in all these revolutions of autonomous intellectuals entailed a radical transformation of the political activities and orientations of major medieval heterodoxies and sects, and in the place of heterodox protest activities in the political process. The essence of this transformation was that instead of the suppression or hemming in of the more radical sectarian and heterodox activities and orientations in special, highly controlled, spaces (such as monasteries, which was characteristic of the medieval period), these activities and orientations were transposed, in the revolutions and in the subsequent modern political process, into the central political arena.

Sectarian activities and heterodoxies developed, as we have seen in chapter 1, in all these civilizations or societies long before the revolutions – although, unlike rebellions and central political struggle, they are not to be found in all human societies; they are indeed only to be found in the Axial Civilizations. In many cases, as for instance in the European Middle Ages and early modern age, some sectarian groups allied themselves with rebellions, whether of peasants or of urban lower classes, and in other cases with some of the actors in the political struggles in the center. But basically most such sectarian activities were confined to, or hemmed into, the more marginal sectors or subterranean sectors of the society.

The Reformation[15] constituted, as we have seen, the crucial point of transformation of the "Catholic" sectarianism in a this-worldly direction: Luther's famous dictum of making the whole world into a monastery – while overtly oriented against the existing monastic orders – did denote a radical transformation of the hitherto prevalent hegemonic tendencies towards sectarian activities in Christianity. Such transformation was taken up even more forcibly by both the radical Reformation and by Calvinism – in which there developed very strong emphasis on the bringing together of the City of God and the City of Man. But Lutheranism did not on the whole give rise to active autonomous political activities, and the radical Reformation and Calvinism were successful – and only for relatively short periods in relatively small communities – in Geneva, in some Dutch and Scottish sects, and in some of the early American colonies.

All these did indeed provide a crucial background for the development of the Great Revolutions. But it was only in the revolutions that such sectarian activities were taken out, as it were, into the broader society and into the centers thereof. It was only in the revolutions that these radical sectarian orientations became interwoven not only with rebellions, popular uprisings, and movements of protest, but also with the political struggle at the center into which they were transposed. In this process the ideological, propagandist, and organizational skills of these intellectuals or cultural elites were of crucial ideological and organizational importance. Without them the entire revolutionary process as it crystallized in these situations would probably not have occurred. Hence they constituted the most crucial element in shaping the political process that developed in these revolutions.

It was all these orientations, as well as the formation, reconstruction, and institutionalization of new types of centers, that distinguished the Great Revolutions and their institutionalization from other movements of protest in history, and which gave them their specific modern connotations.

VII

Yet another central aspect of the revolutionary process was the transformation of the liminal aspects and symbols that were prevalent in various movements of protest. This transformation denoted a far-reaching, radical change in the place of themes of protest, and of violence in the political process. It was not only that many such popular uprisings – best epitomized by the storming of the Bastille – moved into the center and became transposed into it. More important is the fact that in most of these revolutionary processes, the central political arena became, for relatively long periods, shaped in a liminal mode. The center itself became – at least for some periods – as it were a liminal situation or arena, a series of such situations, or the arena in which liminality was played out.[16]

These liminal dimensions of the revolutionary process have been closely connected to the centrality of violence in it. It is not only that violence spread wider and became a component of the central political struggle – in itself a very important and distinct development. What is of crucial importance is that the centrality of violence – and in some cases its ideological sanctification, its sacralization – became, as Merleau-Ponty pointed out, the very essence of the revolutionary process.[17] This centrality of violence signalled the combination of the breakdown of the existing rules of political power, the loss of legitimacy of the existing institutional frameworks, the delegitimization of the existing order, and the search for the establishment of other rules and other symbols of legitimacy. Thus this centrality of violence became transformed into and visible in the very centers of these societies and became highly visible in them. One of the most important aspects of this centrality of violence has been the development and sanctification of terror as one of the recurring components or themes of the revolutionary experience. It was perhaps only in Islam's Order of Assassins and in other Islamic sectarian movements that something approaching such sanctification of violence, of terror, could be found on any large scale.[18] This centrality of violence also infused the liminal characteristics of the revolutionary situations, thus distinguishing them from other liminal situations.

The combination of these most extreme components of the revolutionary process crystallized into political action, aiming at the homogenizing reconstruction of society in their name of a utopian vision crystallized in what would become the Jacobin political vision or tradition. The diverse kernels of this tradition developed in the various Jacobin clubs that emerged during the French Revolution – the common denominator of which emerged as the emphasis on the dictatorship of *salut public*. This emphasis became closely interwoven with the sanctification of violence during the Reign of Terror – epitomized in the figure of Robespierre. This sanctification's predominance in the revolutionary discourse and activity broke down with the Thermidor, but its major premises permitted – in the eyes of both its supporters in different camps and of its opponents – a central component of the modern political discourse, a component that epitomized some of the basic demons of the modern political program and discourse.[19]

The cultural and political programs of modernity: basic premises

VIII

It was in these revolutions and above all with the institutionalization of the post-revolutionary regimes that the basic characteristics of the cultural and political program of modernity became crystallized – especially the combination of orientations of rebellion, protest, and intellectual antinomianism, together with strong orientations to center formation and institution building.[20]

In the background of this program loomed some very powerful, even if sometimes hidden, different meta-narratives of modernity – to follow E. Tiryakian's felicitous expression. There were the Christian, in the sense of affirmation of this world in terms of a higher, not fully realizable vision, the gnostic which attempts to imbue the world with a deep hidden meaning, and the chthonic which emphasizes the full acceptance of the given word and of the vitality of its forces.[21] These different meta-narratives were closely related to the different historical roots of this program.

Among these historical roots the most important have been first the political theories of antiquity and the republican tradition as it developed in the Renaissance (which modeled itself on antiquity even if in fact it differed greatly from it in the Reformation), and the covenantal conceptions as they developed in the Reformation and in the Counter-Reformation's response to them. A second central ideological component of these regimes goes back to, and in many ways incorporates, some of the basic premises of the accountability of rulers to some higher law – the word of God or the Mandate of Heaven – which have been characteristic of the Axial-Age Civilizations, with Europe, of course, being one.[22] The third major ideological component of the modern cultural and political program was the emphasis on the autonomy of the individual, and the closely related if not identical, legitimization of private interests as it developed in concert with the ideology of individualism and was reinforced by the development of new economic forces of the market.[23] Fourthly, there was the tradition of representation and of representative institutions as it developed in Europe during the Middle Ages in the various councils, parliaments, and assemblies of estates – many of them building on traditions of tribal assemblies.

A fifth central ideological component of these regimes rooted in the traditions of Axial civilizations was the utopian eschatological one, the search or quest for an ideal social order. These new modern utopian visions entailed the transformation of Christian eschatology into the secular vision of the unfolding of human destiny. The search for the ways in which the concrete social order could become the embodiment of an ideal order became a central component of the modern political discourse and tradition, and it was closely connected with the charismatization of the center as the arena in which such visions can and should be implemented, a process that crystallized fully in the Great Revolutions. The Great Revolutions can indeed be seen as claimed – even if in an exaggerated way by Eric Voegelin – as the first, or at least the most dramatic, and possibly the most successful, attempt in the history of humanity to implement on a macro-societal scale utopian visions with strong gnostic components.[24]

The various components of this program, with their multiple historical roots, were institutionalized in the aftermath of the Great Revolutions. The institutionalization of this program did not however obliterate the relative autonomy of its various components. On the contrary, this institutionalization gave rise to the development within this program of continual tensions between these components and their ideological and institutional implications.

IX

This program, with its tensions and contradictions, developed and became institutionalized against the background of specific but continually changing historical conditions and processes.

The institutional background of modern regimes, including the constitutional democratic regimes, were the formation in Europe of modern states, the crystallization and constitution of new types of collectivities, and the development of modern market, capitalist, political economies. Common to the first two processes was a very strong emphasis on territorial boundaries; the development of new state–society relations most fully manifest in the emergence of a distinct type or types of civil society; the concomitant transformation of political processes; and the development of capitalist, later industrial-capitalist, types of political economy and the closely connected continual European expansion.

The crystallization of the first modern states in Europe entailed the combination of political administrative centralization with a strong emphasis on the territorial dimensions of the political community, and additionally with a new conception of the political arena – namely as autonomous, even as a distinct ontological entity with relatively clear territorial and symbolic boundaries. This conception, which emerged above all in continental

Europe and in England in close connection with the Wars of Religion, entailed the transformation of the basic conceptions of sovereignty – even if haltingly and intermittently – from the older one of *dominium politicum and regale*.[25] In many of these Continental states, the state was conceptualized in terms of exclusive sovereignty defined in secular terms – even if the absolutist kings claimed some type of divine legitimization or "Divine right of kings." It was the sovereign – the king or the state ("L'état c'est moi") – who was, even if never wholly unchallenged, the embodiment of what could be called the general will, the common good of the society.

In the context of the development of this modern state the most important institutional roots of the modern constitutional democratic regimes were the representative institutions that developed in medieval Europe – the various councils, parliaments and assemblies of estates, many of them building on traditions of tribal assemblies.

The processes of constitution of the new, modern states and of legitimization of the new political regimes were closely interwoven in European societies with those of construction of new types of collectivities, of collective identity or consciousness. The most important dimension of such construction was the crystallization of, above all, secular definitions of each of the components of collective identity; the civil, primordial, and universalistic "religious" ones;[26] the growing importance of the civil and procedural components thereof and a continual tension between such different components; and the development of a very strong emphasis on territorial boundaries as the main loci of the institutionalization of collective identity. The emphasis on the territorial components of collective identity entailed the development of a very strong connection between the construction of states and that of the major, "encompassing" collectivities – a connection which became epitomized in the tendency to construct what was to be called nation states. Such construction entailed a very strong emphasis on the congruence between the cultural and political identities of the territorial population, and the promulgation by the major states of strong symbolic and effective commitments to the center, based on a close relationship between these centers and the more primordial dimensions of human existence and of social life – as these dimensions were reconstructed in that period.

X

The development in Europe of modern states and collectivities and the transformation of the conception of sovereignty were closely related to changes in the structure of power in society – namely to the emergence of multiple centers of economic and political power; and to the development of some nuclei of a distinct type of civil society and of a new type of public arena or sphere.

The development of multiplicity of centers of power and of the nuclei of civil society was closely related to the development of the new type of political economy – of new modes of production, to the development of a market economy, first of commercial and later of industrial capitalism. It was the development in this period of commercial and proto-industrial capitalist economies, of market ideologies,[27] and the strong concomitant emphasis on the rights to private property that created too the nuclei of a new type of relatively independent centers of power. These centers of power were potentially beyond the reach of the political (whether absolutist, republican, or revolutionary communitarian) powers. At the same time these new centers of power often claimed – in line with the older traditions of representative institutions in Europe – the right of autonomous access to the centers of power. Concomitantly there developed potentially autonomous public arenas distinct from the state, as well as from any single ascriptive group of such arenas. It was indeed the continual construction of such public arenas, independent from any single ascriptive sector and from the state – but possibly rooted in many such sectors and above all having an autonomous access to the central political arena, to the state – that constituted the epitome of the new type of civil society that developed in this period in Europe.

XI

The last, but certainly not least, of the processes that were crucial for the formation of modern European societies were those generated by the development of capitalist – first commercial, later on industrial capitalist – political economies.

The development of capitalist economies, of the international capitalist system, and the concomitant continuous expansion of the economy, entailed the creation of new classes and new social strata – of various new "capitalist" classes, industrial workers, and proletariat – and gave rise to concomitant dislocations, new class relations, and class confrontations. These elements and dynamics further gave rise to the continuous international expansion of the capitalist economy as well as to modern political and ideological systems through imperial, colonial, and far-reaching economic means. These developments were closely connected with continual shifts in the distribution of resources and in the modes of access to them, with continual processes of social dislocation and with a continual struggle for the inclusion of different social groups into the central institutional frameworks and arenas or with exclusion from them.

All these processes gave rise to the development of new centers of power which challenged the traditional authorities while generating both new inequalities and tendencies to new concentrations of power and to concomitant dispossession of weaker groups.

All these institutional developments took place within the framework of the emergence of the European state system, which crystallized through political and military responses and within which mobilization of resources for war constituted a central component,[28] and which was to serve also as the jumping-board for political and military expansion beyond Europe. This expansion indeed spawned strong tendencies – rather new and practically unique in human history – to the development of not only universal but also actually world-wide institutional and symbolic frameworks and systems. Several world-wide systems, economic, political, ideological – all of them pluralistic and multi-centered – emerged, each generating its own dynamics and its own reactions to the others. The interrelations among them have never been "static" or unchanging, and the dynamics of these international frameworks or settings gave rise to continuous changes in these societies. This expansion generated continual confrontation between the societies incorporated in the new internal systems, above all between the various hegemonic (initially Western) centers and different peripheries; and between the premises of the cultural program of modernity and the premises of the non-Western European civilization.

A crucial component of this confrontation was the fact that the European expansion gave rise to the construction of a specific European self-conception in relation to other civilizations – a self-conception that entailed a distinct hierarchical ordering of different civilizations with the European on top. Accordingly this conception engendered – despite its universalistic premises and within the framework of these premises – very strong exclusivist tendencies.[29]

All these institutional developments constituted not only the historical background of the crystallization of the cultural and political program of modernity, but also the arenas in which this program – with the antinomial tensions and contradictions inherent in it – was continually played out and institutionalized, and confronted with continually changing institutional developments. All the processes continually confronted the basic premises of the new political regimes.

XII

This program entailed a far-reaching transformation of the conception of the relations between the transcendental and mundane orders and, concomitantly, of the basic conceptions of political realm, of authority, and of center–periphery relations. This program gave rise, perhaps for the first time in the history of humanity, to the belief in the possibility of bridging the gap between the transcendental and mundane orders, of realizing in the mundane orders, in social life, some of the utopian, eschatological visions. All of this thus entailing, as we have seen, the turning upside-down – even if ultimately in secular terms – of the hegemony of Augustinian vision, and the concomitant attempt to implement the heterodox "gnostic" as well as otherworldly and sectarian visions which wanted to bring the City of God to the City of Man. These transformations of the conception of the relation between the transcendental and mundane orders were indeed rooted in the Great Revolutions.

The radical innovation of this cultural program, of this new tradition, even if it could be seen as a transformation of the premises of the preceding traditions, lay in several major, often conflicting, tendencies and premises, all of which shared a strong common denominator: this was the change of the place of God in the construction of both the cosmos and of man, and of belief in God (or in some metaphysical principles) as constituting the starting point for the understanding of both man and cosmos, to the concomitant increasing emphasis on autonomy of reason and man.

The most important components of this program were first the "naturalization" of man, society, and nature; second the promulgation of the autonomy and potential supremacy of reason in the exploration and even shaping of the world; and third the emphasis on the autonomy of man.

Man and nature tended to become "naturalized," or increasingly perceived as no longer directly regulated by the will of God as in the monotheistic civilizations, or by some higher, transcendental metaphysical principles as in Hinduism and Confucianism, or by the universal Logos, as in the Greek tradition. Rather, they were conceived as autonomous entities regulated by some internal laws which could be fully explored and grasped by human reason and inquiry. It was this naturalization of cosmos and of man that constituted the central turning-point from the pre-modern to the modern cosmological and ontological visions and conceptions.

These transformations in the basic conceptions of the relations between man, cosmos, and God, as they developed in early modern Europe, were not initially necessarily anti-religious. Indeed, many of them had very strong religious roots, especially in the Reformation, the Counter-

Reformation, and their repercussions. At first the place of God as the creator of the universe was not denied; rather, these ideological transformations reformulated his place with relation to man, cosmos, and nature. God, insofar as he remained in the picture, was more and more conceived as the creator of a universe that has generated laws of its own – laws that can be fully grasped by human reason and inquiry.

Concomitantly, central to this cultural program was the emphasis on the growing autonomy of man; his – or hers, but in this program certainly "his" – emancipation from the fetters of traditional, political, and cultural authority and the continuous expansion of the realm of personal and institutional freedom and activity. Such autonomy entailed two dimensions: first, reflexivity and exploration, and second, the active, constructive mastery of nature and society.

The exploration of such laws became one of the major foci of the new tradition, providing the key to the working out and exploration of the perennial problems of the reflexive traditions of the Great Civilizations. At the same time it was more and more assumed in this new cultural program that exploration of these laws would lead to the unraveling of the mysteries of the universe and of human destiny.

Such exploration was not purely passive or contemplative. Indeed, a very strong assumption of this cultural vision, or at least of large parts thereof, was that through such exploration not only the understanding, but even the mastery of such destiny, and a concomitant continuous expansion of human environment, could be attained by conscious human effort.

The exploration of nature and the search for potential mastery over it tended also, at least in some versions of this new tradition, and especially in some sectors of the Enlightenment, to extend beyond technical and scientific spheres into the social sphere. Such a view led almost naturally to the emphasis on the exploration and investigation of human nature and of society. It could become connected with the emphasis on the importance and possibility of the application of such knowledge to the social sphere proper; on the relevance of information and knowledge for the management of the affairs of society and into the construction of the socio-political order.

But if the "naturalization" of the cosmos was mostly conceived as being governed by some inherent laws or forces – whether the laws of nature which could and should be scientifically explored, or some kind of inner "romantic" essence – the situation was more complicated with regard to the autonomy of man. Man's naturalization and autonomy was conceived, as Kant has shown, in two contradictory directions.[30] On one hand man was seen as subject to the laws of nature which he himself could explore. On the other, he was characterized by moral autonomy – seemingly at least transcending these laws and preceding a strong critical orientation as a basic component of this order.

Out of the conjunctions of these different conceptions or orientations and within this new modern tradition or cultural program there developed belief in the possibility of active formation – by conscious human activity, participation, and critical reflection – of aspects of social, cultural, and natural orders. Society itself had become an object of conscious human activities and endeavors oriented to its reconstruction. Such reconstruction was also often seen as a basic component of the possibility of extending individuals' mastery over his (or "her" – but here above all "his") own destiny.

Such conscious effort could develop in two – sometimes complementary, sometimes conflicting – directions. One has been the "technocratic" direction, based on the assumption that those in the know, those who mastered the secrets and arcana of nature and of man, of human nature, could devise the appropriate schemes, the appropriate institutional arrangements for the implementation of human good, of the good society. The second such direction promulgated a homogenizing moral-rational vision.[31]

Yet another central component of this vision was a very strong tendency to emphasize the possibility of active participation of various social groups in the formation of a new social and cultural order, as well as a high level of commitment to such orders. Concomitantly, there developed also in this program very strong universalistic orientations – in principle negating the importance and significance of any specific political or national boundaries, but at the same time attempting to define a new socio-political order with broad, yet relatively definitive boundaries.

XIII

Within the framework of this new cultural program the specific political program of modernity developed. The new ontological conceptions promulgated in the cultural program of modernity necessarily transformed the basic characteristics and orientations to tradition and to authority; the basic parameters and premises of the political order, of its legitimization, and of the conceptions of accountability of rulers; as well as those of the structure of centers and of center–periphery relations. This new political program, in close relation to the cosmologies promulgated in these revolutions and to the institutionalization of the new political regimes that crystallized in their wake, entailed a radical transformation of the very conceptions of politics. It gave rise, perhaps for the first time in the history of humanity, to the belief in the possibility of bridging through political action the gap between the transcendental and mundane orders, of realizing in the mundane orders, in social life, some of the utopian, eschatological visions and to the possibility of the transformation of society through political action guided by a distinctive vision. As in the broader cultural program of modernity such vision could be technocratic "engineering" or a "moral-rational" one. The latter entailed the view that the political community is a self-constitutive and self-reflective entity, that society may especially through political actions continuously reconstitute itself in a consciously reflexive way.

At the same time, in close relation to the utopian component in modern political life, far-reaching transformations rooted in the imagery of the Great Revolutions took place in the symbolism and structure of modern political centers as compared with their predecessors or with the centers of other civilizations. The crux of this transformation was the charismatization of the center as the bearer of the transcendental visions inherent in the cultural program of modernity and the combination of such charismatization with the concomitant incorporation of themes and symbols of protest as basic and legitimate components of the premises of these centers, and of their relations with the peripheries of their respective societies.[32]

In contrast with almost every previous civilization, themes and symbols of equality, participation, and social justice became not only elements of protest oriented against the existing center, but also an important component of the political legitimization of *orderly* demands by the periphery on the center.[33] They became central components of the transcendental vision that promulgated the autonomy of man and of reason. Protest and the possibility of transforming some of society's institutional premises were no longer considered to be illegitimate or at most marginal aspects of the political process. They became central components of modern political discourse and practice, as well as of the modern project of emancipation of man, a project that sought to combine equality and freedom, justice and autonomy, solidarity and identity. It was indeed the incorporation of such themes into the center that epitomized their status as central components of the transcendental vision of modernity and which heralded the radical transformation of the sectarian utopian vision into central components of the political and cultural program. Concomitantly, there developed continual tendencies to permeation of the peripheries by the centers and of the impingement of the peripheries on the centers, of the blurring of the distinctions between center and periphery, and of the incorporation of the symbols and demands of protest into the central symbols of the society.

XIV

The transformation of the basic premises of the social and political order became interwoven with a parallel transformation and institutionalization of the ideologies of sovereignty, of citizenship, and of representative institutions in their modern versions.

The transformation of these premises entailed first of all a radical transformation of the basic concepts of sovereignty. The core of this transformation, which took place above all in the Great Revolutions, was the transfer of the locus of sovereignty to the people and the concomitant crystallization of the concepts of popular sovereignty. Likewise, a far-reaching transformation of the concepts and practices of representation, citizenship and accountability of rulers took place. The crucial transformation of "citizenship" was that from an acclamatory or ratifying into a participatory role and a concomitant transformation of representation from a virtual into an actual one.[34] Additionally, the ideology of citizenship became connected with the vesting of political sovereignty in the autonomous community and its members; with the expansion, attained through political struggle and protest, of access to and representation in the center to all citizens in all sectors of society; and with the emphasis on the full institutionalization of the accountability of rulers to the citizens.

As Michael Walzer has shown,[35] one of the most important innovations of the English Civil War was the fact that the king was not simply killed, he was executed after having been tried before a court of law – even if he did not accept the legitimacy of the court. This implied not only that rulers were accountable to some higher law, that they ruled under some Mandate of Heaven – a conception to be found in most Axial Civilizations – but also specified the institutional mechanisms through which the rulers could be called to account. The great institutional innovation here was the location of the supervision and accountability of rulers in specific mundane "routine" political institutions – rather than in *ad hoc* outbursts, in charismatic individuals, or in extra-political institutions, such as the church, which claimed to be the authentic carrier of the higher law.

Closely related was the transformation of the representative institutions and their relations to the accountability of rulers. These institutions became one of the major arenas in which the sovereignty of the people and accountability of the rulers could be implemented – albeit often competing for such place with other arenas.[36] The supervision of rulers increasingly became located in two political institutions, the representative parliamentary and the judicial, both closely related to the conception of some societal (even if not always necessarily popular or democratic) sovereignty.[37]

Later on this conception became transformed into the basic constitutional-democratic premise according to which rulers are continuously elected, and in this way continuously responsible to the people, or at least to the electorate.

The transformations of conceptions of citizenship, sovereignty, and representation, entailed a continual confrontation and cross-cutting or overlapping between three complementary, yet potentially antagonistic conceptions of authority or sovereignty which could be distinguished in the pre-revolutionary period, especially in France. These were the absolutist conception which was promulgated by the central royal-bureaucratic center which could present itself as the bearer of rational enlightenment; the second one which emphasized the place of the representative institutions – parliaments with their juridical bases as in the French case; and the last which vested it in public opinion, ultimately in the popular will.[38] With the institutionalization of the modern post-revolutionary regimes, these different conceptions of authority and sovereignty became, as it were, institutionally fused in the modern constitutional, parliamentary, and judiciary institutions. The tensions between them transferred into those tensions between the premises of representative and republican institutions and those of revolutionary or "national" communal participation – a tension that was at the core of modern regimes, and of the different conceptions of democracy.

XV

Out of the combination of the transformation of center–periphery relations, of the conceptions and practice of accountability of rulers, and the incorporation of the symbols and demands of protest into the central symbols of the society, the continuous restructuring of center–periphery relations has become the central focus of political dynamics in modern societies. The various processes of structural change and dislocation that continually took place in modern societies as a result of economic changes, urbanization, changes in the process of communication, and the like have led not only to the promulgation of various concrete grievances and demands by different societies, but also to a growing quest for participation in the broader social and political order and in the central arenas thereof. This quest of the periphery or peripheries for participation in the social, political, and cultural orders, for the incorporation of various themes of protest into the center, and for the concomitant possible transformation of the center, was often guided by the various utopian visions referred to above and promulgated above all by the major social movements that developed as an inherent component of the modern political process, as we shall see further on.

A central part of this process was the development of autonomous sectors of society as well as of the concept civil society, the latter developing first in Europe.[39] Relatively passive, apolitical sectors of society were transformed into politically active ones promulgating not only the discrete interests of different groups but also different and competing conceptions of the common good. The history of modern polities has in many ways become the history of the incorporation of the symbols and demands of such movements and protests into the centers of their respective societies, the concomitant transformation of center–periphery relations, and the continuous restructuring of the boundaries of civil society and of the political realm.

The cultural program of modernity: antinomies, tensions, and criticisms

XVI

From the eighteenth century onward, the crystallization and institutionalization of this program, with its multiple and continually changing institutional implications, entailed – like the institutionaliziation of any great transcendental vision of social order – multiple antinomies, tensions, and contradictions which were in many ways rooted in the different meta-narratives of modernity referred to above; the Christian, the gnostic, and the pagan. These basic antinomies and tensions in the cultural and political program of modernity – as well as the more "external" criticisms thereof – had their roots in those of the Axial Civilizations, especially in the tension between the search for the implementation of the transcendental vision in the mundane world and the recognition of the imperfectibility of man, a tension which naturally bears on the possibility of such implementation in the cultural program of modernity. In this program these antinomies and tensions became radically transformed into those between the different interpretations of the autonomy and hegemony of man and reason, and of the very possibility of grounding morality and moral order in such autonomy and hegemony. These basic antinomies and tensions gave rise to one of the most intensive discourses on social and political dynamics in human history.

The most important such tensions and antinomies were first those between totalizing and more diversified or pluralistic conceptions of the major components of this program – especially of the very conception of reason and its place in human life and society, and of the construction of nature, of human society, and its history; second, those between reflexivity, autonomy, and active construction of nature and society; third, those between different evaluations of major dimensions of human experience; and fourth, between control and autonomy, between discipline and freedom.

The central focus of the dichotomy between totalizing and pluralistic visions has been between one view that accepts the distinctiveness of different values and rationalities as against another that conflates the different rationalities in a totalistic way, which essentially subsumes value rationality (*Wertrationalität*) or substantive rationalities under instrumental rationality (*Zweckrationalität*) either in its technocratic or moralistic utopian versions. In this conception there developed a very strong tendency to conflate science and technology with ultimate values, to conflate *Wertrationalität* and *Zweckrationalität*, substantive and instrumental rationality, human emancipation with instrumental, even technical, rationality. This tension developed first of all with respect to the very conception of reason and its place in the constitution of human society. It was manifest for instance, as Stephen Toulmin has shown even if in a rather exaggerated way, in the difference between the more pluralistic conceptions of Montaigne or Erasmus as against the totalizing vision of reason promulgated by Descartes.[40]

This tension between totalizing and pluralistic conceptions of human existence and social life also developed with respect to the conception of the course of human history – of its being constructed, especially by some overarching totalizing visions guided by reason or by the "spirit" of different collectivities against the emphasis on multiplicity of such paths. The utopian eschatological conceptions inherent in the belief in the possibility of bridging the gaps or chasms between the transcendental and mundane orders also entailed some very specific ideas of time, especially as related to the course of human history. Among the most important of these conceptions, many of which have been rooted in Christian eschatology but also constituted far-reaching transformations thereof, was a vision of historical progress and of history as the process through which the cultural program of modernity, especially individual autonomy and emancipation, would be implemented. Such progress was defined above all in terms of universalistic values of instrumental rationality, as of reason, science, and technology. But, however future oriented this program was, it also developed references to an imaginary human communal past. It also had a strong evangelistic and chiliastic trend, which, together with its "this-worldly" orientations, gave it a very strong impetus to expansion.[41]

As against such totalizing visions of history there developed those visions – perhaps best represented by Vico, and later by Herder[42] – that emphasized the existence of multiple paths of histories of different societies. This major opposite (romantic) tendency tended to emphasize the autonomy of emotions. In its more conservative view – which developed most strongly in Germany – it emphasized the distinctiveness of primordial collectivities but it shared with the new major cultural program many of the strong utopian, semi-eschatological conceptions, even if certainly not the idea of progress.[43] In many other countries the individualist, anti-institutional revolutionary vision was more predominant – while it faded in Germany.

The second tension that developed within the program was that between different conceptions of human autonomy and its relation to the constitution of society and of nature – especially between reflexivity and exploration on one hand and active construction or mastery of nature, human activity, and society on the other; between the technocratic, engineering conception and the more explorative, reflexive, critical, and morally autonomous conceptions of the construction of society and of attitude toward nature. The emphasis on active construction of society and mastery of nature could become closely connected with the tendency, inherent in cognitive instrumental conceptions, to emphasize the radical dichotomy between subject and object, and between man and nature – reinforcing the radical criticism that claimed that the cultural program of modernity necessarily entailed an alienation of man from nature and society.

The third major tension that developed within the cultural program of modernity concerned the relative importance or primacy of different dimensions of human existence. Of special importance in this context has been the evaluation of the relative importance of autonomy and predominance of reason as against the emotional and esthetic dimension of human existence, often equated with various vital forces, as well as with so-called primordial components in the construction of collective identities. Closely related were tensions between different conceptions of the bases of human morality, especially whether such morality can be based on or grounded in universal principles such as above all on reason, instrumental rationality, or multiple rationalities and multiple concrete experiences of different human communities.

XVII

Cross-cutting these tensions and contradictions in the cultural program of modernity, there developed within this program, and particularly with its institutionalization, a strong continual tension between control and autonomy, between discipline and freedom.

This tension is rooted in the fact that the institutionalization of any onto-logical vision by definition entails the limitations on human creativity through the mechanisms of social control.[44] But beyond this general fact, and in a sense more central to the understanding of the dynamics of mod-ernity, this tension has been rooted in the continual – even if continually changing – contradictions between the basic premises of the cultural program of modernity and the major institutional developments of modern societies, which were to some extent at least inherent in this program.

The first such contradiction has been between emphasis on human autonomy and the strong restrictive control dimension rooted in techno-cratic and/or moral visionary conceptions of the institutionalization of this program – a control dimension forcefully analyzed, even if in an exagger-ated way, from different but complementary points of view by Norbert Elias and Michel Foucault.[45] Among the most important manifestations of this control dimension were the homogenizing tendencies of the modern states, especially the post-revolutionary nation state and the conception of the meaning of being civilized as it crystallized in bourgeois society. This contradiction has been aptly defined by Cornelius Castoriadis as that between ("technocratic") mastery and (human) autonomy.[46]

Closely related have been the contradictions so strongly emphasized by Weber.[47] Thus, the second such contradiction was that between the creative dimension inherent in the visions that lead to the crystallization of moder-nity, the visions of the Renaissance, Reformation, Enlightenment, and the Revolutions and the flattening of these visions, the "disenchantment" of the world inherent in the growing routinization above all in the growing bureaucratization of the modern world.

Third was the contradiction, also stressed by Weber, between an over-reaching vision through which the modern world becomes meaningful and the fragmentation of such meaning generated by the growing autonomy of the different institutional arenas – of the economic, the political, and the cultural.

Fourth was the contradiction between the tendency to self-definition and the construction of autonomous political units – above all states and nation states, and the continual growth of international forces beyond the control of such seemingly autonomous self-constituted political units.

Given the continual social and cultural changes inherent in the develop-ment of modern societies, this tension between control and autonomy con-stituted – as Peter Wagner has shown – a continuous component of these developments.[48]

All these tensions have existed from the very beginning of the promulga-tion of the cultural program of modernity rooted as they were in the transformation of the antinomies inherent in the Axial Civilizations. They constituted a continual component in the development and unfolding of this program – with their latest formulations to be found in the discourse of post-modernism.

XVIII

These as it were internal tensions and contradictions within the cultural and political program of modernity became, in the cultural discourse that developed around it, closely connected with the more extreme radical "external" criticisms thereof.

These more radical criticisms of this program – rooted in the meta-narratives mentioned above and in the premises and antinomies of the "pre-modern" Axial Civilizations – denied the validity of the claims of the promulgators of this program that grounded their premises – and their institutionalization – in transcendental, metaphysical principles and/or denied them the right to see these claims as epitomes of human creativity. The central point of most of these, as it were "external," radical criticisms was the denial of the possibility of grounding any social order, morality, or human creativity in the basic premise of the cultural program of modernity; especially in the autonomy and presumed immanence of man and in the supremacy of reason. Closely related was the denial of the claims that institutional development of modernity was rooted in a transcendental vision and could be seen as the implementation of such vision or of human creativity. These criticisms asserted that contrary to such claims, the institutionalization of these programs denied human creativity and flattened human experience; it led to the disintegration or erosion of moral order, of the moral or transcendental bases of society; and led to the alienation of man from nature from society and to the weakening of human will.

These radical criticisms could be undertaken from two opposite, yet in some ways curiously complementary points of view. The first was the religious or traditional view which espoused the primacy of tradition and religious authority over the claims of reason and human autonomy, emphasizing that it is only the former that can be the bearers of transcendental visions. The other view that criticized the primacy of reason came from those proclaiming that such primacy denies the autonomy of human will and creativity.

It was the connection between the external and internal criticisms of the cultural and political program of modernity – perhaps best epitomized in the works of Nietzsche and in the continual references to him, and later in the works of Ernst Junger or Martin Heidegger[49] – that gave rise to this program's most radical criticism. These criticisms emphasized above all the repressive dimensions or aspects of modern social life as it developed in the nineteenth century and up to the interwar period of the twentieth – especially the "suffocating" materialistic reality of bourgeois society which – as against the spiritual and creative spirits of aristocratic age or the image of free human creativity – undermined the spiritual, moral, and communal dimensions of social life. In many of these criticisms such materialism was seen as embodied in technology that was seemingly the tool of the destruction of the moral and communal fabric of society and often closely related to the dramatization of the world – the development of the Iron Cage. But with the passing of time, with the full institutionalization of modern industrial societies, the attitude to technology among many critics of the cultural program of modernity, especially among the so-called reactionary modernists – such as, for instance, Ernst Jünger, Hans Freyer, Carl Schmitt, and Martin Heidegger – became more complicated.[50] They attempted to "spiritualize" technology, to endow it with communal spirit, to portray it as a great achievement of human will and creativity which was debased only in the depraved bourgeois society.

It is the multiplicity of starting points of both the discourse of the modern cultural and political program and the meta-narratives which influenced the "radical" criticisms thereof, that explains how the program could essentially be accused of generating directly opposite ends or outcomes. Thus, as Mark Lilla has shown,[51] it could be accused – as by the Romantics – of releasing an aggressive form of reason; or by Kierkegaard, Nietzsche, Schopenhauer, and in a different way by Leo Strauss, of subordinating reason to hedonistic drives.[52] Similarly some critics could accuse this program of denying, by absolutization of reason, the place of the sacred in modern societies, while others, like Voegelin, would accuse it of endowing reason with absolute, sacral dimensions.[53] Parallelly some critics would accuse it of depoliticization of authority – while others would fault it for politicizing, in a Jacobin mode, all human relations. The development of such seemingly contradictory criticisms of this program grounded in the narratives of modernity attest to the central importance of these very antinomies as they were rooted in those of Axial Civilizations and transformed in the modern arenas, as a continual aspect of the discourse of modernity. It was indeed the multiplicity of these starting-points of the modern cultural and political program that attest to the fact that modernity was continually perceived, within wide sectors of modern societies, as being – to use Lessek Kolakowski's felicitous expression – on "endless trial."[54]

The tensions in the political program of modernity – pluralistic and Jacobin tendencies

XIX

These tensions and contradictions bore also on the political arena and became manifest in it. The bringing together, above all in the wake of the Enlightenment and the Great Revolutions, of the various ideological and institutional orientations and traditions analyzed above into common cultural institutional frameworks, generated continual ideological and institutional tensions which became inherent components of the cultural and political program of modernity, and of the political dynamics of modern regimes. These tensions have been greatly intensified by their combination with tendencies to the charismatization of the center, to the absolutization of the major dimensions of human existence, with the development of the new center–periphery relations and of a new type of political process in modern societies.

The first such tension was that between a constructivist approach which views politics as the process of reconstruction of society and especially of democratic politics, to follow Claude Lefort or Johann Arnason's formulations, as active self-construction of society, as opposed to a view that accepts society in its concrete construction.

The second such tension, closely related to the first one and also rooted in the overall cultural programs of modernity, was that between an overall totalizing, usually utopian and/or communal vision, usually entailing a strong constructivist approach, and a more pluralistic view which, while not necessarily denying a constructivistic approach to politics, entails the acceptance of multiple patterns of life, of traditions and conceptions of social interests that develop within it. This tension often coalesced with that between the utopian and civil components in the construction of modern political arenas and processes, between "revolutionary" and "normal" politics, and conversely the acceptance of society in its concrete yet continually changing and reconstructed composition.[55] Closely related was the third tension between viewing politics as a totally autonomous dimension of human existence and will as opposed to seeing it as embedded in broader cultural considerations and social frameworks.

XX

The central focus of these tensions as they crystallized within the modern political discourse has been the relation between, on one hand, the legitimacy of the plurality of discrete individual and group interests, of different conceptions of the common will, of the freedom to pursue such interests and conceptions, and, on the other, of totalizing orientations which denied the legitimacy of private interests and of different conceptions of the common good and which emphasized the totalistic reconstruction of society through political actions.

On the ideological level, the development of such pluralistic conceptions was historically connected with growing emphasis on the legitimacy of private interests and conceptions of the common good. This emphasis was rooted in, or connected with, theories of natural rights, with special emphasis on the right to property. The attitude toward property became transformed from the republican view, which stressed its importance for freeing citizens for responsible participation in the political community, to the view of property as embodying "natural rights," almost a precondition of political community, making the political community the guardian of property.[56]

This development was closely connected with a radical change of the meaning of the concept of social contract. First, this idea as it developed in the modern period has been based on the assumption – an assumption that was shared by those such as the Romantics who were opposed to the idea of social contract – that it was human nature that was constitutive of social order, not to be superseded by any other extra-human element. Secondly, the modern idea of social contract could, and often did, imply that the constitution of such a contract could also be connected with the establishment of a good, possibly ideal order – an order understandable in terms of reason and amenable to some sort of scientific investigation. It was possibly with respect to this point that the most radical difference from the conception of social contract in the reflexive tradition of the Great Civilizations has emerged. This conception was connected with the distinction between the civil and political orders, and with the growing perception of civil society as a distinct, autonomous force or congeries of forces.

It would, however, be wrong to assume that the crux of the modern reformulation of the idea of social contract was just to provide the legitimization for individual egoistic interests. The idea of contract could, in itself, be connected with rather different views of human nature and the best social order. It could be seen as in Locke, and later on among the utilitarians, as the harbinger of political liberty. It could be used to justify, as in Hobbes, the construction of a modern Leviathan.

Moreover, the modern reformulations of the conceptions of social contract did not necessarily take for granted the existence of a natural harmony between individual interests and the good of society. The legitimization of the political order in contractual terms based on the rights of individuals did not necessarily entail the sanctification of the will of all as against the common will. The various modern formulations of social contract recognized the potential tensions or even contradictions between the two – and it was this recognition that constituted a central concern of the modern political discourse.

Whatever their concrete political views, most of the modern contractualists searched for ways in which the emphasis on individual rights could be connected with the establishment of a good, possibly ideal, order which is the realization of the vision of reason and good society.

Accordingly, most of the participants in this discourse were concerned with the assurance of the conditions for the development of a responsible citizenry, with individuals seen not only as egoistical, hedonistic, utilitarian beings, but also as at least politically responsible citizens who may also be carriers of some broader visions, courting not only the common wellbeing, but the upholding of civility. This concern could be found, as John Dunn has shown,[57] in Locke's analysis of trust as the basic precondition of human society (curiously reminiscent of Durkheim's conception of pre-contractual elements and solidarity), in the numerous discussions in the Federalist papers, or in J. S. Mill's concern with education. It was probably only in some of the more extreme formulations of utilitarian and recent rational choice approaches that this concern was given up. Moreover, recognition of the legitimacy of private interests entailed not only the recognition and even the legitimacy of plurality of interests, of the will of all, but also, at least implicitly, the plurality of different interpretations of the general will, of the common good.

But at the same time these developments also strongly exacerbated the problem of the relations of such multiple interest to any common will, as in Rousseau's formulation of the famous distinction between the "general will" and the "will of all."[58] This problem of the relations between multiple interests and the promulgation of the general will indeed became exacerbated in modern societies by the transformation of the conceptions of representation and of citizenship. These transformations have made popular sovereignty the bearer or locus of the general will of the common good of the society, but at the same time have sharpened the problematique of the location of the general will; and of the relations between the relative importance of such general vision of the public good – "the general will," on one hand, and the discrete interests of different individuals and groups on the other, and between different conceptions of the common good.

It was indeed in the work of Rousseau, in his analysis of the limits of the possibilities of a balance between the egoistical will of all and the common will of a society; and in the confrontation between the republican political idea of full participation of citizens in the body politic and the individual-istic conception of man as a voluntary member of society, that the tensions between these understandings were brought to their sharpest confrontation and became fully explored.

It is these different conceptions of the relation between the individual and the social order that generated some of the basic tensions in modern political discourse and its dynamics: between liberty and equality; between emphasis on a vision of the good social order and the "narrow" interests of different sectors of the society; between the conception of the individual as an autonomous sovereign and emphasis on the community; between the utopian and the "rational" or "procedural" components of this program and the closely related tensions between "revolutionary" and "normal" pol-itics; and between different bases of legitimization of these regimes. In the political program of modernity, these tensions and antinomies coalesced, above all, in the tension (to follow Lubbe's terminology) between freedom and emancipation which to some extent coincides also with Isaiah Berlin's distinction between negative and positive freedom.[59]

These various tensions in the political program of modernity were also closely related to those between the different modes of legitimization of modern regimes, especially but not only of constitutional and democratic polities – namely between, on one hand, procedural legitimization in terms of civil adherence to rules of the game and, in different "substantive" terms, a very strong tendency to promulgate other modes or bases of legitimiza-tion, above all, to use Edward Shils' terminology, various primordial, "sacred" – religious or secular – ideological components.[60]

XXI

The crucial differences with respect to these concerns between constitu-tional pluralistic as opposed to the different varieties of authoritarian, and above all totalistic or totalitarian orientations or modes of discourse, lay in the respective views about the possibility of development of responsible cit-izenry and leadership through an *open* political process.

The promulgators of the pluralistic conceptions of constitutional democracy were also fully aware of the possibilities of such erosion, but in the constitutional pluralistic conceptions, the individual was recognized as a potentially responsible citizen and not only as purely egoistical, utilitar-ian, or hedonistic being. In the pluralistic conceptions the possibilities of such erosion were seen as possibly counteracted by active participation by citizens in the major institutional – especially political – arenas in which different interests and visions are articulated, aggregated, and transformed into policies in which some visions of common good could be articulated. Accordingly, in contrast to the bearers of the authoritarian and totalitarian conceptions, they searched for appropriate institutional arrangements which could assure the open expression of such different visions as well as of many discrete interests in which the potentially or principled open nature of modern political process and discourse, and the core characteristics of this process as the political self-reflection of society, can be continuously maintained.

XXII

The central dividing point in the modern political discourse has been between the bearers of pluralistic conceptions which accepted and even upheld the legitimacy of multiple private individual or group interests, and of different conceptions of the common good that developed in connection with the tensions inherent in the political program of modernity, and those who denied it.

In the background of these tensions and divisions was concern with the possible erosion, through the overemphasis on narrow individual or group interests, of commitment to the common good.

The concern with such erosion developed within pluralistic democratic and anti-democratic political traditions alike. Such suspicion and preoccupation could be found for instance among the upholders of the constitutional conception of democracy among the Founding Fathers of the American Revolution, in the fear of factions to be found in the Federalist Papers. This fear or suspicion has been even more pronounced among the promulgators of the communitarian participatory conception of democracy and not solely the extreme Jacobin ones – a view that had within itself the seed of "totalitarian democracy."

The mirror images of these pluralistic visions were what may be called various collectivistic orientations or ideologies which espoused the primacy of collectivity and/or of collective vision. Two broad types of such orientations or ideologies were especially important. One was some form of ideology emphasizing the primacy of a collectivity based on common primordial and/or spiritual attributes of – above all – national collectivity. The other, possibly distinctly modern orientation, rooted as we have seen in some of the central ideological components of the Great Revolutions, has been the Jacobin ideology. The essence of the Jacobin orientations and program was the belief in the possibility of transforming society through totalistic political action. These orientations, the historical roots of which go back to medieval eschatological sources, developed fully in conjunction with the political program of modernity and they epitomized the modern transformation of the sectarian attitudes to the antinomies of the Axial Civilizations.

The Jacobin components of the modern political program have been manifest in a strong emphasis on social and cultural activism; on the ability of man to reconstruct society according to some transcendental visions; with the closely connected strong tendency to the absolutization of the major dimensions of human experience as well as of the major constituents or components of social order; and with the concomitant ideologization of politics. Such Jacobin orientations tend to emphasize belief in the primacy of politics and in the ability of politics to reconstitute society. The pristine Jacobin orientations and movements have been characterized by a strong predisposition to develop not only a totalistic world-view, but also over-arching totalitarian all-encompassing ideologies, which emphasize a total reconstitution of the social and political order and which espouse a strong, even if not always often universalistic, missionary zeal.

These orientations have become visible above all in the attempts to recon-struct the centers of their respective societies; in the almost total conflation of center and periphery, negating the existence of intermediary institutions and association of what can sometimes be called civil society, thus conflating civil society with the overall community.

The Jacobin component also appeared in different concrete guises and in different combinations with various political ideological components. The homogenizing tendencies promulgated by most modern nation states, espe-cially those that crystallized after the revolutions, were strongly imbued by such Jacobin orientations. The Jacobin orientation in its pristine modern forms or versions developed first in "leftist" revolutionary movements which often conflated the primacy of politics with the implementation of a technologic or moralistic vision of progress and reason.

But the Jacobin component has been present, as Norberto Bobbio has very often emphasized in his works,[61] not only in socialist but also in nationalistic and fascist movements. These Jacobin orientations could become closely interwoven with movements emphasizing the primacy of primordial communities, as was the case in many fascist and National Socialist movements. The Jacobin components also constitute very strong components of many populist movements.[62] They could also become closely interwoven, as was the case in the fundamentalist movements, with the upholding of the primacy of religious authority. This Jacobin compo-nent could also become manifest in more diffuse ways, as for instance in the intellectual pilgrimage to other societies, in attempts to find there the full flowering of the utopian revolutionary ideal,[63] and in many totalistic attitudes that flourish in different social movements and in popular culture. In these various settings, the Jacobin component has become connected with each setting's respective stance on the different antinomies of modernity developed within them.

Whatever the concrete manifestations of the Jacobin orientation, it constituted a continual component of the discourse of modernity. It is indeed the continual confrontation between this component and orientation and the more pluralistic orientations, as well as between different conceptions of pluralism and different Jacobin ideologies, that constitutes one of the central cores of the discourse of modernity.

XXIII

The contradiction between on the one hand the emphasis on an encompassing revolutionary or technocratic vision and on the other the acceptance of the possibility of multiple views about political and social matters, of the legitimization of multiple patterns of life and interests, and of the strong emphasis on procedural rules that is of the essence of constitutional regimes became fully visible in the later Russian, Chinese, and Vietnamese Revolutions. Likewise, its ingredients could be identified quite explicitly in the Jacobin groups and ideologies in the French Revolution and, more implicitly, in some Puritan groups in England, America, the Netherlands, and in a more tortuous way in France. In all the latter societies it was the constitutional republican option that won the day.[64] The recognition of the legitimacy of multiple interests developed despite the revolutionary origins – with their monolithic, totalistic and exclusive visions – in most of the modern constitutional-democratic regimes. Indeed one of the most important problems in the analysis of those regimes is to understand how the recognition of the legitimacy of multiple views of the good society could develop from such revolutionary origins.

These basic tensions in the political program of modernity – i.e. the tension between the search for the implementation of some overall vision of a better social order on the one hand and the recognition of the legitimacy of discrete "narrow" interests of individuals and sub-groups in the society on the other, and the tension between liberty and equality – have been inherent in all the modern, post-revolutionary regimes, be they authoritarian, totalitarian, or democratic constitutional ones. These tensions have become fully articulated in the different conceptions of democracy – the constitutional and the different participatory ones – and in their attitudes to both the basic institutional frameworks of the modern constitutional democratic regimes and to the bases of legitimization of modern constitutional democratic regimes.

It is the strong historical roots of these tensions and their full articulation in the different conceptions of democracy that explain their close bearing on the dynamics of modern constitutional-democratic regimes. The first, constitutional "Schumpeterian" definition, with all its ramifications, and the closely related pluralistic orientations, were to no small degree rooted in the heritage of constitutional institutions and practices as they crystallized in the early modern age.[65] The various participatory definitions of democracy were rooted in the attempts at the reconstruction of the "republican" traditions of antiquity that crystallized with the Renaissance and the Reformation, but above all in the "communitarian" participatory components of the visions of many heterodox and intellectual movements of the late Middle Ages and early modernity, and especially of the Great Revolutions.[66]

Social movements as bearers of the major antinomies of the cultural and political programs of modernity

XXIV

Just as the antinomies and tensions in the cultural and political program of modernity constituted far-reaching transformations of those of the Axial Civilizations, so also the bearers of these tensions became greatly transformed in the new, modern setting. In place of sects and movements of rebellion, it was above all social and political movements that acted in the open public and political arenas that articulated these dichotomies, tensions, and themes of protest. Such social movements and movements of protest were rooted in the combination of several sources – namely, the political processes that took place in the revolutions and in the subsequent structural and ideological characteristics of modern post-revolutionary regimes; the political program of modernity and the tensions within it; and the institutional dynamics of modern societies – and these movements constituted a continual component of all modern regimes.

It was these movements that were bearers of the major tensions inherent in the cultural and political program of modernity and the major criticisms and oppositions to this program. It was such different movements that constituted in the modern societies one of the main bearers, perhaps the main bearer, of different utopian visions. It was above all in these movements that the utopian dimensions of modern political life, and its relation to modern political frameworks and to the more pluralistic components thereof, have been continually played out.

Many of these movements laid a very strong emphasis on social and cultural activism, on the ability of man to reconstruct society, together with a very strong tendency to the absolutization of the major dimensions of human experience, especially of reason and emotions, as well as of the constituents of collective identity and the legitimization of social order – especially the primordial, civil, and sacred. Concomitantly it was in these movements that the Jacobin components and/or collectivistic orientations could become most prominent and the confrontation with the pluralistic components of the modern political program could be continually articulated. This tendency was closely connected with the charismatization of the center as the major arena in which such visions can and should be implemented.

XXV

The major social movements that constituted the transformation in modern settings of the movements of protest and the sectarian heterodoxies of the earlier arenas, developed against the background of the institutional developments of modern societies and regimes as analyzed above all against the background of the continual tensions and contradictions between the premises of the cultural and political program of modernity and the developments within these institutional arenas. It was these tensions and contradictions that generated the dynamics, crises, and transformations of modern societies.

Several types of such movements developed in modern societies – first of all in Western Europe, then in the Americas, then later in Central and Eastern European, Asian, and African societies. One major type of such movement was center oriented; its major aim was the reconstruction of the centers of the respective societies as embodying the most important charismatic dimensions of the modern socio-cultural order.

Among such center-oriented movements were first those that aimed at changing the distributions of power and its bases within a given society. The most important such movements in modern times were first those that aimed at the growing inclusion through the extension of suffrage of wider strata into the central political framework; and second, the socialist and communist movements which combined such demands with those for reconstruction of the center and patterns of political economy to be effected by reconstruction of economic relations and by abolishment of the more hierarchial premises of their respective centers. Lately many of the new types of social movements – such as women's movements and those of various minorities, all of them demanding changes in principles of allocation of resources and of access to the sources of the distributors thereof – have become very prominent. Many fundamentalist and religious communal movements became, in the last decades of the twentieth century, as we shall see in chapters 3 and 4, the most important center-oriented ones. The second major type of such movements were above all national or ethnic ones which aimed at the reconstruction of the boundaries of the respective political collectivities.

But such center-oriented movements were not the only ones that developed in modern societies. Side by side with these movements developed many others such as religious reform movements; various cooperative or syndicalist movements aimed at the reorganization of some aspects of life of different sectors of society; anarchist movements that opposed the state in principle; and many popular movements which emphasized autonomous participation in the political process as opposed to bureaucratic or center domination.

Many of the movements not oriented to the center emphasized the construction of new spaces to some extent independent of the center, but in many cases also impinging on it. But in most movements there always existed some overlapping between orientation to the center and construction of new spaces. Many of them also developed a total denial of the basic premise of modernity, and above all of its major institutional implications. The concrete themes promulgated by them were not static in their orientation and could in later periods become transposed into center-oriented ones, and could later become appropriated by non-center-oriented movements once again.

All these movements continually intermeshed with more "traditional" types of rebellion as well as popular movements of resistance to the construction of the modern state, industrialism, and market economy. All such movements not only promulgated specific demands but combined them with broader, overarching visions which often entailed strong Jacobin components. Within all these types of movements the major tensions inherent in the modern political process – especially those between the collectively Jacobin or "communal" and the pluralistic components thereof, between different conceptions of the relations between the general will and the will of all, between the primordial, sacred, and civil components of their legitimization, between control and freedom or autonomy – were continually articulated.

The relative importance of these different types of social movements varied greatly in different societies and periods. In some periods, movements not oriented to the center predominated on the political scene. Great differences also developed in different modern societies and in different periods of their history, with respect to the extent and ways in which these movements became interwoven with the other major actors on the political scene, especially with political parties and interest groups.

Social movements: the political process and the continual reconstruction of the realm of the political in modern societies

XXVI

Of central importance for understanding the impact of these movements in modern political dynamics is the fact that they have been closely related to some of the characteristics of the political process that developed within modern regimes. The most important among such characteristics are the emergence of a new type of non-ascriptive, semi-professional "political class" or "classes," the members of which compete openly for power and for broader political support; the development of some continuous organizations for the mobilization of support among the electorate, the most important of which in modern societies have been political parties; the emergence of interest groups working through some representatives (such as different lobby groups), as well as of course social and political movements. Likewise important are the close relations between the promulgation of policies, the regulation of conflicts, and the process of selection of rulers, as well as the fact that these processes have been played out – in contrast with other regimes, with the partial exception of some of the city-states of antiquity – in the public domain, "in the open" and under continuous public scrutiny.

But it was above all two additional aspects of the political process in modern societies – rooted in the combination of the political program of modernity and the structural characteristics of modern societies – namely the tendency to the politicization of many social problems and conflicts, and second the continuous redefinition of the scope of the "political," that are of crucial importance for the understanding of the central importance of the various social movements in modern political dynamics.

Modern political regimes have been characterized by the generally high level of politicization of the many problems and demands of various sectors of society and of the conflicts between them – a characteristic unparalleled in all other regimes, with perhaps the very partial exception of some of the city-states of antiquity.

These tendencies to politicization have been exacerbated by the fact that in all modern regimes the boundaries of what is considered the appropriate scope of political action, the boundaries of the political, of the legitimate, open political arena and action, have been continuously changing. The transition from a laissez-faire conception of the state – never, of course, fully implemented in reality – to the post-Second World War Keynesian regulatory policies and the institutionalization of the welfare state is perhaps the best illustration of such change – but it constitutes in a sense only the tip of the iceberg. In fact such changes have been continuous in these regimes throughout their histories, and as the illustration of the welfare state shows, they have been closely related to the specification of the different entitlements due to the different sectors of societies.[67]

The specification of such changes, the drawing of the boundaries of the political, has in itself constituted – unlike in most other political regimes in human history – one of the major foci of open political contestation and struggle, as articulated above all in periods of intensive change by different movements. The changes in the realm of the political usually entailed promulgation of different conceptions of the common good and of the basic entitlement to which all citizens and various such sectors may make claim. Such demands for the redefinition of the boundaries of the political have usually been promulgated by various movements of protest arising often in periods of change, but also in more "stable" periods.

XXVII

These numerous, continually changing movements developed first of all in Europe, then in the Americas, and later throughout the world, in close relation to the problems arising out of the contradictions between the basic premises of the cultural and political program of modernity and the actual processes of its institutionalization in multiple concrete historical settings in Western Europe and beyond it. They arose above all in relation to the processes of industrialization and development and expansion of capitalism; of the construction of new modern political regimes and formations and international systems; and of the concomitant new types of collectivities – nations and nation states. Beyond Western Europe these process movements arose in relation to the expansion of modernity throughout the world in its imperialist, economic, military, and ideological dimensions, and to the confrontation between Western hegemony and the Central and Eastern European, Asian, and African traditions and civilizations.

All these movements addressed themselves critically to different aspects or dimensions of the political and cultural program of modernity and to the basic antinomies of modernity, and they entailed specific modes of selection from among the major themes of the cultural program of modernity and their political and institutional repercussions and interpretations.

Thus with respect to the first major types of movements that developed in European societies, the criticisms of the existing order of modernity promulgated by the socialist movements were mostly couched in terms of the non-completion of the original project of modernity, not of its negation, and was oriented toward its fuller implementation. The national movements built on those components of the revolutionary heritage that emphasized the right to self-determination of a collectivity – stressing above all highly particularistic primordial terms. The national or nationalistic movements aimed above all at the reconstruction of the boundaries of newly crystallizing collectivities. They entailed the confrontation between the universalistic and more particularistic or ascriptive components of legitimization of the modern regimes and could couch their criticism of the existing order in extreme negations of the universalistic components of the cultural program of modernity. The extreme nationalist movements denied the universal and universalistic orientations of these regimes and espoused in an extreme ideological way the primordial racial orientations. Unlike the conservative movements which predominated throughout most of the nineteenth century on the "right" wing of the political spectrum, these "new" extreme nationalist fascist movements evinced strong Jacobin, mobilizatory tendencies. Other combinations and themes, such as various religious, communal, or universalistic ones, would become, in later periods, the most important center-oriented themes.

These various continually changing and emerging movements developed side by side, often competing and in conflict with one another but always constituting a central component of modern political and social dynamics and of the discourse of modernity as it developed from the late eighteenth century on. They were complementary as they both were rooted first in the historical experience of their countries, and of the modern international systems or frameworks. But different movements developed in conjunction with the various aspects or dimensions of this experience, emphasizing different problems and contradictions between the premises of this program and its institutionalization. The various movements promulgated different visions of modern life, of modern social and political order, and of modernity. All these movements articulated some of the antinomies and tensions inherent in the cultural and political program of modernity and of its institutionalization in the different historical settings and contexts. Accordingly, they could also under some conditions oppose and contradict one another, and come into intensive ideological and political conflicts with one another – as was the case in the fierce ideological and political struggle between communist and fascist movements in the 1930s or between communist and democratic ideologies during the Cold War.

The concrete contours of such movements – their origins and ideologies, the major actors active within them, the bases of their support, and the extent of their being center oriented – has been continually changing in different modern societies. But they constituted a continual component of the modern political scene and of modern political processes. While the concrete problems to which these movements were oriented and their concrete aims and ideologies were continually changing, such continually changing orientations and ideologies promulgated by these movements were always focused on some of the major components of the modern cultural and political order, its antinomies and tensions.

It was indeed these various movements that posed the most important challenges to the newly emerging modern regimes which slowly crystallized first against the *ancien régime* and to no smaller – possibly an even greater – extent to the different modern, post-revolutionary regimes. It was in the continual encounter between these movements and the different modern regimes in which they developed that the basic characteristics – as well as problems, tensions, and contradictions – of the modern political process and of the political program of modernity became fully articulated.

3

Fundamentalism as a modern Jacobin anti-modern utopia and heterodoxy – the totalistic reconstruction of tradition

Introduction: the historical settings

I

Modern fundamentalist movements constitute one of the major social movements which developed in the framework of modern civilization and of modernity. The ideologies promulgated by the fundamentalist movements constitute a part of the continually changing discourse of modernity, especially as it developed from the end of the nineteenth century onwards. These movements continually interacted with other such movements often constituting mutual reference points to one another. These fundamentalist movements developed in a specific historic context (as did other social movements), one characterized by both a new historical phase which crystallized in the second half of the twentieth century in the confrontations between the Western European and Non-Western civilizations, and by the intensification within the Western countries of discourse concerning the internal antinomies of the cultural program of modernity – particularly those regarding the different conceptions of reason and rationality (as we shall see in greater detail in chapter 4).

Within the broad panorama of the multiple modern movements and discourses of modernity, the fundamentalist movements developed some particular characteristics that rendered them potentially one of the most extreme, yet distinctively Jacobin forms of social movements. These characteristics, which distinguish these movements from the proto-fundamentalist ones, existed in embryonic form in most of them and came to full fruition under specific historical conditions in the more "visible" and active movements.

II

The first modern movements which were called fundamentalist developed as we have seen in the United States during the last decades of the nineteenth, and in the beginning of the twentieth centuries, but their seeds went back to earlier periods – to the Protestant settlement in the colonies.

Appearing first in Europe, Protestantism itself and sectarian Protestantism in particular exhibited a potent mixture of strong proto-fundamentalism and fundamentalist tendencies which were manifest in many groups of the radical Reformation such as the Münster Anabaptists, and to some extent in Calvin's Geneva and among some Dutch Calvinist communities. Similar, even stronger tendencies were also manifest in some of the early colonies in the United States. These totalistic Jacobin fundamentalist orientations were transformed, and hemmed in, through their institutionalization in more pluralistic settings of which the United States provides the best example. But fundamentalist tendencies continued to be very strong in the United States, and the American Protestant fundamentalist movements constitute a continual component on the American political scene up to this very period. They crystallized against the background of a long history of evangelistic Protestant movements which developed in the colonies and have been present in the USA from its very inception.

The term "fundamentalism" came into common usage in the second decade of this century, with the publication of a series of pamphlets called *The Fundamentals*, which appeared between 1910 and 1915, and through a set of conferences of the World's Christian Fundamentals Association in 1919. Historians of American religion agree that fundamentalism's classic period followed in the 1920s.

The most helpful point of general departure is provided by George Marsden who both demonstrates that the fundamentalist movement of the 1920s went considerably beyond millenarian circles, and goes on to define "fundamentalism" in its heyday as "militantly anti-modernist Protestant evangelicalism." "Militant opposition to modernism," he says, "was what most clearly set off fundamentalism from a number of closely related traditions, such as evangelicalism, revivalism, pietism, the holiness movements, millenarianism, Reformed confessionalism, Baptist traditionalism, and other denominational orthodoxies."[1]

Revivalist evangelical and fundamentalist groups witnessed a revival in the middle of this century. Among the most important of such groups were the Christian Coalition, led by Ralph Reed; its predecessor, the Moral Majority, led by Rev. Jerry Falwell; and to some extent, the PTL, led by Pat Robertson – all of which aimed to promote the Christian agenda of morality and became politically active.[2]

In Europe there developed, albeit to a much smaller extent, different modern sects with strong fundamentalist tendencies, especially in the Scandinavian countries, as well as in Germany whose sects were closely related to the pietist traditions that were very prominent in the Lutheran tradition.

In a similar manner, these fundamentalist tendencies developed among the various Protestant groups, especially the evangelistic and pentecostal ones, that started to "infiltrate" Latin America around the turn of the century and gathered momentum in the period after the Second World War.[3]

III

In Jewish communities, fundamentalist tendencies and groups started to develop from the mid-nineteenth century on; in Islamic countries especially in the twentieth century. In modern Jewish history, and in the more contemporary scene in Israel and the various Jewish communities in the Diaspora, several major fundamentalist trends developed. The first, strong fundamentalist or at least highly intensified proto-fundamentalist tendency has developed in some sectors of Neo-Orthodoxy in Central and Eastern Europe, under the impact of the Enlightenment, the struggle for Jewish emancipation, the development of modern Reform trends in Judaism, and in continual confrontation with the latter. This trend was best epitomized perhaps in Hungary, especially in the personality of the Hatam Sofer and in his famous saying: "The new is forbidden from the Torah . . ." [4]

Given the objective socio-political situation of the Jewish communities – their living in alien, often hostile, environments – such fundamentalist tendencies were mostly oriented toward the regulation of the internal religious and communal life of their communities, and of their ritual and symbolic relation with the outside world. The situation has changed in the State of Israel, and to some extent in the Jewish communities in contemporary liberal societies – especially, but not exclusively, in the United States.

In Israel, from about the seventies on there developed two major trends – with many divisions within them – that demonstrated very strong, even if varying fundamentalist tendencies. Both constituted responses to the disintegration of the initial cultural and institutional Zionist, especially labor, mold which was predominant in Israel till the mid or late seventies. However, they developed from different vantage points with respect to this mold. The first are the ultra-nationalist Zionist groups epitomized in Gush Emunim (Block of the Faithful) – who constituted the spearhead of the settlement in the West Bank and Gaza. The second group which developed strong fundamentalist overtones has been the anti- or non-Zionist ultra-orthodox, which started in this period to move out of their self-imposed relative segregation into more active political directions evincing many fundamentalist tendencies.[5] Common to both are challenges in the name of some pristine, potentially fundamentalist vision to the basic symbolic premises of the central premises and the institutions of the State of Israel. Further, each group only partially accepts (often for opposite reasons) the legitimacy of the Israeli State's premises and institutions. In both cases, these tendencies were closely related to their attempts at the reconstruction of relations between the primordial, historical and religious components of Jewish collective identity – with each acting in different directions. In the case of Gush Emunim such partial acceptance has been rooted in the full acceptance of the Zionist vision, through the imbuing of that vision with a full Messianic legitimacy. This partial acceptance was evident in the emphasis on the supremacy of the higher law, in this case a law which they proclaimed stressed the sanctity of Eretz Israel, as against the law of the land – that is, against any political compromise with respect to the West Bank, Judea and Samaria, which would deny the sanctity of the contemporary era. Second among them is an emphasis, though in many ways a weaker one, on the sanctity of the Halakhah.

The developments in the Gush Emunim took place within the basic Zionist symbolic framework or repertoire, even if they gave rise to far-reaching changes in the relative importance and concrete definitions of many of the components of this repertoire. The situation was different with respect to the various anti-Zionist, or at least non-Zionist, religious orientations, as articulated by Agudat Israel and other extreme Orthodox groups. In the case of the non-Zionist Orthodox groups – originally concentrated around the Agudat Israel Party in what was increasingly called the "Haredi" sector – there developed, not from the beginning of the state, but from the beginning of the Zionist movement, the non-acceptance of the legitimacy of the Zionist vision and later the state and its institutions, including that of the chief rabbinate. They often portrayed their existence in Eretz Israel as existence in the "spiritual Galuth, Exile." Most of them have accepted the existence of the state at most in a de facto manner. Their attitude to the state has been purely instrumental, attempting to receive as many resources from state agencies as possible without granting them any basic legitimacy.

Although they shared with Gush Emunim an emphasis on the primacy of the Holy Law, of Halakhah, their vision of this supremacy differs greatly from that of the Gush. It is devoid, with the exception of some Hasidic groups, of any Messianic political orientations and activism. Originally, they were in some sense apolitical – i.e. they did not attempt to engage in political activity beyond either trying to demand resources from the state, or to further and support demands for religious legislation made by the

Religious Zionists. The fundamentalist components of their vision have been inwardly directed, manifest above all, as Haim Soloveitchik and S. Heilman have shown,[6] in a growing ideologization and rigidification of tradition, of emphasis on more totalistic conceptions and regulations on their members, and on constructing very rigid boundaries which would distinguish them from other sectors of society.

Yet even here there simultaneously took place a very interesting transformation of the original negative attitude of the ultra-Orthodox groups to the Zionist movement. Truly enough, the basic negative attitude to the "revolutionary" dimensions of Zionist ideology – those dimensions focused on the reconstruction of Jewish tradition – continued, and some of the more extreme among the ultra-Orthodox groups became even more intensified in rather strong sectarian, potentially fundamentalist directions.

These fundamentalist potentialities became gradually, yet continually, reinforced and brought out into the open due to the growing *active* participation of the ultra-Orthodox groups in the political life in Israel. At the same time, more and more of the ultra-Orthodox not only accepted *de facto* the State of Israel but to some extent started to legitimize it in terms of settlement in Eretz Israel, thus treating it as a viable, existing Jewish community which has to be guarded and protected. They increasingly participated in political life, making more demands not only for financial allocations for their institutions, but also for imposing their own conceptions on public life in Israel. Many of them tended to become close to more "rightist" groups that held "hawkish" tendencies with respect to relations with the Palestinians – and while they did develop some incipient fundamentalist overtones, they lacked the strong political Messianic activism of the Gush Emunim.

These fundamentalist tendencies became strengthened and intensified after the 1996 elections when the various religious parties, most of whom increased their membership in the Knesset, became important partners in the new government coalition. As a consequence they became much more militant than before, and started a series of strong campaigns to impose religious ways on many public spheres in Israel.

Parallel intensive fundamentalist movements – very similar to the Haredi sectors in Israel, in fact very closely interwoven with them – developed in the Jewish communities in the USA and Europe, with their activities being often more oriented to the Israeli scene than to the countries in which they live.[7]

IV

In the Muslim world multiple and diverse fundamentalist movements developed from the late nineteenth century – gathering special momentum

in the latter part of the twentieth century. In the background of these movements was probably the prior pristine proto-fundamentalist renovative
movements, the Wahabis, the founders of what was to become Saudi
Arabia – and even further back to the Mahdi regime that crystallized in
Sudan in the late nineteenth century. If the Wahabi movement can be seen
as the last and most vivid case of "classical" Islamic, in our terms "proto-
fundamentalist" movement, it is useful to consult Voll again (paraphrasing
him a bit):

the case of Muhammad Ahmad, the Sudanese leader who proclaimed his mission
as Mahdi and drove the Ottoman-Egyptian forces out of his country in the
1880s . . . is the most evocative model for today's fundamentalist activities. His
mission was to create a more purely Islamic society by eliminating the innovations
introduced by outsiders, even though they called themselves Muslims. The
Sudanese Mahdi rejected the corrupt practices of the Turko-Egyptian rulers and
fought the British, but he did not reject modern military technology. Although he
is frequently described as an opponent of foreign rule and an enemy of Western
intrusions into the Islamic world, he also opposed certain local religious customs,
engaged in ijtihad, and in other ways recalled the example of Ibn 'Abd al-Wahhab.
Although he envisioned his mission in messianic terms, he stands well within the
heritage of Sunni fundamentalism.
   Although the Mahdi himself died in 1885, he created a state which lasted until
British and Egyptian forces conquered the Sudan in 1898. The Mahdist movement
remained an important force in Sudanese society throughout the twentieth century.
In the 1940s, the Mahdist movement became the basis for one of the major
Sudanese political parties, and a great grandson of the Mahdi, Sadiq al-Mahdi,
served as prime minister of the independent Sudan in the 1960s and again in the
1980s. The political dynamism of the Mahdist movement, in both the nineteenth
and twentieth centuries, has provided Muslim intellectuals throughout the Islamic
world with an example of effective Islamic political activism.[8]

   In the twentieth century there started to develop, against the background
of the multiple reform movements, also strong fundamentalist movements
in Sunni Islam.
   All these movements constituted part of the continual confrontation
between Islam and the West, and represented the multifaceted responses of
various groups of Muslim intellectuals and leaders throughout the Muslim
lands to the impact of the West.[9]
   Among the most important of these movements were, to follow Mumtaz
Ahmad's list:

The Muslim Brotherhood in the Arab countries, Jamaat-i-Islami in Pakistan, India
and Bangladesh, Dar-ul-Islam in Indonesia, Islamic National Front in Sudan,
Islamic Literary Society in Tunis, Parti Islam Se-Malaysia in Malaysia, and the
Rafah party in Turkey.[10]

In the seventies such movements developed in Shi'i Islam especially in Iran, but also in Iraq. In this period it was above all Iran, Algeria, North Africa, and Sudan that became the center-stage of these movements – spreading in the eighties and nineties through the Muslim diasporas in Europe and beyond. One of the most important of such developments from about the late sixties on was in Turkey, the only (formerly?) Muslim country in which a militant secular regime crystallized.[11]

One of the strongest of such movements developed in Afghanistan – there constituting a mixture of "classical" Islamic proto-fundamentalist movements based on tribes, with more modern organizational, but very limited mobilizatory tendencies – the Taliban. Several such movements started to emerge after the breakdown of the Soviet Union, sometimes out of some of the more traditional ones in Central Asia – but there developed strong rifts between the leadership that had developed under the aegis of the former Soviet Union and that of the new leaders in the framework of the fundamentalist movements. As mentioned above, Muslim fundamentalist movements developed also in India and in Pakistan. In Pakistan, and to some extent Malaysia, these movements developed within the framework of an ideologically Islamic state – a state that, according to these movements, did not go far enough in imposing an Islamic vision and law.

In many African countries – in East and West Africa alike – radical Islamic movements with strong fundamentalist orientations continually developed within the broader framework of the expansion of Islam. They were in continual interaction – cooperative and contestational alike with the many other Muslim movements in these countries – gaining very high visibility in Kenya and Uganda in East Africa, in Guinea, Mali, Ivory Coast and Senegal in West Africa, and predominance in Sudan. All these movements were in one way or another much more closely interwoven than the Wahhabi – and even than the Mahdi one in Sudan – with anti-colonial struggles, with struggles against Western dominance in its various guises and hence also with national movements. Many of them also portrayed themselves as being such national movements.

Strong fundamentalist movements also developed in many parts of the Muslim diasporas – in Europe, especially in France, Germany and England, in the Caribbean, Canada and to some extent in the USA. Significantly enough it was within these groups that some of the most extreme conceptions of the Muslim ummah were promulgated.

At the same time, in the last three or four decades of the twentieth century, many communal-religious national movements developed or gathered strong momentum in many South and Southeast Asian countries after the first stages of decolonization and the establishment of independent states which were initially presumably based on some modern secular premises. Among them were, in India, first the Area Samaj, later the contemporary BJP (Bharatia Janatar Party) and parallel movements in Sri Lanka which developed some seemingly fundamentalist-like, totalistic orientations and ideologies. These movements were often characterized, to follow Nikkie Keddie's nomenclature,[12] by strong religious–communal orientations. These communal-national movements share some very important characteristics with fundamentalist movements such as their attempt to construct a new religious communal identity, attempts to construct communal boundaries, their tendencies to ritualization of violence, and their promulgation of a strong anti-secular stance. As for the latter, these movements also denote a shift from the hegemony of some of the ideals or premises of the Enlightenment in the construction of modern nation states, their institutions, and in the collective consciousness or identity of modern societies. Yet, as we shall see in greater detail later, most of these movements differ in several very crucial ways from the "pristine" fundamentalist movements analyzed above.

Already the preceding illustrations indicate clearly, as has also been the case with proto-fundamentalist movements, that even within the same society and civilization, both in different periods of their histories and in the same period, there develop a great variety of and heterogeneity of fundamentalist movements. They also indicate that the "same" movements – as for instance some of the Haredim in Israel, or many Muslim groups in Central Asia or in Africa, may acquire at a certain period strong fundamentalist characteristics which they did not have before – and may perhaps shed them in other periods.[13] Thus all these movements are in continual flux and in close continual interaction with many other religious, ethnic, and national movements that burgeoned in all these societies. Indeed, to reiterate, these movements cannot be understood except as part of the general, multifaceted dynamics of these societies, as interacting with the development and unfolding of multiple social and political movements, and not as isolated, self-enclosed entities.

All these facts notwithstanding, it is possible to point out some features which characterize – even if necessarily in an ideal-typical way – the fundamentalist movements or the fundamentalist tendencies in such movements.

The distinct sectarian utopian characteristics of modern fundamentalist movements

V

The core characteristics of the modern fundamentalist movements constitute a radical transformation, in a distinct modern mode, of some of the basic structural and ideological characteristics – especially the sectarian utopian – and orientations of the proto-fundamentalist movements that developed in the various Axial Civilizations which we have analyzed above. Similar to those of the proto-fundamentalist movements, the basic onto-logical conceptions promulgated by modern fundamentalist movements have been characterized by – to follow Emmanuel Sivan's analysis[14] – attempts at the appropriation and construction of space and time accord-ing to their respective utopian visions. These utopian visions have often been imbued with very strong eschatological components which place them at the end of history, with a message of messianic redemption often follow-ing an imminent catastrophe – an ontology which comes to full fruition in their specific "enclave" culture.

These movements also share with the proto-fundamentalist ones several of the basic characteristics of utopian sectarianism, namely the tendency to construct sharp boundaries between the "pure" inside and the "pol-luted" outside, as well as their self-perception as the "elect." Concomitantly they continually promulgate images of an enemy or ontological enemy, one that is about to pollute them or against whom one should be on constant alert – as for instance the assimilationist Jews and the secular world for the Jewish, especially Haredi-fundamentalists; or the USA, Israel, and Zionism for the Muslim fundamentalists. Significantly enough, although in some cases it was particularistic groups such as the Jews or the USA that were/are designated as such enemies, it is usually their being the bearers of some bad, polluted, or satanic universalism that is singled out.[15]

Similar to many other sectarian-ideological movements as well as many authoritarian movements of both the left and the right, the fundamental-ist movements also exhibit a very low threshold of tolerance for ambiguity on both personal and collective levels.

All of these characteristics, as well as their persistent emphasis on tradi-tion – on what they proclaimed to be pristine traditions of their respective religions – and their basic sectarian utopian tendencies, make them seem-ingly very similar to proto-fundamentalist movements. And yet these char-acteristics which the fundamentalist movements share with the proto-fundamentalist ones have become radically transformed in the modern fundamentalist movements, making them a distinctly modern phe-nomenon. In some, even if in paradoxical ways, many of the fundamental-ist groups can be seen (as we shall indicate later) as parallel to the most extreme "secular" Jacobin movements and regimes – namely the Communist ones.

Also, the composition of these movements (as we shall see in greater detail in chapter 4) greatly differs from that of the proto-fundamentalist movements of earlier periods, and is very much in line with the composition of some of the more militant modern, especially Jacobin movements.

It is above all, however, with respect to some of their ideological features that the relations between fundamentalist movements and modernity are revealed and the modern characteristics of these movements become most conspicuous; ideological features such as both the mode of construction of their ideologies of traditions – which constitute the core of their ideologies – and these ideologies' institutional implications. The most important of these features is the appropriation by these movements of some central aspects of the political program of modernity, particularly of various – especially Jacobin – participatory, totalistic, and egalitarian orientations (even if this egalitarian component is in most of these situations confined to men). This crucial feature stands side by side with the anti-Enlightenment aspect of their ideology, and with the denial of claims of the sovereignty and autonomy of reason and of the perfectibility of man.

It is this vision that generates within these movements not only a strong predisposition to the development of a totalistic world view and organization which is characteristic of many "traditional" sectarian movements, including the proto-fundamentalist ones, but also overarching totalitarian all-encompassing ideologies. These ideologies emphasize a total reconstruction, organized basically by political action, of the social order. Many of these movements also, at least potentially, espouse a strong very often missionary zeal. Thus, it is not just the various components of their ontology listed above but rather the bringing together of these components in a distinct sectarian-utopian Jacobin vision that constitutes the distinctive features of these movements. Concomitantly, in at least partial contrast to most pre-modern historical sects and proto-fundamentalist movements, the enclave culture they construct exists in constant tension with their more expansionist tendencies which are closely related to their distinct modern characteristics.

This tension is indeed rooted in some of the distinctly modern characteristics of these movements. The first of these is, as Raymond Grew has strongly emphasized (private communication), the very strong emphasis on choice, on the freedom – and necessity – to make a conscious moral choice in joining and adhering to these movements – thus at least implicitly emphasizing the autonomy of human will. This emphasis on moral choice is conceived in terms of the necessity to combat the evils of the modern Western world – evils rooted in the weakness of human nature but reinforced when given a free rein in modernity with its presumed assumption of the perfectibility of man.

This emphasis on moral choice, on confronting the evils of the modern world, can be also found among seemingly traditionalistic enclaves – like many of the Haredim – once they are drawn into confrontations with the secular world and its institutions. Closely related is the tendency among members of many of these movements to present the joining of such movements and participation in them as the act or process of conversion.[16] Thus the conception of the autonomy of human will acquires in the fundamentalist movements some distinct modern features rooted in the combination of their specific Jacobin orientations and anti-Enlightenment doctrines.

Second, this tension between the mentality of the beleaguered enclave and strong expansionist tendencies is rooted in the necessity of most such movements to mobilize continually new membership and to face the tension between the upholding of a pristine vision and the more mundane interests and behavior of large parts of such membership. It is this tension that, as Raymond Grew and Peter van der Veer have shown,[17] gives rise in these movements to strong tendencies to engage in ritual violence that continually reemphasizes the exclusiveness of the movements and the closure of their boundaries against the polluted world, against the enemy. These two tendencies – the emphasis on the necessity of moral choice in the battle against the evils of the modern world and continual mobilization of wider sectors – are not of course limited to the fundamentalist movements. They are indeed characteristics of many modern movements – including the various communal-religious ones. They become however most fully articulated in a distinct mobilizatory and Jacobin way in the fundamentalist movements which promulgate, in the name of a moral-religious vision, the construction of a new collective and individual identity, not only through religious, but also through political processes and action.

VI

The strong, potentially totalitarian, Jacobin components or tendencies which can be identified – even if to varying degrees per movement and per historical period – are manifest first in the attempts to reconstruct their respective societies; and second, in the almost total conflation of center and periphery, negating the existence of intermediary institutions and association, thus conflating what can sometimes be called civil society with the overall community. Third, such potential Jacobin orientations can be found in the strong tendency to the sanctification of the reconstruction of the center as a continuous liminal arena, with this sanctification often connected with ritual violence and terror.

As in the case of the Great Revolutions and "leftist" totalitarian movements, the pure pristine fundamentalist movements tend also to minimize, in principle at least, the importance of primordial components of collective identity – or at least to make them secondary in relation to the universalistic religious ones – as for instance the Islamic against the Iranian ones, or as in Sudan, the Islamic against the local and African ones. The emphasis on primordial components in these movements becomes strong only in special cases, as in Judaism, in which the primordial orientations constitute a basic component of the universal religion. The picture among the communal-religious nationalist movements, which developed especially from the sixties on in India and in Buddhist countries in South and Southeast Asia, has been rather different, as we shall see in greater detail later.

The roots of these distinctive modern characteristics of the fundamentalist movements, of the combination of utopian sectarianism with strong Jacobin political tendencies, are to be found in the close relation of these movements to the cultural and political program of modernity and to modern political processes as they developed in the Great Revolutions, especially in the post-revolutionary regimes. Just as the Great Revolutions were closely related to, indeed rooted in, some of the heterodoxies of their respective Axial Civilizations, so within the fundamentalist movements, especially those which developed in the monotheistic civilizations, the heterodox tendencies of the proto-fundamentalist groups have been transformed into potentially fully-fledged modern political programs with potentially missionary visions. Above all, many of the fundamentalist movements share with the Great Revolutions the belief in the primacy of politics, albeit in their case, religious politics – or at least of organized action – guided by a totalistic religious vision to reconstruct society, or sectors thereof. It is indeed, as we have indicated above, the ideological and political heritage of the Revolutions that epitomized the victory of gnostic heterodox tendencies to bring the Kingdom of God to Earth, as an attempt to recognize that the world constitutes the crucial link between the cultural and political program of modernity and fundamental movements.

Truly enough, such a totalistic orientation did not necessarily always entail the development of an active political stance beyond the fundamentalist movements' own confines. Thus indeed many of these fundamentalist movements, as for instance the "original" Protestant ones that developed in the USA, often espoused visions of withdrawal from the world, of internal reconstruction of the self and of the community, as against becoming involved in the polluted political world, and strongly emphasized that it is mainly, perhaps only, through such internal purification that the pollution of the external world can be overcome. Similarly some of the grass-roots fundamentalist movements in Pakistan or Malaysia – and the different evangelistic movements above all in societies like in Latin America in which the dominant religion is not that espoused by these movements – do not develop distinct political activities and often promulgate a principled withdrawal from politics, and they also often emphasize the importance of internal reconstruction. Indeed most of these movements have put very strong emphasis on the development of schools and various social services. It was by virtue of these activities that they were able to attract large sectors of the population – and it was through these organizations that they were able to promulgate and propagate their specific religious orientations.

Within these fundamentalist groups very strong Jacobin-like tendencies were oriented above all to the reconstruction of at least their internal life. But these tendencies could also harbor some seeds of potentially expansive political activity, of a strong tendency to engage in some type of political activity rooted in attempts to construct a new identity based on a religious moral vision oriented to the broader society. Thus for instance the ideology of jihad, promulgated openly by some of the Muslim fundamentalist movements, very often found a strong resonance among many of those which have developed in Muslim societies.

The surge and intensity of such political activity depends on the concrete historical and institutional settings of the various fundamentalist movements and may develop in a variety of ways – for instance, as designated by Almond, Sivan and Appleby,[18] those of World Conqueror, World Creator, World Transformer, and the extreme antipolitical mode – that of World Renouncer. While this last mode has been relatively strong in many of the earlier modern movements and can, of course, also be found in the contemporary scene – in the latter more political and active orientations have become more predominant.

The Jacobin components and characteristics of the modern fundamentalist movements

VII

Many of the components of the fundamentalist movements, such as the utopian, eschatological orientations, the emphasis on a strict interpretation of a holy script, sectarian attitudes and the like, can be found in many of the other modern-oriented movements as well as in the popular cultures that developed in their respective societies – with which the fundamentalist movements interacted continually, often in confrontational ways. But it is above all in fundamentalist movements that these components come together so as to define the very nature of these movements. Needless to say, even in these movements the relative importance of these components may vary greatly, and these components may become interwoven in different ways with other themes which themselves may become, under appropriate historical circumstances, either more prominent or more diluted.

Because of all these facts there has developed in the literature on fundamentalism a continual far-ranging controversy as to the legitimacy of calling all these movements fundamentalist. On the most general level it has been claimed that it is inappropriate to apply a term coined in a specific setting – that of American fundamentalism – to movements in other religions or civilizations.[19] On more concrete levels, it has been pointed out that many of the supposedly central characteristics of fundamentalism – such as emphasis on the literal interpretation of, and adherence to, a holy script – are either not fully applicable to all of these movements or can be found also in other ones. It would be beyond the scope of this book to go into all the details of these controversies. Suffice it to point out that, while many of these criticisms of the use of the term fundamentalism are indeed well taken, they do not face up to what are indeed the core characteristics of these movements which distinguish them from other, relatively similar ones. The common core of these movements, as was the case with respect to the proto-fundamentalist movements, lies not in the various details – such as adherence to a literal reading of a holy text which may indeed greatly vary – but in their specific type of sectarian-utopian Jacobin tendencies. Such tendencies may indeed allow for a great variation in details, and needless to say their strength also varies between such different movements and between different periods in the history of each such movement. Indeed, there may also be great differences in the extent to which any movement develops at any given point in time all the ideal typical "fundamentalist" characteristics or, on the contrary, the extent to which these may become blurred. But all these caveats notwithstanding, it is these specific Jacobin tendencies or characteristics that constitute the most important common characteristics of these movements and which justify, in our mind, the use of the term fundamentalism for all of them. At the same time, just because of this common core which can be found in most of these movements it seems to us, as we shall see yet in greater detail later on, that the application of the term fundamentalism to the numerous national communal religious movements which have developed lately is not appropriate.

VIII

One of the most interesting and paradoxical manifestations of this combination of the modern Jacobin mobilizatory dimension of modern fundamentalist movements and regimes with an "anti-modern," or at least anti-liberal ideology, can be found in their attitude to women. On one hand, most of these movements, as Martin Riesebrodt has shown in his incisive analysis,[20] promulgate a strong patriarchal, anti-feminist attitude which tends to segregate women and to impose far-reaching restrictions on them – seemingly, but only seemingly, of a type which can be found in many of the Arab regimes like Saudi Arabia, the roots of which were traditional proto-fundamentalist ones. On the other hand, in stark contrast to such traditionalistic regimes, the modern fundamentalist ones mobilize women – even if in segregation from men – into the public sphere, be it in demonstrations, paramilitary organizations, or the like.

Indeed the reshaping of the social and cultural construction of women, and the construction of a new public identity rooted in the Islamist vision, constituted a very important component in the fundamentalist programs in Iran and Turkey, and were very often promulgated by educated and professional women who felt alienated in the preceding secular public space. In the 1996 elections in Iran, women not only voted and stood as candidates to the parliament, some were elected – one of them (Ms Rafsannghani, the daughter of the then President) claiming that there is nothing in Islamic law which forbids women to take public office. Significantly enough, one of the first acts of the new government installed by the Afghan group of the Taliban – which evinced more proto-fundamentalist than modern fundamentalist Jacobin tendencies – in early October, 1996 was to force women from the public sphere, out of schools, and even from work.[21] Additionally, in June 1997, the Taliban rulers in Kabul ordered the Iranian Ambassador to leave the country accusing Iran of attempts to undermine Taliban rule.

The strong modern components of many of the fundamentalist movements can also be seen in some aspects of their institutionalization as regimes. When the Islamic revolution triumphed in Iran, it did not abolish most of the modern institutions – those without any roots in Islam – such as the parliament, the majilis, and both elections to it and even to the Presidency of the Republic. The importance of these elections was demonstrated in May 1997 when, against the (even if implicit) advice or recommendation of the clerical establishment, a more "open-minded" candidate, Muhammad Khatami, was elected – seemingly by the vote of women and younger people. It even promulgated a new constitution – something which some of the earlier traditionalists opposed vehemently. Both the majilis and the mode of election to it were reconstructed – with some very strong

Jacobin elements, clothed in an Islamic garb. Interestingly enough, one of these garbs – the institutionalization of a special Islam court or chamber to supervise "secular" legislation – was not so far removed from the special place of juridical institution which is characteristic of modern constitutional regimes, even from the principle of judicial revision.[22] Moreover, the basic mode of legitimation of this regime as promulgated in the constitution contained some very important modern components. It declared two different sources of sovereignty – God and the people – without attempting to reconcile the two.[23]

Significantly enough, among many of the apolitical evangelical, especially Pentecostal movements in Latin America, the construction of new modes of life according to their visions of the Gospel entailed the growing autonomous participation of women and the weakening of the prevalent "machoist" culture.[24]

Indeed, in more general terms, as M. E. Yapp has succinctly put it: "(Islamic) fundamentalists want a strong state as a major investment in education and modernity but everything to be done according to the shara. Most fundamentalists are unconcerned by the contradiction evident in this combination."[25]

IX

It is the combination of these different components of fundamentalist visions with very strong Jacobin orientations that also explains the very paradoxical attitude of these movements to tradition and to modernity. While in many ways the fundamentalist movements are reactive (as many scholars have pointed out),[26] yet this general designation can also be applied to other, especially various modern-reformist, movements. Hence, this distinction does not delineate the specific characteristics of the fundamentalist movements; the distinct ways in which such fundamentalist movements and groups reconstruct tradition and select – and reconstruct – different themes from the cultural and political repertoire of tropes available to them. The anti-modern, or to be yet again more precise, anti-Enlightenment attitude and the specific way of promulgating tradition that develop within the fundamentalist visions are not just a reaction of traditional groups to the encroachment of new ways of life, but a militant ideology which is basically couched in highly modern idiom and is oriented to the mobilization of wide masses. They are, as Frank J. Lechner and Martin Riesebrodt among others have pointed out,[27] very strongly oriented against the social and institutional differentiation of modern societies, promulgating a highly de-differentiated, monolithic, vision of the world.

The paradoxical attitude of modern fundamentalist movements to tradition; essentialized tradition as modern totalistic ideologies

X

Thus, although seemingly traditional, these movements are in fact in some paradoxical ways anti-traditional. They are anti-traditional in that they negate the living traditions, with their complexity and heterogeneity, of their respective societies or religions and instead uphold a highly ideological and essentialistic conception of tradition as an overarching principle of cognitive and social organization.

This attitude to tradition is manifest in two very closely connected facts. First, the often conservative existing religious establishment of their respective societies constitutes one of the major foci of criticism of these movements – up to the point where these establishments are even seen as one of those establishments' major enemies. Second, and closely related, is the fact that the younger sectors, especially within the cities, be it in Turkey or in the Muslim diasporas in the West, which are drawn to fundamentalist movements, distance themselves from their traditionalist parents. The traditionalist way of life of their parents or grandparents is seen by them as not pure enough and as a simple-minded compromise with the secular society.[28]

Most fundamentalist groups tend to espouse a principled denial of the continued unfolding of tradition and of its interpretation – which does, of course, in itself constitute a very distinct, new, and innovative mode of interpretation. The fundamentalists are in principle oriented against any innovation or lenience within the existing traditions – even if such innovation has been a continuous component in such tradition. For instance, the Hatam Sofer's – a major figure, the promulgator of proto-fundamentalist orientations in modern Eastern European Jewish orthodoxy in the first half of the nineteenth century – famous injunction that "anything new is forbidden from Torah" to which we have referred above went against the great and continuous tradition of interpretation and innovation which characterized the classical (medieval and early modern) Jewish tradition. Such injunctions and attitudes were in fact themselves innovations – but innovations presented as representing simple, pristine "old" tradition.[29] It is also very significant that the nature of such innovations, of the exact interpretation of what is new and what is old varies greatly between various fundamentalist movements that develop within the same religion or civilization, and constitute a bone of contention between them.

Thus, fundamentalist traditionalism is not to be confused with a "simple" or "natural" upkeep of a given living tradition. Rather, it denotes an ideological mode and stance oriented not only against new developments, against different manifestations of modern life, but also against the continually changing and diversified tradition. Such attitude of these movements can be seen, as we have pointed out above, in their attitudes to both the more conservative religious leaders of their respective traditions, as well as to the more popular manifestations thereof. Thus while for instance the Jamaat-i-Islam in Pakistan does not differ in its concrete demands from the more conservative Ulema, yet the whole tenor of their demands when espoused by the Jemaat is radically different from that of the conservative Ulema. Thus, to follow Mumtaz Ahmad:

But fundamentalists do differ from the conservative ulama in their concept of Islam as a *deen*, which they interpret as a "way of life." The Jamaat-i-Islami criticizes the conservative ulama for reducing Islam to the five pillars – profession of faith, prayer, fasting, almsgiving, and pilgrimage. The Jamaat views Islam as a complete [. . .] and a comprehensive way of life which covers the entire spectrum of human activity, be it individual, social, economic, or political. For them, Islam means the total commitment and subordination of all aspects of human life to the will of God.

As a revitalized formalism, the Jamaat-i-Islami seeks to replace the folk and popular practices of Sufi Islam with the approved rituals of orthodox Islam. In line with Islamic modernism, fundamentalists militate against the fatalistic quietism of the sufi fraternities. They present Islam as a dynamic and activist political ideology which must acquire state power in order to implement its social, economic, and political agenda.

This brings us to one of the most important defining characteristics of the Jamaat-i-Islam and other Islamic fundamentalist movements: *unlike the conservative ulama and the modernists, the fundamentalist movements are primarily political rather than religious intellectual movements.* While both the ulama and the modernists seek influence in public policy-making structures, the fundamentalists aspire to *capture* political life . . ."

The Jamaat-i-Islami set as its objective 'the establishment of the Islamic way (*Deen*) so as to achieve God's pleasure and seek salvation in the Hereafter.' In order to achieve this objective, the Jamaat set out the following five programs for itself:
1. To construct human thought in the light of the ideals, values, and principles derived from divine guidance.
2. To "reform and purify" individual members of society so as to enable them to develop a truly Islamic personality.
3. To organize these individuals under the leadership of the Jamaat and to prepare and train them to invite humanity to the path of Islam.
4. To take all possible steps to reform and reconstruct the society and all of its institutions in accordance with the teachings of Islam.
5. To bring about a revolution in the political leadership of society, reorganize political and socioeconomic life on Islamic lines, and finally, establish an Islamic state.[30]

XI

It is not, however, just the selection and reconstruction of certain themes of tradition as the only legitimate symbols of the traditional order and their upholding of them against the existing situation, and against others, that is characteristic of the various fundamentalist movements. What is crucial here is the attempt to essentialize tradition in terms of these themes and symbols, and in name of a basic premise or pristine vision embodied in some text – whether in the form of a book or a message, an exemplary personality, or an event in an idealized period – and concomitantly to total-ize this vision in a utopian mode.

Such ideological stances also entail a denial of the unfolding of a histor-ical process and instead promulgate an essentialist, non-historical concep-tion of a religious civilization, and of tradition.

Aziz Al Azmeh, in his analysis of the Islamic movements, points out some of the most important aspects of this transformation, which in prin-ciple apply also to non-Islamic ones:

> Eschatology and past example become utopia when they become activist, when they become a chiliasm, with a sense of total imminence. They become utopia when legalism and moralism give way to total political contestation. This occurs when the fundamentalist movement as distinct from historical Islam is ascendant among par-ticular groups in society. Islamic political and social ideals based on primitivist models become utopian when these models are activated and valorized, when fun-damentalism ceases to be a cliché and takes on programmatic specifications and, as a precondition of this specification, acquires a social and political constituency. Historically, this has taken two main forms. In the Islamic Middle Ages, radical fun-damentalism was, as far as I know, invariably chiliastic, associated with the complex of ideas generically known as Mahdism. North African history is especially replete with Mahdism both Sunnite and Shi'ite: the Idrisids, the Fatimids, the Almohads, Sufi politics like that of Ibn Qasi (d. 1151), a thaumaturge who established a short-lived state in the Algarve, and countless others. These have already been mentioned briefly, and associated with Ibn Khaldun's theory of kinship.
>
> The second form of activist utopianism is contemporary Islamic radicalism, for which there is no precedent in Islamic history. Like chiliasm, it relies on the specification of fundamentalism, that is to say, on the precise and imminent inter-pretation of the pristine model, be that divine pronouncement or utopian example. This is quite natural in all utopias, for by their very nature these have to establish a constituency by affirming the univocality of texts and examples which are, in them-selves, naturally multivocal: Plato specified his Republic in the *Laws*, Rousseau his Contract with his projected Corsican constitution.
>
> Similarly, Islamic radicalism, a very recent phenomenon indeed and the illegiti-mate offspring of Islamic reformism and Wahhabite-Mawdudian fundamentalism,

was born of a particular specification. It specified *jahiliyya*, the non-Islam that is to be converted into Islamic order, as an actual presence. Of course each movement in this fundamentalism provided particular specifications consonant with its social, political and cultural import. Wahhabite fundamentalism in Arabia, from the beginning until the definitive establishment of utopia by the Imam (later King) Abd al-Aziz (the foundation of Saudi Arabia) and the suppression of the Ikhwan Wahhabite militia in 1927, decreed all territory identified for absorption by the expanding Saudi polity as *jahiliyya* – and by territory I mean geographical territory to be subjugated, socio-political territory to be linked to the House of Saud in a tributary fashion, and of course religious territory defined by the diversity of local cults whose centralization and homogenization under the title of *shari'a* was a cultural precondition for political centralization. *Shari'a* here is of course in the main Hanbalite, characterized by a moralistic rigor which homogenizes public life on the one hand, and an economic liberalism on the other, much like some early Protestant politics.

The difference between Arabian and, say, Egyptian Muslim utopianism arises from distinct historical worlds to which they belong. Arabian utopianism imagines the chiliastic order in terms of miracle and without necessary political reference to the state; this is very much in keeping with medieval Islamic habits. Egyptian utopianism, on the other hand, regards its relation to the state as fundamental. It seeks immediately to take the state by force, as with the radicals professing notions like *takfir*. It also seeks, as with the Muslim Brothers in their fundamentalist mode, to work a rhetorical reconciliation of the notion of *shura* (a form of Medinan consultation) and of liberal political notions with the aim of gaining power.[31]

XII

Such essentialization and totalization of tradition – often in a utopian mode, which is characteristic of the modern fundamentalist movements – entails the concomitant arrangement – in a hierarchical, relatively undifferentiated way – of different aspects and layers of tradition according to the presumed implications of this single vision.

Accordingly fundamentalist movements are characterized by a *principled* – though not easily observed in practice – differentiation between layers of "tradition" in terms of their relation to the pristine vision, and by the ideological symbolization of many customs – such as pattern of dress, calendric observance, and the like – which can be used as markers of collective identity to demarcate the boundaries between internally pure and externally polluted spaces. In practice they may often waver between, on the one hand, a sharp segregation between "traditional" (ritual, religious) and non-traditional spheres of life, without developing any strong connective symbolic and organizational bonds between the two, on the one hand; and a strong predisposition or demand for some clear unifying principles which would connect and unify both arenas, on the other. As a result, there develops within these movements a strong tendency toward "ritualization" of the symbols of traditional life on both the personal and collective levels alike. Increasing attempts to impose traditional symbols on the mundane, often secular world in relatively rigid, militant ways may then alternate with the total isolation of these traditional symbols from the impurities of that world.[32]

The rather paradoxical attitude of these movements to tradition is shaped by their basic ideologies; especially by the nature of their criticism of modernity; their stand with respect to the basic antinomies of modernity; and the closely related characteristics of their attempts to appropriate modernity in their own terms according to their distinct sectarian and utopian vision with strong political orientations. It is these characteristics that give rise to these movements' tendencies to construct, in a totalistic mode, an ideologized, essentialized conception of tradition.

XIII

This attitude to tradition prevalent in many of the fundamentalist movements is closely connected with yet another paradox which characterizes the modern fundamentalist movements – a paradox that could be found among the proto-fundamentalist movements but became more fully articulated in the modern setting. The essence of this paradox is that although these movements present themselves as the pure pristine orthodoxy of their respective religion, there are in fact, in any given situation, heterodoxies which are in sharp conflict with the existing religious establishment, with the prevailing ways of life, and with the preceding tradition. In many cases the leaders of the fundamentalist movements are intellectuals with strong antinomian tendencies – with their antinomianism being oriented not only toward the secular elites of their respective countries but also, as in countries like Pakistan or Malaysia or Morocco, against the prevalent modes of interpretation of tradition by the more orthodox Islamists.

The basically heterodox nature of the fundamentalist movements is evident also in the fact that within any religion or civilization there tend to develop, at any single point, not one but several fundamentalist movements, and among such movements there tend to develop continual sectarian quarrels and schisms – with such confrontations tending to generate even greater emphasis on degrees of choice and human will.

Truly enough, such variety may be due to different socio-political circumstances or to changing constellations of the relations between the various fundamentalist groups and the political rulers, and the closely connected possible incorporation of some of the fundamentalist themes or symbols by the existing regimes.[33] But beyond such various contingent reasons, such variety is also inherent in the very nature of the religious sectarian dynamics of the fundamentalist movements. Despite the fact that each such movement claims to be the only representative of the original pristine vision of its religion, they are all in fact new constructions which may, and often do, differ with respect to which aspect or symbol of their religion they portray as the essence of the original pristine vision. Thus, as we have seen, the almost coterminous development of different fundamentalist movements in the fold of the same religion can be found in contemporary Israel, where both the anti-Zionist "Haredim" and the ultranational Gush Emunim claim to present the pristine vision of Judaism.[34] Similarly, among the Protestant fundamentalist movements in the USA there developed continuous differences and conflicts with respect to sources of authority – over texts, and de facto which or whose interpretation of the text – and over whether or not the proclaimed vision was in fact the true representation of the pristine vision.

Such variety is even greater given the widespread geopolitical range of Islam in the Muslim countries where such variety could already be found in the many proto-fundamentalist or revivalist Islamic movements in the eighteenth century and prior.[35] It is not only that fundamentalist Muslim movements develop in different political regimes – including ones like Pakistan or Malaysia which define themselves as Muslim – but that, as the condemnations by Iran of the Taliban movements in Afghanistan attests to, there may develop strong contestations between different Muslim fundamentalist movements or regimes.[36] Significantly enough, in all these cases there also develop different interpretations of the literal understanding of texts, and different emphases on various parts of such texts.

These different interpretations are not confined to dissensions among the fundamentalist movements – they constitute a part of the wider discourses on tradition and modernity that take place in all these societies, be they Muslim, Jewish, or especially, but not only, Protestant-Christian or sectors thereof. This yet again attests to the continual interweaving of these movements with the broader settings in which they act and to the multiple intellectual and political movements and streams within them.

XIV

The upshot of all these tendencies is that these movements are not political in the instrumental or technical sense but rather in their attempts, albeit at times via political means, to implement an overall moral vision, to construct a new collective identity, and to appropriate modernity in their own terms. Nilufer Göle presents a very incisive analysis of Islamic fundamentalism in Turkey in these terms.

A return to the original sources – comprising of references to the Quran itself and the Sunna and Hadith (sayings and traditions of the Prophet) and the "asr-i saadet" period (the age of the Prophet Muhammed and the four orthodox caliphs (622–661) – is a common feature of almost all islamist movements, calling for revivalism and struggling against the contamination of "pure" Islam by customary practices. The ways in which islamist movements situate themselves in relation to western modernity marks the main difference of the new generation of islamists from the nineteenth century modernist islamists. While the latter, as in the writings of Muhammed Abduh, Jamal al-Din al-Afghani, Rashid Rida, tried to accommodate islamic values with democratic and modern values, the contemporary radical islamists take a non-apologetic and an anti-modernist stand, in the name of an islamic alternative. The search for an alternative in Islam, especially endows muslim intellectuals with a very strong quest for an authentic identity and provides them with the emotional, moral and intellectual tools with which they direct a critique to permissiveness, consumerism, pollution, corruption and nationalism, all considered as sinful outcomes of western modernity and civilization.

Contemporary islamism is situated at the crossroads of the critique of traditional interpretations of Islam on the one hand and of modernism on the other. Hence, islamism is neither a direct outcome of religious and cultural traditions, nor a straightforward representation of muslim identity. On the contrary, it stems from the problematization of muslim traditions and identity. Islamism is a cultural and political deconstruction of the category of "muslim"; consequently one "becomes" an islamist when one engages in a critique and refuses to be a muslim the way one is naturally "born" into it. Islamism implies therefore, a critique and even a discontinuity with the given categories of muslim identity; it is an endeavour to rename, to reconstruct muslim identity, by freeing it from traditional interpretations and by challenging modernism. It is "radical" both in its critique of traditions, considered as responsible for the passivity and the "enslavement" of muslim people, and in its desire to instaure a radically different civilization, that is a revolutionary change comprising the islamization of spheres of life ranging from conceptions of self, to organizations of life-world and politics of government.

Islamism, both in its ideological formulations and sociological practices posits new hybridations between tradition and modernity, religion and secularism, community and religion. The new actors of islamism, both in their sociological profiles and social practices incarnate the paradoxical, ambivalent nature of contemporary islamism. Especially the new intellectual and professional elites owing their identity and social visibility on the one hand to modern education that they have acquired recently, and on the other, to islamist movements in which they have been taking part in the last twenty years, is of particular interest.

Hence, I am arguing that it is in this realm of habitus, cultural-codes and life-styles, that the stakes of power struggle between the republican elites and the others are rooted. In other words, the question of life-styles is not a trivial matter of fashion, trends, individual choices but reveals relations of intersubjectivity, relations of stratification, relations of power linked to the domain of habitus. One can argue that upper middle-class kemalist women in particular but also kemalist men, who acquire education and a professional career and who cultivate their body-language and way of life in a "secular," that is non-muslim manner, obtain prestige, social recognition, therefore "symbolic capital" and form, a distinct social status group. Hence such a definition of social distinction and social status, rooted in the exclusion of the islamic life-world, forms the main social and political discord between the secularists and the islamists. In other words, in order to become part of the elite, one has to master the western code of conduct, discourse and living. Ways of education and ways of living distinguish the republican elites as "civilized" and as "progressist" in counter-distinction to parochial elites who are attached to traditional, local and religious manners and customs . . .[37]

The power of the Jacobin component of the fundamentalist movements

XV

It is these movements' attitudes to tradition and their attempts to implement by political means a moral-religious vision that explain what may seem as a paradox of our analysis – namely that these religious movements, with their strong emphasis on tradition, have yet acquired characteristics which have been associated with one of the most extreme, modern, secular visions – namely the Jacobin.

On the phenomenological level, the answer to this paradox lies in the fact that it is not the secular dimension of the Jacobin or the "religious" dimensions of the fundamentalists that are crucially important. Rather, it is their totalizing, absolutizing tendencies which they share that explains this paradox. These tendencies are rooted in the basic antinomies of the Axial Civilizations as they were promulgated above all by some heterodox – especially the proto-fundamentalist – movements with strong gnostic orientations. In the Great Revolutions these heterodoxies became thoroughly politicized and moved from peripheries into the center. It was such politicization and movement into the center that constituted the core of the Jacobin movement or orientation and greatly influenced the modern political agendas of the many social movements including the fundamentalist ones.

What explains the Jacobin tendencies that distinguish the modern fundamentalist movements from the proto-fundamentalist ones are the former's development within the framework of modern political agendas; both their promulgation of a distinct stand with respect to the modern cultural and political program and the ways in which they attempted to reconstruct tradition in terms of such attitudes to modernity; and their appropriation of the modern political frameworks on their own terms.

The fundamentalist and the Communist regimes – a comparison of two modern Jacobin movements and regimes

XVI

Given these very distinctive Jacobin characteristics and tendencies of the modern fundamentalist movements, it will be worthwhile to compare them to other distinctive Jacobin movements or regimes to develop a more nuanced understanding of them. First, it will benefit us to compare them to Communist ones with which they share some paradoxical and some mirror-like characteristics, and secondly, we shall compare them to the major types of nationalistic movements or regimes, especially fascist and national-social ones, that developed in modern societies.

Communist and fundamentalist movements and regimes share the tendency to promulgate a very strong salvationist vision or gospel. The visions promulgated by both these types of regimes contained a strong tendency to combine different themes of protest with the construction of a new ontological definition of reality, with a total world view rooted in the respective salvationist vision. Although the content of this vision varied greatly between them – they promulgated opposite and to a large extent mutually exclusive visions – they did share the view that the implementation of this vision was to take place in this world, in the present. Instead of the – basically unfathomable – future, the implementation of this vision was, as that of all the Great Revolutions, to be achieved in the present, and thus, present and future became in many ways conflated.

These visions entailed the transformation both of man and of society, and of construction of new, personal and collective identities. It was in the name of salvation that these movements and regimes demanded total submergence of the individual in the general totalistic community, the total reconstruction of personality and of individual and collective identity. It was in the name of such vision that they developed their Jacobin features, above all the view that many aspects of the social and political orders can be continuously reconstructed by conscious human, above all political, action. Both the Communist and the fundamentalist regimes emphasized the active construction, by political action, of a new social and cultural order, the active participation of most sectors of society in such order, as well as a high level of commitment to it.

In both cases, the institutionalization of such visions gave rise to regimes characterized by strong mobilizatory orientations and policies aiming at transforming the structure of society in general, and of center–periphery relations in particular. Both types of movements and regimes aimed such efforts at transformation and mobilization, with the sanctification of violence and terror against internal and external evil forces and enemies – especially those rooted in the internal dynamics of modern Western "bourgeois" society.

Both types of regimes aimed at the total transformation of the symbols of collective – and personal – identity, of the institutional structure of the society, and at the establishment of a new social order, rooted in the revolutionary universalistic ideological tenets, in principle transcending any primordial, national, or ethnic units – even if not denying these units' partial legitimacy, and even if in fact being very closely related to national concerns, and even if in fact many of them developed as part of national reactions to Western imperialism and expansion in its different forms. At the same time these ideologies defined new socio-political collectivities with broad, yet relatively definitive, boundaries. In the case of the Communist regimes, these new collectivities, the collectivities of "workers" and "intellectuals," embraced all mankind, or at least those parts of mankind willing to both accept the basic premises of the "gospel" and to define themselves in terms of the vision presented in this gospel. In the case of the Islamic fundamentalist regimes, the whole realm of Islam is seen as their arena. Indeed a new conception of the *ummah* beyond any specific place was often promulgated in sectors of these movements with strong appeal, especially to the Islamic diaspora communities in Europe and Asia. Given the unusual combination of primordial and universalistic components in the construction of Jewish collective consciousness in Jewish fundamentalist movements, there developed a continual tension and oscillation between these two components. However, contrary to, for instance, the contemporary communal national movements in South Asia, there did not develop within most communist and fundamentalist movements a total negation of universalistic orientations. In this context it is important to note that both the communist and the fundamentalist movements – mostly but not only the Muslim ones – were international, transnational movements, activated by very intensive, continually reconstructed networks, be it of various socialist and communist movements or of Muslim, Jewish and Protestant networks, and of scholars, pilgrims, or the like. These networks were composed of many different elements among which the fundamentalist Jacobin characteristics were only one part. But the very existence of such networks facilitated the expansion of these groups' social and cultural visions as well as their universalistic messages, while at the same time continually confronting them with other competing visions.

It was the salvationist visions promulgated by these movements and regimes that constituted the ultimate legitimization of the regimes, and their respective elites were seen as the bearers of the salvationist mission. In this sense both regimes were based, as Martin Malia[38] has put it with respect to the Communist regimes, on legitimization from the top – i.e. on legitimization which seemingly was in no need of popular approbation, not unlike that of the bearers of many transcendental religions. And yet the legitimization of both the Soviet regime and the fundamentalist movements differed in several crucial respects from that of either traditional religious salvationist groups, or from that of historical absolutist regimes – the pre-revolutionary *ancien régimes*. In contrast to these regimes, the legitimation of the Communist and fundamentalist regimes alike contained very strong, far-reaching revolutionary and participatory components, combined with strong mobilizatory policies, and hence implied a new type of accountability of rulers. In principle it was the entire community that was not only the object but also the bearer of the salvationist vision or mission. The elite "only" represented it – possibly instituting it – while promulgating the "real" will of the society,[39] or the holy vision of the community even if the proper interpretation of the vision could be vested in one person or group. In the Soviet case the elite seemingly represented the universal revolutionary vision and were accountable to the people to carry it out. In the Iranian case – probably the clearest hitherto illustration of a fully institutionalized fundamentalist regime – the constitution promulgated by Khomeini, itself a great innovation in the realm of "traditional" Islam, declared in 1982 two different sources of sovereignty – God and the people.[40] The interpretation of this sovereignty and its institutional repercussions certainly entailed a different mode of legitimation than the traditional one. It entailed a much higher degree of participation of the different groups of clerics in interaction with broader sectors of the population, and continual struggles between different groups of clerics about the correctness of their respective interpretations of the salvationist vision.

These two types of movements and regimes also shared several of the basic characteristics of utopian sectarian groups to which we have referred above – namely the tendency to constitute sharp boundaries between the "pure" inside and the polluted outside and the continual constitution of an image of ontological enemy. The enemy is often the same, or very similar, for both types of movements – world capitalism in the West, above all the United States, and even Zionists, usually other "universalisms" – as epitomes of evils of modernity. But the grounding for such enmity differed greatly between these two movements or regimes. In the Soviet case it is the non-completion or perversion of the original vision of modernity, of the Enlightenment, while for the fundamentalists it is the basic premises of the Enlightenment that constitute the major characteristics of the enemy. Additionally, these two movements, many other such sectarian-ideological movements, many authoritarian movements of the right and left alike, and fundamentalist ones, all exhibit a very low threshold of tolerance for ambiguity on both the personal and collective levels. This low tolerance of ambiguity was closely connected, in both these types of movement (as well as in the fascist-national socialist one) with the denial of the pluralistic components of modern political institutions.

XVII

These two types of movements and regimes also faced at least some rather parallel problems attendant on their institutionalization – among them the growing contradictions between the salvational vision and the exigencies of maintaining some type of orderly political and modern economic regime; between their tendencies of totalization and the necessity to face, even to some degree promote, the processes of structural differentiation against which they were oriented; the problems attendant on the potential corruption of their elites and the general even if partial "regression" from the universalistic-missionary vision to the primacy of concrete demands of statehood. But above all, in distinction from pre-modern regimes which developed from sectarian groups, these two regimes also faced the tensions inherent in the relations between their Jacobin tendencies and their acceptance and adoption of some of the basic institutional frameworks of modern constitutional regimes – for instance, constitutions; elections, if even highly regulated or controlled ones; and parliamentary and juridical institutions. Needless to say, there also developed far-reaching differences between these two regimes with respect to the problems attendant on their institutionalization, some of which were rooted in their different ideologies. As Ernest Gellner has very succinctly pointed out,[41] the Achilles heel of the Soviet regime was the fact that its salvationist mission was oriented only in this world, to be tested in society by economic performance, while in the Iranian case the more "other-worldly" components of the vision provided a rather strong, even if certainly not absolute, safety net for the regime.

Thus, all these movements continually face problems stemming from their interweaving with the broader settings in which they develop – while on the one hand they continually attempt to appropriate for themselves these broader frameworks and set their agendas, on the other they must continually accommodate themselves to these settings. Indeed their very attempt to appropriate these modern settings continually confronts them with the demands and premises of many of these settings. Thus within these regimes and movements there develops continual tension between the more modern – economic, institutional, potentially secular orientations, often borne by professional groups who were among the active participants in the formative stages of these movements or the newly mobile social groups which their own policies generate, and the more radical religious and/or political Jacobin leadership.

XVII

But there were, of course, radical differences in their respective visions. As Raymond Grew has put it (private communication), the phenomenological starting point of the fundamentalist vision is the individual recognition of and devotion to religious truth.

The outline of such a society, in turn, puts it in competition and conflict with the larger society, which produces a series of demands: first, that the larger society at least not inhibit the fulfillment of the new spiritual enclave. Then it demands that the benefits enjoyed by the larger society must also be available to the fundamentalist one, then comes to see itself as a program for reform of the dominant society and an alternative to it. Possession of fundamentalist truth becomes a basis for challenging established ways on every front (although in practice this is attempted very selectively). This insertion into the larger society furthermore creates the need to define boundaries, lest the fundamentalist community be dissipated or undermined by the corrupting influences around it.

In the Communist case it is the recognition of the social evils of the larger society, the quest to reconstruct it in the name of a secular vision, and the social political organization devoted to the implementation of such a vision that constitute such a starting point – even for the individual quest. For the Communist, salvation lies in society; for the fundamentalist it basically remains individual, even if its attainment is regulated by the movement or by the regime. Moreover, while the Communist vision was oriented to the implementation of social-historical change, of "progress," the fundamentalist aim was at an outcome that will stop change. Of crucial importance is that the fundamentalists do not accept, indeed strongly deny the perfectibility of man which stands in sharp contrast to the original Jacobin, indeed to the very premises of the Enlightenment and the subsequent socialist and Communist, and to some extent the extreme Fascist and National-Social regimes (I owe this observation to Bjorn Wittrock).

XVIII

The differences between the two types of Jacobin – the Communist and the Iranian Fundamentalist – regimes are manifest above all in their attitudes to modernity, in their criticism of it, in their attitudes to its basic antinomies, and in their appropriation, rejection, and interpretation of this program's cultural and political components.

The salvationist vision promulgated in the Communist revolutions and regimes – especially of the Soviet regime, and to a smaller extent in China – was rooted in the basic premises of the cultural program of modernity, above all in its Enlightenment component with strong emphasis on the perfectibility of man. It followed the criticism of modernity of the existing order as it was promulgated by the socialist movements, which did not entail the negation of the original project of modernity but criticized its non-completion by bourgeois society and was oriented toward its fuller implementation. The Communist movement and regimes did not deny the primacy of instrumental rationality and technology. Rather, they appropriated these themes for themselves and presented their regimes as the sole bearer of the pristine vision of such instrumental vision, of progress, of technology, of mastery of nature, and of the rational, emancipatory restructuring of society. This criticism of modernity also entailed the construction of a specific pattern of cultural collective identity attendant on the encounter of non-Western European societies with the West and with modernity. This pattern of collective identity entailed a far-reaching denial of the claims made, for instance, by the Slavophiles – or of their parallels in various Eastern European and Asian countries – which promulgated total opposition to the Enlightenment and to instrumental reason, technology and mastery of the environment, as these elements stood against the authentic spirit or tradition of their respective societies.

As against this ideological stance the basic ideologies of the fundamentalist movements entailed the negation of some of the basic tenets of modernity as a civilizational form. These movements are indeed fully oriented against some of the basic premises of the Enlightenment, especially against the change of the place of God (or some metaphysical principles) in the construction of the cosmos and of man; especially against the premise of individual autonomy and freedom, and of the perfectibility of man; against the concomitant emphasis on the sovereignty of reason and of the legitimation of social and political order in such terms; and against the emphasis on change, on progress.

But at the same time the utopian sectarian criticisms of modernity and the anti-modern – or rather anti-Enlightenment – stance of the fundamentalist movements, are closely connected with a highly selective appropriation, transformation, and reinterpretation of various aspects or dimensions of modernity in very distinct ways which differ greatly from those of the other major types of modern social movements. The core of this selectivity is the appropriation of the mobilizatory and participatory dimensions of the modern political program and some of their basic institutional formations – like parliaments, elections, and constitutions – while at the same denying their legitimation in "secular" terms, above all in terms of the sovereignty of autonomous individuals. Moreover, the very emphasis on these participatory dimensions entails also the paradoxical and perhaps inadvertent acceptance of the autonomy of human will and choice.

Fundamentalist, fascist and national-socialist, and contemporary communal national movements

XIX

The basic attitudes of the fundamentalist movements to modernity can be compared not only to those of the socialist or communist ones, but also, even if briefly, to those of Fascist or National-Socialist character, which also aimed at the construction of new collective identities, new collective boundaries, as well as to implement a new vision via political action. The Fascist and National Socialist movements differed however in their basic attitudes to modernity both from the socialist and communist movements which they actually confronted as well as from the later fundamentalist ones. These national or nationalistic movements, especially the extreme fascist or national-socialist ones, aimed above all at the reconstruction of the boundaries of modern collectivities, which entailed the confrontation between universalistic and more particularistic or ascriptive components of construction of collective identity of the modern regimes. Their criticism of the existing modern order entailed an extreme negation of the universalistic components of the cultural program of modernity, especially in its Enlightenment version – hence they also showed less missionary zeal over transcending national boundaries. Yet significantly enough, the universalistic components of the cultural and political program of modernity – which they negated – constituted such an important reference point to them that in some ways they attempted to transpose them into their particularistic visions, often attempting to present these visions in some semi-universalistic terms of which, paradoxically enough, race could be one.[42]

A rather similar picture developed with respect to the attitudes of fascist and national socialist movements to technology. In their acceptance of the technological or instrumental aspects of modernity, together with the denial of any sovereignty or autonomy of reason and of the individual, they were seemingly similar to the fundamentalist ones. However, the fascist and national–socialist movements strongly emphasized the primacy and autonomy of human will – even if not of reason, indeed standing in many ways against abstract reason – thus sharing a basic Enlightenment component of the cultural program of modernity. As against this, the fundamentalist movements criticized this program from the outside by emphasizing, in principle, the submission of human will to divine commandments – even if at the same time emphasizing, paradoxically enough in a very strong modern mode, the importance of moral choice.

XX

Here it might be worthwhile to compare the fundamentalist movements with some of the more extreme, seemingly fundamentalist-like, nationalist movements designated by Nikkie Keddie as communal religious movements which have become very prominent recently – even though having earlier historical roots – in many Asian countries, especially in India and in Buddhist countries in South and South East Asia, which have been often lumped together with the fundamentalist ones.

These communal-national movements share with the fundamentalist movements some very important characteristics, especially the attempts to construct new religious communal identity, communal boundaries, tendencies to ritualization of violence, and a strong anti-secular stance. They constitute, together with fundamentalist movements and with many movements in the West, a shift from the hegemony of some of the ideals of the Enlightenment in the construction of modern nation states, its institutions and in the collective consciousness or identity of modern societies. Yet, most of these movements differ in several very crucial ways from the "pristine" fundamentalist movements analyzed above – as well as from the European fascist and national–socialist movements. First, their major orientations are particularistic and primordial. Indeed, they are consciously anti-universalistic, emphasizing the distinctiveness of their community from other such communities, and also, to no small extent, from the secular order of modernity, which constitute their major "others." However, unlike the European fascist or national–socialist movements, the universalistic components of the cultural and political program of modernity do not for these communal national movements constitute an *internal* reference point, or a component of the constitution of their internal cultural face – they are in a way "negated" as external components.

Second, they do not espouse strong conceptions of the reconstruction of the social order according to a vision rooted in an ontological perspective. In the case of these communal-national religious movements, the construction of strong communal boundaries and the promulgation of many sectarian tendencies, symbols, and rituals – especially those which emphasize the distinctiveness of and purity of its own collectivity as against the pollution of the others – do not necessarily entail a totalitarian reconstruction of society. Most of them harbor strong particularistic visions of exclusion, but only very few develop into a fully totalistic-Jacobin direction; thus they do not develop strong Jacobin tendencies to the reconstruction of society by a politically active center.

Truly enough, some of these seemingly fundamentalist movements attempted to develop new doctrinal moral contents or canons – in ways contrary to whatever was seen as the center of "classical" Hinduism. Such inventions entailed attempts at a soteriological revaluation of the political arena far beyond what was prevalent in the historical tradition of these civilizations. The Hindu movements, which attempted to construct such a totalistic view, tended usually to invent some of the religious elements like the holy scripts which are central in the fundamentalist movements. But the promulgation of such religious overtones and themes was not on the whole very successful or, as in the case of the reconstruction of Vedic rituals, limited to only some sectors of the population.

The same is true to a smaller extent of Buddhist countries – even given the stronger political implications of Theravada Buddhism – especially of Sri Lanka, even if (as G. Obeyskeyere has shown) there may in these circumstances develop other apolitical fundamentalist orientations, groups or movements.[43] It is only insofar as such national components are closely interwoven with strong universalistic orientations based, as is the case, on scriptural exegesis, that such movements, most notably the Jacobin ones, develop such strong Jacobin orientations and organizational characteristics.

XXI

Thus, the major difference between the various nationalist, Fascist and National–Socialist, and more recent communal religious national movements on the one hand, and the fundamentalist movements on the other, lies in the fact that the latter espoused very strong universalistic orientations. In this espousal they were similar to the Socialist and Communist movements and ideologies. Additionally, just as these latter movements, the fundamentalist movements espoused universalistic orientations and attempted to ground their legitimation in such universalist "transcendental," religious, or "secular" bases and to construct some universalistic communities – be they the new "ummah" as espoused by some Islamic fundamentalist, the modern universalistic community of the workers, or proletarians espoused by the Communists. But the bases of their respective universalisms differed greatly between those of the socialist or communist and the fundamentalist movements. The socialist and communist movements were fully set within the framework of the cultural program of modernity, above all of the Enlightenment and of the Revolutions, and their criticism of this program was made in terms of its incompleteness. As against this the universalistic orientations of the fundamentalist movements were seemingly outside that program, ideologically opposed to it, denying some of its major premises – such as, for instance, the insistence on progress and on the march of history.

But at the same time the utopian sectarian criticisms of modernity and the anti-modern stance of the fundamentalist movements is combined paradoxically with the adoption of very strong Jacobin orientations, with their strong emphasis on the reconstruction of society through political action and through political participation of wider strata, thus at the same time appropriating many of the participatory and constructivist components of the cultural program of modernity and, implicitly at least, the emphasis on the autonomous exercise of moral choice. Because of this specific type of Jacobin tendency or predisposition, these movements face continuous tensions – tensions which are inherent in most sectarian movements, but which are exacerbated in the modern fundamentalist ones – between the strong participatory orientations rooted very much in the modern conceptions of center-periphery relations which develop within them, and the authoritarian ones inherent in their basic sectarian ideologies. Concomitantly there developed in these movements a continual tension between the more instrumental and pragmatic, potentially secular orientations and the more radical Jacobin religious-political ones.

A brief analytical-typological summary: proto-fundamentalist, fundamentalist, and communal-national movements

XXII

It might be worthwhile at this point to bring out fully the major analytical characteristics of the various movements which constituted the focus of our analysis – above all the proto-fundamentalist, the (modern) fundamentalist, and the communal-national ones.

The proto-fundamentalist movements which developed in the premodern period in the Axial, above all monotheistic civilizations, shared with the modern fundamentalist movements the strong sectarian-utopian elements oriented to the implementation of a vision of the pristine features of their respective religions.

It is these orientations that distinguished the proto-fundamentalist movements from other sectarian movements that developed in their respective civilizations as well as the fundamentalist movements from other modern social movements.

The crucial difference between the proto-fundamentalist and modern fundamentalist movements has been in the strong – even if in some cases potentially strong – political Jacobin orientations and characteristics of the latter. The most important of these orientations was the strong emphasis on the reconstruction, through political means and action, of state, society, and the individual alike. The roots of those Jacobin tendencies of the fundamentalist movements are to be found in the Great Revolutions – the Puritan, American, and above all the French, and in the later Russian and Chinese revolutions. In strong contrast to the proto-fundamentalist movements, the fundamentalist ones moved in the wake of the Great Revolutions into the very center, into the central political arena linking them with the quest to bring the Kingdom of God to Earth.

The fundamentalist movements shared their Jacobin tendencies with other leftist, above all Communist, movements and regimes, and to some extent with the rightist fascist and national-socialist movements. They differed however from these movements, as we have shown in the preceding section, in their basic premises, and above all in their attitudes to the premises and antinomies of the cultural and political program of modernity.

Of special interest from the point of view of our analysis is the difference between these "pristine" fundamentalist movements and the communalnational ones which have burgeoned above all in South Asia and are often compared to the fundamentalist ones. As we have seen, the major difference of these religious communal movements from the fundamentalist view was that their major orientations are particularistic and primordial. Indeed, they are consciously anti-universalistic, emphasizing the distinctiveness of their community from other such communities – and to no small extent also from the secular order of modernity – which constitute their major "others." For these movements, unlike however the European fascist or national–socialist movements, the universalistic components of the cultural and political program of modernity do not constitute an *internal* reference point, or a component of their constitution of their internal cultural face – they are in a way "negated" as external ones.

Second, these communal-national-religious movements do not espouse strong conceptions of the reconstruction of the social order according to a vision rooted in ontological conception. The construction of very strong communal boundaries and the promulgation of many sectarian tendencies, symbols and rituals that take place in these movements – especially those which emphasize the distinctiveness of and purity of its own collectivity as against the pollution of the others – do not necessarily entail a totalitarian reconstruction of society. Most of them harbor a strong particularistic vision of exclusion, but only very few develop into fully totalistic-Jacobin direction; they do not develop strong Jacobin tendencies to the reconstruction of society by a politically active center.

XXIII

The different movements referred to above which developed under specific historical conditions in the overall development and expansion of modern civilization, varied greatly with respect to their basic attitudes and different components of the cultural program of modernity, its tension and antinomies, and criticisms thereof, but at the same time they shared a common reference to this program.

They varied with respect to their universalistic as opposed to communal or particularistic primordial components of this program; with respect to the premises of autonomy of man, of human will, reason, with respect to sources of authority. All these variations entailed different attitudes of the basic antinomies of this program and criticism thereof – but at the same time they shared the emphasis on participation and equality and, paradoxically, on certain issues of free will and choice inherent in the autonomous conceptions of man.

These variations were not fixed in their contents. Rather, for all of these movements there developed in all these dimensions a continuous reconstruction and renovation of concrete new themes and tropes, attesting to the continual dynamics of modernity – and at the same time added to this fact is that the cultural program of modernity constituted a common positive or negative reference point for all of them.

These various movements developed under different historical conditions. The socialist and the national or nationalistic movements, as well as, of course, many others, arose and crystallized in Europe under specific structural conditions such as the basic contradictions in the institutionalization and development of the post-revolutionary regimes and capitalist industrial political economies. The socialist movements arose under the conditions which brought out the contradiction between on the one hand the democratization of modern regimes, and on the other the expansion of capitalism – that is, the slow, and to some extent intermittent expansion of the new economic capitalist system along with the continuous struggle for equality of access to the center and for the possible reconstitution of the center according to more egalitarian premises. The national-fascist movements built on those components of the revolutionary heritage which emphasized the right to self-determination of a collectivity – above all in highly particularistic primordial terms. As against this the fundamentalist movements develop either in the context of the full institutionalization of this program, as in the USA; or, as in the case of Muslim, Jewish, and other Axial Civilizations, in connection with the expansion of Western modernity and the global confrontation between it, in its original Western version, and non-Western European (or American) civilizations. This brings us to a more detailed analysis of the broader historical contexts in which these movements develop.

4

Historical setting and variability of fundamentalist movements

The intercivilizational setting of fundamentalist movements – the hegemony of the West and the premises of the Western program of modernity

I

The modern fundamentalist movements developed in specific historical conditions, have been borne by distinct types of leaders and elite groups and supported by distinct social groups. Some of the conditions under which they developed – especially those relating to intercivilizational confrontations – were indeed in a very general way rather similar to those we have identified with respect to the development of proto-fundamentalist movements. The social activists and ideologues that led to development of the modern fundamentalist movements – as was the case for both the various communal-religious and the prior proto-fundamentalist movements – perceived the increasing diversity of ways and styles of life taking place in their countries or civilizations as undermining the existing "traditional" ways and as threatening to their self-conceptions. These situations and changing conditions were perceived and interpreted by relatively large, vocal sectors of their societies, and especially by strategically placed elites and influentials as onslaughts on, and threats to their civilizations – perspectives and interpretations to which large sectors of their respective societies were responsive. These conditions, combined with the weakening of existing – in this case modernizing – secular regimes due to internal pressures and struggles, external pressure, and usually through a combination of both, provided the background for the development of the modern fundamentalist movements.

The distinctive characteristic of the broad historical contexts in which these fundamentalist and the various communal-religious movements developed was of course that of the expansion of modernity, above all through colonial and imperialist processes of the West and its encounter and confrontations with many non-Western European religious traditions or civilizations. But these movements developed in very specific constellations of this expansion and of these confrontations.

From its very beginning this expansion gave rise first to the continual confrontation between the cultural and institutional premises, and the concomitant antinomies and contradictions of Western modernity, with those of other civilizations – of other Axial Civilizations, including Eastern European, as well as non-Axial ones, the most important of which has been Japan. Second, this expansion generated continual confrontations between the claims to hegemony and the facts thereof of Western European and North American states as bearers of the programs of modernity, and the search of the various non-Western societies for an autonomous independent place in the new world system and for appropriation by them of many dimensions of the cultural and political program of modernity. Third, this expansion generated both the continuous – but shifting – crystallization of hegemonies within the new, modern, international systems as well as challenges to them. These confrontations and challenges constituted a continuous and central aspect of these new intercivilizational dynamics.

The concrete historical constellations which served as the background for the development of the fundamentalist movements constituted a new phase, a marked shift in some of the major characteristics of these confrontations. They entailed a far-reaching shift in the relations between, on the one hand, the hegemony of Western societies in the international systems which crystallized with the expansion of modernity, and on the other, the social and national movements and regimes which crystallized in non-Western European (or North American–US) countries and civilizations which developed within the framework of this new political, economic, and ideological world-system.

II

In the overall period of the nineteenth and twentieth centuries – and in particular, up to the end of the Second World War, during the Cold War, and thus through the 1950s to the 1980s – this expansion and these confrontations were characterized by some distinct features – despite natural variations among, and intensive changes within these periods – which are of great importance from the point of view of our discussion. This long period, with the great variations and changes that took place within it, was characterized by the globally (nearly) unchallenged political, economic, and ideological hegemony of Western modernity – except for the continual, intensive local resistances to this program's imperialist expansion and its political, economic, and cultural impositions.[1]

First, it was demonstrated by the fact that this program constituted the most important, nearly universal reference point for most of the elite groups and leaders of the different social movements in non-Western European societies who were concerned with the reconstitution of their collective identities in the new global frameworks. Second, this hegemony was evident in the fact that most of these reconstructive attempts were oriented to the incorporation of these societies into these frameworks – to no small degree according to their premises, i.e., according to the premises of the cultural and political program of modernity; further, even those groups which challenged this program did so with reference to its basic premises, while indeed at the same time continually reinterpreting them. At the same time these attempts were often combined with challenges to the hegemony or hegemonies of the West and with confrontations with it. In the period between the two world wars these confrontations and challenges were closely connected with the growing ideological confrontations between the major political movements and ideologies that crystallized in Europe – between on the one hand liberal and social democratic ones, and on the other fascism and communism, as well as between these latter two. Still later in the period of the Cold War, these challenges and confrontations were interwoven with the confrontations between the West, especially the USA, and the Communists, as embodied in the Soviet, and to a lesser extent, the Chinese regimes. All these confrontations were played out both within the different states and on the international scene, the two being closely connected as became most clearly visible in the Spanish Civil War, and later on in the period of the Cold War in the many insurgencies and changes of regimes throughout most parts of Asia, Africa, and Latin America – and they were set fully within the framework of the original cultural program of modernity, of its premises, and antinomies.

These confrontations were closely related to the far-reaching processes of social change that developed in all these societies. The general characteristics of these changes have been analyzed abundantly and in detail in the vast social science and historical literature, and are, at least in their general outlines, well known.[2] In this long period of time, and in all the non-Western European and (North) American regimes which were incorporated within the new international systems (with the exception of the "white dominions" such as Canada, Australia and New Zealand, or rather of the predominant white sectors in these societies), there took place far-reaching economic and social changes and dislocations of major social sectors. There likewise developed many new types of modern capitalist political economies which were characterized by different modes of relatively dependent status in the new international systems, and within which there continually developed many possibilities of direct linkages between such various internal sectors and "outside" international sectors.

Additionally, in all these societies, new political frameworks and states crystallized. Some of these new states were initially constructed through colonial expansion by the Western, especially European powers, and later became transformed through anti-colonial struggles into new independent states – often building, like in India and Burma or Indonesia, on indigenous political traditions. In other societies, such as China, Thailand, and Japan, new states were constructed through the internal transformation or adaptation of existing regimes.

They were also based on the homogenizing premises of the modern nation states – i.e., on the attempt to create a common, homogeneous cultural mode of citizens or subjects who are socialized by various agencies – educational, military, media – into a uniform mold and who also stand in direct relation to the State and to the national-territorial community in an unmediated fashion. They also attempted to construct narratives of national histories of the cultural programs of (Western) modernity.

Most of these states were also shaped, at least on some of the more formal levels, according to the premises of modern constitutional regimes with their implicit emphasis on the rule of law and on the accountability of rulers – thus undermining many central aspects of the traditional modes of legitimation. In most if not all of these regimes, the basic premises, themes and symbols of the Western cultural and political program, as well as the major Western institutions – representative, legal, and administrative – have indeed been appropriated by their major elites and institutionalized within their respective societies, even if such appropriation entailed continual transformations of these premises and institutions. Also, in many of these regimes as in Europe, major symbols of protest, among them the symbols of the great revolutions, were incorporated into their basic symbolic repertoire.

Simultaneously, out of both the continual interaction and confrontation between these processes of change and dislocation, and the crystallization of the new institutional premises, there developed in all these societies many social movements of protest and of resistance that were much more intensive than in earlier periods of these societies.[3] The major themes of these movements were to no small degree taken – and reinterpreted – from the new repertoire of the new modern civilization, but also often built on the traditions of protest and heterodoxies that had existed in all these civilizations. A continual focus of these movements was the confrontation between the premises of Western modernity and those of their respective civilizations, a confrontation that focused on the attempt to forge out for their respective societies autonomous places and room for their cultural authenticity in the new international system. Yet another such aspect has been the challenge before the Asian, Eastern European, Latin American, and later African societies, of being "really" modern, of "catching up" with the West, and of finding niches within the international system in which they can develop their own autonomous institutions, without being continually in a dependent or inferior position.

III

All these problems and challenges were continually taken up by the major movements of collective, "national" resistance, by those movements that developed as the major responses within these societies, as it were, to the Western expansion that impinged on them, and by the different regimes that crystallized in these societies. From the second half of the nineteenth century through the first half of the twentieth, various liberal and reformist movements seemed to occupy the center stage of the political arenas in these societies. Later on – especially after the Second World War – socialist, communist, or revolutionary movements became more prominent, all of them interwoven with continual movements of local resistance. At the same time, especially since the end of the nineteenth century, various national movements continually developed throughout these periods. In most, if not all, of these societies, revolutionary and national symbolism have become an inherent part of the repertoire of symbols of protest; likewise, social movements presenting themselves as revolutionary and/or nationalist became very prominent in many of these societies. In some cases, as in China or Vietnam, the national and the socialist or revolutionary movements did coalesce. In others, they were either antithetical to one another, or the various socialist movements were subsumed under the broader national ones.[4]

The attraction of these themes of protest – liberalism, socialism, and nationalism – beyond Western and Central Europe was rooted in the fact that the adoption or appropriation and consequent reinterpretation of these themes enabled the respective groups of non-Western European nations to attempt to participate actively in both the new modern (i.e. initially Western) universal tradition, as well as in the new international systems of rebellion against many of its concrete institutional and ideological aspects, especially of Western "control" and dominance. It was the appropriation and incorporation of some of these themes and of the major modern Western institutions that made it possible for various elites and the broader strata of these non-Western European societies to appropriate some of the universalistic elements of the Western program of modernity, and to claim participation in it. At the same time, such appropriations enabled these groups to rebel against the international and institutional realities of the new modern civilization in terms of its own symbols and premises, and to uphold their own continually reconstructed authenticity, often presented by them as their distinct "spirituality" in terms of universalistic themes promulgated by this program.[5]

Such rebellion was facilitated by the fact that the appropriation of the symbols of liberalism, socialism, as well as as to some degree nationalism, was based on the transposition of the struggle between hierarchy and equality to the international scene. Although initially couched in European terms, these themes could also find resonance in the political traditions of many of these societies, above all in the conceptions of accountability of rulers. While appropriating these themes and symbols, the various groups, social movements, and elites within the non-Western European societies or civilizations were able to refer to the traditions both of protest and of center-formation in their respective traditions and historical experience, and to cope with problems of reconstructing their own centers and traditions in terms of a new historical reality. A central aspect of such appropriation of these themes by these various elites and movements was the reconstruction of their histories as national ones defined in the terms of European Enlightenment and Romanticism. This symbolic transposition of the ideologies of nationalism and socialism from European to non-European settings was reinforced by the combination – especially in the socialist tradition, and to some extent in the nationalist movements – of orientations of protest with strong tendencies to institution-building and center-formation. In these ways the appropriation of these themes could serve as a signal of participation in this new civilization, or at least to some of its premises, but also as a verdict against the realities of the new situation when judged according to the very premises of this civilization.[6]

At the same time there also developed in these periods more extreme movements which promulgated extreme "nativistic" or "proto-nationalistic" communal religious themes which denied many of the basic premises of the modern program. On the more intellectual level, such themes were voiced for instance by the Slavophiles in Russia who promulgated the total denial of the Enlightenment elements presented as materialistic, egoistic and soulless, as against the quintessential spiritual essence of their respective civilizations.[7] On the more popular level, there developed the numerous populistic and "nativistic" movements which expressed in this way their resistance to the imposition of the modern programs.

The – often very fierce – confrontation between these movements and those which promulgated the different types of "secular" versions of collective identity constituted a continual focus of the ideological and political modern discourse that developed in all these societies; but in this long period it was on the whole the promulgation of secular collective identity formulated in some "Enlightenment" or modern Romantic terms that prevailed in most of these societies. In this long period, the more "nativistic" and proto-fundamentalist movements which acquired some more modern orientations during this period were on the whole secondary, seemingly marginal and local.[8] The same was true of the numerous movements of resistance which also continually developed in the multiple peripheries of the newly constructed nation state – be it among the indigenous populations of the Latin American societies or the various peasant groups and/or ethnic minorities in South or Southeast Asia.

National and Communist movements and regimes: the incorporation of socialist symbols and the crystallization of different programs of modernity

IV

Thus, however great the differences between them, common to most of these movements and the regimes they established was emphasis on strong secular components of collective identity, very often couched in terms derived from the different streams of the Enlightenment and/or of Romanticism; on a relatively homogeneous conception of the new political and national collectivity and its history; and on direct, unmediated relations between the "state" or nation and its members or citizens. But at the same time there developed within these movements different modes of appropriation and reinterpretation of the various themes of the cultural and political programs of modernity which continually crystallized in different concrete ideological and institutional patterns.

The most important among such patterns up to the first half of the twentieth century were first, the "later" Communist Revolutions of Russia, China, and Vietnam,[9] and second, the various national movements which promulgated the establishment of modern-territorial states – these latter states developed through either anti-colonial struggle as in India and Burma, or through internal transformation of previous political entities as occurred much earlier in Japan and Thailand.[10]

The "later" Communist Great Revolutions – which gave rise to the crystallization and institutional and ideological hegemony of the totalitarian Jacobin regimes of the "left," with their specific salvationist mission, to which we have briefly referred above in chapter 3 – constituted one of the most radical attempts of non-Western European societies to become integrated into the emerging international system. These revolutions challenged the domination and hegemony of the Western program of modernity in the name of the very premises of this program. The cultural-political visions and programs promulgated in these revolutions entailed a far-reaching denial of the claims of different "nationalistic" or "nativistic" groups such as the Slavophiles or their equivalents in Asian countries which promulgated, in name of the authentic spirit or tradition of their respective societies, total opposition to the Enlightenment and to instrumental reason and rationality, technology, science, and emphasis on mastery of the environment.

The collective identity promulgated by the Soviet regime was couched in terms that placed national identity as secondary, even if it is in fact the Russian (or the Han in China) components that were predominant in the construction of their collective identity. But in principle the various national components were subsumed under the universalistic salvationist themes promulgated by these regimes even while continuing to be very strong in a subterranean way. However, these components were, in highly reconstructed ways, to re-acquire greater, often crucial importance with the dismemberment of the Soviet regime. In China, in the post-Mao period, these national and regional identities acquired greater importance, but on the whole were closely connected with the economic and technological orientations.

V

The distinct program of modernity promulgated in these regimes was closely related to the historical conditions under which these revolutions crystallized – both of which distinguish them from those of the first revolutions, as well as from those in which there developed some modern national regimes and the contemporaneous fundamentalist and communal-national movements.

Both the earlier and later revolutions occurred within societies that developed within the framework of Axial Civilizations and where combinations of this – and other-worldly soteriological conceptions were predominant – or, as in China, where a highly this-worldly vision has been promulgated. They differed, however, with respect to the conceptions of social order and citizenship prevalent in them. First of all, these revolutions occurred, to a much greater extent than their predecessors, under the impact of international political, economic, and ideological forces. Second, they already had various revolutionary models before them and did not have to invent one – although needless to say they transformed these models greatly. They were also led by much more well-organized intellectual and political groups usually already established in party-like frameworks – with highly developed organizational and mobilizatory skills.

Third, the first revolutions occurred in societies in which rather strong nuclei of conceptions of citizenship, as well as a partial conception of an "ex-parte" view of social order existed. As against this, the latter revolutions took place in societies in which conceptions of citizenship were either very weak or entirely absent, and in which "ex-toto" conceptions of social order prevailed. However, these revolutions developed in pure Imperial (not Imperial feudal) societies and in conditions of relatively – in modern terms – backward economies. The first revolutions – which had no other revolutionary model before them – developed in relatively centralized, absolutist, or semi-absolutist regimes which grew out of the Imperial-feudal background and in which the relative multiplicity of autonomous elites and sub-elites were continually active.

The later revolutions crystallized in highly centralized Imperial regimes in which the secondary elites were closely supervised and segregated. These differences, as well as the class constellations of these societies, influenced the shape of the post-revolutionary regimes that developed in these societies. The first revolutions can be seen as in some way continuing the processes of reconstruction of the centers and the boundaries of collectivities that had been taking place in Europe throughout the Middle Ages, although they gave rise to the most radical types of such reconstructions. Accordingly, the post-revolutionary regimes in Western Europe evinced a relatively smaller discontinuity from the pre-revolutionary ones, although the break from the past constituted at least one important component in their ideologies. The later revolutions constituted within their respective societies much more radical breaks, and were characterized by greater symbolic and institutional discontinuity from their preceding regimes. They also developed in societies whose levels of economic development were, relative to their periods, rather weak and in which the rulers attempted to make up for this by speedy and selective modernization. Hence the major social forces which were active in them – peasants, first or second generation industrial workers, and very weak middle-class elements – differed greatly from those prominent in the first revolutions.

VI

The other most important pattern consisted of the appropriation and reinterpretation of the different themes of the cultural and political programs of modernity – albeit in a much more diversified manner than in the Communist regimes and ideologies – which were promulgated from the late nineteenth century through the 1950s in a great variety of ways: especially by the national movements that developed in Asian and late African societies that promulgated the establishment of national-territorial states and that later established such states either through anti-colonial struggles as in South and Southeast Asia, or through the internal transformation of the previous political regimes as in Japan and Thailand.

Most of the national movements and new regimes which crystallized in the major Asian countries in the second half of the nineteenth century and the first half of the twentieth entailed the promulgation of rather secular conceptions of nationalism, constructed very much in terms of the Enlightenment and of Romanticism, and set within the basic framework of the cultural and political program of Western modernity.

This was true first of all of the numerous national movements and regimes which developed in Eastern Europe before the First World War and especially in the period between the two wars – many of which had some distinct fascist and/or semi-romantic features. Beyond Europe, the construction of Indian national identity by the Congress Party, and later by Gandhi and Nehru – perhaps the most interesting and important illustrations of this tendency – were predominant during this anti-colonial struggle and in the early stages of post-colonial independence in most of these societies. This was so even in many Muslim societies where the relation between their respective nationalisms and the universalistic claims of Islam constituted a continual problem.[11]

Particularistic primordial and religious communal components or symbols were often promulgated by these nationalist and even by socialist movements – but they were on the whole secondary to the more secular national or revolutionary ones; that is, they were subsumed under the latter and did not constitute the distinctive markers of the collective identity and consciousness of these movements.

Indeed, many of these movements emphasized that their own traditions were the bearers of the pristine universalistic values espoused by the cultural program of modernity and were much more faithful to these values than the West with its imperialist exploitation and practices – and very often the national histories that were written in this period were couched in such terms. Thus, significantly enough, many of the reformist religious movements that developed in this long period – be it the Brohmo Samaj founded in 1827, the Arya Samai (Society of Arians) founded in 1875, or the Muslim reformists like Muhamm'd Abdul's and Jamal-al-Din of Afgani – while calling for the revival, seemingly in a traditional way, of the pristine traditions of their respective civilizations, often portrayed these traditions in highly humanistic or rationalistic terms, as being compatible with science and calling for the purification from superstitious beliefs or practices.[12]

VII

These movements and regimes crystallized in conditions which differed in many respects from those of the late revolutions. Most of these movements and early modern regimes developed, with the exception of Thailand and Japan, within the framework of the European imperial-colonial Empires and as the most important challenges to these Empires. They usually developed in societies in whose historical experiences some mixture of imperial and patrimonial regimes was predominant.[13] The regimes – again with the exception of Japan and Thailand – which developed as a result of anti-colonial movements, built on these earlier patrimonial or patrimonial-imperial historical experiences, the most important characteristics of which were some form of segregated – regional, ethnic, and religious – sectors; a relatively weak permeation of the center into the periphery, and of impingement of the periphery on the center; and the prevalence – especially in these sectors – of multiple patterns or bases of legitimation. Closely related to these tendencies in many of these civilizations and societies were the relatively weak traditions of autonomous access of different sectors to the political center, of conceptions of citizenship, and of an autonomous civil society. Such access was in these societies controlled by the center itself, and within them – with the partial exception of Muslim countries – there developed at most only kernels of a conception of law as an autonomous area distinct from the political and administrative arenas, or as not fully embedded in communal practice.

A great variety of regimes developed in these societies ranging from conservative modernizing, to semi-revolutionary nationalistic ones, such as the Nasserist regime in Egypt, the Ba'ath movements and regimes in Syria and Iraq, or similar regimes existing for some period of time in Burma, and in some African countries like Tanzania. Unlike the Communist regimes, the various national movements and regimes did not promulgate distinct social or economic visions. In many of them there developed, after the attainment of independence, strong statist regimes which attempted to regulate the capitalist economies that had become predominant in them under the impact of Western expansion. In the more radical regimes, "revolutionary" themes were promulgated in conjunction with statist orientations – in others more conservative modernizing regimes were predominant.

VIII

In their emphasis on the superiority of their own traditions over the universalist premises of the cultural program of modernity, the nationalist conceptions promulgated by most of these movements and regimes constituted, in a way, the mirror image of the socialist or communist ones. At the same time socialist themes and symbols were also incorporated in many of the national movements – albeit in distinct ways. In the nationalist regimes, the socialist and communist themes and symbols did not become, as was the case in the Communist regimes, the central, hegemonic collective symbols of an entire regime and in the construction of the collective identities thereof, but developed in distinct ways in different societies.

The differences in the relative importance of socialist symbols in the construction of the collective identity of the different non-Western European societies have been very closely related to different modes of construction of the new, modern collective identities that crystallized in them; and to their basic orientations to the cultural and political programs of modernity to the West and to Western hegemony, thus indicating different attempts to define their own standing in these hegemonic international systems.

Societies in which the symbols of socialism were incorporated into the central repertoire or where such incorporation was attempted at early periods include Russia, China, to some extent Burma under U Nu and Ne Win, as well as some African countries such as Tanzania in the 1960s and 1970s. In Japan and in Thailand such symbols were not incorporated into the symbol systems of the collectivity. The same is basically true of India, despite the fact that many socialist declarations and policies were undertaken in Nehru's, and to some extent in Indira Gandhi's time.

The extent of appropriation of socialist symbols as components of new collective identities by the major elites and protest groups of these societies depended on the degree to which the predominant, basic ontological conceptions and premises of social order promulgated by the respective hegemonic elites contained the following components: strong universalistic elements, strong this-worldly utopian and millenarian elements and orientations, and the extent to which tensions between hierarchy and equality were of great symbolic and institutional importance in these societies. Thus socialist symbols were incorporated into the central symbols in a "pluralistic" way in Western Europe; in a totalistic way in Russia, China, and to some degree in the Middle East where universalistic and utopian elements were very strong; and they were absent in Japan, and in India – where either other-worldly orientations were predominant or utopian orientations did not focus on the political realm.

Additionally, the incorporation of socialist symbols into the central premises and symbol systems of these societies depended on the extent of internal cohesion between their elites in the new international situation; the ways in which they were incorporated into the new European-dominated international setting; and the degree to which there developed a strong discrepancy between their aspirations to participate in the new universalistic program of modernity together with their desire to maintain the strong universalistic components of their own traditions. Thus, indeed, the standing of Russia and China as centers of a great, potentially universalistic civilization was sharply undermined by this encounter, giving rise among many of their elites to a strong predisposition to the incorporation of such symbols. In the case of Japan, on the other hand, where modern collective cultural identity was successfully reconstructed, albeit mostly in primordial terms with very weak universalistic tendencies, side by side with the attainment of strong international standing, the predisposition to incorporate socialist symbols into its central symbols was much weaker, and limited to marginal elites which were unable to influence the center and/or broader groups. This weakness of socialism was reinforced by the prevalence of the premises of hierarchy, as well as by the weakness of a strong transcendental dimension in the basic definition of the ontological realm prevalent in Japan.

In African and Middle Eastern societies, different and changing constellations of some of these factors affected the incorporation of different aspects of socialism. In most African societies, colonialism has drawn into the international orbit, political and cultural units mostly from pre-Axial Civilizations with very weak universalistic orientations and has involved – at least among the more educated and urbanized elites – a very strong predisposition to participate in the broader setting of the new modern civilization. The ideology of African socialism developed in this context, later to recede with the development of a more negative attitude toward the West.

In the central Islamic, and above all in the Middle Eastern Arab countries, the predisposition of different elite groups and regimes like the Ba'ath ones in Syria and Iraq to incorporate socialist symbols into the central symbols of their societies was connected with the weakening of many elements of their own Great Traditions and especially with the uncertainty about relations between the new emerging political centers and the universalistic claims of Islam. At the same time, the persistence of this ambivalence, combined with the fact of Islam's being a universalistic civilization, resulted in the selection in the post-Second World War period of some socialist symbols and broad socialist political programs – albeit with a tendency to legitimize them in terms of the Islamic tradition and symbols. These symbols became less important with the resurgence of Islamic identity and of so-called Islamic fundamentalism – although in these movements claims were often made that Islam contained the pure non-materialistic aspects of social justice, and significantly enough, such claims were made not in terms of the premises of the Western program of modernity but in those of their own authentic civilization. In this context, it is very interesting to note that many of the activists in various Muslim Arab countries who were drawn to different socialist themes and movements became later very active in the fundamentalist movements of the eighties and nineties. It is significant that the predisposition to incorporate socialist symbols has been on the whole weaker in those African societies with a strong, traditional, or more modern Islamic identity, which gave them the possibility of participating in an already existing Great Tradition.

IX

Whatever the differences in incorporation of socialist symbols into the basic collective symbols of these societies, in most of them socialism was not closely connected either with highly developed industrialization or with the working classes. Hence, quite obviously, many important differences from the European pattern emerged in the organizational structure of socialist parties or movements.

One of the most important characteristics common to most of the socialist or communist parties or movements in these societies has been their weak and intermittent relation to any broad social bases and the prevalence within them of professional or semi-professional political agitators with varying degrees of organizational effectiveness. These factors also affected the nature of class symbolism in the socialist movements of these societies. In countries like Burma, in many of the African countries, and in some Islamic ones, where there was only a weak tradition of active politically-oriented class-consciousness, it was the welfare-distributive aspect of socialism that was emphasized – sometimes even with a denunciation of any emphasis on class conflict, as against a strong emphasis on collective harmony and collective well-being. In some of these societies or revolutionary movements, class-consciousness was stronger and attempts were made by some leaders of some of the revolutionary movements to connect it at least symbolically to the working class.

The socialist movements and themes were not the only ones that attracted different groups in these societies. The same has been true in the interwar period and in the early stage of the Second World War of fascist movements and themes, which were appropriated by different elite groups in these societies as yet another mode of rebellion against the West – and its hegemony – but also mostly promulgated in Western terms. Significantly enough, however, numerous fascist groups developed not only in the Eastern European societies but also in the various Asian countries, and fascist-like corporatist themes were often promulgated by the nationalist movements or regimes though their overall impact was not very great. This was probably due to the fact that the pristine fascist or national-social movements that developed in Europe promulgated distinctive ideologies of primordiality and particularism that were specifically bound to the Western tradition or identity and were not easily universalized beyond the West. From this point of view it is interesting that they found greater resonance in Latin American countries.

X

From the end of the Second World War until the 1960s and 1970s, these different movements and regimes which occupied the center stage of their respective political scenes appropriated and continually reinterpreted many of the themes and antinomies of the cultural program of modernity, giving rise to different combinations of these themes and to different institutional patterns. Whatever the differences between these societies (which were indeed very great), during that long period most of them were set within the basic framework of the original Western European cultural and political program of modernity.

But again, such appropriation of these themes and institutional patterns was not a simple process of duplication. Rather, it entailed the continual selection, reinterpretation, and reformulation of such themes with different emphases on different components of this program. Such different symbolic interpretations have been continually developing with respect to these programmatic interpretations; in these societies' conceptions of themselves and their pasts; in their constructions of new collective identities; and with regard to their negative or positive attitudes to modernity in general, and to the West in particular.

Or, in greater detail, these different interpretations entailed selective emphases or interpretations of different components of these programs such as man's active role in the universe; the relation between *Wertrationalität* and *Zweckrationalität*; the conceptions of cosmological time and its relation to historical time; the belief in progress; the relation of progress to history as the process through which the cultural program of modernity may be implemented; the relation between the individual and the collectivity; and between reason and emotions.

In many of these civilizations the basic meaning of "modernity" was rather different from the original Western vision rooted in the ideas of Enlightenment and that suggested progress, the unfolding of the great historical vision of reason, self-realization of individuals, and social and individual emancipation. While within many of the non-Western European (or North American–US) societies, modernity was conceived as growing in participation both on the internal and international scene, particularly with regard to ideas of equality and participation, the other dimensions – especially those of individual liberty, of social and individual emancipation, of individual autonomy as closely related to the historical unfolding of reason – all of which were constitutive of the Western European discourse on modernity from the Enlightenment on – were not necessarily always accepted.

The crystallization of such changing programs entailed a continual reinterpretation of these themes in relation, on the one hand, to the major components of the modern cultural or political program, its antinomies and contradictions and, on the other, to attempts to define the authenticity of their own cultural heritage in the new modern situation and to appropriate modernity in terms of this heritage. The search for their own authenticity in the new setting and of their relation to the hegemonic programs of modernity as promulgated by Western powers, constituted a major focus of such continual reinterpretation that moved continually between several basic poles. One such major pole was the tendency to negate modernity – especially Western modernity – as undermining the true spirit or pristine nature of their respective civilizations. The other such pole was the appropriation of modernity by these civilizations and the concomitant attempts to identify theirs as truer than the other Western one, and at the same time to assure that their societies will indeed live up to the different and continually changing images of modernity. Sometimes situations would develop such as in Japan whereby technological success was seen as proof of the superiority of their spiritual sensibilities.

These differences between the different cultural programs of modernity were not purely "cultural" or academic. They were closely related to some basic problems inherent in construction of modern institutions. In the political realm, these different cultural programs of modernity also entailed different conceptions of authority and of its accountability, different modes of protest and of political activity, and different modes of institutional formations. They were concomitantly closely related to the tension between the utopian and the civil components in the construction of modern politics; between "revolutionary" and "normal" politics; between the general will and the will of all; between civil society and the state; and between individual and collectivity.

Changing intercivilizational settings, globalization, the weakening of Western hegemony and new challenges to it – the development of communal-religious and fundamentalist movements

XI

Whatever the differences between the socialist, communist, and national movements and regimes with regard to the relative importance of socialist symbols in the construction of collective identity, all of these movements and regimes were set, as we have seen above, within the basic framework of the cultural and political program of Western modernity.

The development and seeming predominance, or at least very high visibility, of the fundamentalist and communal-religious-national movements on the contemporary scene signal a far-reaching change or shift in the nature of the confrontation between the non-Western European civilizations and the West and its basic premises of the modernity program. It is this far-reaching change or shift with respect to the position of the West and the premises of the cultural and political program of modernity that distinguishes the new contemporary national, communal-religious, and above all, modern fundamentalist movements from the various socialist, communist, and national movements.

As against the seeming acceptance of these premises combined with the continual reinterpretation thereof that was characteristic of the earlier movements, the contemporary fundamentalist and most communal-religious movements promulgated a seeming negation of at least some of these premises, a markedly confrontational attitude to the West, and attempts to appropriate the global system on their own terms couched in the modern, non-Western, often anti-Western, mode.

Above all these latter movements promulgated a radically negative attitude to some of the central Enlightenment – and even Romantic – components of the cultural and political program of modernity, especially to the emphasis on the autonomy and sovereignty of reason and of the individual. They, especially the fundamentalist ones, promulgated a totalistic ideological denial of these "Enlightenment" premises, and a basically confrontational attitude not only to Western hegemony but to what was defined by them as Western civilization usually conceived in totalistic and essentialist ways. In these movements, confrontation with the West did not take the form of searching to become incorporated into the new hegemonic civilization on its own terms, but rather to appropriate the new international global scene for themselves, for their traditions or civilizations – as they were continually promulgated and reconstructed by the impact of their continual encounter with the West. The communal-national movements built on the earlier "nativistic," "Slavophile"-like countries – but reinterpreted them in radical, political, modern, communal-national ways. The fundamentalist movements, while minimizing in principle, if not in practice, the particularistic components of the communal-national movements, grounded their denial of the premises of the Enlightenment in the universalistic premises of their respective religions or civilizations, as newly interpreted by them.[14]

Significantly enough, in these movements socialist or communist themes or symbols were no longer strongly emphasized. Themes of social justice were usually promulgated in terms of their own autochthonic traditions – often portrayed as inherently superior to the materialistic socialist ones. In this context, it is worth reiterating that the activists especially in various Muslim Arab countries who were drawn to different socialist themes and movements became very active in the communal fundamentalist movements of the eighties and nineties.[15]

XII

These far-reaching changes in the mode of confrontation between these movements and the West developed in a new historical context. The most important aspects of this context, some of which were commented on in great detail by Nikkie Keddie, were: first, changes in the international systems and shifts of hegemonies within them, above all weakening of the Western ones; secondly, the exhaustion of the Cold War's ideological and political confrontations culminating in the disintegration of the Soviet regime; thirdly, the development throughout the world, but especially in non-Western societies, of a series of highly destabilizing processes in connection with the multiple processes of economic and cultural globalization of a series of highly destabilizing processes; fourthly, ideological and institutional developments in Western societies of what has been often designated as a post-modern direction; and fifthly, the closely connected decline or transformation of the ideological and institutional premises of the modern nation state, and the development of strong tendencies to multiculturalism.[16]

To enlarge now on these points: First, these movements developed in the period of the disintegration or at least weakening of the "old" Western hegemonies and of weakening of the modernizing regimes in different non-Western societies; often in situations in which the perception of such weakening became relatively strong among active elites in the non-Western countries – as for instance after the October War and the oil shortage in the West.

This perception of the weakening of Western hegemony was connected with important, economic changes in the West, and in global economy. The general economic features of this period was the demise in the West of the Keynesian Welfare State, with its combination of steady and reasonably rapid economic growth, near-full employment, rising real wages and standards of consumption, government intervention through monetary and fiscal policies, the development of welfare systems and some socialist experiments (especially in Britain), and by the domination of the American dollar and the American economy. These changes in the internal economies of these societies were connected with the relative decline in America's economic hegemony as manifest in the greater economic consolidation of Europe, and above all by the growing power of Japan as an economic force, followed by the emergence of Asian countries – South Korea, Taiwan, Hong Kong, and Singapore – as forces in world trade.

Secondly, a crucial event on the international scene was the demise of the Soviet Union and accordingly of the salience of the ideological confrontation between Communism and the West – a confrontation which was set, as we have seen, within the framework of the original cultural and political program of modernity. This demise, which also gave rise to multiple, often very aggressive, ethnic and regional conflicts, could be interpreted, perhaps paradoxically from the point of view of the promulgators of the "end of history" thesis, as an exhaustion of the Western cultural program of modernity.[17]

Thirdly, in close relation to these changes, there also took place processes of globalization of the economy manifested in growing movements of capital and labor forces and manifest in intense movements of international migration, seemingly beyond the control of national governments, and accompanied by growing parallel processes in the cultural arena – be it in matters of consumption and media, giving rise to a continual flux of patterns of entertainment and dress. Fourthly, and in close relation to the preceding, a series of highly destabilizing processes developed on a global scale. The most important among them were as Nikkie R. Keddie has pointed out:[18] highly uneven developments by region, class, race, and gender; economic slowdown or stagnation in the developed world, the

Middle East, much of South Asia, Africa, and Latin America; and fifthly, increasing internal and international migration; greater choice for women in lifestyle, marriage, and motherhood; rising divorce; growing education and urban growth which allow many people to express discontents more effectively; the concomitant skewing of the population toward the very young age-groups, and strong tendencies to global cultural homogenization, to what has been called de-traditionalization, or decoupling between cultural and local identities. Some of the most interesting manifestations of such developments has been connected with the emergence of new diasporas – such as the Muslim or Indian ones in Europe or the United States; or with the extension and growing self-consciousness of older ones – such as the Chinese or Asian ones.

Sixth, at the same time a rather paradoxical situation developed on the internal political scenario of many societies all over the world. On the one hand there developed in most societies a continual strengthening of the "technocratic" rational secular policies in various arenas – be it in education, family planning, and the like. But on the other hand these policies were not able to cope adequately with most of these new problems attendant on the processes analyzed above. All these processes became closely connected with the weakening or transformation of the basic ideological and institutional premises of the hitherto prevailing model of the modern nation state, giving rise in many parts of the world to different combinations of strong tendencies to multiculturalism with growing ethnic national and religious conflicts.

XIII

But it is not only within the societies of Asia, Latin America, or Africa that developments took place which went beyond the initial model of Western modernity and of the modern nation state. At the same time in Western societies themselves there took place new developments and discourses which have both greatly transformed the initial model of modernity in what has often been designated as a post-modern direction and have undermined the original vision of modern society and of the modern nation state.[19]

These developments signalled rather far-reaching changes in the understandings of modernity in Western societies, entailing the weakening in Europe of both the till then hegemonic and homogenizing conceptions of the project of modernity as embodied in the modern nation and/or revolutionary state, and in the strength of the secular components in the construction of collective identities as they developed – or were perceived as having developed – in the West. In the United States these changes gathered momentum in the sixties in the context of the weakening of the religious components in the American public sphere and consciousness and of the seemingly successful institutionalization of what was seen by many groups as godless rational modernity.

On the cultural level these developments entailed first, a growing tendency to distinguish between *Zweckrationalität* and *Wertrationalität*, and to the recognition of a great multiplicity of different *Wertrationatitäten*. Cognitive rationality – especially as epitomized in the extreme forms of scientism – has become dethroned from its relatively hegemonic position, as has been the idea of the "conquest" or mastery of the environment – whether of society or of nature. Second, these developments also entailed a very important shift of the utopian orientations predominant in these societies from the construction of modern centers to other arenas.

These developments were closely connected to far-reaching social and cultural changes, signalling the decomposition of the preceding "bourgeois" culture, with its strong regulative tendencies so forcefully depicted by Max Weber and from different points of view by Norbert Elias and Michel Foucault.[20] There developed a weakening of the former, relatively rigid, homogeneous definition of life patterns, and hence also of the boundaries of family, community, or of spatial and social organization. Occupational, family, gender and residential roles have become more and more dissociated from "Stände," class, and party-political frameworks, and tend to crystallize into continuously changing clusters with relatively weak orientations to such broad frameworks in general, and to the societal centers in particular. In the political sphere and in the conception of the citizenship role there have developed tendencies to the redefinition of boundaries of collectivities: to a growing dissociation between political centers and the social and cultural collectivities, and to the development of new nuclei of cultural and social identities which transcend the existing political and cultural boundaries.

One of the most important institutional changes connected with those tendencies has been the development of various structural, semi-liminal enclaves within which new cultural orientations, new modes of search for meaning – often couched in transcendental terms – tend to be developed and upheld, partially as counter-cultures, partially as components of new cultural scenes.

As a result of these processes and changes, there continually developed new types of social and economic cleavages and restructurings of the social strata and the relations between them. Additionally, from about the 1970s there developed a new underclass of those who seemed to become unemployable in the age of economic and technological globalization.

Concomitantly a weakening occurred in the distinction between the political "left" and "right," and through reconstruction, the political center that was strong at least in Europe and Japan weakened – likewise, political discourse became increasingly focused on a narrower range of issues, which were increasingly de-ideologized, above all in their relation to the center.

All these developments have culminated in a shift in the nature of protest movements – as manifested in the development of the new movements of protest that developed from the sixties on, starting from the student rebellions, up to the women's and the ecological movements, all of which stressed growing participation in work, different communal orientations and the like. Instead of a conflictual–ideological focus on the center and its reconstitution or on economic conflicts, both of which characterized the earlier "classical" social movements of modern and industrial societies, the new movements were oriented at what one scholar has defined as the extension of the systemic range of social life and participation; or by the emphasis on construction of new social spaces as against orientations to the center.

All these changes have been connected with a far-reaching shift from viewing the political centers and the nation state as the basic arenas of the charismatic dimension of the ontological and social visions. While the political center of the nation state continues to be the major arena for the distribution of resources, it no longer constitutes the major focus of the charismatic dimensions and utopian orientations of various social movements – or of large sectors of the society. This shift was connected with increasing confrontations in many societies, in both local and global scenes and arenas, between the original Western conceptions of modernity as embodied in the modern nation state or revolutionary state, and the newly emerging local, regional, and transnational conceptions of collective identity.[21] In Western Europe there took place many processes of "transnational" Europeanization. While these processes weakened the cultural and political homogeneity of the Western European nation states, they generated tendencies to new exclusiveness – either on the local level or on the "European" level – oriented against Eastern Europe, "Islam," and/or the United States. At the same time in Eastern Europe, in the wake of disintegration of the Soviet Union, national tendencies and consciousness became intensified. Concomitantly throughout Europe there emerged different new diasporas and minorities, often giving rise to the intensification of "ethnic" or "religious" confrontations. All these gave rise to continual discussions – above all in the West, but spreading very quickly beyond it, that placed a strong emphasis on multiculturalism as a possible supplement to the modern nation state model or as possibly displacing it.[22]

It was these changing situations that constituted the major background for the development and growth of the fundamentalist movements – in the United States and in the non-Western European countries alike. In these situations, the encounter with fundamentalist movements became part of the internal Western discourse. It was in this discourse that these movements were dubbed as fundamentalist, and the confrontations between them and the predominant secular or religious groups have sometimes been portrayed in terms of an internal "Western" cultural discourse, and have often been perceived as internal cultural critique. In the non-Western societies and movements the confrontation with the West did not take the form of a search, on the part of the non-Western elites, to become incorporated into the new hegemonic civilization according to the prevalent themes or premises thereof. Rather, it signalled a search for new modes of incorporation in the emerging global framework of modernity. While on the one hand these movements dissociated themselves ideologically from this global framework, yet on the other hand this framework continued in fact to constitute a basic ideological and institutional point of reference for them. Accordingly, these movements tried to appropriate this new framework on their own terms, in terms of their newly reconstructed collective identities, often presented in essentialistic, universalistic civilizational terms as distinct from the West and opposed to it.[23]

XIV

In close relation to these new historical circumstances, in which the modern fundamentalist and communal religious movements developed which distinguish them from the historical contexts in which the proto-fundamentalist movement or those in which the social movements of earlier stages of modernity developed, parallel differences can be also identified with respect to the social groups or categories which promulgate the various fundamentalist or communal-religious visions and those which have been responsive to such promulgation. While these groups and the ways in which they came together necessarily varied greatly in different societies and in different historical situations, and these variations still have to be systematically analyzed, several common characteristics can be pointed out.

The common denominator of these groups has been that they have undergone rather distinct processes of far-reaching social, cultural, and economic dislocation. While the nature of such dislocation, on the whole, differed between the more active promulgators of such visions and those responsive to them, there naturally may develop different degrees of overlapping – varying in different situations – among them. With respect to both groups it is not just "simple" economic deterioration or dispossession that is of importance, although such deterioration may greatly help in generating fundamentalist predispositions and the possibility of mobilization of broader sectors of the population by fundamentalist or communal-religious activists. It is rather dislocation from either the centers of these societies or from relatively secure, embedded social and economic frameworks or niches that is of crucial importance.

As in the case of the proto-fundamentalist movements, the major promulgators of these fundamentalist or communal-national religions or visions tend to come mostly from sectors dislocated from the cultural, political, and social centers of their respective societies. In contrast, however, to the pre-modern situations, in which the major bearers of the proto-fundamentalist visions came usually from some sectors of the traditional religious leaders and communities – in the modern fundamentalist movements, a very important part was played also by various "modern" educated groups – professionals, graduates of modern universities, and the like – who find themselves dispossessed from access to the centers of their respective societies or from their cultural programs. Thus, for instance, it was not only the dislocation of the Shia clergy from strong positions in the cultural center or close to it, that has been important in the success of the Khomeini revolution. Of no smaller importance was the fact that highly mobile, modernized, occupational and professional groups, which developed to no small extent as part of the processes of modernization, were controlled by the Shah and barred from any autonomous access to the new political center or participation in it – very much against the premises inherent in these processes.[24] Such groups were especially visible in Turkey, India, Pakistan, and in many of the Muslim diasporas in Europe – but they were also important in other Muslim or South Asian societies.

The broader social sectors which tended to be responsive to such messages consisted mostly of those economically dispossessed groups, which were caught up in distinctive modern economic processes – processes closely related to the dynamics of globalization analyzed above. These were not necessarily the lowest economic echelons – peasants, or urban lumpenproletariat – but rather groups from the middle or lower echelons of more traditional economic and broader sectors, who experienced continuous social and occupational mobility into urban centers especially into the new occupations.[25]

These groups often find themselves in a situation of social anomie in which old ways of life have lost their traditional standing. They are caught in the pressure for the greater economic efficiency that is demanded by globalization and international markets, they are losing their security nets, and the programs promulgated by the existing modernizing regimes are not able, for the reasons analyzed above, to provide them with meaningful interpretations of the new reality. A very important group which may be highly susceptible to communist-religious or fundamentalist messages consists of younger generations of seemingly hitherto well-established urban classes who distance themselves from the more secular style of life of their relatively successful parents. But even more important are the relatively recent members of second-generation immigrants to the larger cities from provincial urban and even some rural centers, as M. E. Yapp has put it:

In general, one may say that the fundamentalists are young, poor and urban, and that they are products of modernization and in particular of urbanization and the great educational expansion which that has allowed . . . Fundamentalism is an attractive formula for them because it has resonances from the traditional society of their upbringing and a program for success in the modern world. In different times, socialism, fascism, communism, or even liberalism might have charmed their minds, and may yet do so, but fundamentalism is the currently fashionable alternative to the tired Western-style program of the existing elite.[26]

The attraction to fundamentalist movements among these social sectors is very visible also in various sectors of the Muslim diaspora – especially, but not only, in Europe.[27] Here also it was those groups which underwent processes of dislocation to modern occupational and cultural settings, combined with blockages to full political and cultural integration in their respective host societies, and with a very ambivalent attitude to the cultural program and collective identity of these societies, that became most prone to join the fundamentalist groups.

Nulifer Göle has analyzed very incisively major characteristics of the groups in Turkey:

The new actors of islamism, both the leaders and the followers in almost all Muslim countries such as Egypt, Iran, Turkey, Pakistan, are among the recently urbanized and educated social groups. They often become "islamist" by following a common path: after their move from little provincial towns to cities, they encounter, during their years in high school and the university, the works of some authors which would define the landmarks of contemporary islamist ideology, such as Pakistani Abu al-Ala Mawdudi, Egyptian Sayyid Qutb, Iranian Ali Shariati, and more particularly for Turkey, Ali Bulac and Ismet Ozel.

The formation of new islamic actors can be traced to the post-1983 period in Turkey when islamist engineers rose to political power within the ranks of the Motherland Party, islamist veiled women became visible in modern university campuses of big cities, a flourishing publication of islamist periodicals, newspapers and books shifted the current intellectual agenda in Turkey from the dominance of leftist intellectuals to that of islamist ones. These new agents incarnated the move

of Islam from the periphery of the system to its center to the extent that they themselves were the products of that center, of its educational institutions and urban life.
Such a move is not taking place without cultural tensions, social conflicts leading
to political disputes over new issues. As these new actors of islamism are beginning
to obtain the same cultural capital with the republican elites, share the same university classes with them, occupy the ranks of parliament and participate in equal
terms to public debates at television, they start to gain public visibility, social recognition, legitimation and prestige. The republican secular elites, they react primarily in political terms and struggle against islamic fundamentalism ("theriatcylyk")
in defense of secularism ("laiklik"); yet there is a realm of class conflictuality which
escapes to the linguistic consciousness but constitutes a fundamental threat to their
social power and privilege to be an elite. . .

. . . The radical rupture with the local culture renders the process of identification
of rising peripheral classes with the established elites difficult. Such a cultural gap
between the elites of the center and the peripheral groups – which does not necessarily imply economic deprivation but a symbolic one – is another feature of assy-
metrical realities and trajectories between the western and the non-western
modernities and politics. The very project of modernization, resourcing itself from
external references alien to local morality, gender identities and daily spatial practices, perverts the relationships between the elites and the people. The established
elites do not provide a familiar model for the projection and identification of aspirations and of guidance for life and professional strategies of the newly rising
groups.

One common feature of these authors is their effort to redefine islamic "authenticity" in a manner that would no longer be apologetic to western modernity. A
return to the original sources – comprising of references to the Quran itself and the
Sunna and Hadith (sayings and traditions of the Prophet) and the "asr-i saadet"
period (the age of the Prophet Muhammed and the four orthodox caliphs [622–661]
– is a common feature of almost all islamist movements, calling for revivalism and
struggling against the contamination of "pure" Islam by customary practices. The
ways in which islamist movements situate themselves in relation to western modernity marks the main difference of the new generation of islamists from the
nineteenth-century modernist islamists. While the latter, as in the writings of
Muhammed Abduh, Jamal al-Din al-Afghani, Rashid Rida, tried to accommodate
islamic values with democratic and modern values, the contemporary radical islamists take a non-apologetic and an anti-modernist stand, in the name of an islamic
alternative. The search for an alternative in Islam, especially endows muslim intellectuals with a very strong quest for an authentic identity and provides them with
the emotional, moral and intellectual tools with which they direct a critique to permissiveness, consumerism, pollution, corruption and nationalism, all considered as
sinful outcomes of western modernity and civilization.

The veiling of women emerges as the most visible symbol of the islamization of
the life-world because islamist body-politics defines a distinct sense of self ("nefs")
and community, where the central issue becomes the control of women's sexuality

and the social separation of sexes. But, in addition to that, other social forms, such as beards for men, taboos on chastity, promiscuity, homosexuality, alcohol consumption and the like, define new moralist practices and the semiology of the islamic way of life.

Islamic faith and the islamic way of life become a reference point for the re-ideologization of seemingly simple social issues such as the covering of girl students at the university, the permission for prayer spaces in public buildings, the construction of a mosque at the center of Istanbul, the non-mixity in the public transportation system, the censorship on erotic art and the discouragement of alcohol consumption in restaurants. All these demonstrate the islamist political problematization of cultural issues and criticism of a "secular way of life." Islamism rather than being in continuation with traditional interpretations and practices of muslims in general, expresses an exacerbation of muslim identity and its reconstruction in and "vis-à-vis" the modern world. Furthermore, localizing the partners and the source of this dispute as "Islam versus the West" would be an oversimplification, disregarding the significance of the indigenous conflictuality between the secular elites and the islamist counter-elites.

In other words, islamist movements render visible a realm of conflictuality, one whose terms are defined by different discursive constructs and normative values of ethics, gender relations, and life-styles. Therefore, islamists and secularists are disputing the hegemony over the cultural model which is not separable from class conflictuality . . . .[28]

XV

These processes of dislocation differed greatly from those which developed in earlier periods, in the period of the burgeoning of the national, socialist, and Communist movements analyzed above. The processes of dislocation that developed in those periods gave rise to movements focusing on the restructuring of the respective centers which were also seen as capable of coping with the results of these processes of dislocation, and these sectors did not conceive their dislocation as being directly related to broader international, global forces. This situation has radically changed with the development of distinct processes of globalization which have been taking place in the contemporary scene, and with the inability of the nation states to cope with many of the problems attendant on these processes.

It is in such situations of double dislocation that in many social sectors there developed an acute sense of onslaught, challenge, or threat – be it military, political and/or cultural – above all by the promulgation in name of "Godless" reason, of extra-religious vision, often in combination with the acceptance of, or giving in to, utilitarian, mundane concerns, of their respective civilizations. In many such situations the combined impact of internal change and impingement of external forces is seen by these groups

as undermining, in the name of autonomous reason and/or of purely egoistical hedonistic impulses, the basic religious premises and their religion or
tradition, giving rise to a diversity of ways and styles of life together with
potentially degenerative tendencies. It is the crystallization of such situations and perceptions that provides the most propitious background for the
development of modern fundamentalist and communal-national movements, and it becomes intensified when existing regimes – in this case above
all the various secular-national regimes – became weaker through internal
strife or external pressure. It is these specific characteristics of these processes of dislocation that explain the specific features of the totalistic ideologies and orientations of these movements.

XVI

Such processes of dislocation have been abundantly illustrated – even if
perhaps not studied systematically enough – within various Middle Eastern
and some Southeast Asian societies. Parallel processes of dislocation lie
also in other societies, even if differing in details, in India in connection
with respect to the recent upsurge of Hindu national-communal movements, as well as – significantly enough – in the USA.

To follow Douglas R. Spitz's review of some recent studies on Hindu
Nationalism:

The main thrust of the authors' argument is that the rise of the BJP [Bharatiya
Janata Party] is basically due to two complementary trends. First is the growing
alienation of Hindus – especially those of the rapidly increasing educated middle
classes – from the essentially western rationalistic Nehruvian vision of India as a
centralized secular state, based on a "composite" cultural inheritance. Second is the
increasing attractiveness to these alienated classes of the Hindu nationalist vision
of India as a nation-state based on the indigenous dominant Hindu culture. In
accounting for these trends the authors suggest that the Nehruvian concept may be
unsuited to Indian realities because it ignores the primacy of religious identities in
the lives of most Indians. Moreover, its advocates placate Muslim and Christian
sensibilities by downplaying "the religious and cultural content of Hinduism as the
mainspring of Indian civilization" (p. 222). This, along with the progressive degeneration of Indian political life under the aegis of the increasingly unprincipled
Gandhi-dominated Congress party and its secularist allies, gave impetus to the
Hindu nationalist revival which was already underway, fueled by growing Hindu
middle class apprehension about increasing Muslim political assertiveness, the
political mobilization of *dalits* and tribal peoples, and the threat posed by Sikh and
Kashmiri separatists to India's territorial integrity. The organizational and mass
consciousness-raising activities of the RSS and VHP spearheaded this revival. The
BJP was able fully to exploit these developments after 1984 when, under the lead-

ership of L. K. Advani, it abandoned its platform of Gandhian Socialism and reverted to the earlier Bharatiya Jana Sangh program of unambiguous Hindu nationalism and Integral Humanism. This restored the credibility of its Hindu nationalist credentials with the RSS, whose cadres are essential to the BJP organization.

The authors conclude that, with its solid base in the urban Hindu middle classes and growing but still "soft" support among rural and poor Hindus, the BJP is a potent national force in Indian politics, despite its failure as yet to penetrate deeply South India. However, they feel that its ideology is too narrowly Hindu and anti-Muslim to form a viable alternative to Nehruvian secularism, and that its use of Hindu religious symbols will prove of limited electoral appeal, especially if it is unable to restrain the violent "lumpen" militancy of the VHP.[29]

XVII

Parallel processes of dislocation, again naturally differing in concrete details, have been also identified in the seemingly most developed modern society – the United States – with respect to those sectors which have been the most anti-governmental or anti-statist orientations among large, white sectors of American society.

To follow Thomas B. Edsall's report in the *Washington Post* (10/20/96, p. A13),

A new mapping of the American electorate shows that voter hostility to government is most concentrated in the white, small-town middle class.

In face-to-face interviews with 2,047 adults, the Gallup Organization found majorities who believe that the "governing elite" is "insensitive to the people's concerns (64 percent), unconcerned with values and morality (59 percent), unconcerned with the common good (54 percent) and only concerned about the elite's own agenda (69 percent).

The survey was conducted for a study called "The State of Disunion" run by James Davison Hunter, a sociologist at the University of Virginia and author of "The Culture Wars" and "Before the Shooting Begins."

"Those who are most worried, upset and angry about America in general – indeed, those with the most negative sentiments all around – are the white, well-educated middle classes who are most prominently from small towns in the East Central states and the West," Hunter wrote. "Those at the bottom of the socioeconomic spectrum are, in fact, the least upset with the US government."

Hunter wrote that people in the West, more than in any other region, are discontent with the governing elite, as are evangelical Christians.

One of the survey's findings is that members of the activist Christian right are far more upscale and better educated than both evangelical voters generally and the entire population. One-third of the religious right has a college degree or better compared to one-fifth of the general public, 42 percent holding professional jobs compared to 20 percent of all those surveyed and 14 percent with incomes in excess of $75,000 a year, compared to 8 percent for everyone, according to the survey.

Hunter, working with Carol Bowman, director of Survey Research at Bridgewater College, defined the Christian right as "evangelicals who describe their political beliefs as conservative, identify themselves as supporters of the conservative Christian movement in politics, favor allowing voluntary prayer in public schools, believe homosexual relations are 'wrong for all,' believe that abortion during the first three months is 'wrong for all' [and] believe that abortion is murder."

The survey also found that the Christian right is the most torn in its views about the United States. On the one hand, its constituents rank among the highest of all groups in terms of their "respect for the political institutions in America." But at the same time, "the Christian right articulates a remarkable pessimism about the current state of affairs in American society. This pessimism is unrivaled among other Americans . . . 81 percent of Christian right supporters said they thought America was either in a strong to moderate decline, compared to 51 percent of the total population," and the perception of decline among Christian right supporters extended to the areas of family life, the work ethic, spiritual life and education.

The Hunter study sought to determine not only distrust of government, but also the degree to which voters view government in "malevolent" and hostile terms. "Of the two-thirds to three-quarters of Americans who generally suspect that the government is run by selfish, big interests, only a minority repeatedly expresses unequivocally conspirational allegations [in response to a series of questions]. Still, one-quarter of the population repeatedly express the conviction that the government is run by a conspiracy."

These conspirational views are held most strongly by those living in towns of less than 10,000 (31 percent compared to 21 percent for those living in cities of 50,000 or more). The survey said "strong suspicions of conspiracy flourish in the West, fade as they move eastward, and perish on their trek across the Alleghenies."

On the subject of homosexuality, the survey detected a general pattern of "public ambivalence," Hunter wrote. Of those surveyed 60 percent disagreed with the statement that "homosexual couples should have the right to marry," and 65 percent disagreed with "homosexual couples should be allowed to adopt children." Conversely, 64 percent disagreed with the statement that "homosexual behavior should be against the law if it occurs between consenting adults," 69 percent disputed the view that "AIDS is God's way of punishing homosexuals," and 51 percent disagreed with the statement that "landlords should not have to rent to homosexuals if they are morally opposed to homosexuality."[30]

XVIII

Rather parallel, even if much more complex and varied, developments took place in various Latin American countries, which saw, as we noted above, a very widespread expansion of Protestant, especially evangelistic and pentecostal, movements.[31] The broader historical contexts in which these movements developed were rather similar to those which were connected with the development of the fundamentalist and communal-national religions ones – namely the weakening of different secular modernizing in Latin America, above all patrimonial-bureaucratic constitutional, or military authoritarian regimes, and widespread processes of dislocation attendant on the various processes of globalization analyzed above. The development of these movements in many Latin American countries has to be understood also in the context of the prolonged alliance of most of the higher echelons of the Catholic church with the more conservative oligarchic and authoritarian elements in these regimes and the slow but continual inroads from at least the beginning of the twentieth century of Protestantism into the heartlands of Catholicism. Given these specific characteristics, the great religious effervescence that developed from about the sixties on was not confined to Protestant groups alone – although these, especially evangelistic and pentecostal groups continually gathered momentum then. Indeed, as D. H. Levine has shown, these movements can be seen as part of a broader intensive religious effervescence which also encompassed the broader majority Catholic sectors.[32]

Ontological conceptions and the development of fundamentalist and communal-religious movements – some comparative indications

XIX

The preceding analysis has identified two sets of conditions – namely broad global, social, economical, and cultural processes and the closely related distinct processes of social dislocation of different elite groups and social sectors – as being of crucial importance in explaining the upsurgence of the religious components in the construction of collective identities in many non-Western societies as well as in the Americas. But while these conditions seem to develop in most of the countries analyzed, their "results" – i.e., the nature of the movements that developed within them and the impact of these movements – vary greatly between them. Thus it is, of course, necessary to distinguish, first, between the conditions conducive to the development of the communal-national and fundamentalist movements, and second, between the different impacts which these movements have in their respective societies.

As was also the case with respect to the development of proto-fundamentalist movements, four conditions are of great importance in the development within the broad panorama of the resurgent religious identities of the more distinctive fundamentalist ones. First, the basic ontological premises and conceptions of social order prevalent in these civilizations, especially the relative centrality of the political arenas in these conceptions; second, the closely related importance of political utopias in the political tradition of these societies; third, the concomitant conceptions of accountability of rulers predominant in these societies or civilizations; and fourth, the relative strength of institutions mediating the access to the sacred.[33]

Thus, among the modern and contemporary societies it is above all within the societies which crystallized in the framework of monotheistic civilizations or sectors thereof that there developed the strongest tendencies to the development of the fundamentalist movements with strong totalistic-Jacobin tendencies. These tendencies, as those to the development of proto-fundamentalist movements, were connected first of all to the fact that it was within these civilizations, even in their modern post-revolutionary permutations, that the political arena has been perceived as the major arena of the implementation of the transcendental utopian visions. Even were such visions couched in modern secular terms, they were rooted in the interweaving in their historical experience of this and other-worldly orientations to the construction of the mundane world. Similarly, as with respect to the proto-fundamentalist movements, the tendency to the development of modern fundamentalist ones was strongest in those societies in which there did not develop strong institutions mediating the access to the sacral. Accordingly within (Western) Christianity the divide, as we have seen already above, has been between Catholicism and Protestantism, and it is in the latter that have developed strong semi-Messianic utopian stances focused on the political arena.

The importance of the prevalence of such ontological premises and conceptions of social order for the development of fundamentalist movements stands out clearly in the country in which the first modern fundamentalist movements developed – which were also the first to designate themselves as such, and probably invented the term fundamentalism – namely, the United States. It is the prevalence in the United States of ontological conceptions rooted in the Protestant tradition that provides at least a partial clue to the seemingly rather puzzling situation in which a strong tendency to the development of fundamentalist movements developed in the very core of modernity. At the same time, as we shall yet see in greater detail later on, the analysis of the American case is important not only for the understanding of the conditions conducive to the development of fundamentalist movements, but also for understanding the different paths of their development, and their impact in their respective societies.

XX

Of special interest from the point of view of the continual interaction between the fundamentalist movements and the broader setting in which they develop are the Muslim fundamentalist movements which developed within states based on Islamic ideology – Pakistan, Bangladesh, and to a smaller extent Malaysia – as well as contemporary evangelical Protestant movements above all in the United States. The Islamic ideology promulgated in these states by different regimes – however much of their intellectual roots, especially in Pakistan, are to be found in some of the earlier Islamic modern fundamentalist thought, above all in the writings of Mawdudi[34] – tended, initially at least, on the whole to espouse a more communal-religious nationalism, and much less a Jacobin fundamentalist one. In these regimes the promulgation of Islamic laws – sometimes in its most extreme aspects, such as cutting off the hands of thieves – constituted more an attempt to use traditional regulations as markers of communal identity, and not as part of a broader program for instruments for the totalistic reconstruction of society. In many of these regimes non-Islamic, "secular" laws continued to be upheld in many arenas. It was just because of this fact that these regimes could become objects of attack of more extreme fundamentalist groups which developed within them. It is, however, very significant from the point of view of our analysis that such tendencies developed in Islamic societies and communities.

The situation in the various contemporary, evangelical, missionary, Protestant movements, most of which originated in the United States,[35] which have lately burgeoned throughout the world, is more complicated but in principle, though certainly not in detail, similar to the situation in Muslim societies. Within these movements there tend to develop strong

Jacobin orientations, certainly inward, but often also under appropriate circumstances, outward-oriented. These orientations are grounded in the Protestant tradition with its strong universalistic orientations and political orientations; in their scriptural emphases and the emphases on direct access to the sacred. Their vision and mission is conceived in highly universalistic terms, even if very often with a very strong emphasis on America as the bearer or incarnation of this mission, but in line with a continual theme of American collective identity as the bearer of the universalistic mission. Significantly enough their enemies, the "other" of these groups are not some other communal or national groups – but competing universalisms, some with very strong fundamentalist or at least Jacobin tendencies – namely Islam, Communism, Catholicism-and-feminism.[36]

At the same time, while eschatological evangelical themes are very strong among most of them, not all of them develop full Jacobin tendencies. It is not only that most of them are active in pluralistic settings and institutions which do not facilitate the full development of such tendencies. Even internally many of them tend often to emphasize more revivalist or millennialist themes and only secondarily Jacobin ones. Moreover, fully-fledged, externally oriented, political Jacobin tendencies tend to develop mainly in those societies in which their own religion is hegemonic and in which these movements constitute "internal" heterodoxies challenging the existing orthodoxy. When the development of these movements constitutes, as in Latin American countries, a part of the permeation of Protestantism into countries in which Catholicism has been predominant, most of the evangelistic, pentecostal, with potentially Jacobin tendencies, movements tend not to develop fully-fledged autonomous political activities oriented to the reconstruction of their entire societies. Rather they tend to ally themselves with the more conservative political forces – even if on the ground they reconstruct the traditional modes of life and social spaces. But the transition between the internal and external Jacobin emphases – in both directions – is much easier in the cases of the various Protestant and Islamic groups than in that of the communal-utopian national movements in Asia.

XXI

As against the strong tendency to development of fundamentalist movements in many sectors of monotheistic civilizations – this tendency, as well as that to the development of communal-religious national groups, has been much weaker, as was also the case with respect to proto-fundamentalist ones, in the realm of Confucian civilization or civilizations – in contemporary (mainland) China (PRC), Taiwan (RC), and Singapore. All these regimes developed from within a civilization in which transcendental visions were constructed in wholly secular and this-worldly terms, thus minimizing the possibility of development of fundamentalist tendencies from within the cultural or intellectual, even potentially dissident, cores of these regimes.[37]

True enough, all these societies saw the continuous development of many semi-subterranean cults, including some Christian evangelist ones, but fundamentalist tendencies were relatively weak not only in mainland China but also in Taiwan and Singapore. Likewise, these cults and tendencies seem to have been rather muted and dispersed with relatively weak impact. Needless to say, the heavy hand of totalitarian or authoritarian regimes played an important role in the mostly subterranean or marginal existence of most such groups. Similarly, the wide promulgation of the official ideologies might have generated some, even if only passive, acceptance of these regimes.

It was indeed with the weakening of the authoritarian regime in Taiwan that many such cults, and above all many Christian evangelical groups, became much more widespread and started to flourish, as happened also in PRC. However, these cults or religious revivals do not appear to have evinced, at least till now, strong fundamentalist tendencies.[38] It is only among the continually growing Christian evangelical groups that the beginning of some such tendencies could be identified. At the same time the strong nationalistic tendencies which started to develop there with the weakening of the Communist regime and of their hitherto hegemonic ideologies tended also to be couched mostly in secular-nationalistic, and not religious, terms.

The developments in Korea – especially of the continual growth of evangelical Protestant groups since the late nineteenth century, and their gaining of great momentum while adding strong fundamentalist tendencies in more contemporary periods – are of great interest from the point of view of our analysis.[39] While systematic research on these developments is still in the very beginning, the continual success of such groups in Korea has been attributed, even if in rather general terms, to the decay of the last Confucian royal regime in the nineteenth century; the strong identification of many of these churches with the Korean national traditional resistance, especially under the Japanese regime; the very weak legitimization of the post-Second World War regimes; and the growing modernization and concomitant far-reaching social dislocations that took place under these regimes. Indeed, it seems plausible to suggest that it is

the loss of legitimation of the regime and the weakness of central institutional structures, combined with very intensive processes of social change
that provided a fertile ground not only for the acceptance of Christianity
among wide sectors of the Korean population but especially for greater
susceptibility to the more evangelistic, potentially fundamentalist, sects.
Yet given the fact that these movements developed in a society and political order in which the basic premises were certainly not Christian or
Protestant, and therefore could not constitute "internal" heterodoxies –
and whose cultural elites were greatly depleted and weakened during
the Japanese occupation – their Jacobin tendencies were confined more to
the reconstruction of the internal life of these communities or toward the
creation of wider spaces for their communities than to the reconstruction
of the overall political and social order.

XXII

The tendency to the development of fundamentalist movements, ideological politics, and to the ideological reconstruction of the political center in
a Jacobin mode, has been much weaker in those civilizations with "other-
worldly" orientations – especially in India and to a somewhat smaller extent
in Buddhism – in which the political order was not perceived as an area of
the implementation of the transcendental vision. Indeed, in these societies
it was above all communal-religious, often national movements, that tended
to develop as the major contemporary, center-oriented movements. Given,
however, the centrality of the political dimension in the expansion of modernity – even in other-worldly civilizations, such as Buddhism and
Hinduism – the religious communal movements which develop within these
have very strong political orientations or dimensions.[40] Many such political movements tended to clothe themselves in religious, often fundamentalist garb – to which several trends of so-called Hindu-fundamentalism
attest.[41] But most of these movements differ in several very crucial ways
from the "pristine" modern fundamentalist movements analyzed above.
First their major orientations are particularistic, primordial, and not universalistic. Most of them harbor some particularistic vision of exclusion,
but only very few develop a fully totalistic-Jacobin direction. They do not
promulgate, or at least promulgate only very weak conceptions of reconstruction of the social order according to any social vision rooted in an
ontological perspective. The "others" – to be excluded or distanced from –
are other national, ethnic, and religious communities, instead of other
"universalistic" communities, civilizations, or religions. But even if the
Jacobin fundamentalist tendencies are relatively weak in these movements,

there may indeed develop tendencies to very intensive inter-communal violence, to no small extent rooted in the tendency to politicization of religion which is very strong in all of them.[42]

These differences between the communal-national religious and fundamentalist movements are closely related to the characteristics of the bearers or carriers of these visions – especially to the prevalence of autonomous religious or intellectual groups in the fundamentalist movements as against carriers of solidarity in the communal-religious ones.

The puzzle of the weak development of fundamentalist movements in Japan

XXIII

The case of Japan is of great interest from the point of view of the comparative analysis of fundamentalist movements, especially for the understanding of the relations between proto-fundamentalist and fundamentalist movements, and for understanding the antinomies of both the Axial Civilizations and of the cultural program of modernity.

While nationalistic movements and ideologies have continuously developed in modern Japan, it is rather difficult to discern the development of fundamentalist groups with extreme Jacobin ideologies and orientations. The many new religions, nationalist movements, and various extreme terrorist sects that have developed in early modern – the Tokugawa and early Meiji periods – and in contemporary Japan, did not develop into fully fledged fundamentalist groups with distinctive Jacobin ideologies and patterns of organization and orientation. Most of these sectarian movements, as well as those which developed in Japan in earlier periods, did not evince some of the main characteristics of the sects and heterodoxies which developed in the various Axial Civilizations and of their modern transformations. But at the same time, Japan's sectarian movements have all constructed new spaces to which their members could escape, as it were, from the restrictions of the existing order, and develop lifestyles of their own, and in which new types of activities and modes of discourse developed and many potentially subversive themes were promulgated.

This development was very much in line with the characteristics of the numerous Buddhist and even Taoist sects which developed throughout Japanese history. Most of these sects underwent a process of "de-Axialization" – and, as we have in our analysis strongly emphasized the close relation between the development of fundamentalist movements and some core characteristics of the Axial Civilizations, it would be of great interest from the point of view of this analysis to explore the roots of these processes of de-Axialization.

XXIV

Both Confucianism and Buddhism have greatly influenced the entire cultural and social ambience of Japanese society.[43] Their influence was very far-reaching. But the nature of this influence and the impact of Confucianism and Buddhism in Japan were different from that of Confucianism in China, Korea, and Vietnam, or of Buddhism in, above all, Southern Asian countries.

Institutionally in Japan neither Confucianism nor Buddhism has changed the structure of the center or of the ruling elites. In Japan, the "importation" of Confucianism did not develop those central institutional aspects that shaped the Confucian regimes in China, Korea, and Vietnam – namely the examination system and the crystallization through this system of the stratum of literati and of the imperial bureaucracy, who recruited to a large extent through these examinations. Buddhism also developed some very distinct characteristics in Japan that distinguished it from those Buddhist communities in India, China, and Southeast Asia. The most important of these characteristics was the development of very strong this-worldly orientations and of a very sectarian, familistic, organizational structure of Buddhist groups or sects.

In close relation to such far-reaching institutional changes, some of the major premises or concepts of Confucianism and Buddhism were also transformed in Japan in a highly this-worldly direction. The ontological conceptions that stressed (as in all Axial Civilizations) the chasm between the transcendental and mundane orders, between "culture" and "nature," were shifted in a more "immanentist" direction.[44] This meant a much stronger emphasis on the mutual embeddedness of the cultural and natural orders and on nature as given.

The ideological transformation of Buddhism and Confucianism in Japan was probably most fully manifest with respect to the conception of a national collectivity and its relations to the broader Buddhist and Confucian civilizations, as well as with respect to conceptions of authority, especially Imperial authority. The crux of this transformation was the redirection of the universalistic orientations of Buddhism and Confucianism to a more particularistic, primordial direction.

Neither Confucianism nor Buddhism changed the distinctive definition of the Japanese collectivity which had predominated for many centuries in the hegemonic discourse in Japan – it being constructed in terms of sacred liturgical community, with emphasis on its sacredness or divinity and on the uniqueness of the Japanese collectivity or nation. The strong universalistic orientations inherent in Buddhism, and more latently in Confucianism, were subdued and "nativized" in Japan. This conception of a divine nation, of sacred particularity – to follow Z. J. R. Werblowski's felicitous expression – while obviously emphasizing the sacredness and uniqueness of Japan, did not entail, as was the case in the monotheistic religions and civilizations, the connotation of it being uniquely "chosen" in terms of a transcendental and universalistic mission. It did not entail the conception of responsibility to God to behave according to such precepts or commitments.[45] When Japan was defined as a divine nation, this meant a nation protected by the Gods, as being a chosen people in some sense, but not a nation carrying God's universal mission.[46]

Parallel developments took place with respect to the basic conceptions of political authority and of the accountability of rulers – which constituted, as we have seen, core components of Axial Civilizations. Unlike in China (and Korea and Vietnam), where in principle the Emperor, even if a sacral figure, was "under" the Mandate of Heaven, in Japan he was sacred and seen as the embodiment of the Gods and could not be held accountable to anybody. Only the Shoguns and other officials could be held accountable, and then in ways not clearly specified and only in periods of crisis, as for instance at the end of the Tokugawa regime.

At the same time, and in close relation to the tendency to "Japanize" the different universalistic religions, has been the fact that Japan has never become, in its own eyes and in the collective consciousness of most of its sectors, an integral part of other, broader civilizations, even if it has continually been oriented to them. Throughout its history, although continuously in contact with other civilizations, Japan has perceived itself as mostly a self-enclosed civilizational and national entity.

One crucial derivative of this definition of the Japanese collectivity has been the impossibility of becoming Japanese by conversion. The Buddhist sects or Confucian schools – seemingly the most natural candidates for channels of conversion – could not serve as such in Japan. True enough, in the pre-Heian period and in later times, Koreans as well as other groups became assimilated into the different regional Japanese settings. But these earlier experiences of assimilation did not entail a "conversion" or *principled* acceptance into a common collective entity sharing a specific transcendent vision. When more articulated conceptions of such a collective consciousness have developed in modern times, they have excluded even the possibility of such assimilation.[47]

XXV

This process of transformation of the basic Confucian and Buddhist conceptions or premises in Japan was closely related to a parallel process of transformation of the respective cultural elites which were the carriers of these conceptions.

On mainland Asia, the Confucian and Buddhist elites were relatively, sometimes highly, autonomous. The Confucian elites constituted a new, distinct, autonomous political-cultural stratum recruited in principle, if not always in practice through the examination system, the basic contents of which were promulgated and set up by them. The Buddhists, at least in the religious arena, were also highly autonomous and not embedded in the existing structures of power or family.

In contrast, in Japan both the Confucian scholars and the Buddhist sects were deeply embedded in the existing power structure and kinship and family settings. Although the Confucian academies in Japan were often relatively independent institutions, they were highly dependent on the rulers for any offices for their teachers or students. The Confucian scholars served in Japan at the courts of the rulers according to the criteria set up by the rulers, and they served at the rulers' will. The Buddhist sects became strongly embedded in the familistic setting predominant in most sectors of Japanese society.

Linked to these characteristics of the Confucian and Buddhist groups was the relative weakness of autonomous cultural elites – the potential bearers of utopian orientations. True, many cultural actors or specialists – priests, monks, scholars, and the like – participated in such coalitions. But the cultural, religious, and intellectual elites, while often engaged in very sophisticated cultural activities and discourse, evinced little autonomy in the social and political realm, i.e. as actors upholding values and orientations not embedded in existing social frameworks, but enunciated and articulated by them, and according to which they are recruited.

One of the most important outcomes of all these processes of transformation, of the de-Axialization of Confucianism and Buddhism in Japan, was that the type of confrontation between orthodoxy and heterodoxy that developed in various ways in the different Axial Civilizations did not develop in Japan.

Thus, the central aspects of the processes of de-Axialization of Confucianism and Buddhism in Japan have been the immanentization of the transcendental; particularization of the universalistic orientations; the weakness of autonomous cultural elites, and of the concomitant weakening of the potential for challenging both the premises of the existing order and of authority in name of those transcendental principles according to which rulers could be judged and called to accountability.

Concomitantly, the numerous movements of protest that developed in Japan in pre-modern and contemporary periods alike, did not usually challenge the basic premises of the system – but were very effective in creating spaces for new types of social and cultural activities. The numerous "new religions" that developed in Japan from the Tokugawa period to the present are very good illustrations of these tendencies. Their accommodative stance, with its very strong emphasis on the good life in the present, was in many ways the opposite of fundamentalist orientations – even if some of them developed very strong nationalist orientations.

XXVI

Japan's encounter with the West evinced a pattern rather similar to that of Confucianism and Buddhism. Of special interest from the point of view of the comparative analysis of modern fundamentalist movements is both the Meiji Restoration – which has often been compared to the Great Revolutions[48] (revolutions which, as we have seen, provided a central component in the development of various Jacobin, including fundamentalist, modern movements) – and this Restoration's impact on the possibility of the development of totalitarian tendencies in Japan. Here of special interest is the examination of the relation between the weakness of full fledged Jacobinistic movements and orientations in Japan and the basic characteristics of the Meiji Ishin which distinguish it from the Great Revolutions – despite the great similarities between them.

The basic long-range processes and causes leading to the downfall of the Tokugawa regime were very similar to those of the Great Revolutions. Similarly, just as in the Great Revolutions, the Meiji Ishin ushered in not only a new mode of legitimation, but a new – essentially modern – overall cultural program which encompassed most arenas of life, changed the composition of the ruling class entirely, and moved in the direction of structural change and modernization.

And yet from the very beginning the Meiji Ishin differed in some very crucial ways from the European, American (and later on the Russian and Chinese) revolutions. The first such difference is of course manifest in its very name – even if the term Ishin is possibly closer to Renovation, or to "being pulled in a new direction," rather than simply Restoration as it has been called in Western literature.

Above all, the cultural and political program promulgated by different groups which were active in the Meiji Ishin differed greatly from that of most of the Great Revolutions. Indeed, the crux of this difference was rooted in, or closely connected with, the Axial and non-Axial roots of the Great Revolutions and the Meiji Ishin, respectively. It was in a way the reverse image of those of the Great Revolutions – and in many ways it was no less radical. The Meiji Ishin was proclaimed a renovation of an older, archaic system which in fact never before existed, and not as a Revolution aiming to change the social and political order; to totally reconstruct the state and society alike in accordance with transcendental principles proclaiming a new direction.

To reiterate, the cosmology and ontology entailed in the new cultural programs were promulgated as the renovation of an older archaic system, which in fact never existed, not as a revolution aimed at changing the social and political order in an entirely new, universalistic direction. While millenarian restorative themes were prominent in different sectors of the uprisings before and during the Restoration, utopian, future-oriented orientations, rooted in a universalistic-transcendental vision, were, in contrast to the other revolutions, very weak and almost nonexistent.

Concomitantly, in the Meiji Ishin there did not develop – as was the case in the Great Revolutions in Europe, the USA, Russia, and China – a universalistic, transcendental, missionary ideology, or any components of class ideology, two elements which were also very weak in the peasant rebellions and movements of protest of the Tokugawa period. The cultural program promulgated in the Meiji Ishin – and later on by the Meiji state – consisted of a mixture of pragmatic orientations to the question of how to adapt to the new international setting with strong Restorationist components or orientations. It constituted a combination of the restorationist nativistic vision with what may be called functional prerequisites of modern society, such as efficacy, achievement, and equality.

XXVII

These distinct characteristics of the Ishin ideology were closely related to some of the structural characteristics of the revolutionary renovative process itself – which again distinguished it from that of the Great Revolutions. The most important of these characteristics which distinguish the revolutionary processes that toppled the Tokugawa bakufu from those of the Great Revolutions were the relatively weak connections between different rebellious groups, their relative segregation, the almost total absence of sacralization of violence and the construction of the center in a liminal mode.

Indeed, what is perhaps most distinctive about the Meiji Restoration as compared to the Great Revolutions was the almost total absence of distinct, *autonomous*, religious or secular, intellectual groups as active, independent elements in the political process of the Restoration acting not simply as the background for the revolutionary process – which stands out in marked contrast to the Puritans in the English Revolution and their descendants in the American one, the ideologues in the French Revolution, or the Russian Intelligentsia.[49]

XXVIII

It was this cultural program of modernity, rooted as it was in the non-Axial, immanentist ontologies prevalent in Japan, that guided the crystallization of the Meiji state, the later development of modern Japanese society, and to some extent at least, the specific characteristics of the major institutional formations of modern Japan.

One of the most important repercussions of this program can be found in the political arena in the strong tendency to conflate national community, state, and society – a tendency which has become especially prevalent in the modern and contemporary arenas.

Such conflation has had several repercussions for the structuring of the ground rules of the political arena. The most important of these repercussions have been the development, first, of a weak concept of the state as distinct from the broader, overall, in modern terms, national community (national being defined in sacral, natural, and primordial terms), and second, of a societal state characterized by both a strong tendency to emphasize guidance rather than direct regulation and the permeation of the periphery by the center.

Closely related has been a very weak development of an autonomous civil society, although, needless to say, elements of the latter, especially the structural and organizational components thereof (such as different organizations) have not been missing. One of the most interesting corollaries of this embedment of the political arena and civil society, unlike within the overall community, has been the absence in the historical ("feudal") and early modern conceptions of autonomous legal rights and of representative institutions. In Japan, however, unlike in many absolutist, or totalitarian systems, the absence of such institutions was not connected with a strong symbolic distinction of the center, of the state, or with strong efforts by the center not only to control, but also to restructure and mobilize the periphery – according to a new vision destructive of the values hitherto prevalent in the periphery.

The specific type of civil society that developed in Japan is perhaps best illustrated by the continual construction of new social spaces which provide semi-autonomous arenas in which new types of activities, consciousness, and discourse develop, which, however, do not impinge directly on the center. Those participating in them do not have autonomous access to the center, and are certainly not able to challenge its premises.

This weakness of civil society was not due to its suppression by a strong state, but rather to the continual conflation of state and civil society with the national community. Rather, the relations between state and society have been effected in the mode of patterned pluralism, of multiple dispersed social contracts.

Closely connected to these characteristics of the major institutional arenas of modern Japan is the development of a rather distinct pattern of political dynamics, especially concerning the impact of movements of protest on the center. The most important characteristic brought about by the relatively weak-principled ideological confrontations with the center – confrontations characterized above all by the lack of success in mobilizing wide support by those leaders who promulgated such ideological confrontation – was the quite far-ranging success in influencing, if often indirectly, the policies of the authorities and the creation of new, autonomous, yet segregated social spaces in which activities promulgated by such movements could be implemented.

The processes of democratization and the continual diversification of sectors and elites that took place after the Second World War have expanded the access of broader sectors of society to the organs of government and imbued these organs with a greater respect for the legal specification of the rights of citizens and for legal procedure. They have not, however, greatly expanded the scope of an autonomous civil society which could promulgate its own criteria of legitimation and impose them on the state in the name of principles transcending the state and the national community alike.

It was these characteristics of the modern Japanese society, especially of the Japanese State, civil society, and of the relations between them, that explain why the seemingly liberal tendencies that developed in the Taisho period never gave rise to a full-fledged – in the Western case – liberal regime. Similarly, it is these characteristics that explain why the repressive military regime that developed in the thirties never developed, despite the use of many fascist symbols and themes, into a full-fledged fascist regime with a mobilizing party and mass movements oriented at the total reconstruction of society.[50]

XXIX

It is all these specific characteristics of the modern Japanese society, rooted as they are in the distinct cultural program of modernity and in the distinct characteristics of the Japanese political system, that explain the weakness or non-development of fully-fledged Jacobin fundamentalist movements in Japan – very much in line with parallel developments of sectarianism in pre-modern Japan.

The ultimate roots of this non-development (or at most the very weak development) of fundamentalist movements with full-fledged Jacobin characteristics in Japan, are found in the processes of the de-Axialization of the impact of the Axial Civilizations, and later of the universalistic modern orientations – and attest to the close relation between the development of proto-fundamentalist and fundamentalist movements and the antinomies inherent, first, in the Axial Civilizations and second, in the Axial roots of the cultural program of modernity.

The bracketing out of universalistic and transcendental orientations and of the continual confrontations between such orientations and the civil or primordial ones in the construction of modern Japanese collective consensus, has weakened – indeed undermined – the possibility of development of full-fledged Jacobin ideologies with their strong tendency to the absolutization of central aspects of human experience. Additionally, the conflation of state and civil society has minimized the possibility of development of that component of the Jacobin vision which entailed the totalistic reconstruction of society through political action.

The various religious and/or nationalistic groups which can be seen as having contained the seeds of such fundamentalistic orientations went the way of most movements of protest in Japan throughout most of the Japanese historical experience – namely, as we have seen, there developed the relatively weak principled ideological confrontation with the center – these were characterized above all by the lack of success of leaders of such confrontation movements to mobilize wide support; which resulted in the concomitant creation of new autonomous but segregated social spaces in which activities promulgated by such movements could be implemented.

Collective identity, institutional formations and the development and impact of fundamentalist and communal-religious movements – the USA

XXX

The potentialities for the development of the conditions under which these religious movements in general, and fundamentalist ones in particular, take form could indeed be found in all those civilizations in which the basic ontological premises were conducive to such developments. Indeed, from this point of view there existed great similarities between the proto-fundamentalist and the modern fundamentalist movements. In contrast to the former, however, modern movements were characterized by some distinctive features – by the potential Jacobin tendencies of the fundamentalist movements, and the highly politicized totalistic ones of the communal-national movements, and by their appropriation, albeit in highly restrictive and extreme anti-pluralistic terms, of the homogenizing tendencies of the modern territorial state.

However, beyond these common features, the characteristics of modern movements varied greatly between civilizations and societies with regard to their scope of development, the nature of their impact on their respective societies, and the extent to which certain types of movements were able to predominate over others. Likewise, these features varied greatly between different periods in the modern and contemporary history of these societies. In all these societies and civilizations, fundamentalist ideologies constitute only one mode of response to processes of changes attendant on the crystallization and expansion of modernity, and their importance and impact vary greatly in different situations and settings.

The extent to which there develop within these movements the ideal typical fundamentalist orientations and characteristics, and above all the nature of the impacts of these movements on their respective societies, have been greatly influenced not just by the ontological premises and premises of social order that are prevalent in these societies and their respective bearers, but by the interrelation between these premises, the construction of collective identities, and the strength of the structure of political institutions of the respective societies or civilizations.

Here a closer look at the American (USA) case is of great interest and importance. It is, as we have seen, the prevalence of ontological conceptions rooted in the Protestant tradition that provides at least a partial clue to the rather puzzling situation in which a strong tendency to the development of fundamentalist movements developed in the very core of modernity, in a society often conceived by many of its members and by others as the epitome of modernity. However, the analysis of the American case is important not only for the understanding of the conditions conducive to the development of fundamentalist movements, it is also important for its ability to lend understanding to both the different paths of these movements' development, and their various impacts in different societies. Of central importance here is, of course, the fact that the fundamentalists never did "take over" in the United States despite seemingly strong attempts by many such groups. They were not able to monopolize the public agenda and political life. They always had to play within the constitutional framework and its basic premises and contours, and within the framework of the basic components of the American collective identity. This combination, in the United States, of the tendency to develop fundamentalist movements with their rather specific and seemingly, especially in comparison with some Muslim countries, limited impact on the broader institutional settings, can be better understood only when related to the place of Protestant ontological conceptions and premises of social order in the construction of the American (USA) collective identity, political order, and the symbolic and institutional premises of its political order.

The mode of the constitution of collective identity and institutional order that crystallized in the USA distinguishes it not only from non-Western modes but from the original Western European ones, thus attesting to the fact that already within the West there developed different programs of modernity. The American (USA) collective consciousness constructed a civilization which was based on a political ideology transformed from a religious experience but maintaining its religious orientations – a hitherto unique occurrence in the history of humankind. Unlike the case in the Roman Empire, where the common citizenship was defined in secular-legal terms, with some undertones of a certain common cultural ambience, in the USA, the religious roots and components of the common bond were crucial.

The American civilization and "way of life" were constructed in terms of a common political ideology with religious roots and an emphasis on Christian heritage, rather than, as was the case in Europe, in terms of a combination of religious tradition with historical, ethnic, and national identity with almost no territorial or historical components. The collective consciousness was not related to a common historical origin, to common historical memory, mythical or actual – i.e. it did not comprise strong primordial components. Instead, it was the rather specific type of civil religion defined by Robert N. Bellah that constituted the core of this collective identity.[51]

In Samuel Huntington's words,

For most people national identity is the product of a long process of historical evolution involving common conceptions, common experiences, common ethnic background, common language, common culture and usually common religion. National identity is thus organic in character. Such however is not the case in the United States. American nationality has been defined in political rather than organic terms. The political ideas of the American creed have been the basis of national identity . . . . The United States thus had its origins in a conscious political act, in assertion of basic political principles and in adherence to the constitutional agreement based on those principles.[52]

Concomitantly the premises of this civilization entailed the constitution of a social order, of a collectivity whose collective identity was not couched in hierarchical terms, that is, in which the problems of the hierarchical orders of the society were not related to the problems of the constitution of the body politic.

XXXI

Religion played a central and rather paradoxical role in the construction and dynamics of the American cultural and political programs, its collective consciousness, and its identity. The paradoxical nature of this role has been manifest in the fact that on the one hand this program has been to no small extent developed from religious, above all Protestant traditions, and from the strong totalistic components thereof, while on the other hand one of its major institutional derivations has been the separation of church and state. This separation was not based on secular, anti-religious premises, which could be found especially in the European Enlightenment. Rather, insofar as it was rooted first in the Enlightenment, it was based on the deistic premises – and above all on the strong opposition to any established (state) church – as part of the opposition to strong government. Second, it was rooted in the historical experience of escaping from the wars of religion, the concomitant recognition of the impossibility of imposing any single religion on the multiplicity of sects, and the consequent strong emphasis on religious tolerance between different religious groups – even if in the first colonies the established church was initially institutionalized.

Thus religion was seemingly pushed into the realm of the private – but in fact it was pushed into the realm of the non-governmental, associational public arena where it played a most central role, and thus found its way into the political arena. As Wendy F. Naylor has put it, the separation of church and state did not necessarily entail the separation of religion from politics.[53]

Religion – religious organization, symbols, and discourse – constituted a continual component of the public and political discourse. It is not only that American society has been the most religious Western society in terms of the acceptance of religious beliefs, membership in religious organizations, and attendance at religious services – facts which by themselves attest to the importance of the religious component in the public associational life. But beyond this, the religious component and imagery played a continual role in the structuring and construction of the symbolic dimension of American collective identity and politics. This dimension was indeed very closely related to the specific utopian and future-oriented components in the American cultural and political program and in the construction of American collective identity. This religious component further constituted a continual component not only of the "cultural" but also of the political arena in the United States.

Religious symbolism and discourse constituted central components of the emphasis on the necessity to preserve the purity of the American commonwealth against the various attempts of the forces of evil threatening it from the inside or outside – a theme which was continually promulgated by American politicians. Similarly American individualism in its specific dimension was very often promulgated in religious terms and symbols.

Above all the religious component was continually interwoven with the reinterpretation of the American collective consciousness, and at the same time the construction of the American collective consciousness and identity constituted a central part of the agenda of many religious associations and activities in the United States.

This was the case, as Christopher Adamson has shown, already in the very beginning of the Republic:

Following the American Revolution, the social foundation supporting a settled ministry and sustaining the Old World tradition of an established state church began to crumble, prompting Alexis de Tocqueville to observe that in the United States, "the ideas of Christianity and liberty are so completely intermingled that it is almost impossible to conceive of the one without the other." Large numbers of ordinary Americans who had internalized egalitarian, anti-aristocratic attitudes while advancing the patriot cause began to search for and find spiritual meaning in evangelical forms of religious expression. Indeed, the revivals sweeping the northern and western states between the American Revolution and the Civil War have been described as "the Revolution at work in religion." . . . The Second Great Awakening sacralized the meaning of the American Revolution, so that American nationalism prior to the Civil War rested not just on the power of national symbols, such as the face of George Washington or the flag, but on the pervasive influence of evangelical Christianity. The operation of thousands of voluntary religious organizations helped to create a common world of experience which defined what it was to be an American. Whereas revivalism helped to forge a national identity south of the border, Protestant Christianity in Upper Canada was a far less cohesive force, largely because its evangelical, pietistic potential did not survive political reactions to the War of 1812. The counterpoint to the Christian republicanism of the Americans was a fundamental Christian Loyalism. "Loyalty with us", declared the leading Wesleyan Methodist, Matthew Richey, "is an integral and essential part of religion.". . . Republican Christianity was defined by an evangelical conception of the church as a voluntary society of converted believers. This conception threatened the fundamental premises of Christian Loyalism north of the border. Given that the colony's political survival hinged on the preservation of close ties with Britain, evangelical and non-evangelical Upper Canadians were forced to work out a modus vivendi.[54]

This rather unusual place of religious components in the construction of the American collective identity has been very closely related to the special attitudes to authority and to the basic institutional frameworks, especially as embodied in the constitution. The strong religious, utopian dimension of the American cultural and political program and the overall ideological format of this program, gave rise to one of the most important aspects of American society – a combination of a very strong and emphatic acceptance of the basic institutional, especially constitutional framework on the one hand, with a very strong suspicion of those in authority and of distrust of the government on the other – generating a very specific mode of combination of moralism and pragmatism in political life. The overall community – the Republic or Commonwealth – and its basic institutional-symbolic frameworks could easily become the foci of the charismatic-utopian dimension or orientation of the search for the pure, unpolluted community, or of the covenant binding it together, while the concrete political institutions, process, and office-holders could easily become the focus of mistrust. Such mistrust was closely connected to the very strong populist orientations prevalent in America and could give rise to the search for participatory politics undiluted by the political process – a theme promulgated lately for instance by Ross Perot with his emphasis on symbolic electronic town meetings.

Concomitantly there developed in the United States a rather unusual combination of, on the one hand, the center being defined much more in terms of the overall community, of the republic with its constitutional arrangements, and much less in terms of the concrete political institutions or activities, and on the other, the fear of expansion of government – a combination that constituted a continual theme in American political discourse. This combination could sometimes be seen in different designations of the country: "America" would often be used to designate the overall community the bearer of the strong utopian vision, while the United States would designate the more mundane concrete governmental institution (I owe this observation to Tom Burns).

This attitude to authority was very closely related to a more general characteristic of American politics and political discourse – a continual oscillation between on the one hand a pragmatic, "realistic" attitude most fully epitomized on the one hand in pork and barrel politics, and in a very unsentimental, sometimes brutal attitude to the political game, and on the other, a highly moralistic, often missionary, self-justifying, and sanctimonious attitude. This oscillation generated in the USA, in S. P. Huntington's words, the continuous "promise of disharmony"[55] – but a disharmony based on full acceptance of the premises of the center and of the search for the reestablishment of the utopian harmony inherent in these premises.

XXXII

All these factors have been important in explaining the major characteristic of the movements of protest that developed in the USA, of which the various revivalist, evangelist, and later fundamentalist movements constituted a continual component. Protest was indeed built in to the very premises and institutional framework of the American political arena as promulgated in its "myth" or creed, and it was the basic American political and constitutional discourse and its tensions that have also provided the basic framework of themes and movements of protest that developed from very early in the USA, and continue till today.

The major themes of protest that developed in the USA were set very firmly within these basic parameters of the American political and constitutional discourse. The major themes of protest crystallized in such movements – be it in the various revivalist movements, the abolitionists, or the first movements of displaced farmers or industrial workers that developed in the first half of the nineteenth century – and focused on the identification and the exposition of the evils threatening the basic premises of the American system. They were oriented against those aspects of social life which were seen as contaminating the purity of American life – against the pollution of this purity by various evil forces (especially those mentioned above) – and to the elimination of this pollution. Most of these movements shared many of the basic premises of the American cultural program: its strong future orientation, messianism, this-worldliness, emphasis on active participation and commitment to the social order. The strong interweaving of these themes of protest with the constitutional and legal debates and discourses did, of course, greatly reinforce this tendency to the acceptance by most of these movements of the basic premises of the American civilization. The two most important evils exposed by many such movements – and in the general political discourse – were first, those of unbridled egoism and second, the concentration of power and wealth – both of which were seen as undermining the basic foundation of Americans' life, of the covenant which brings the American people together. The negation of the inequality generated by such concentration of wealth or power was couched not in class terms but in terms such as "producers" as opposed to "parasites," or later in the twentieth century, in terms of denial of access to the possibilities of competition, to the fruits of the good life, and to full and equal participation in the political and moral life of the community.

These themes, which were couched in terms of the basic premises of the American creed and constitutional discourse, were upheld by almost all of the movements of protest that developed in the USA – with each movement naturally emphasizing different themes and combining them with different concrete social and economic ones, which naturally varied greatly in different periods. Whatever the differences between these movements, they were not oriented to the reconstruction of the center and the community but rather to their purification; to bringing them up to the fuller realization of the utopian vision of the American community. Indeed the most distinctive characteristic of the major movements of protest that developed in the USA was that they were above all oriented to the upholding of the premises of the American vision, which constituted a central component of the American collective consciousness and political creed.

XXXIII

It is all these factors – the modes of construction of American (USA) collective identity, the premises of its social and political role, and the basic characteristics of the movements that developed in them – that constituted the background for the continual tendency for revivalist, evangelical, and later fundamentalist movements to develop in the USA, and these movements constitute a continual component of American political life.[56] The fundamentalist movements which started to develop from the 1920s on, constituted a distinctly new type of such movements – although they built on the earlier millennial and evangelical ones, and continually overlapped and interacted with the many such movements which burgeoned together with them. These new fundamentalist movements and ideologies developed over a period when the older "synthesis" between the religious, republican, and liberal components in the American collective consciousness weakened and the "secular liberal" or "scientistic" became predominant – a process which started with the progressive era and continued to gather momentum after the Second World War.

These movements spread and became increasingly oriented to the broader social and political arenas at the same time that dissociation and even confrontations between many sectors of American society were on the rise, especially between what Robert Wiebe referred to as the local against the national class. These confrontations developed in conjunction with growing government intervention, with the movement of the courts in what was perceived by many sectors of the local classes as a liberal-secular, "godless" direction, and with far-reaching changes taking place in American society and in the political institutions, especially the parties. These movements, from the 1970s on, became closely connected with, and continual and central components of the American right and the upsurge of American conservatism – and exhibited, especially with respect to their attitudes toward government and governmental action and in their strong ideological orientations, some very specific characteristics which distinguish them from, for instance, contemporaneous European "conservative" movements.

Jason Epstein in his review of two books by Lind and Hodgson[57] on recent American conservative movements with their strong religious "right" component, brings out forcibly some of the major characteristics of these movements and their place on the broad American scene.

From the suburbs of Mecca to pools of Beverly Hills, there is no wonder that rootless multitudes now yearn increasingly for the absolute and submit to its avatars, who flourish as disorder accumulates. This yearning, now so prevalent in the United States, has resulted not in the classic conservatism of Plato and Burke but in its degenerate form, the intolerant worship of idols and dogma whether promoted by the falsified Islam of the Muslim Brotherhood or the falsified Christianity of Pat Robertson, whose invariable companions are self-deception and the deception of others. True conservatism, on the other hand, demands that the levers of change be placed beneath the world as it is, not as we would like it to be.

Lind and Hodgson show how for the past half century or so a band of quixotic counter-revolutionaries – Jacobins of the right attacking the symptoms of modernity – descended in the North from Joe McCarthy, the John Birch Society, and William F. Buckley and in the South from Strom Thurmond and George Wallace – has attempted to distract Americans from their actual challenges, including their obligations to their own poor and to the solvency of their children and their children's children, by turning them against a "demonized version of their government and toward the recovery of a grossly fictitious golden age, the residue of sermons, films, and editorials in the *Wall Street Journal*. The result is a puritanical politics of simpering virtue versus hellish depravity, in which the middling condition of actual lives is ignored.[58]

Epstein continues with the analysis of some of the distinct themes espoused by these groups:

In his very useful survey of right-wing populism in postwar America, Godfrey Hodgson identifies as its three main components anti-communism, racism, and the fear of social disintegration: in other words a reaction to the intrusion of the outside world upon the long-isolated enclave of white male dominance. In a positive sense, one might say that the experience of the American right, as Hodgson presents it, has been its irritable and reluctant awakening from the long dream of exceptionalism to find itself alongside a disreputable and no less irritable bedmate called history, from whom there is no possibility of divorce, while a century's dirty dishes are piled in the kitchen below. Whether the bedmates reconcile or prolong their quarrel is an open question. Should the quarrel continue, however, the loser will not be history.

The American right, Hodgson notices, comprises two incompatible components: authoritarian traditionalists, who are usually members of fundamentalist or evangelical religions, and radical individualists, including "libertarian" businessmen, speculators, and their journalistic and academic apologists in departments of economics, particularly at the University of Chicago. Hodgson makes too much of their incompatibility. What binds the two is their hostility to federal regulatory and taxing power or, in a larger sense, their shared conviction that the United States ought to be a largely homogeneous culture, a fairy-tale version of its disheveled self, a Disneyland whose brave citizens are free to make their fortunes no matter what the damage to competing interests, where differences are settled man to man, where women sing in church when they are not at their stoves incubating embryos, where overt non-conformists are not welcome and the income tax has been repealed.

In fact, an actual invasion of America had been under way since the early 1960s, one that had nothing to do with sexuality, Communists, or desegregated schools. This was the invasion of foreign goods, which were often better made, cheaper, and more useful than American ones. By the 1970s, this invasion would devastate much of the old industrial economy of the United States, including the high wages for industrial workers which for years Americans had taken for granted. This unprecedented competition, implemented by new technologies in transport and communication, within the once largely impregnable American market, would indeed turn the world upside down for most Americans and contribute to the selfishness and xenophobia of the Republican right. "But the structural decline in American economic growth that began in 1973 would not only be ignored, its profound consequences for the United States would repeatedly be denied by the radical right and its publicists even as American productivity growth and hourly wages remained stagnant or fell and federal indebtedness continued to mount."[59]

XXXIV

Thus the preceding analysis indicates that it was the combination of deep-rooted Protestant orientations prevalent in many sectors of American society which constituted a basic component of its premises and perceptions in many sectors of American society of the weakening of the religious components in the construction of American collective identity that has given rise to evangelistic, later the fundamentalist movements in this society. At the same time, however, it was the continual prevalence in the United States of an interweaving between the religious and civil components of collective identity (even though tension always existed between them and their relative importance varied in different periods); the prevalence of the US "civil religion"; the continual working of pluralistic institutions; and the autonomy and cohesiveness of the center and its openness to broader strata, that has assured the relatively limited impact of these movements on their society – particularly when compared to many Muslim societies, and also, to some extent, to Israel and Jewish communities in the USA and Europe. Thus indeed while the fundamentalist tendencies with potential Jacobin orientations have been stronger from the sixties or seventies on, they never "took over" in the United States despite seemingly strong attempts by many such groups. They were not able to monopolize the public agenda and political arena – even if they were greatly influential – because of the basic institutional, constitutional, and federal structure, the strong pluralistic or open dimensions in the construction of the American collective identity, and the basic premises of the American political system. They always had to play within the constitutional framework and its premises and basic contours. Thus, for instance, a banner carried by one of these active "rightist-fundamentalist" groups after Oklahoma proclaimed "Reno is the best reason to uphold the second amendment" – and while this may appear bizarre to many, it is the legitimization of their demands in constitutional terms, in terms of the Bill of Rights, that is highly significant here.[60]

Collective identity, institutional formations and the development and impact of fundamentalist and communal-religious movements: Asian societies, with a comparative look at Europe

XXXV

The analysis of the American case indicates that the impact of fundamentalist movements on their respective societies is greatly influenced not just by ontological premises and the premises of social order that are prevalent in these societies, but by the interrelation between these premises; the construction of collective identities; the strength of the structure of political institutions; the autonomy of the major elites; the structure, autonomy, cohesiveness, and accessibility of the center – and the mutual openings and trust between these different elites and broader social strata in the structuring of the center of the respective societies or civilizations. The importance of these conditions could be identified already in earlier historical periods with respect to the conditions conducive to these movements' development, and in the impacts of proto-fundamentalist movements in these various societies, as briefly alluded to in chapter 1.

Many of the "historical" Muslim societies in the Middle East and beyond in Western and Central Asia, were characterized by the prevalence within them of patrimonial regimes, or as in the case of the Ottoman Empire, of imperial regimes with very strong patrimonial tendencies. These regimes shared with the patrimonial regimes which developed in such non-Axial Civilizations as Mesoamerica, and the Ancient Near East of (Hinduized) South Asia, strong tendencies to the development of rather pluralistic institutional arrangements, especially in the form of segregated – regional, ethnic, and religious – sectors; a relatively weak permeation of the center into the periphery and impingement of the periphery on the center; as well as the prevalence, especially in these sectors, of multiple patterns or bases of legitimation.[61]

There exists, however, a rather important difference between the patrimonial-like systems which developed in the framework of the Axial Civilizations, like in Christianity and above all in the realm of Muslim civilization, and those which developed in the realms of non-Axial Civilization, especially in South and Southeast Asia. In the latter cases, the basic structure and orientations of the hegemonic elites, especially the weakness or nonexistence of autonomous cultural or intellectual elites and the embedment of most elites in the broader ascriptive settings, did not facilitate the development of religious movements oriented to the reconstruction of the political arena. The story was different in those societies, like the many Muslim societies, or parts of Christianity (in the Russian Empire, or in a different vein in Ethiopia) in which the development of patrimonial regimes was due more to historical contingency or to political-ecological conditions. In these societies the existence of strong, even if for a long period only latent, orientations to the reconstruction of the political arena was manifest in such movements as the proto-fundamentalist ones in Islam, or revolutionary ones as in Russia or China.

This does not mean that any of these civilizations (or religions), especially that of Islam, as has been often claimed in the controversies around the interpretation of contemporary fundamentalist movements, is inherently fundamentalist. What it does mean, however, is that given appropriate historical conditions which lead, under the combined impact of intercivilizational processes to which we have referred above, to the weakening of the more patrimonial or neo-patrimonial regimes, the chances of development of proto-fundamentalist, and in modern times, of fundamentalist movements, and their attaining an important place in the center-stage of the political arena are very great. This is to some extent at least in contrast to those patrimonial regimes in which these pluralistic-semi-patrimonial characteristics persisted even if in continually changing forms, as was the case to some extent in the modern regimes which developed in the framework of "other-worldly" civilizations as we shall see in greater detail later on – India being one of the most interesting cases.

XXXVI

The importance of these conditions – i.e., of the interweaving between different components of collective identity, of pluralistic institutional frameworks, and cohesiveness of centers – can be identified even more clearly and forcefully with respect to the development of modern fundamentalist and religious-communal movements with their distinct modern characteristics, and above all with respect to their impact on their respective societies. It is indeed the modern characteristics of these movements rooted in their close relation to the political program of modernity and its institutional implications, that intensified the importance of these conditions on the development of these movements, as well as their own impact on these respective societies.

In the various contemporary Muslim, South, and Southeast Asian societies referred to above, it was the weakening under the impact of the more global conditions and pluralistic features analyzed above, as well as the growing rigidity of the centers and the weakening of the solidary relations between the center and the various elites and broader social strata, that has provided a fertile ground for the development of fundamentalist or of South Asian communal-national religious movements. It is the combination of these factors that greatly influenced the scope and intensity of both the feeling of dispossession of many sectors from the respective centers of their societies, and of perception of threat to their respective civilizations. Given the nature of the premises and processes of the modern political order, and the potentially inherent politicization of all social movements, there developed in all these societies the possibility of a continual feedback between these movements and the continual weakening of the pluralistic institutional arrangements.

Under such conditions the impact of these movements on their respective societies may be reinforced by several factors. First, they may be reinforced by the very weak tradition in many of these civilizations and societies of access to the political center and of weakness of the conceptions of citizenship and autonomous civil society, paradoxically those very conditions which have in earlier periods minimized within them the potentialities of development of revolutionary movements.

Second, the development of fundamentalist or communal-religious tendencies among groups of intellectuals and political activists with strong totalistic orientations were often reinforced in many non-Western societies by the prevalence within them of the *ex-toto* conceptions of social order; the suspicion of autonomous individuals and civil society; the grave concerns over the eroding possibilities in the public order of discrete private and group interests; and by a very strong suspicion of the legitimacy of discrete private and group interests, and of "normal" politics. Such concerns constituted, in a sense, a mirror image of similar concerns among centers of constitutional democracies in the West – they were closely connected with suspicion of representative institutions and of legitimacy rooted in observance of the rules of the game. However, unlike the constitutional democracies in the West, in many of the Asian and African societies, these concerns were not set within the context of a strong tradition of citizenship, civil society, and of representative institutions.

XXXVII

A brief comparative look at the historical experience of modern Europe as it bears on our problems might be of interest here.[62] Extreme fundamentalist movements did not develop to any great extent in most Western European countries and whenever movements with such tendencies did develop – for instance in Scandinavian countries and in some Calvinist enclaves, especially in the Netherlands – they never attained the importance that they did in either the United States or Muslim societies. The study of such movements is not very developed, and the reasons for these movements' relatively weak development in European countries and the variations in their development have not been systematically investigated. Following, however, the preceding analysis, I would like to suggest that one possible starting point for the explanation of the relative weakness of such movements – beyond their being hemmed in, in Catholic countries, by the centuries old regulative institutions of the Church – are some of the historical characteristics of the construction of collective identities in Europe.

One of the most important characteristics of the construction of collective identities in European historical, and especially modern experience, has been the continual interweaving of primordial, civil, and universalistic components. It was such continual interweaving that has minimized the chances of development of religious fundamentalist movements in most European countries, and of those movements which did develop, to penetrate the center stage of the political arena. But as we have seen already in chapter 2, many extreme "left" and "right" Jacobin nationalist movements – and regimes – did develop in Europe, and it might be worthwhile to have a brief look at the relations between the development of these movements and the different models of construction of collective identities in different European nations.

The central aspect of the construction of collective boundaries and identities, which influenced the strength or weakness of the tendencies to the development of such extreme Jacobin exclusivist movements and regimes in Europe was the way in which modern universalistic or civic components of collective identity were combined not only with the older religious ones, but also with newly reconstructed – in a modern way – primordial ones. In all modern European societies the primordial components of such identity, continuously reconstructed in such modern terms as nationalism and ethnicity, were confronted by the modern universalistic and by civil components. The mode of interweaving these different components of collective identity greatly shaped the scope of pluralism that developed in them.

It was in those societies in which the primordial components were subsumed relatively successfully under the civil and universalistic ones and all were "peacefully" interwoven in the construction of their respective collective identities, that a relatively wide scope of pluralistic arrangements were allowed.

It was the contrary tendencies to the absolutization of the major dimensions of human experience and social order and concomitant principled exclusivity that provided a propitious background for the development of various extreme movements with strong Jacobin tendencies – the leftist revolutionary, the extreme nationalistic, as well as the extreme religious ones – among some of which there existed potentialities for fundamentalist movements in various European Protestant countries such as the Scandinavian countries, the Netherlands, or Switzerland. But as in England, Holland, Switzerland and in the Scandinavian countries, the crystallization of collective identity was characterized by the close interweaving of the primordial and religious components with the civil and universalistic ones, without the former being denied, allowing a relatively wide scope for pluralistic arrangements, the impact of the potentially fundamentalist movements was relatively weak. In Catholic countries it was the Catholic Church with its "traditional" techniques of hegemony which was crucial in hemming in the impact of potentially fundamentalist tendencies in the central political arena.

In those societies or sectors within which there developed strong tensions between the primordial and the civil universalistic components in the construction of the collective identities of the modern nation-state (as was the case in Central Europe, above all in Germany and in many social movements in Western Europe) there developed a stronger tendency to crises and breakdowns of different types of pluralistic arrangements. The tension between the primordial, civil, and universalistic components in the construction of their collective identity gave rise in these societies and movements to strong emphasis on the centrality of the primordial components in construction of the modern collective consciousness, very often combined with extreme absolutist Jacobin tendencies.[63]

XXXVIII

The importance of yet another dimension of the construction of collective identity and institutional formations in influencing the impact of fundamentalist movements is their development and impact in countries, like Korea or Latin American ones, in which basic religious or civilizational premises differed from those of the fundamentalist movements – i.e., in these societies such movements did not constitute *internal* heterodoxies confronting the predominant orthodoxies. In both these cases, the potential Jacobin tendencies of such movements were mostly confined to the reconstruction of the internal life of these communities rather than towards either the creation of wider spaces for their communities, or the reconstruction of the overall political and social order.

As we have seen, in many of the Latin American countries there developed a far-reaching overlap in the concrete religious practices and orientations between the developments in the Protestant and the Catholic sectors, and very often the boundaries between the two were blurred. Yet on the whole the Protestant sectors, especially the evangelical and Pentacostal, tended to be basically in a minority position, and to develop stronger collective identity and boundaries. Some of the differences between these Catholic and Protestant groups were closely connected to the different patterns of dislocation of the people which were attracted to these groups.[64]

The most important such difference was that, given the fact that these societies were predominantly Catholic, not only was it the Catholic groups which were by far the most widespread, but it was above all different sectors within the Catholic elites which were the carriers of many of the Catholic movements such as Liberation Theology. The leaders of various Protestant groups did not on the whole come from such centers, and accordingly, the whole manner of their involvement in the broader political arenas and impact on them developed in rather distinct ways. They were often dubbed or designated as a-political. Insofar as such designation entails the development of strong tendencies toward the reconstruction of the central premises of the political arena, it was on the whole correct. The weakness of such tendencies was also to no small extent reinforced by the more conservative forces with which these groups tended to ally themselves. But at the same time their designation as apolitical seems to be misleading insofar as it implies that they had no impact on the broader political arena or culture of their societies. Not only did they introduce an element of heterogeneity and religious pluralism, and hence of political dissent – which was hitherto very weak in these societies. Of even greater importance is the closely related fact that in their own spaces and confines they introduced – as did, but possibly to a lesser extent, the Catholic popular groups – a very strong egalitarian and participatory element – including, as we have seen, a growing participation of women and weakening of the patriarchal-machoist components of the political culture.[65]

Collective identity, institutional formations, and the development and impact of fundamentalist and communal-religious movements: the historical and contemporary experience of India

XXXIX

The importance of these conditions – i.e. of the interrelations of ontological visions, the construction of collective identities, and the patterns of legitimization of political regimes – to both the development of communal-religious and fundamentalist movements, as well as these movements' impacts on their respective societies can be greatly illuminated by an analysis of modern Indian historical experience, and paradoxically through its comparison with the American experience.

The most important starting point for such an analysis is the rather surprising persistence of a constitutional democratic regime in India since independence – together with Israel, and partially Sri Lanka, as the only such "post-colonial" post-Second World War regimes. The fact that India has remained a democratic constitutional regime since independence in 1947 has confounded many prophets of doom who had predicted the demise not only of the constitutional regime in India, but also of the Union of India as such. To give only one illustration, in *India, The Dangerous Decades*, a very incisive and influential book published in 1960, Selig Harrison made two predictions.[66] One was that the level of conflicts – inter-caste, inter-regional, or inter-linguistic would increase in India, and the other was that because of the intensification of conflicts, the Union of India would be put in great jeopardy. The interesting fact is that while the first prediction did come true, the second did not, at least not until now. Moreover, the Union of India continued despite numerous turbulences to be a constitutional democracy – the largest such democracy in the world.

Several reasons seem to be of special importance for explaining this rather astounding fact. The most important such reason for this rather surprising fact is the highly accommodative stance of the center to the potentially conflictual demands by numerous social groups and movements – indeed demands rooted in many of the conflicts observed and predicted by Selig Harrison and many other scholars[67] – be they economic demands, especially of peasants and industrial workers; economic conflicts focused on demands on affirmative action, especially with respect to positions in civil service for unscheduled or lower castes; and demands for cultural or linguistic autonomy and recognition for the numerous regional and linguistic groups. This accommodative stance was to some extent suspended during Indira Gandhi's Prime Ministership in 1966–1977 and 1980–1984 – to be returned to after her assassination.

This relatively high level of accommodation of the center was based on a very pragmatic attitude, with relatively weak ideological components. This attitude was to some extent contrary to the experience of many European states, whether in the Austro-Hungarian and Russian Empires, or needless to say to the experiences in Eastern Europe in more recent times. This pragmatic accommodative attitude entailed relatively widespread acceptance – among the elites and the broader sectors of society – of the legitimacy of the demands of various groups for participation in the political arena, and the concomitant acceptance of the central political institutions and their legitimation by many such sectors of the society. It was indeed the continual development of this accommodative stance, that lies at the heart of India's hitherto continuity as a constitutional state.

The roots of the development of this pragmatic attitude in India can be found in some very important aspects of the pre-colonial Indian historical experience, aspects that were further reinforced by several elements of India's colonial experience under the British and its struggle for independence. The most important aspects of this historical experience have been the conceptions, definitions, construction, and legitimization of political arena, and the relations of this to other institutional arenas.

The basic legitimization of this arena developed in two interwoven directions – one rooted in the conception of dharma, or the duty of subjects to rulers, as well as the duties of rulers to listen to the demands or problems of subjects; and second, the pragmatic judgment of the performance of rulers.

Different sectors' places in the social order were in principle prescribed by their ritual standing in the purity-auspiciousness schemes, but at the same time the relative autonomy and continual reconstruction of the various community and caste frameworks enabled the development of continual political dynamics, and the acceptance by the rulers of the legitimacy of the claims of different groups.

At the same time the interrelations between the political and other arenas were characterized by the *relative* autonomy of the major social groups and elites, the complex of castes and villages, and the networks of cultural, economic, and political communication, which were characterized by a high degree of autonomy – but an autonomy embedded in ascriptive, albeit wide and continuously reconstructed, frameworks.

The nature of this autonomy has been captured by R. Inden, who defines the various local and caste groups as both subjects and citizens who, although taxed and controlled by the kings were also allowed a high degree of self-regulation: they "had an inherent, but limited and partial capacity (we might call it rights) to combine within and among themselves and order their own affairs."[68]

Given these characteristics of the relations between the political and other arenas in India, there developed no basic ideological confrontation between state and society – until recent times, under the impact of European rule – and no wars of religion.

These conceptions of the political arena have had far-reaching repercussions on the political dynamics that developed in India, two of which are of special interest in a comparative framework. The first is that in India – despite its "empires" – there never developed a conception of statehood as a distinct, absolutist, ontological entity. Secondly, there were – until modern times – no wars of religion.

Political imagery nonetheless played a very important role in the construction of the Indian collective consciousness – especially in encounters with other, above all Islamic, civilizations. Such encounters, as Sheldon Pollock has shown, have, for instance, intensified the importance of the cult of Rama in large parts of India since about the twelfth century, and that of the political components in the self-definition of both the Indians and the new "others." Significantly, however, even the intensification of this political component did not give rise to attempts to impose one Axial vision (Hinduism) on the other (Islam) – that is, to confront the other civilizations with the universalistic exclusiveness of one's own.[69]

XL

The development of the modern Indian polity – which started under the British and fully crystallized with the establishment of the Union of India after the independence in 1947 – in tandem with partition and the creation of Pakistan has, of course, given rise to a uniform political framework in which the possibility of confrontation between different groups became much greater than before. This development created the potentiality of the numerous conflicts and confrontational stances predicted by the various scholars and observers.

It has, however, been the unique characteristic of the development of India – in contrast with most other post-colonial countries – that it was hitherto able to minimize the disruptive effects of such confrontations on the political order and to keep them within the respective constitutional-colonial and post-colonial frameworks – that of the Union of India.

This ability was connected with the fact that with the establishment of the Union of India, the distinct characteristics of the relations between the political and other institutional arenas were not radically different from those that were prevalent in the previous periods, even though, given the basic democratic and constitutional premises of the system, they changed considerably. The basic conceptions of rulership did not necessarily change but became more and more reformulated in modern semi-welfare terms.[70] The relative non-ideological, highly pragmatic approach to the political arena reinforced the acceptance of the legitimacy of the claims of various sectors of the society. Such claims became transformed into legitimate political demands based on more autonomous and "open" bases – providing a very strong push for democratic participation in the political process.

The major reason for the fact that the numerous confrontational possibilities that developed in India did not give rise to continual breakdowns of the modern Indian political system, was that building on the earlier historical experience as well as on the colonial one, the constitutional democratic system that developed in India was characterized, as Arend Lijphart has shown in his incisive analysis, by several consociational-like features based on power-sharing principles. The most important such features were: (1) grand coalition governments that include representatives of all major linguistic and religious groups, (2) cultural autonomy for these groups, (3) proportionality in political representation and civil service appointments, and (4) a minority veto with regard to vital minority rights and autonomy.[71]

Second was the prevalence of the seemingly secular civil legitimization of the Indian state promulgated by Gandhi, Nehru, and the Congress Party.[72] In this conception the Hindu component of the new collective identity was defined not so much in primordial communal terms but rather as a sort of general "humanistic" secular dimension of the Indian constitutional order, of the secular Indian state. India was conceived as a territory – not as sacred ground. While the more communal-religious components of Hindu collective identity were continually promulgated by many groups and movements, such as the Vishna Shindu, their conceptions were for a long period bracketed out – even if not totally denied – of the central political arena, the official construction of the Indian collective consciousness, and above all, of the legitimation of the Indian state as they were promulgated by the Congress.[73]

XLI

It is the combination of all these factors – above all of the continual accommodational, power-sharing tendencies, the relatively weak sanctification of the political sphere rooted in the "other-worldly" components of the ontological conceptions prevalent in India, and the continual semi-secular pattern of legitimation of the state – that explains the relatively secondary place of communal religions and the weakness of fundamentalist movements in India in the first phases of independence. It is above all the combination of two factors that provided for the development of the intensive communal national movements epitomized by the BJP Party: first, the weakening and erosion of the institutional arrangements of this political system, as for instance of the political parties – a process which became intensified during and after Indira Gandhi's regime – and resulted to no small extent from the paradoxical results of these accommodative policies; and second, the connection between growing economic expansion and the continual discrepancy and tensions between different sectors of the population, tensions exacerbated by the various "affirmative action policies" undertaken as part of numerous accommodative policies.[74]

It was in this situation that there developed processes of dislocation which, as suggested in the quotations from D. R. Spitz above,[75] were in principle very similar to those connected with the rise of the fundamentalist movements with strong Jacobin tendencies that developed within many of the Muslim societies and, in a different way, in the United States, as indicated by T. B. Edsall. Moreover, the rise of such movements was connected – in perhaps surprisingly parallel ways to that of the fundamentalist movements in the United States – with changes in the relations between the components of modern collective identity, especially between the "secular" and different communal components of their respective collective identities, generating also a weakening of the legitimation of the Indian state in terms of a secular vision, as originally promulgated by Gandhi and Nehru – and further, touched on the central aspects of both of these constitutional regimes.

It was all of these developments that provided the background to continual development in India of communal-religious movements from the seventies on. All these developments did indeed give rise to a very great increase in the promulgation of communal-religious Hindu identity; to growing intra-communal violence above all against the Muslims of India, epitomized in both the burning of the Ayodhya Mosque in 1990 and the communal riots in Agra City in 1992; to a very strong contestation about the construction of national identity; and to a very marked shift in the bases of legitimation of the Indian political system.[76] Significantly enough, however, these developments did not give rise in India to pristine fundamentalist movements, but to – often virulent and violent – communal-religious national ones. Most of them harbor, as we have indicated already above, very strong particularistic visions of exclusion, but only very few develop into a fully totalistic-Jacobin direction. Also, they have only very weak – if any – conceptions of reconstruction of the social order according to any social vision rooted in an ontological conception. The orientations of these movements which developed in India among the Hindu population are, as we have already seen above, particularistic, primordial, and not universalistic.

The fundamentalist and communal-religious challenge to modern pluralistic regimes

XLII

Whatever the outcome of all these processes – whether communal-national or fundamentalist-Jacobin – they all attest to the growing importance of the religious component in the reconstitution of the collective identities in many contemporary societies. These movements have put the problem of the place of these components (in their great variety), and the relations between them and to other such components – such as the civil and various pluralistic ones – in the very center of the agendas of their respective societies.

In the United States these problems were put on the central agenda by the many fundamentalist movements which burgeoned in the last two decades. The fact that these movements continually acted within the constitutional framework of the USA does not mean that they were not influential. Not only have they carved out wide spaces for themselves, they have also infused many of their demands and issues in the political arena and discourse. But at the same time, the fact that they have been continually playing in this constitutional ground has also greatly influenced their structures and orientations, especially by discouraging or dampening the Jacobin tendencies of many – if not of all, especially of the more extremist groups among them – and by making many of them proclaim more open universalistic religious and political orientations. Truly enough, a close reading of many of the texts promulgating such openness does indicate that the totalistic, potentially Jacobin tendencies have not entirely disappeared. They were rather put in some brackets, and while some of them have become continually diluted, others seem to be continually, as it were, simmering.

In contemporary Europe this problem was lately put on the central agenda, above all by different immigrant communities – especially those coming from non Christian-Muslim or Indian communities. In Israel, Turkey, and in almost all the Muslim societies this problem was continually articulated by the fundamentalist revivalist movements which have continually developed in all these societies. It was only in two Muslim societies/states and in Iran and Sudan that fundamentalist regimes were established, but they constituted a central component in the political process of the societies.

In several African countries – in Sudan, Kenya and Uganda in East Africa and in Mali, Guinea or Ivory Coast, and Senegal in West Africa – the more radical Islamist movements have been continual components of the more general tendencies of expansion of Islam, and have had to confront and cooperate with not only the initial post-colonial "secular" regimes, but also with many of the other Islamic movements in the processes of the construction of their respective states and societies.[77]

In all these societies the fundamentalist movements have been continuously interwoven with other movements – among them the often called "reformist" movements that have attempted to reinterpret their respective traditions, be they Protestant, Muslim, or Jewish – in the contemporary scene. Such movements have been continuously interwoven not only with one another, but also with existing secular regimes with which they are in continuous contact, and among them there have developed continual processes of mutual accommodation and confrontation alike. The concrete contours of these processes and patterns of accommodation vary greatly between different societies, different periods in the history of each, and according to the specific constellation of the various forces analyzed above.

With the exception of the United States and lately of Europe – most of these movements developed in those states which were established, like Kemalist Turkey, after the First World War, or in colonial-imperial states, which were constituted by the various national movements that developed after the Second World War.

In some of these regimes – India, Israel and basically also in Turkey – these movements acted within the framework of the continual constitutional democratic regimes. In many of the other states these movements developed and acted in the frameworks of modernizing, secular, semi-constitutional, usually autocratic regimes. In all these states, but especially in the latter, there developed a continual, paradoxical relation between these movements and processes of democratization in their respective societies, a relation which in many cases highlighted one of the most important challenges to these regimes.

The Khomeini revolution in Iran and to a small extent the establishment of the fundamentalist regime in Sudan, have also been connected with growing demands for the opening up of autocratic regimes. Similarly in Pakistan the Jama'at Islam was often involved in struggles against the autocratic regimes. Indeed, it was the secular, modernizing, autocratic regimes that constituted the butt of the fundamentalist movements. In Algeria there developed a continual confrontation and contestation between the "secular"-military regime and the Islamic fundamentalist movements which may well lead to the breakdown of the Algerian state.[78] The contestation in Algeria has brought out the paradoxical relation between democratization and "Islamization." The fundamentalist movements in Algeria rose to prominence as a result of democratic elections – giving rise to the paradoxical discussion whether to support the suppression of elections in order to turn the tide of Islamization which would, according to this view, abolish the constitutional state.[79]

Most of these regimes employed a great variety of combinations of repressive and accommodative measures towards these – as well as against other opposition – movements.[80] In at least some of these societies it was the extent of such accommodation and openness that was very important in hemming in, as it were, the more extreme fundamentalist tendencies. As S. V. R. Nasr has put it, even if in possibly somewhat exaggerated ways, with respect to Pakistan and Jordan:

It has capitalized on popular political discontent to take the political process unawares. Protracted involvement with the political process, as has been the case with the Jama'at in Pakistan, will elicit concessions from the ruling order in terms of new laws or distribution of political and economic power – Islamization. But it will also create barriers to further progress of revivalism and immunize the political process to its ultimate challenge. It will compel revivalism to turn to pragmatic politics in lieu of ideological posturing, will encourage other political forces to respond to the revivalist threat, and also will provide them with sufficient time to do so. Similarly, it enables the state to formulate policies that would accommodate dissent at the expense of revivalism. The Jama'at's meager parliamentary representation over two decades . . . bears ample testimony to this fact. Similarly, the Jama'at experience echoes that of Jordan's Muslim Brotherhood. In the November 1993 elections in that country, the second one in which the Brotherhood has participated openly, the party lost seats to other political forces.

This is an important point to bear in mind. Revivalists have by and large responded positively to the burgeoning democratization process in many parts of the Muslim world, from Algeria to Jordan, Lebanon, Malaysia, Bangladesh, and Pakistan, and they have abandoned their anti-state platforms of earlier times and become involved with the political process. They are an important element in the civil society that will serve as the pillar of democracy. However, the reaction to this development in the ruling regimes in the Muslim world and among Western policymakers and academicians has not been positive.

Democracy engenders exactly the kind of protracted involvement with the political process, which was the case of the Jama'at which became enfranchised in the early 1950s. It joined the political process in Pakistan and since then has participated in that process during its democratic periods (1951–1958, 1971–1977, and 1988 to the present) as well as authoritarian ones (1958–1971 and 1977–1988). By abandoning its anti-state posture and endorsing the state and the political process, the Jama'at became subject to the influence of those political forces that govern the ebb and flow of the political process. Its revolutionary image faded, and it became bogged down in debates, policy decisions, compromises, and political maneuvering that have stymied its progress and constricted its maneuverability. This has been particularly true during the country's democratic periods, when open political debate has forced the Jama'at to elaborate on its ideology and conversely has provided other political forces with the opportunity to immunize themselves to its challenge. During the democratic periods, moreover, the Jama'at has been forced to divert its attention from opposition to the government to competition with an array of other political forces, with the effect of diffusing its political energies. In the long run, this has been the single most important cause of the Jama'at's constructed political development . . .[81]

Rather similar tendencies can be identified in other Muslim societies like Malaysia. In yet other societies, like Egypt or Tunisia, much more repressive measures have been continually undertaken by the regimes – especially against the extreme, radical, and terrorist group – but these regimes have also been obliged to deflect wider support of the fundamentalist movements by promulgating stronger "Islamic" religious or economic policies.[82] At the same time, in all these regimes the challenges of the fundamentalist movements, especially but not only of the more extreme terrorist groups among them, have continually tested the limits of pluralistic toleration and openness that may develop within them.

XLIII

The paradoxical relations between processes of democratization, fundamentalist movements and the constitution and continuity of modern pluralistic political frameworks, are fully visible in those "new states" within which democratic frameworks were continually maintained.

Indeed, yet another look at the situation in India is of great interest. The most recent – 1996 – elections, which can in many ways be seen as a watershed in the development of Indian constitutional democracy, point to some aspects of the impact and intensity of communal-religious orientations on the broader institutional frameworks, especially, in this case, on the continuity of the Indian democratic constitutional system. In these elections the Congress party lost its dominant position and it was the BJP, the Indian nationalist party that became the largest, and thus the first party to be asked by the President to form the government. Its leader, Atal Behari Vejpayee, became Prime Minister and sought the Parliament's vote of confidence for his government. When he could not get it – in face of the opposition of various "secular" parties which were afraid of the BJP's attitude toward the Muslim party – the task was given to H. D. Deve Gonder, the leader of the Centered Front, a coalition of disparate regional and low caste parties.[83]

What was then the impact of the last election on the future of Indian democracy? There arises the problem of whether these changes denote the breakdown of political institutions in India, or their transformability in a more decentralized direction, or the continuation of power sharing and its adaptation to new circumstances. Indeed the very high participation in the elections (about 65 percent of the electorate), the relatively few accusations of corruption, and the low level of violence seem to attest to the vitality not only of democratic political participation, but also to some of the constructive dimensions of the public sphere in India.

A rather similar contradictory or open picture emerges with respect to the shift in the bases of legitimation of the political regime. There took place an important shift in a "nationalistic" direction. V. S. Naipaul's comments in the *New York Herald Tribune* of May 6, 1990 are very appropriate here:

A Strong Hindu Response to Historical Humiliation. India was trampled over, fought over. You had the invasions and you had the absence of a response to them. There was an absence even of the idea of a people, of a nation defending itself. Only now are people beginning to understand that there has been a great vandalizing of India.

In pre-industrial India, people moved about in small areas, unaware of the dimension of the country, without any notion of nation. People seemed to say: We are all right here. The rest of the world may be disastrous, but we are not affected. Now, however, things seem to be changing. What is happening in India is a mighty, creative process. Indian intellectuals, who want to be secure in their liberal beliefs, may not understand what is going on.

But every other Indian knows precisely what is happening: Deep down he knows that a larger response is emerging to their historical humiliation.

The new Hindu attitude, the new sense of history being attained by Hindus, is not like Mohammedan fundamentalism, which is essentially a negative, last-ditch effort to fight against a world it desperately wishes to join.

The movement is now from below. It has to be dealt with. It is not enough to abuse these youths or use that fashionable word from Europe, "fascism."

There is a big, historical development going on in India. Wise men should understand it and ensure that it does not remain in the hands of fanatics.[84]

It is not clear whether this shift denotes a break with the existing framework of legitimation or a shift of components within it. Indeed, the leader of BJP, who has become for a short while Prime Minister, and who has been known as a relative moderate, stressed in one of his speeches after the election a strong commitment to the constitutional arrangements and observing the rights of minorities. While seemingly indicating a trend toward the domestication, as it were, of these extreme nationalistic tendencies, however, he also announced that he would adhere to the parties' religious policies.

The problem here, as in many other democracies, is the prevalence and continual transformation of some consensual orientations – of some common texts – made beyond the rules of the game, but which legitimize the actual rules, and without which the actual rules of the game may not be always upheld. Such orientations did exist and were relatively effective in the historical experience of India, in the legitimization of the political arena in terms of the basic conception of the dharma, or under Nehru and the Congress rule when a mild secular conception of Indian polity legitimated the coexistence of different cultural groups. Nevertheless, the maintenance of such common text became somewhat harder with the continual weakening of both the political institution and the constitutional-democracy in India. It is too early to judge the outcome with respect to all these problems of democracy in India but they have been highlighted by the 1996 elections, and they will become even more visible in the 1998 elections which were called after the disintegration of the various governments based on different "secular" coalitions.

XLIV

A picture which is much more complex but in principle rather similar emerges in Israel. While, as we have seen, various fundamentalist movements gained strength from the seventies on and while within many of them there developed attempts of the legitimation of the state – the culmination of which was the assassination of Prime Minister Rabin in November 1995 by a man close to these groups and promulgating their ideologies. Yet on the whole these movements except for some extreme groups remained within the constitutional framework. Significantly enough at the same time there took place a continual incorporation of religious symbols and themes into the repertoire of central symbols of the society. Such incorporation did not always abate, indeed in some ways, it intensified the demands made by these movements.

A very complicated situation developed in this respect in Turkey. Turkey has been the only Muslim society in which a secular revolution, establishing a secular state with very strong militant homogeneous tendencies, was established by the Kemalist revolution, disestablishing Islamic institutions and attempting to take out Islam from the public sphere and discourse. The continual upsurge of Islamicist tendencies and movements that took place in Turkey from the seventies on, gathering momentum from the eighties on, which was due in general to the social processes of globalization, dislocation and change analyzed above, seemed to threaten the secular foundations of the Turkish Kemalist republic. The success of the Islamist party in the elections leading to the formation in 1996 of a coalition government under the premiership of the leader of the Islamist party increased the feeling of this threat by various secular sectors of the population and by the army which has always looked on itself as the guardian of the Kemalist heritage – ultimately, in the summer of 1997, this coalition was brought down and replaced by a government based on a secularist coalition. At the same time, charges were made against the Islamist party as being opposed to the basic premises of the Turkish republic, and demands to outlaw it were brought before the Turkish institutional court, which has indeed outlawed it, on these grounds, in January 1998. Whatever the concrete outcome of these confrontations, they highlight the problems and tensions – and possible confrontations – that can develop between the secular premises, the constitutional democratic system and processes, and the development in these societies of – in close relation to these processes – the processes of democratization which constitute an important background of the fundamentalist movements.

In all these societies, these movements sought to construct open spaces for themselves, to gain more open access to public spaces, sometimes to demand the incorporation of many of their religious symbols and themes into the repertoire of collective identity in their respective states, and to promulgate some specifically "religious" policies – such as the policies of "Islamic economics," which constituted, as Timur Kuran has shown, the basic promulgation of the collective Muslim identity.[85]

The outcomes of such policies point to the dilemmas and problems of the relations between these movements and the continuity of pluralistic constitutional regimes. On the one hand, such policies of these movements could to some extent assure their remaining within the basic constitutional framework. But such incorporation also pointed to the possibility that the totalistic dimensions of these movements could take over the constitutional regimes,[86] undermining their basic premises and institutional frameworks.

The other side of the confrontation between the pluralistic and totalistic programs of modernity is the problem – which was indeed central with respect to the Soviet regimes, and continues to be so with respect to the Chinese one – of the extent to which such regimes are able to incorporate within the framework of the premises of their own cultural and institutional programs of modernity, the more pluralistic tendencies inherent in modernity. One of the interesting problems in this context is the conditions under which the potentially "secularizing" tendencies of the more professional groups active within the fundamentalist movements, such as engineers, will counteract, as Nulifer Göle suggests, the totalistic tendencies of these movements.[87] It seems a plausible hypothesis that such potentialities are greater when movements do not succeed in becoming the predominant rulers of their countries, than in situations in which they do, as in Iran. From this point of view, it would be of great interest to watch closely the recent developments in Iran, after the election and inauguration of President Khatami – as well as the developments in the various African – as well as Central Asian – countries referred to above.

Whatever the outcome of all these processes, they all attest to the growing importance on the contemporary world scene of the religious – whether fundamentalist-Jacobin or communal-national – component as promulgated by different fundamentalist or communal-religious movements or regimes, in the reconstitution of the collective identities in contemporary states.

XLV

These movements developed, as we have seen, in new historical settings or phases of the expansion of modernity and with the structural transformations attendant on it, and crystallized out of the combination of the changes in the historical context of the encounters and confrontations between the Western and non-Western civilizations, of the changes in the global economic and political systems and the processes of dislocation related to these processes analyzed above.

The concrete development of these movements – especially whether they develop as communal-national or fundamentalist ones – depends on the combination of several factors which were also crucial in the crystallization of proto-fundamentalist movements. As with respect to these earlier movements, their intensity and impact greatly depend on the combination of the ontological visions and conception of social order that have been prevalent in the respective societies or civilizations and on the relative importance of their respective carriers, the autonomous religious elite as against the carriers of communal solidarity. The relative strength of the impact of these movements has been above all influenced by the processes of construction of collective identities, the strength and flexibility of the central institutions of these societies and factors which enhance or weaken the strength of the respective regimes, especially concerning their components of civility and pluralism. But given the inherent modern characteristics of the fundamentalist movements and the fact that they constitute an inherent component of the discourse and institutional developments of modernity, their impact on the dynamics of modern regimes has been much greater than that of the proto-fundamentalist movements or their respective regimes – with the possible exceptions of those which were at the background of the Great Revolutions.

XLVI

We may now bring together the major lines of our analysis of the modern fundamentalist movements. The fundamentalist and the communal-nationalist movements signaled a new phase or shift in the development of the discourse and institutional dynamics of modernity as it expanded and became continually transformed throughout the world. They promulgated – just as did the various liberal constitutional and social democratic regimes, and the Communist and various nationalist fascist movements in the period between the two world wars – distinct programs of modernity and different visions both of modern life and of modern social and political order.

These movements articulated, as did the various major social movements which developed in earlier stages of modernity, some of the antimonies and tensions inherent in the cultural and political program of modernity and of its institutionalization in different historical settings and contexts. All these movements emphasized different problems and contradictions between the premises of the cultural and political program of modernity and between these premises and the process of institutionalization in different historical settings that developed in conjunction with the expansion of modernity. Within all these movements the major tensions inherent in the cultural and political program of modernity – especially those between the collectively Jacobin or "communal" and the pluralistic components thereof, between different conceptions of the relations between the general will and the will of all, between control and freedom or autonomy – were continually articulated.

The distinctive characteristics of these fundamentalist movements, and to a smaller extent of the communal-national ones, were, as we have indicated above, the promulgation of a radically negative attitude to some of the central Enlightenment components of the cultural and political program of modernity especially, to the emphasis on the autonomy and sovereignty of reason and of the individual. These movements promulgated a totalistic ideological denial of these "Enlightenment" premises, and adopted a basically confrontational attitude not only to Western hegemony but to the West as such conceived in totalistic and essentialist ways. In these movements, the confrontation with the West did not take the form of a search to become incorporated into the new hegemonic civilization on its own terms but rather of a totalistic ideological denial of the "Enlightenment" premises of this civilization and of attempts to appropriate the new international global scene for themselves, for their traditions or civilizations – even though the ways in which these traditions were promulgated by them were indeed reconstructed under the impact of their continual encounter with the West.

The upsurge of the fundamentalist movements and regimes constituted a new phase in the continual confrontations in the development of modernity between different types of pluralistic and Jacobin regimes – both of which constitute an inherent component of modernity.

Just as the situation in the thirties with respect to fascist and communist regimes, there developed in all the societies in which these movements crystallized rather paradoxical relations, between processes of democratization and the challenges of the totalistic movements to the existing pluralistic or constitutional regimes. Just as in the twenties and thirties of this century, the growing democratization and political activization of broader sectors created the challenges of their incorporation in the constitutional or semi-constitutional pluralistic frameworks – challenges which bore within themselves the possibilities both of their transformability as well as of their breakdown.

These movements constituted one of the major challenges to the institutionalization and continuity of modern constitutional pluralistic regimes – perhaps the most important challenge on the contemporary scene, beyond those attendant on the transitions to democracy from authoritarian regimes in Eastern Europe and Latin America and East Asia – challenges which are in a way parallel to the challenges of the extreme Jacobin or nationalist movements presented to the constitutional-democratic regimes in the thirties in Europe.

These challenges constitute – as did those of the fascist and communist movements in the thirties – a clear illustration of the continual problems of transformability of modern especially constitutional democratic societies and of the points of their vulnerability and potential breakdown. Indeed, it is here that some of the challenges and the points of vulnerability of modern constitutional – or even semi-constitutional – regimes become fully visible. The test of such transformability as opposed to the breakdown of these regimes is – as was the case with respect to the challenges of the extreme Jacobin or nationalist movements presented to the constitutional-democratic regimes in the thirties – whether incorporation of the religious-communal or fundamentalist symbols and promulgation of some "religious" ones will entail the subsumption of such symbols under the basic institutional premises of the regimes – as happened for instance in Scandinavian countries in the thirties with respect to fascist and extreme communist regimes alike, as against the possibilities of these regimes being taken over,[88] through far-reaching accommodation of the fundamentalist movements or disintegrating through the overall repercussions of these challenges. The possibility of such transformability is contingent on the capacity of the constitutional or semi-constitutional regimes to develop accommodative tendencies that may be able to hem in, mitigate, and transform – to some extent at least – either the pristine Jacobin orientations of the fundamentalists, or the more communal-national ones, and to weaken their appeal to wider strata, thus enabling the continual development of different types of pluralistic regimes or patterns.

But it is not in all contemporary societies that these movements occupy the center stage of the political arena; their role has been, as we have seen, much smaller in those societies like the major East Asian societies – China, Japan, Eastern European, or even in most Latin American countries, very much in line, as we have seen, with their historical premises and historical existence of these societies. In these societies the dynamics of modernity as they develop in the contemporary scene differ greatly from those in which the fundamentalist and national-communal movements and ideologies develop. But in all of them, these movements give rise not to "closed" civilizations but to a great variety of continually interacting modern civilizations in which even the inclusive tendencies are constructed in typically modern ways, and articulate continually, in different concrete ways in different historical settings, the antinomies and contradictions of modernity.

5

Some considerations on modernity

I

The preceding analysis of the Jacobin component in modern fundamentalist movements, and the place of these movements among other modern social movements and in the discourse of modernity, attests not only to the modern characteristics of these movements, but also sheds some light on some basic features of modernity, on modern cultural programs, and on modern civilization. This analysis attests to both the multiplicity of modern cultural programs and to their continuous dynamics. Indeed, as we are approaching the end of the twentieth century, new visions and understandings of modernity and of modern civilization are emerging throughout the world, be it in the West – Europe, the United States – where the first cultural program of modernity developed, or among Asian, Latin American, and African societies. All these developments demand a far-reaching reappraisal of the classical visions of modernity and modernization.[1]

Such a reappraisal should be based on several considerations. It should be based first of all on the recognition that the expansion of modernity has to be viewed as the crystallization of a new type of civilization – not unlike the expansion of Great Religions, or great Imperial expansions in past times. However, because the expansion of this civilization almost always and continually combined economic, political, and ideological aspects and forces to a much larger extent, its impact on the societies to which it spread was much more intense than in most historical cases.

This expansion indeed spawned a tendency – practically unique in the history of mankind – to the development of universal, worldwide institutional and symbolic frameworks and systems. This new civilization that emerged first in Europe later expanded through the world, creating a series of international frameworks or systems, each based on some of the basic premises of this civilization, and each rooted in one of its basic institutional dimensions. Several economic, political, ideological, almost worldwide systems – all of them multi-centered and heterogeneous – emerged, each generating its own dynamics, its continual change in constant relation to the others. The interrelations among them have never been "static" or unchanging, and the dynamics of these international frameworks or settings gave rise to continuous changes in these societies.

Just as the expansion of all historical civilizations, so also the civilization of modernity undermined the symbolic and institutional premises of the societies incorporated into it, opening up new options and possibilities. As a result of this, a great variety of modern and modernizing societies, sharing many common characteristics but also evincing great differences among themselves, developed out of these responses and continual interactions.

The first, "original" modernity as it developed in the West combined several closely interconnected dimensions or aspects: first, the structural, organizational one – the development of the many specific aspects of modern social structure, such as growing structural differentiation, urbanization, industrialization, growing communications and the like, which have been identified and analyzed in the first studies of modernization after the Second World War; second, the institutional one – the development of the new institutional formations, of the modern nation-state, of modern especially national collectivities, of new and above all capitalist-political economies; and last and not least, of a distinct cultural program and closely related specific modes of structuration of the major arenas of social life.

The "classical theories" of modernization of the 1950s, indeed the classical sociological analyses of Marx, Durkheim, and to a large extent even of Weber – or at least in one reading of him – have implicitly or explicitly conflated these different dimensions of modernity; these approaches assumed that even if these dimensions are analytically distinct, they do come historically together becoming basically inseparable. Moreover, most of the classics of sociology as well as the studies of modernization of the forties and fifties have assumed, even if only implicitly, that the basic institutional constellations which came together in European modernity, and the cultural program of modernity as it developed in the West, will "naturally" be ultimately taken over in all modernizing societies. The studies of modernization and of convergence of modern societies have indeed assumed that this project of modernity with its hegemonic and homogenizing tendencies will continue in the West, and with the expansion of modernity, prevail throughout the world. Implicit in all these approaches was the assumption that the modes of institutional integration attendant on the development of such relatively autonomous, differentiated institutional spheres, will be on the whole similar in all modern societies.

But the reality that emerged proved to be radically different. The actual developments indicated that in all or most societies the various institutional arenas – the economic, the political, and that of family – exhibit continually relatively autonomous dimensions that come together in different ways in different societies and in different periods of their development. Indeed, the developments in the contemporary era did not bear out this assumption of "convergence" and have emphasized the great diversity of modern societies, even of societies similar in terms of economic development, like the major industrial capitalist societies – the European ones, the USA, and Japan. Sombart's old question: "Why is there no socialism in the US?" formulated in the first decades of this century attests to the first, even if still only implicit, recognition of this fact. Far-reaching variability developed even within the West – within Europe itself, and above all between Europe and the Americas – the USA, Latin America, and Canada.[2]

The same was even more true with respect to the relation between the cultural and structural dimensions of modernity. A very strong, even if implicit, assumption of the studies of modernization – that the cultural dimensions or aspects of modernization, the basic cultural premises of Western modernity are inherently and necessarily interwoven with the structural ones – became highly questionable. While the different dimensions of the original Western project have indeed constituted the crucial starting and continual reference points for the processes that developed among different societies throughout the world, the developments in these societies have gone far beyond the homogenizing and hegemonic dimensions of the original cultural program of modernity.

Modernity has indeed spread to most of the world, but did not give rise to a single civilization, or to one institutional pattern, but to the development of several modern civilizations, or at least civilizational patterns, i.e. of civilizations which share common characteristics, but which tend to develop different even if cognate ideological and institutional dynamics. Moreover, far-reaching changes which go beyond their original premises of modernity have been taking place also in Western societies.

II

The civilization of modernity as it developed first in the West was from its very beginning beset by internal antinomies and contradictions, giving rise to continual critical discourse which focused on the relations, tensions, and contradictions between its premises and between these premises and the institutional development of modern societies. The importance of these tensions was fully understood in the classical sociological literature – Tocqueville, Marx, Weber or Durkheim – and was later taken up in the thirties, above all in the Frankfurt school in the so-called "critical" sociology – which was, however, focused mainly on the problems of fascism, but this importance then became neglected in post-Second World War studies of modernization. Lately it came yet again to the forefront to constitute a continual component of the analysis of modernity.[3]

The tensions and antinomies that have developed within the basic premises of this program were first, between totalizing and more diversified or pluralistic conceptions of the major components of this program, of the very conception of reason and its place in human life and society, and of the construction of nature, of human society, and its history; secondly, between reflexivity and active construction of nature and society; thirdly, those between different evaluations of major dimensions of human experience; and fourthly, between control and autonomy.

In the political arena these tensions coalesced with those between a constructivist approach which views politics as the process of reconstruction of society and especially of democratic politics, or as active self-construction of society as opposed to a view which accepts society in its concrete composition; between liberty and equality; between the autonomy of civil society and the charismatization of state power; between the civil and the utopian components of the cultural and political program of modernity; between freedom and emancipation in the name of some, often utopian, social vision; above all between Jacobin and more pluralistic orientations or approaches to the social and political order; and between the closely related tension between, to use Bruce Ackerman's formulation, "normal" and "revolutionary" politics.[4]

These various tensions in the political program of modernity were closely related to those between the different modes of legitimization of modern regimes, especially but not only of constitutional and democratic polities – namely, between, on the one hand, procedural legitimation in terms of civil adherence to rules of the game and on the other, and in different "substantive" terms, a very strong tendency to promulgate modes of legitimation based on – above all, to use Edward Shils' terminology – various primordial, "sacred," religious or secular-ideological components.[5]

It was around these tensions that there developed the critical discourse of modernity. The most radical "external" criticism of modernity denied the possibility of the grounding of any social order, of morality, in the basic premises of the cultural program of modernity especially in autonomy of individuals and supremacy of reason; it denied that these premises could be seen as grounded in any transcendental vision; it also denied the closely related claims that these premises and the institutional development of modernity could be seen as the epitome of human creativity. Such criticisms claimed that these premises and institutional developments denied human creativity and gave rise to both the flattening of human experience and to the erosion of moral order – of the moral and transcendental bases of society; and gave rise to the alienation of man from nature and from society. The more internal criticisms of this program, which could often overlap or become interwoven with the "external" ones, evaluated the institutional development of modern societies from the point of view of the premises of the cultural and political programs of modernity as well as from the point of view of the basic antinomies and contradictions inherent in this program. Of special importance here was both the multifaceted, continual, and continually changing confrontation of the claims of the program to enhance freedom and autonomy with the strong tendency to control; and this program's relation to inequality and the continual dislocation of various social sectors that developed with the crystallization of modern institutional formations.

III

All these antinomies and tensions developed from the very beginning of the institutionalization of modern regimes in Europe. The continual prevalence of these antinomies and contradictions also had – as the classics of sociology were fully aware of, but as was to no small extent forgotten or neglected in the studies of modernization – far-reaching institutional implications and were closely interwoven with different patterns of institutional constellations and dynamics that developed in different modern societies. With the expansion of modern civilizations beyond the West, in some ways already beyond Europe to the Americas, and with the dynamics of the continually developing international frameworks or settings, several new, crucial elements have become central in the constitution of modern societies.

Particularly noteworthy in this context was the relative place of the non-Western societies in the various – economic, political, ideological – international systems, societies that differed greatly from that of the Western ones. It was not only that Western societies were the "originators" of this new civilization. Beyond this, and above all, was the fact that the expansion of these systems, especially insofar as it took place through colonialization and imperialist expansion, gave Western institutions a hegemonic place in these systems. But it was in the nature of these international systems to generate a dynamics which gave rise to both political and ideological challenges to existing hegemonies, as well as to continual shifts in the loci of hegemony within Europe, from Europe to the United States, then also to Japan and East Asia.

But it was not only the economic, military-political and ideological expansion of the civilization of modernity from the West throughout the world that was important in this process. Of no lesser, possibly even of greater importance, was the fact that this expansion has given rise to continual confrontations between the cultural and institutional premises of Western modernity with those of other civilizations – those of other Axial Civilizations, as well as non-Axial ones, the most important of which has been, of course, Japan. Truly enough, many of Western modernity's basic premises, symbols, and institutions – representative, legal, and administrative – have become indeed seemingly accepted within these civilizations, but at the same time far-reaching transformations and challenges have taken place, and new problems have arisen.

The attraction of these themes – and of some of these institutions, for many groups within these civilizations – lay in the fact that their appropriation permitted many groups in non-European nations, especially elites and intellectuals, to actively participate in the new modern (i.e. initially Western) universal tradition. However, this appropriation was combined with the selective rejection of many of these themes' aspects and of Western "control," and hegemony. The appropriation of these themes made it possible for these elites and broader strata of many non-European societies to incorporate some of the universalistic elements of modernity into the construction of their new collective identities, without necessarily giving up either specific components of their traditional identities – often also couched in universalistic, especially religious terms which differed from those that were predominant in the West – or their negative attitude towards the West.

The attraction of these themes of political discourse to many sectors in the non-Western European countries was also intensified by the fact that their appropriation in these countries entailed the transposition to the international scene of the struggle between hierarchy and equality. Although initially couched in European terms, it could find resonances in the political traditions of many of these societies. Such transposition of these themes from the Western European to Central and Eastern Europe and to non-European settings was reinforced by the combination, in many of the programs promulgated by these groups, of orientations of protest with institution-building and center-formation.

Such transposition was generated not only by the higher hierarchical standing and actual hegemony of the Western countries in these new international settings, but also by the fact that the non-Western civilizations were put in an inferior position in the evaluation of societies which was promulgated by the seemingly universalistic premises of the new modern civilizations.

Thus various groups and elites in Central and Eastern European, and in Asian and African societies were able to refer to both the tradition of protest and the tradition of center-formation in these societies, and to cope with problems of reconstructing their own centers and traditions in terms of the new setting. From this perspective, the most important aspect of the expansion and appropriation of these themes beyond Western Europe by different groups in these societies lay in the fact that these acts made it possible to rebel against the institutional realities of the new modern civilization in terms of its own symbols and premises.

IV

The appropriation of different themes and institutional patterns of the original Western modern civilization in non-Western European societies did not entail their acceptance in their original form. Rather, it entailed the continuous selection, reinterpretation, and reformulation of such themes, giving rise to a continual crystallization of new cultural and political programs of modernity, and the development and reconstruction of new institutional patterns. The cultural programs that have been continually developing in these societies entailed different interpretations and far-reaching reformulations of the initial cultural program of modernity and its basic conceptions and premises. These formulations entailed different emphases on different components of this program on its different tensions and antinomies, and the concomitant crystallization of distinct institutional patterns. They entailed the continual construction of symbols of collective identities; their conceptions of themselves and of their roles; and their negative or positive attitudes to modernity in general and to the West in particular.

These differences between the different cultural programs of modernity were not purely "cultural" or academic. They were closely related to some basic problems inherent in the political and institutional programs of modernity. Thus, in the political realm, they were closely related to the tension between the utopian and civil components in the construction of modern politics; between "revolutionary" and "normal" politics, or between the general will and the will of all; between civil society and the state; and between individual and collectivity. These varying cultural programs of modernity also entailed different conceptions of authority and its accountability, different modes of protest and political activity, and questioning of the basic premises of the modern order and different modes of institutional formations.

In close relation to the crystallization of the different cultural programs of modernity there has been taking place in different modern societies a continual process of crystallization of different institutional patterns and of different modes of critical discourse, which focused on interrelations and tensions between different institutional arenas, and between them and the different premises of the cultural and political programs of modernity and their continual reinterpretations.

The preceding considerations about the multiple programs of modernity do not of course negate the obvious fact that in many central aspects of their institutional structure – be it in occupational and industrial structure, in the structure of education or of cities – in political structures very strong convergences have developed in different modern societies. These convergences have indeed generated common problems but the modes of coping with these problems, i.e the institutional dynamics attendant on the development of these problems, differed greatly between these civilizations.[6]

But it is not only with the societies of Asia or Latin America that developments took place which went beyond the initial model of Western society. At the same time in Western societies themselves there have developed new discourses which have greatly transformed the initial model of modernity and which have undermined the original vision of modern and industrial society with its hegemonic and homogenizing vision. There has emerged a growing tendency to distinguish between *Zweckrationalität* and *Wertrationalität*, and to recognize a great multiplicity of different *Wertrationalitäten*. Cognitive rationality – especially as epitomized in the extreme forms of scientism – has certainly become dethroned from its hegemonic position, as has the idea of the "conquest" or mastery of the environment – whether of society or of nature.

V

These different cultural programs and institutional patterns of modernity were not shaped by what has been presented in some of the earlier studies of modernization as natural evolutionary potentialities of these societies; or, as in the earlier criticisms thereof, by the natural unfolding of their respective traditions; nor by their placement in the new international settings. Rather they were shaped by the continuous interaction between several factors. In most general terms they were shaped by the historical experience of these societies in civilization, and by the mode of both the impingement of modernity on them, and their incorporation into the modern political economic and ideological international frameworks.

In greater detail, these programs were shaped by several continually changing factors. First, they were shaped by basic premises of cosmic and social order, that is, the basic "cosmologies" that were prevalent in these societies in their "orthodox" and "heterodox" formulations alike as they have crystallized in these societies throughout their histories. A second shaping factor was the pattern of institutional formations that developed within these civilizations through their historical experience, especially in their encounter with other societies or civilizations.

Third, these programs were shaped by the encounter and continual interaction between these processes, and the new cultural and political program of modernity; the premises and modes of social and political discourse that were prevalent in the different societies and civilizations as they were incorporated into the new international systems and the continual interaction of these societies with these processes. In this encounter, of special importance were the internal antinomies and tensions or contradictions in the basic cultural and, above all, political program of modernity as it developed initially in the West – and even within the West in a great variety of ways, and as it became transformed with its expansion.

The fourth set of factors shaping this program was the dynamics, internal tensions, and contradictions that developed in conjunction with the structural-demographic, economic, and political changes attendant on the institutionalization of modern institutional frameworks, and between these processes and the basic premises of modernity.

It was the constant interaction between these factors, as well as their continual reinterpretation, that generated the continual changes in the cultural programs that developed in these societies. It is also these factors that influenced the major components of their institutional formations and the different configurations of civil society and public spheres, the different modes of political economies – and the constitution of the boundaries of their respective collectivities and the components of collective consciousness and identity, or what has been designated as nationalism or ethnicity.

The major actors in such processes of reinterpretion and formation of new institutional patterns were various political activists, intellectuals, in conjunction above all with the social movements. Such activists, intellectuals, and leaders of movements promulgated and reinterpreted the major symbols and components of the cultural programs of modernity, and themselves addressed the antinomies and contradictions within these programs and between them and institutional realities.

In all modern societies, such movements arose in relation to the problems that developed attendant on the institutionalization and development of modern political regimes, their democratization, and of modern collectivities. Likewise, such movements arose especially in relation to the contradictions which developed between, on the one hand, the expansion of capitalism and the development of new economic and class formations, and on the other, the premises of the cultural and political program of modernity and its institutionalization. It is above all these movements which promulgated the antinomies and tensions inherent in the cultural and political programs of modernity and which attempted to interweave them with the reconstruction of centers, collectivities, and institutional formations.

Whatever the concrete details of these agendas, they highlighted the continual challenge of the contradiction between on the one hand, encompassing, totalistic, potentially totalitarian overtones based either on collective, national, religious and/or Jacobin visions, and on the other, a commitment to some pluralistic premises. None of the modern pluralistic, constitutional regimes has been able to do entirely away – or even can possibly do away – with either the Jacobin component especially with its utopian dimension, with the orientation to some primordial components of collective identity, or with the claims for the centrality of religion in the construction of collective identities or in the legitimization of the political order. The ubiquity of this challenge has also highlighted the possibility of crises and breakdowns as inherent in the very nature of modernity.

VI

Thus within all modern societies there continuously developed new questionings and reinterpretations of different dimensions of modernity – and in all of them there have been continually developing varying cultural agendas.

All these developments attest to the growing diversification of the visions and understanding of modernity, of the basic cultural agendas of the elites of different societies – far beyond the homogenic and hegemonic visions of modernity that were prevalent in the fifties. While the common starting point of many of these developments was indeed the cultural program of modernity as it developed in the West, more recent developments gave rise to a multiplicity of cultural and social formations which go far beyond the very homogenizing and hegemonizing aspects of this original version.

Thus, many, if not all, of the components of the initial cultural vision of modernity have been challenged in the last decade or so. These challenges claimed that the modern era has basically ended and given rise to a post-modern one – challenges that were in turn counter-challenged by those like Jurgen Habermas, who claimed that the various post-modern developments basically constitute either a repetition, in a new form, of criticisms of modernity which existed there from the very beginning, or constitute yet another manifestation of the continual unfolding of modernity.[7] Indeed, it can be argued that the very tendency or potential to such radical reinterpretations constitutes an inherent component of the civilization or civilizations of modernity.

This is even true, as we have seen throughout the book, even if in a very paradoxical manner, of the most extreme anti-modern movements that developed in the contemporary period – namely the communal-religious and fundamentalist movements (particularly the latter), even if the core of their ideologies are (highly essentialized) tradition and their ideas are anti-modern and anti-Enlightenment. The basic structure or phenomenology of their vision and action is in many crucial and seemingly paradoxical ways a modern one, just as was the case with the totalitarian movements of the twenties and thirties, and these movements bear within themselves the seeds of very intensive and virulent revolutionary sectarian, utopian Jacobinism, seeds which can, under appropriate circumstances, come to full-blown fruition.

Whatever the ultimate verdict of these developments, there can be no doubt that they all entailed the unfolding of the civilizations of modernity, even if many of these movements and trends entailed a radical transformation of some of the initial premises of Western modernity and, above all, of the modes of structuration of social activities and institutional arenas that characterized the first "bourgeois" (and paradoxically also the later Communist) modern societies.

VII

Thus, while the spread or expansion of modernity has indeed taken place throughout most of the world, it did not give rise to just one civilization, one pattern of ideological and institutional response, but to at least several basic variants – and to continual refractions thereof. Again, in order to understand these different patterns, it is necessary to take into account the pattern of historical experience of these civilizations.

But the importance of the historical experiences of the various civilizations in shaping the concrete contours of the modern societies which developed in their historical spaces does not mean, as S. P. Huntington seems to imply in his influential *The Clash of Civilizations*, that these processes give rise on the contemporary scene to several closed civilizations, civilizations which basically constitute mere continuations of their respective historical pasts and patterns. It is not only, as Huntington correctly indicates, that modernization does not automatically imply Westernization. What is of crucial importance is that on the contemporary scene there has taken place the crystallization of continually interacting modern civilizations in which even the inclusive particularistic tendencies are constructed in typically modern ways, ways which attempt to appropriate from modernity on their own terms, and to continually articulate in different concrete ways and in different historical settings, the antinomies and contradictions of modernity. But it is not only that there continually developed multiple modern civilizations – rather, these civilizations, which shared many common components which constituted mutual reference points, have been continually developing, unfolding, and giving rise to new problematiques and continual reinterpretations of the basic premises of modernity. Within all societies there continuously developed new questionings and reinterpretations of different dimensions of modernity – and in all of them there have been developing different cultural agendas. All of these factors attested to the growing diversification of the visions and understandings of modernity, of the basic cultural agendas of different sectors of modern societies – far beyond the homogenic and hegemonic visions of modernity that were prevalent in the fifties. The fundamentalist – and the new communal-national – movements constitute one such new development in the unfolding of the potentialities and antinomies of modernity.

Indeed, such developments may give rise to highly confrontational stances – especially to the West – but these stances will be promulgated in continually changing modern idioms and they may entail a continual transformation of these indications and of the cultural programs of modernity.

Such diversity certainly undermined the old hegemonies, yet at the same time it was closely connected, perhaps paradoxically, with the development of new, multiple, common reference points and networks – with a globalization of cultural networks and channels of communication far beyond what existed before.

At the same time, the various components of modern life and culture were refracted and reconstructed in ways which went beyond the confines of any institutional boundaries – especially those of the nation-state – giving rise to the multiple patterns of globalization and diversification studied by such scholars as Arjun Appendurai, Ulf Hannerz, and Roland Robertson.[8]

It is this combination of, on the one hand, the growing diversity of the continuous reinterpretations of modernity with, on the other, the development of multiple global trends and mutual reference points, that is characteristic of the contemporary scene.

Notes

1 Heterodoxies, sectarianism, and utopianism

1. On these various movements, see the respective chapters in the five volumes of the Fundamentalism project of the American Academy of Arts and Sciences, and the articles in *Contention*, nos. 11 & 12. See also G. Kepel, *The Revenge of God: The Resurgence of Islam, Christianity and Judaism in the Modern World*, Philadelphia, The Pennsylvania State University Press, 1994; P. van der Veer, ed., *Conversion to Modernities: The Globalization of Christianity*, New York, Routledge, 1996; W. Shea, "The Catholic Tribe and Fundamentalism as a Stranger," in F. Nichols, ed., *Christianity and the Stranger: Historical Essays*, Atlanta, Scholars Press, 1995, pp. 221–286; M. Jungensmeyer, *The New Cold War?: Religious Nationalism Confronts the Secular State*, Berkeley, University of California Press, 1993; H. Munson Jr., review of Mark Jungensmeyer *The New Cold War?: Religious Nationalism Confronts the Secular State, International Journal of Middle East Studies*, 27, 3, 1995, pp. 341–401; R. Grew, "On Seeking the Cultural Context of Fundamentalism," University of Michigan, draft.

2. P. van der Veer, *Religious Nationalism: Hindus and Muslims in India*, Berkeley, University of California Press, 1994; D. Allen, ed., *Religion and Political Conflict in South Asia: India, Pakistan, and Sri Lanka*, Westport, Greenwood Press, 1992; C. F. Keyes, L. Kendall, and H. Hardacre, eds., *Asian Visions of Authority: Religion and the Modern States of East and Southeast Asia*, Honolulu, University of Hawaii Press, 1994; E. Cohen, "Christianity and Buddhism in Thailand: The 'Battle of the Axes' and the 'Contest of Power'," in *Social Compass*, 38, 2, 1991, pp. 115–140. See also C. Stewart and R. Shaw, eds., *Syncretism/Anti-Syncretism: The Politics of Religious Synthesis*, London, Routledge, 1994.

3. S. N. Eisenstadt, "The Axial Age: The Emergence of Transcendental Visions and Rise of Clerics," *European Journal of Sociology*, 23, 2, 1982, pp. 294–314; S. N. Eisenstadt, ed., *The Origins and Diversity of Axial Age Civilizations*, New York, State University of New York Press, 1986; K. Jaspers, *The Origin and Goal of History*, New Haven, Yale University Press, 1965.

4. See M. Weber, *Gesammelte Aufsätze zur Religionssoziologie*, Tubingen, J. C. B. Mohr, 1922, 1978; and G. Roth and W. Schluchter, *Max Weber's Vision of History, Ethics and Methods*, Berkeley, University of California Press, 1979.

5. E. Shils, "Center and Periphery; and Society and Societies – The Macrosociological View," in E. Shils, ed., *Center and Periphery, Essays in Macrosociology*, Chicago, University of Chicago Press, 1975, pp. 3–11.

6. The concept of Great Tradition is derived from R. Redfield, *Human Nature and the Study of Society*, Chicago, University of Chicago Press, 1962.

7. Eisenstadt, ed., *The Origins and Diversity of Axial Age Civilization*; S. N. Eisenstadt, ed., *Kulturen der Achsenzeit*, Frankfurt, Suhrkamp Verlag, 1992, 3 vols.; and *Civilta Comparata*, Naples, Liguori, 1991.

8. See S. N. Eisenstadt, "Cultural Traditions and Political Dynamics, The Origins and Modes of Ideological Politics," *British Journal of Sociology*, 32, 2, 1981, pp. 155–181; Eisenstadt, ed., *The Origins and Diversity of Axial Age Civilizations*.

9. Ibid.

10. E. Voegelin, *Order and History*, Baton Rouge, LA., Louisiana State University, 1954.

11. See E. Tiryakian: "Three Meta Cultures of Modernity: Christian, Gnostic, Chthonic," *Theory, Culture and Society*, 13, 1, 1996, pp. 99–118.

12. S. N. Eisenstadt, R. Kahane and D. Shulman, eds., *Orthodoxy, Heterodoxy and Dissent in India*, New York, Mouton, 1984; S. N. Eisenstadt, "Transcendental Vision, Center Formation, and the Role of Intellectuals," in L. Greenfeld and M. Martin, eds., *Center, Ideas and Institutions*, Chicago, University of Chicago Press, 1988, pp. 96–109.

13. A. Seligman, "The Comparative Studies of Utopias," "Christian Utopias and Christian Salvation: A General Introduction," and "The Eucharist Sacrifice and the Changing Utopian Moment in Post Reformation Christianity," in Seligman, ed., *Order and Transcendence*, Leiden: E. J. Brill, 1989, pp.1–44; S.N. Eisenstadt, "Comparative Liminality: Liminality and Dynamics of Civilization," in *Religion*, 15, 1985 pp. 315–338; Voegelin, *Order and History*; M. Lasky, "The Birth of a Metaphor: On the Origins of Utopia and Revolution," *Encounter*, 34, 2, 1970, pp. 35–45 and 3, 1970, pp. 30–42; Lasky, *Utopia and Revolution*, Chicago, University of Chicago Press, 1976.

14. Voegelin, *Order and History*; N. Cohn, *In the Pursuit of the Millennium*, New York, Harper, 1961.

15. M. Weber, *Ancient Judaism*, Glencoe, Free Press, 1952.

16. S. N. Eisenstadt, "Cultural Traditions and Political Dynamics," *British Journal of Sociology*, 32, 1981, pp. 155–181.

17. G. Eichinger Ferro-Luzzi, "The Polythetic-Prototype Approach to Hinduism," in G. Sontheimer and H. Kulke, eds., *Hinduism Reconsidered*, New Delhi, Manohar, 1989, pp. 187–196; D. Ludden, ed., *Contesting the Nation*, Philadelphia, University of Pennsylvania Press, 1996.

18. On Hinduism, see M. Stutley and J. Stutley, *A Dictionary of Hinduism, its Mythology, Folklore and Development, 1500BC–AD1500*, Bombay, Allied Publishers, 1977; P. Bowes, *The Hindu Religious Tradition. A Philosophical Approach*, London, Routledge and Kegan Paul, 1978.

On Jainism, see C. Gaillat, "Jainism," in *The Encyclopedia of Religion*, New York, Macmillan and Free Press, 1987, Vol. 7, pp. 507–514; A. L. Basham, "Jainism and Buddhism," in T. W. DeBary, ed., *Sources of Indian Tradition*, New York, Columbia University Press, 1958, pp. 37–93.

On Bhakti, see J. B. Carman, "Bhakti," in *The Encyclopedia of Religion*, vol. 2, pp. 130–134; J. Lele, ed., *Tradition and Modernity in Bhakti Movements*, Leiden, E. J. Brill, 1981. On some of the earlier but persistent heterogeneous trends in Indian religion, see J. Gonda, *Visnuism and Sivaism*, London, Athlone Press, 1970.

19. On the major aspects of Buddhism relevant for this point of view see P. A. Pardue, *Buddhism: A Historical Introduction to Buddhist Values and the Social and Political Forms They Have Assumed in Asia*, New York, Macmillan, 1971; W. T. DeBary, ed., *The Buddhist Tradition in India, China and Japan*, New York, Modern Library, 1972; P. Levy, *Buddhism: A Mystery Religion?*, New York, Schocken, 1968.

20. On the caste system and networks, see M. Singer and B. S. Cohn, eds., *Structure and Change in Indian Society*, Chicago, Aldine, 1968; D. G. Mandelbaum, *Society in India*, Berkeley, University of California Press, 1970; R. Fox, *Kin, Clan, Raja and Rule: State-Hinterland Relations in Preindustrial India*, Berkeley, University of California Press, 1971; N. B. Dirks, "The Conversion of Caste: Location, Translation, and Appropriation," in Van der Veer, ed., *Conversion to Modernities*, pp. 115–136.

21. On the dynamics of Indian and Buddhist society and the place of sects within them, see J. C. Heesterman, *The Inner Conflict of Tradition: Essays in Indian Ritual, Kinship and Society*, Chicago and London, The University of Chicago Press, 1985; specially Heesterman, "Brahmin, Ritual and Renouncer," pp. 26–44; *The Ancient Indian Royal Consecration*, The Hague, Mouton and Co., 1957; and *The Broken World of Sacrifice: An Essay in Ancient Indian Ritual*, Chicago, University of Chicago Press, 1993; T. N. Madan, ed., *Way of Life: King, Householders and Renouncer*, Delhi, Vikas Publishing House, 1982, pp. 251–272; R. Thapar, "Householders and Renouncers in the Brahmanical and Buddhist Traditions," ibid., pp. 273–298; S.T. Tambiah, "The Renouncer: His Individuality and His Community," ibid., pp. 209–309; N.B. Dirks, "Political Authority and Structural Change in Early South Indian History," in *Indian Economic and Social History Review*, 13, 2, 1976, pp. 125–157. G. Goodwin, "Portrayal of India, Caste Kingships and Dominance Reconsidered," in *Annual Review of Anthropology*, 17, 1988, pp. 497–552.

On sects in Hinduism and Buddhism see F. Hardy, *Virama Bhakti: Early Development of Krsna Devotion in South India*, Oxford University Press, 1981; Lele, ed., *Tradition and Modernity in Bhakti Movements*; K. Schormer and W. H. McLeod, eds., *The Saints, Studies in a Devotional Tradition of India*,

Berkeley, University of California Press, 1985; J. B. Carman and F. A. Margolin, eds., *Purity and Auspiciousness in Indian Society*, Leiden, E. J. Brill, 1985; S. C. Malik, ed., *Dissent, Protest and Reform in Indian Civilization*, Simla, Indian Institute for Advanced Study, 1973.

22. See K. Ishwaran, ed., *Change and Continuity in India's Villages*, New York, Columbia University Press, 1970; Singer and Cohn, eds., *Structure and Change in Indian Society*; P. Chatterjee, *The Nation and Its Fragments: Colonial and Postcolonial Histories*, Princeton, Princeton University Press, 1993; and *Nationalist Thought and the Colonial World: A Derivative Discourse?*, Zed Books, United Nations University, 1986.

23. On the Chinese civilization, see E. D. Reischauer and J. K. Fairbank, *A History of East Asian Civilization*, Vol. 1, *East Asia: The Great Tradition*, Boston, Houghton Mifflin, 1960; M. Weber, *The Religion of China: Confucianism and Taoism*, trans. H. Gerth, New York, Free Press, 1964; C. K. Yang, "The Functional Relationship between Confucian Thought and Chinese Religion," in J. K. Fairbank, ed., *Chinese Thought and Institutions*, Chicago, University of Chicago Press, 1957, pp. 269–291; A. F. Wright, *The Confucian Persuasion*, Stanford, Stanford University Press, 1960; D. S. Nivison and A. F. Wright, eds., *Confucianism in Action*, Stanford, Stanford University Press, 1959; and A. F. Wright, ed., *Studies in Chinese Thought*, Chicago, University of Chicago Press, 1953. See also: J. Gernet, "Introduction," in S. R. Schram, ed., *Foundations and Limits of State Power in China*, London, University of London, School of Oriental and African Studies, 1987, pp. xv-xxxvii; D. McMullen, "View of the State in Du You and Liu Zonngyuan," in ibid., pp. 59–86; B. L. Schwartz, "The Primacy of the Political Order in East Asian Societies: Some Preliminary Generalizations," in ibid., pp. 1–10; A. Hulsewe, "Law as One of the Foundations of State Power in Early Imperial China," in ibid., pp. 11–32; M. Loewe, "Imperial Sovereignty: Dong Zhongshu's Contribution and His Predecessors," in ibid., pp. 33–58; H. Franke, "The Role of the State as a Structural Element in Polyethnic Societies," in ibid., pp. 87–112.

24. J. C. T. Liu, "An Early Sung Reformer, Fan Chun-yen," in J. K. Fairbank, ed., *Chinese Thought and Institutions*, pp. 105–132; and *Reform in Sung China, Wang An-Shih, 1021–1086 and his New Policies*, Cambridge, Cambridge University Press, 1959; W. T. DeBary, "Some Common Tendencies in Neo-Confucianism," in D. Nivison and A. F. Wright, eds., *Confucianism in Action*.

25. See H. Fingarrette, "Human Community as Holy Rite. An Interpretation of Confucius' Analects," *Harvard Theological Review*, 59, 1, 1968, pp. 53–67; and *Confucius, The Secular as Sacred*, New York, Harper & Row, 1972; J. G. A. Pocock, "Ritual, Language, Power: An Essay on the Apparent Political Meanings of Ancient Chinese Philosophy," in Pocock, *Politics, Language and Time, Essays on Political Thought and History*, New York, Atheneum, 1973, pp. 42–80; DeBary, *Neo Confucian Orthodoxy and the Learning of the Mind and Heart*; Metzger, *Escape from Predicament – Neo-Confucianism and China's Evolving Political Culture*.

26. On the impact of Buddhism and Taoism on Chinese society, see Reischauer and Fairbank, *A History of East Asian Civilization*; M. Kaltenmark, *Lao Tzu and Taoism*, Stanford, Stanford University Press, 1969; A. F. Wright, *Buddhism in Chinese History*, Stanford, Stanford University Press, 1959.

27. On the political structure and dynamism of the Chinese Empire see: Reischauer and Fairbank, *A History of East Asian Civilization*; C. O. Hucker, ed., *Chinese Government in Ming Times: Seven Studies*, New York, Columbia University Press, 1969; J. T. C. Liu, "An Administration Cycle in Chinese History," in J. A. Harrison, ed., *China: Enduring Scholarship*, Tucson, University of Arizona Press, 1972, vol. 1, pp. 75–90; Eisenstadt, *Political Systems of Empires*, especially chapters 10, 11; and "Innerweltliche Transzenden und die Strukturierung der Welt. Max Weber Studie über China und die Gestalt der chinesischen Zivilisation," in W. Schluchter, ed., *Max Webers Studie über Konfuzianismus und Taoismum. Interpretation und Kritik*, Frankfurt am Main, Suhrkamp, 1983, pp. 363–411; A. F. Wright and D. Twitchett, eds., *Perspectives on the Tang*, New Haven, Yale University Press, 1973; J. A. Langlois, Jr., ed., *China under Mongol Rule*, Princeton, Princeton University Press, 1981; J. D. Spence and J. E. Wills, eds., *From Ming to Ching*, New Haven, Yale University Press, 1979; F. Wakeman, Jr., *The Great Enterprise: The Manchu Reconstruction of the Imperial Order in Seventeenth-Century China*, Berkeley and Los Angeles, University of California Press, 1986; Schram, ed., *The Scope of State Power in China*.

28. Weber, *Ancient Judaism*; S. N. Eisenstadt, *Jewish Civilization. The Jewish Historical Experience in a Comparative Perspective*, New York, State University of New York Press, 1992.

29. S. N. Eisenstadt, "The Disintegration of the Medieval Jewish Civilizational Framework in the Modern Period and the Integration of Jews in European Societies," in Eisenstadt, *Jewish Civilization. The Jewish Historical Experience in a Comparative Perspective*, New York, State University of New York Press, 1992, pp. 85–108.

30. See H. Ben-Sasson, ed., *The Story of the Jewish People*, Cambridge, MA, Harvard University Press, 1972; G. Scholem, *The Messianic Idea in Judaism*, New York, Schocken Books, 1971.

31. H. A. R. Gibb, *Studies in the Civilization of Islam*, Boston, Beacon Press, 1962; I. M. Lapidus, *A History of Islamic Societies*, Cambridge, Cambridge University Press, 1987; H. Laoust, *Les schisms dans l'Islam*, Paris, Payot, 1965.

32. Aziz Al Azmeh, *Islams and Modernities*, London, Verso, 1993.

33. Henry Munson, Jr., *Islam and the Revolution in the Middle East*, New Haven, Yale University Press, 1988.

34. Lapidus, *A History of Islamic Societies*; and "State and Religion in Islamic Societies," *Past and Present*, 151, 1996, pp. 3–27.

35. C. Lindholm, "Despotism and Democracy: State and Society in the Premodern Middle East," in John A. Hall and Ian Jarvie, eds., *The Social Philosophy of Ernest Gellner*, Amsterdam, Rodopi, 1996, pp. 329–355; S. Akhavi, "Sayyid Qutb: The Poverty of Philosophy and the Vindication of Islamic Tradition," in

S. Mardin, ed., *Cultural Transitions in the Middle East*, Leiden, E. J. Brill, 1994, pp. 130–152; S. A. Arjomand, "Constitutions and the Struggle for Political Order: A Study in the Modernization of Political Tradition," in Mardin, ed., *Cultural Traditions in the Middle East*, pp. 1–49; E. Sivan, *Interpretations of Islam: Past and Present*, Princeton, The Darwin Press, 1985; and *Radical Islam: Medieval Theology and Modern Politics*, New Haven, Yale University Press, 1990.

36. Munson, Jr., *Islam and Revolution in the Middle East*; G. Warburg, "Mahdism and Islamism in Sudan," *International Journal of Middle East Studies*, 27, 2, 1995, pp. 219–236.

37. S. A. Arjomand, "Unity and Diversity in Islamic Fundamentalism," in M. Marty and R. Scott Appleby, eds., *Fundamentalisms Comprehended*, Chicago, The University of Chicago Press, 1995, pp. 179–198; and "Shi'ite Jurisprudence and Constitution Making in the Islamic Republic of Iran," in M. Marty and R. Scott Appleby, eds., *Fundamentalisms and the State*, Chicago, The University of Chicago Press, 1993, pp. 88–110; and *Authority and Political Culture in Shi'ism*, New York, State University of New York Press, 1988; and "The Consolation of Theology: Absence of the Imam and Transition from Chiliasm to Law in Shi'ism," *Journal of Religion*, 1996, pp. 548–571; and "The Crisis of the Imamate and the Institution of Occultation in Twelver Shi'ism: A Sociohistorical Perspective," *International Journal of Middle East Studies*, 28, 1996, pp. 491–515.

38. Munson, Jr., *Islam and Revolution in the Middle East*.

39. E. Landau-Tasseron, "The 'Cyclical Reform': A Study of the mujaddid tradition," in *Studia Islamica*, 70, 1989, pp. 79–118. H. Lazarus-Yafeh, "'Tajdid al-Din': A Reconsideration of Its Meaning, Roots and Influence in Islam," *The New East*, 31, 1986, pp. 1–10; N. Levtzion, "Eighteenth Century Renewal and Reform Movements in Islam," *The New East*, 31, 1986, pp. 48–70; Levtzion and J.O. Voll, eds., *Eighteenth Century Renewal and Reform in Islam*, Syracuse, Syracuse University Press, 1987; Levtzion and G. Weigert, "Religious Reform in Eighteenth-Century Morocco," *Jerusalem Studies in Arabic and Islam*, 19, 1995; John Voll, "Fundamentalism in the Sunni Arab World: Egypt and the Sudan," in M. Marty and R. Scott Appleby, eds., *Fundamentalisms Observed*, Chicago, University of Chicago Press, 1991, pp. 345–403.

40. B. Lewis, "Islamic Concepts of Revolution," in Lewis, *Islam in History*, London, Alcove Press, 1975, pp. 253–266; E. Gellner, *Muslim Society*, Cambridge, Cambridge University Press, 1981; Ibn Khaldun, *The Muqadimmah*, London, Routledge and Kegan Paul, 1988.

41. Voll, "Fundamentalism in the Sunni Arab World: Egypt and the Sudan"; S. T. Hunter, ed., *The Politics of Islamic Revivalism: Diversity and Unity*, Bloomington, Indiana University Press, 1988; T. Kuran, "The Economic Impact of Islamic Fundamentalism," in M. Marty and R. S. Appelby, eds., *Fundamentalisms and the State: Remaking Polities, Economies and Militance*, Chicago, University of Chicago Press, 1993, pp. 302–341; and, *Theoretical*

Economics, 153, 1, 1997; W. Watt, *Islamic Fundamentalism and Modernity*, London, Routledge, 1988.
42. Voegelin, *Order and History*.
43. S. N. Eisenstadt, *European Civilization in a Comparative Perspective*, Oslo, Norwegian University Press, 1987.
44. On heterodoxies in Christian civilizations and on the most important heterodoxy to develop in Catholic Europe – Protestantism – see G. Lewy, *Religion and Revolution*, New York, Oxford University Press, 1974; J. LeGoff, *Hérésies et Sociétés dans l'Europe pre-industrielle*. . ., Paris, Mouton, 1968; M. Waltzer, "Puritanism as a Revolutionary Ideology," in B. Laughlin, ed., *Studies in Social Movements*, New York, The Free Press, 1959.
45. See S. N. Eisenstadt, *Revolutions and the Transformation of Society*, New York, The Free Press, 1978.
46. M. Douglas, *Purity and Danger*, London, Routledge & Kegan Paul, 1966.
47. Many of the implications of these differences were explicated in Eisenstadt, *The Origins and Diversity of Axial Age Civilizations*; Eisenstadt, ed., *Kulturen Der Achsenzeit*, and Eisenstadt, *Civiltà Comparata*.
48. T. N. Madan, "The Double Edged Sword: Fundamentalism and the Sikh Religious Tradition," in Marty and Appelby, eds., *Fundamentalism Observed*, pp. 594–628.
49. D. K. Swearer, "Fundamentalistic Movements in Theravada Buddhism," in Marty and Appleby, eds., *Fundamentalism Observed*, pp. 628–691; Allen, ed., *Religion and Political Conflict in South Asia: India, Pakistan and Sri Lanka*.
50. On the distinction between orthodoxy and heterodoxy in general, see Eisenstadt, "Heterodoxies, Sectarianism and Dynamics of Civilizations"; and Eisenstadt, ed., *Kulturen der Achsenzeit*, and *Civiltà Comparata*.
51. On Sects in Hinduism and Buddhism see Hardy, *Virama Bhakti: Early Development of Krsna Devotion in South India*; Lele, ed., *Tradition and Modernity in Bhakti Movements*; Schormer and McLeod, *The Saints: Studies in a Devotional Tradition of India*; Carman and Margolin, eds., *Purity and Auspiciousness in Indian Society*; Malik, ed., *Dissent, Protest and Reform in Indian Civilization*.
52. P. Mus, "La Sociologie de Georges Burvitch et l'Asia," *Cahiers Internationaux de Sociologie*, 43, 1967, pp.1–21.
53. LeGoff, *Hérésies et Sociétés dans l'Europe pre-industrielle* . . .; F. Heer, *The Intellectual History of Europe*, Garden City, Doubleday, 1968.
54. R. Scott Appleby, *Spokesmen for the Despised*, Chicago, University of Chicago Press, 1997.
55. On the general historical background of the Karaites see: S. Baron, *A Social and Religious History of the Jews*, vol. 6, New York, Columbia University Press, 1952–1933; R. Nemoy, ed., *Karaite Anthology – Excerpts from Early Anthology*; Sh. Hoffman, "Karaites," in *Encyclopedia Judaica*; Z. Ankori, *Karaites in Byzantium*, New York, Columbia University Press, 1959.

56. Schwartz, "Law and Truth: On Qumran-Sadducean and Rabbinic Views of Law."

On relevant aspects of the Karaite Halakhah see also: Y. Erder, "Mercaziuta shel Eretz Israel beHugei Ha-Karaut Ha'Kduma le-Or Hilchotav shel Mishwaya Al'Aukbari" ("The Centrality of Israel among Ancient Karaism according to Mishwaya Al'Aukbari"), *Zion* 1955, pp. 37–67; and "The First Date in 'Megillat Ta'anit' in the Light of the Karaite Commentary on the Tabernacle Dedication," *The Jewish Quarterly Review*, 82, 3–4, January–April 1992, pp. 263–283; and "The Karaite-Sadducee Dilemma," *Israel Oriental Studies*, 14, 1994, pp. 195–215.

57. Erder, "Mercaziuta shel Eretz Israel beHugei Ha-Karaut Ha'Kduma le-Or Hilchotav shel Mishwaya Al'Aukbari" [in Hebrew] ("The Centrality of Israel among Ancient Karaism According to Mishwaya Al'Aukbari"); and "The Karaites-Sadducee Dilemma."

58. H. Ben Shamai, "Return to the Scriptures in Ancient and Medieval Jewish Sectarianism and Early Islam," in E. Patlagean and A. Le Boulluec, eds., *Les retours aux écritures fondamentalismes présents et passés*, Paris, Peeters Louvain, 1993, pp. 319–342.

59. See the introductory essay to Levtzion and Voll, eds., *Eighteenth Century Renewal and Reform in Islam*; Landau-Tasseron, "The 'Cyclical Reform': A Study of the Mujaddid Tradition"; Levtzion and Weigert, "Religious Reform in Eighteenth-Century Morocco."

60. E. Sivan, "In God's Cause," in the Erasmus Ascension Symposium, *The Limits of Pluralism. Neo-Absolutism and Relativism*, Amsterdam, Praemium Erasmianum Foundation, 1994, p. 16. See also Sivan "Jihad, Text, Myth, Historical Realities," in Patlagean and Le Boulluec, eds., *les retours aux écritures fondamentalismes présents et passés*, pp. 83–100.

61. E. Kolberg, "Authoritative Scriptures in Early Imami Shi'ism," in Patlagean and Le Boulluec, eds., *Les retours aux écritures fondamentalismes présents et passés*, pp. 295–312. H. Lazarus-Yafeh, "Muslim Medieval Attitudes towards the Qur'an and the Bible," in Patlagean and Le Boulluec, eds., *Les retours aux écritures fondamentalismes présents et passés*, pp. 253–268.

62. Al Azmeh, *Islams and Modernities*, p. 98.

63. Voll, "Fundamentalism in the Sunni Arab World: Egypt and the Sudan," p. 351.

64. Cohn, *In Pursuit of the Millennium*; H. Oberman, *The Dawn of the Reformation: Essays in the Late Medieval and Early Reformation Thought*, Edinburgh, T. and T. Clark, 1986; and *The Impact of the Reformation: Essays*, Grand Rapids, MI, William B. Eerdmans, 1994; and *The Reformation: Roots and Ramifications*, Edinburgh, T. & T. Clark, 1994; L. Kolakowski, *Chrétiens sans église*, Paris, Gallimard, 1969.

65. See S. N. Eisenstadt. "Origins of the West. The Origins of the West in Recent Macrosociologial Theory. The Protestant Ethic Reconsidered," *Cultural Dynamics*, Leiden, E. J. Brill, 1991, pp. 113–147.

2 The Great Revolutions and the transformation of sectarian utopianism

1. E. Voegelin, *Enlightenment and Revolution*, ed. John H. Hallowell, Durham NC, Duke University Press, 1975; *The New Science of Politics*, Chicago, University of Chicago Press, 1952; *Die politischen Religionen*, Munchen, Wilhelm Fink Verlag, 1996; idem, *Das Volk Gottes*, Munchen, Wilhelm Fink Verlag, 1994; R. Gould, *Insurgent Identities: Class, Community, and Protest in Paris from 1848 to the Commune*, Chicago, University of Chicago Press, 1995.
2. S. A. Arjomand, "Iran's Islamic Revolution in Comparative Perspective," *World Politics*, 38, 3, 1976. See also S. N. Eisenstadt, "Frameworks of the Great Revolutions: Culture, Social Structure, History and Human Agency," *International Social Science Journal*, 133, 1992, pp. 385–401; and *Revolutions and the Transformation of Societies*, New York, Free Press, 1978.
3. M. A. Shaban, *The Abbasid Revolution*, Cambridge, Cambridge University Press, 1970; M. Sharon, *Black Banners from the East*, Jerusalem, Magnes Press, 1983; E. Gellner, *Muslim Society*, Cambridge, Cambridge University Press, 1981, especially pp. 1–185; A. S. Ahmed, *Millennium and Charisma among Pathans*, London, Routledge & Kegan Paul, 1979.
4. On the primacy of politics in the Great Revolutions see C. Leforte, *Democracy and Political Theory*, Minneapolis, University of Minnesota Press, 1988, pp. 57–163; *Totalitarian Democracy and After – International Colloquium in Memory of Jacob L. Talmon*, Jerusalem, June 21–4, 1982, The Hebrew University, 1984, pp. 37–56; François Furet, *The French Revolution*, New York, Macmillan, 1970; and *Interpreting the French Revolution*, Cambridge, Cambridge University Press, 1981; and *Rethinking the French Revolution*, Chicago: University of Chicago Press, 1982; B. Singer, *Society, Theory, and the French Revolution: Studies in the Revolutionary Imaginary*, New York, St. Martin's Press, 1986. For the primacy of politics in many contemporary Islamic fundamentalist movements see: B. Tibi, *The Crisis of Modern Islam*, Utah, University of Utah Press, 1988.
5. J. A. Goldstone, "Revolutions dans l'histoire et histoire de la revolution," *Revue française de Sociologie*, 3, 4, 1983, pp. 405–430.
6. Eisenstadt, "Frameworks of the Great Revolutions: Culture, Social Structure, History and Human Agency"; and *Revolutions and the Transformation of Societies*.
7. J. A. Goldstone, *Revolution and Rebellion in the Early Modern World*, Berkeley, University of California Press, 1991.
8. C. Tilly, "Does Modernization Breed Revolution?" *Comparative Politics*, 5, 3, 1973, pp. 425–47. J. A. Goldstone, "Revolutions dans l'histoire et histoire de la revolution"; and *Revolution and Rebellion in the Early Modern World*; N. R. Keddie, ed., *Debating Revolutions*, New York, New York University Press, 1995.
9. E. Hobsbawm, *The Age of Revolution*, London, Weidenfeld & Nicholson, 1964.
10. C. Hill, *The Origins of the English Intellectual Revolution Reconsidered*, Oxford, University Press, 1997.

11. A. Cochin, *La Révolution et la libre pensée*, Paris, Plon-Nourrit, 1924; and *L'esprit du Jacobinisme*, Paris, Presses Universitaires de France, 1979; Furet, *French Revolution*; and *Interpreting the French Revolution*; and *Rethinking the French Revolution*; M. Ozouf, *La Fête Revolutionnaire*, Paris, Gallimard, 1982; Singer, *Society, Theory, and the French Revolution: Studies in the Revolutionary Imagery*.

12. V. C. Nahirny, *The Russian Intelligentsia: From Torment to Silence*, Rutgers, NJ, Transaction Publications, 1981; K. Riegel, "Der Marxismus-Leninismus als politische Religion," in H. Maier and M. Schäfer, eds., *"Totalitarismus" und "Politische Religionen"*, Munich, Ferdinand Schöningh, 1997, pp. 75–139; P. Pomper, *The Russian Revolutionary Intelligentsia*, New York, Crowell, 1970; F. Venturi, *Roots of Revolution. A History of the Populist and Socialist Movements in Nineteenth Century Russia*, Chicago, University of Chicago Press, 1983; E. Sarkisyanz, *Russland und der Messianismus der Orients*, Tubingen, Mohr, 1955.

13. In greater detail, see S. N. Eisenstadt, "Transcendental Vision, Center Formation and the Role of Intellectuals," in L. Greenfeld and M. Martin, eds., *Center and Ideas and Institutions*, Chicago, University of Chicago Press, 1980, pp. 96–109.

14. Ibid.

15. H. Oberman, *The Dawn of the Reformation: Essays in the Late Medieval and Early Reformation Thought*, Edinburgh, T. & T. Clark, 1986; and *The Impact of the Reformation: Essays*, Grand Rapids, MI, William B. Eerdmans, 1994; and *The Reformation: Roots and Ramifications*, Edinburgh, T. & T. Clark, 1994.

16. See for instance Ozouf, *La fête revolutionnaire*.

17. M. Merleau-Ponty, *Humanism and Terror*, Boston, Beacon Press, 1969.

18. See Laoust, *Les Schisms dans l'Islam*; and M. Rodinson, "Terrorisme et Politique dans l'Islam Médiéval" (trans. from English by Annick Pelissier), in B. Lewis, ed., *Les Assassins*, Paris, Berger-Levrault, 1982.

19. F. Furet, "Jacobinisme," in Furet and M. Ozouf, eds., *Dictionnaire Critique de la revolution française*, Paris, Flammarion, 1988, pp. 751–762; and *French Revolution*; and *Interpreting the French Revolution*; and *Rethinking the French Revolution*; R. Aron, *Machiavel et les tyrannies modernes*, Paris, Editions de Fallois, 1993.

20. See Voegelin, *Enlightenment and Revolution*.

21. See E. Tiryakian, "Three Meta Cultures of Modernity: Christian, Gnostic, Chthonic," *Theory Culture and Society*, 13, 1, 1996, pp. 99–118.

22. On the Axial-Age Civilizations, see S. N. Eisenstadt, "The Axial Age: The Emergence of Transcendental Visions and the Rise of Clerics," *European Journal of Sociology*, 23, 2, 1952, pp. 294–314; Eisenstadt, ed., *The Origins and Diversity of Axial-Age Civilizations*, Albany, NY, SUNY Press, 1986.

23. T. Ball and J. G. A. Pocock, eds., *Conceptual Change and the Constitution*, Lawrence, KS, University of Kansas Press, 1988; J. G. A. Pocock, *The Machiavellian Moment*, Princeton, Princeton University Press, 1975; and *Virtue, Commerce, and History*, Cambridge, Cambridge University Press, 1985.

24. Voegelin, *Enlightenment and Revolution*; and *The New Science of Politics*; and *Die politischen Religionen*; and *Das Volk Gottes*.

25. See on this H. G. Koenigsberger, "Riksdag, Parliaments and States General in the Sixteenth and Seventeenth Centuries," in Nils Stjernquist, ed., *The Swedish Riksdag in a Comparative Perspective*, Stockholm, The Bank of Sweden Tercentenary Foundation, 1979, pp. 59–79.

26. S. N. Eisenstadt and B. Giesen, "The Construction of Collective Identity," *European Journal of Sociology – Archives européennes de sociologie*, 36, 1, 1995, pp. 72–102; Shils, "Primordial, Personal, Sacred, and Civil Ties".

27. W. Reddy, *The Rise of Market Culture. The Textile Trade and French Society*, Chicago, University of Chicago Press, 1984.

28. C. Tilly, *Coercion, Capital, and European States, AD 990–1990*, Cambridge, Basil Blackwell, 1990; B. Downing, "Constitutionalism, Warfare, and Political Change in Early Modern Europe," *Theory and Society*, 17, 1988, pp. 7–56.

29. T. Todorov, *The Morals of History*, Minneapolis, University of Minnesota Press, 1995; and *The Conquest of America: The Question of the Other*, New York, Harper and Row, 1984.

30. C. Bigger, *Kant's Methodology: An Essay in Philosophical Archeology*, Athens, Ohio University Press, 1996; Ch. Taylor, *Hegel and the Modern Society*, Cambridge, Cambridge University Press, 1989.

31. A. Salomon, *In Praise of Enlightenment*, Cleveland, World Pub. Co., 1963; and *The Tyranny of Progress: Reflections on the Origins of Sociology*, New York, Noonday Press, 1955; S. Toulmin, *Cosmopolis, The Hidden Agenda of Modernity*, New York, Free Press, 1990.

32. Eisenstadt, "Transcendental Vision, Center Formation and the Role of Intellectuals"; "Frameworks of the Great Revolutions: Culture, Social Structure, History and Human Agency"; and *Revolutions and the Transformation of Societies*.

33. See Eisenstadt, "Transcendental Vision, Center Formation and the Role of Intellectuals"; and *Modernization, Protest and Change*, Englewood Cliffs, Prentice Hall, 1966; Shils, "Primordial, Personal, Sacred and Civil Ties," in Shils, ed., *Center and Periphery, Essays in Macrosociology*, Chicago, University of Chicago Press, 1975, pp. 111–126; M. Lacey and K. Haakonssen, eds., *A Culture of Rights. The Bill of Rights in Philosophy, Politics, and Law. 1791 and 1991*, Cambridge, Cambridge University Press, 1991.

34. P. Rosanvallon, *Le Sacré du citoyen. Histoire du suffrage universel*, Paris, Editions Gallimard, 1992.

35. M. Walzer, ed., *Regicide and Revolution: Speeches at the Trial of Louis XVI*, London, Cambridge University Press, 1974.

36. Helen Cam, *The Hundred and the Hundred Rolls: An Outline of Local Government in Medieval England*, London: Methuen, 1930; C. McIlwain, *Constitutionalism and the Changing World: Collected Papers*, London, Cambridge University Press, 1939; *Constitutionalism*, rev. ed., Ithaca, NY,

Cornell University Press, 1947; and *The Growth of Political Thought in the West*, New York, Macmillan, 1932; G. Jacobson, *Apple of Gold: Constitutionalism in Israel and the United States*, Princeton, Princeton University Press, 1993.

37. Rosanvallon, *Le Sacré du citoyen*.

38. K. M. Baker, *The French Revolution and the Creation of Modern Political Culture*, Oxford, Pergamon Press, 1987.

39. J. Schmidt, "Civil Society and Social Things: Setting the Boundaries of the Social Sciences," *Social Research*, 62, 4, 1995, pp. 899–932; J. Cohen and A. Arato, *Civil Society and Political Theory*, Cambridge MA, MIT Press, 1992; V. Perez Diaz, *The Return of Civil Society. The Emergence of Democratic Spain*, Cambridge MA, Harvard University Press, 1993.

40. Toulmin, *Cosmopolis*.

41. D. Outram, *The Enlightenment*, Cambridge MA, Cambridge University Press, 1995; Salomon, *In Praise of Enlightenment*; and *The Tyranny of Progress: Reflections on the Origins of Sociology*.

42. M. Lilla, *Making of an Anti-Modern*, Cambridge MA, Harvard University Press, 1993; and "Was ist Gegenaufklärung?," in *Merkur*, 566, 1966, pp. 400–411; I. Berlin, "Two Concepts of Liberty," in *Four Essays on Liberty*, London, Oxford University Press, 1975, pp. 118–172; *Vico and Herder*, New York, Hogarth Press, 1976; idem, *Against the Current*, New York, Hogarth Press, 1980; and *The Crooked Timber of Humanity*, New York, J. Murray, 1991; G. Vico, *The New Science of Giambattista Vico*, abridged and rev. ed., Garden City NY, Anchor Books, 1961; J. Herder, *J. G. Herder on Social and Political Culture*, Cambridge, Cambridge University Press, 1969.

43. Toulmin, *Cosmopolis*; J. Habermas, *The Philosophical Discourse of Modernity*, Cambridge, MA, MIT Press, 1987; H. Blumenberg, *Die Legitimät der Neuzeit*, Frankfurt, Suhrkamp, 1987; S. N. Eisenstadt, ed., *Post-Traditional Societies*, New York, Norton, 1972; Taylor, *Hegel and the Modern Society*; and *Sources of the Self: The Making of the Modern Identity*, Cambridge, MA, Harvard University Press, 1989.

44. See for greater detail S. N. Eisenstadt, *Power, Trust and Meaning*, Chicago, University of Chicago Press, 1995, especially chapter 3.

45. N. Elias, *The Court Society*, Oxford, Blackwell, 1983; and *The Civilizing Process*, New York, Urizen Books, 1978–1982; M. Foucault, *The Birth of the Clinic: An Archaeology of Medical Perception*, New York, Vintage Books, 1973; *Technologies of the Self: A Seminar with Michel Foucault*, Amherst, University of Massachusetts Press, 1988; *Surveiller et Punir: Naissance de la prison*, Paris, Gallimard, 1975; and *Madness and Civilization: A History of Insanity in the Age of Reason*, New York, Pantheon Books, 1965.

C. Castoriadis, *Philosophy, Politics, Autonomy*, Oxford, Oxford University Press, 1991 especially chapters 7, "Power, Politics, Autonomy," pp. 143–174, and 8, "Reflections on 'Rationality' and 'Development'," pp. 175–218.

46. Castoriadis, *Philosophy, Politics, Autonomy*.

47. M. Weber, *Die Protestantische Ethik: Kritiken und Antikritiken*, Gütersloh Germany, Gütersloher Verlagshaus, 1978; and *Politik als Beruf*, Berlin, Duncker and Humblot, 1968; and *On Charisma and Institution Building: Selected Papers*, Chicago, University of Chicago Press, 1968; and *The Rational and Social Foundations of Music*, Carbondale, Southern Illinois University Press, 1958; W. G. Runciman, ed., *Max Weber: Selections in Translation*, Cambridge, Cambridge University Press, 1978.
48. P. Wagner, *A Sociology of Modernity: Liberty and Discipline*, London, Routledge, 1994.
49. See for instance, F. W. Nietzsche, *On the Genealogy of Morality*, Cambridge, Cambridge University Press, 1994; and *The Will to Power*, New York, Vintage Books, 1967; and *Beyond Good and Evil*, Chicago, Gateway, 1955; and *The Living Thoughts of Nietzsche*, London, Cassell, 1942; for a good selection, see W. Kaufmann, ed., *The Portable Nietzsche: Selected and Translated*, New York, Viking Press, 1965. See also S. Aschheim, "Nietzsche and the German Radical Right, 1914–1933," in Z. Sternhell, ed., *The Intellectual Revolt Against Liberal Democracy 1870–1945*, Jerusalem, Israel Academy of Sciences and Humanities, 1996, pp. 159–176.

E. Junger, *Feuer und Blut*, Magdeburg, Stahlhelm Verlag, 1925; and *Der Kampf also inneres Erlebnis*, Berlin, Mittler, 1929; and "Der Arbeiter," in his *Werke*, VI, Stuttgart, E. Klett, 1964.

M. Heidegger, *Hegel's Phenomenology of Spirit*, Bloomington, Indiana University Press, 1988; and *The Fundamental Concepts of Metaphysics*, Bloomington, Indiana University Press, 1995; and *German Existentialism*, New York, Philosophical Library, 1965; one of the best works on Heidegger is G. Steiner, *Martin Heidegger*, New York, The Viking Press, 1979.
50. J. Herf, "Reactionary Modernism Reconsidered: Modernity, the West and the Nazis," in Sternhell, ed., *The Intellectual Revolt Against Liberal Democracy 1870–1945*, pp. 131–158; J. Muller, "The Radical Conservative Critique of Liberal Democracy in Weimar Germany: Hans Freyer and Carl Schmitt," in Sternhell, ed., *The Intellectual Revolt Against Liberal Democracy 1870–1945*, pp. 190–218. Junger, *Feuer und Blut*; and *Der Kampf also inneres Erlebnis*; and "Der Arbeiter". H. Freyer, *Theorie des objektiven Geistes: Eine Einleitung in die Kulturphilosophie*, Leipzig, B. G. Teubner, 1923; and *Die Industriegesellschaft in Ost und West: Konvergenzen und Divergenzen*, Mainz, V. Hase and Koehler, 1966.

C. Schmitt, *Politische Theologie: Vier Kapitel zur Lehre von der Souveränität*, Munich, Duncker and Humblot, 1922; and *Political Romanticism*, Cambridge, MA, MIT Press, 1986; and *Die Diktatur: Von Den Anfängen des modernen Souveränitätsgedankens bis zum Proletarischen Klassenkampf*, Berlin, Duncker and Humblot, 1989; and *The Concept of the Political*, New Brunswick, Rutgers University Press, 1976; and *The Crisis of Parliamentary Democracy*, Cambridge, MA, MIT Press, 1988.

Heidegger, *Hegel's Phenomenology of Spirit*; and *The Fundamental Concepts of Metaphysics*; and *German Existentialism*. One of the best works on Heidegger is Steiner, *Martin Heidegger*.

51. Lilla, "Was ist Gegenaufklärung?"
52. See for instance S. A. Kierkegaard, *Two Ages: The Age of Revolution and the Present Age*, Princeton, Princeton University Press, 1977; and *Fear and Trembling and the Sickness unto Death*, Princeton, Princeton University Press, 1974.

    Nietzsche, *On the Genealogy of Morality*; and *The Will to Power*; and *Beyond Good and Evil*; and *The Living Thoughts of Nietzsche*; for a good selection, see Kaufmann, ed., *The Portable Nietzsche: Selected and Translated*. See also Aschheim, "Nietzsche and the German Radical Right, 1914–1933."

    A. Schopenhauer, *On the Basis of Morality*, Providence, Berghahn Books, 1995; and *The World as Will and Representation*, New York, Dover Publications, 1966; and *Essay on the Freedom of the Will*, Indianapolis, Bobbs-Merrill, 1960.

    L. Strauss, *The Rebirth of Classical Political Rationalism. An Introduction to the Thought of Leo Strauss*, Chicago, University of Chicago Press, 1989; and *The Concept of the Political*, New Brunswick, Rutgers University Press, 1976; and *The City and Man*, Chicago, University of Chicago Press, 1978; and *What is Political Philosophy? And Other Studies*, Glencoe, The Free Press, 1959; and *Thoughts on Machiavelli*, Seattle, University of Washington Press, 1969; and *The Political Thought of Hobbes: Its Basis and its Genesis*, Chicago, University of Chicago Press, 1973.
53. Voegelin, *Enlightenment and Revolution*; and *The New Science of Politics*; and *Die politischen Religionen*; and *Das Volk Gottes*.
54. L. Kolakowski, *Modernity on Endless Trial*, Chicago, University of Chicago Press, 1990.
55. C. Lefort, *Democracy and Political Theory*, Minneapolis, University of Minnesota Press, 1988; see also J. P. Arnason, "The Theory of Modernity and the Problematic of Democracy," *Thesis Eleven*, 26, 1990, pp. 20–46; J. Dryzek, "Political Inclusion and the Dynamics of Democratization," *American Political Science Review*, 90, 3, 1996, pp. 475–487; J. Dunn, *The History of Political Theory and Other Essays*, Cambridge, Cambridge University Press, 1996.
56. J. Nedelski, *Private Property and the Limits of American Constitutionalism*, Chicago, University of Chicago Press, 1990.
57. J. Dunn, *Locke*, Oxford, Oxford University Press, 1984; and *Rethinking Modern Political Theory*, Cambridge, Cambridge University Press, 1978, especially part I.
58. J. Rousseau, *The Social Contract and Discourses*, ed. and intro. G. D. H. Cole, New York, Dutton Everyman's Library, 1968.
59. I. Berlin, "Two Concepts of Liberty," in *Four Essays on Liberty*, London, Oxford University Press, 1975, pp. 118–172; H. Lubbe: *Freiheit statt Emanzipationszwang. Die Liberalen Traditionen und das Ende der marxistischen Illusionen*, Zurich, Edition Interfrom, 1991.
60. Shils, "Primordial, Personal, Sacred and Civil Ties."

61. N. Bobbio, *Il futuro della democrazzia*, Turin, Giulio Einaudi Editore, 1984; and "Postfazione," in Bobbio, *Profilo Ideologico del Novecento Italiano*, Turin, Giulio Einaudi, 1986, pp. 177–185; and *L'eta dei diritti*, Turin, G. Einaudi, 1990; N. Matteucci, "Democrazia e autocrazia nel pensiero di Norberto Bobbio," in *Per una teoria generale della politica – Scritti dedicatti Norberto Bobbio*, Florence, Passignli Editori, 1983, pp. 149–179.
62. On the Jacobin elements in modern polities see: Cochin. *La révolution et la libre pensée*; and *L'esprit du Jacobinisme* and J. Baechler, preface in idem, pp. 7–33; Furet. *Rethinking the French Revolution*; J. L. Talmon, *The Origins of Totalitarianism Democracy*, New York, Praeger, 1960; See also J. L. Salvadori and N. Tranfaghia, eds., *Il modelo politico giacobino e le rivoluzione*, Florence, La Nova Italia, 1984; and M. Salvador, *Europe, America, Marxismo*, Turin, Einaudi; 1990, chapter 7. See also E. Frankel, "Strukturdefekte der Demokratie und deren ünberwindung" and "Ratenmythos und soziale Selbstbestimmung," in Ernest Frankel, ed., *Deutschland und die Westlichen Demokratien*, Frankfurt am Main, Suhrkamp, 1990, pp. 68–95 and 95–137, respectively. A very strong statement against the emphasis on "common will" in the name of "emancipation" can be found in Lübbe: *Freiheit statt Emanzipationszwang. Die Liberalen Traditionen und das Ende der marxistischen Illusionen.*
63. Eisenstadt, *Transcendental Visions*.
64. B. Fontana, ed., *The Invention of the Modern Republic*, Cambridge, Cambridge University Press, 1994.
65. Cam, *The Hundred and the Hundred Rolls: An Outline of Local Government in Medieval England*; McIlwain, *Constitutionalism*; and *The Growth of Political Thought in the West*.
66. On the modern classical revolutions and their background see: Eisenstadt. *Revolutions and the Transformation of Societies*; and "Historical Sociology Revolutions," in *International Social Science Journal*, 1992; M. Lasky "The Birth of a Metaphor: On the Origins of Utopia and Revolution," *Encounter*, 34, 2, 1970, pp. 35–45 and 3, 1970, 30–42; and *Utopia and Revolution.* Chicago: University of Chicago Press, 1976.

On the Revolutions and modernity, see for instance the special issue on The French Revolution and the Birth of Modernity, *Social Research*, 1989.

On the role of groups of heterodox intellectuals in some of the revolutions and in the antecedent periods, see: Cochin, *La révolution et la libre pensée*; and *L'esprit du Jacobinisme* and J. Baechler, preface in idem, pp. 7–33; Furet, *Rethinking the French Revolution*; Nahirny, *The Russian Intelligentsia: From Torment to Silence.*
67. See C. S. Maier, ed., *Changing Boundaries of the Political*, Cambridge, Cambridge University Press, 1987; and A. Przeworski, *Capitalism and Social Democracy*, Cambridge, Cambridge University Press, 1985.

3 Fundamentalism as a modern Jacobin anti-modern utopia and heterodoxy

1. G. Marsden, *Fundamentalism and American Culture*, New York, Oxford University Press, 1980, p. 4.
2. The most important religious fundamentalist groups in America have been:

> **American Center for Law and Justice** Legal organization of the contemporary Christian Right, assiciated with Pat Robertson and spearheaded by Jay Sekulow. The ACLJ files lawsuits on behalf of Christians who believe they have faced discrimination. Founded in 1990.
>
> **American Council of Christian Churches** Militant fundamentalist organization, formed in 1941 by Carl McIntyre. The ACCC denounced Communist infiltration in society and in mainline Protestant churches and provided resources to the anti-Communist groups of the 1950s.
>
> **American Family Association** Founding date unknown. Organization of the contemporary Christian Right, originally known as the National Federation of Decency, headed by Donald Wildmon. The AFA focuses primarily on monitoring sex and violence on television and on countering anti-Christian stereotypes on television. It organizes consumer boycotts of the sponsors of offending programs.
>
> **Bible Crusaders of America** Anti-evolution organization of the 1920s. The BCA was well funded, linked to Baptist churches, and active primarily in the South.
>
> **Bible League of North America** Organization formed in 1902 that fought the teaching of evolution through arguments and publications.
>
> **Catholic Alliance** Organization launched in 1995 by the Christian Coalition to attract Catholic support for the Christian Right.
>
> **Christian Coalition** Organization of the contemporary Christian Right, headed by Pat Robertson and Ralph Reed. The Christian Coalition is the largest extant group and is generally more moderate than other organizations. Founded in 1989.
>
> **Christian Crusade** Anti-communist organization of the 1950s.
>
> **Christian Voice** Christian Right organization founded in the late 1970s by Robert Grant with the help of Pat Robertson. The Christian Voice was known for its lobbying and ridiculed for its voters' guides, which nonetheless served as precursors for more sophisticated contemporary efforts. The organization exists today.
>
> **Church for Excellence in Education** Founding date unknown. Organization of the contemporary Christian Right, headed by Robert Simonds. The CEE opposed the teaching of secular humanism and witchcraft in schools and programs to establish national education standards, such as outcomes-based education.
>
> **Concerned Maine Families** Organization of the contemporary Christian Right that sought to pass a referendum in Maine in 1995 that would

have barred local jurisdictions from passing laws forbidding job discrimination against gays and lesbians.

Concerned Women for America Organization of the contemporary Christian Right, headed by Beverly LaHaye. CWA is composed primarily of women and takes a special interest in women's issues. Founded in 1979.

Defenders of the Christian Faith Anti-evolution organization of the 1920s, active primarily in the Midwest.

Eagle Forum Anti-feminist organization headed by Phyllis Schlafly. Eagle Forum was organized to fight the Equal Rights Amendment in the 1970s and now focuses on opposing feminism, the teaching of secular humanism, and legal abortion.

Family Research Council Organization of the contemporary Christian Right, headed by Gary Bauer. The FRC was once the political arm of Focus on the Family, although the two groups are now separate for tax reasons. The FRC specializes in providing detailed research on policy issues.

Flying Fundamentalists Founding date unknown. Arm of the Defenders of the Christian Faith that sponsored anti-evolution rallies in the Midwest. In 1926 the Flying Fundamentalists appeared in more than 200 cities in Minnesota alone.

Focus on the Family Founding date unknown. Radio ministry and organization of the contemporary Christian Right, headed by James Dobson. The group's political arm is the Family Research Council.

Home School Legal Defense Association Founding date unknown. Organization that defends rights of homeschooling parents, most of whom are Christian Conservatives. The HSLDA is headed by Michael Farris.

Moral Majority Premier Christian Right group of the 1980s, headed by Jerry Falwell. The Moral Majority established paper organizations in all states but was primarily a direct-mail organization that received substantial media attention.

National Association of Evangelicals Organization of evangelical denominations, formed by new evangelicals in 1942 and active today.

Old Time Gospel Hour Founding date unknown. Jerry Falwell's televized sermons from the Liberty Baptist Church in Lynchberg, VA.

Operation Rescue Founding date unknown. Anti-abortion group that specializes in blockading abortion clinics. Members try to prevent women from entering the clinics by physically blocking their path and by harassing them verbally. The organization attracts members of Christian Right groups but also a few pro-life liberals.

Oregon Citizens Alliance Founding date unknown. Organization of the contemporary Christian Right that continues to attempt to amend the Oregon Constitution to allow job discrimination against gays and lesbians and to condemn homosexuality.

People for the American Way Founding date unknown. Organization
founded by Norman Lear to oppose the Christian Right.

Religious Roundtable Christian Right group from the 1980s.

700 Club Founding date unknown. Pat Robertson's television program,
which features interviews with guests of varied religious backgrounds,
an African-American co-host, and political commentary by Robertson.
The *700 Club* provided the financial nucleus of Robertson's 1988 presi-
dential campaign.

Trading Values Coalition Founding date unknown. Organization of the
contemporary Christian Right, headed by Louis Sheldon. TVC focuses
primarily on opposing laws that protect gays and lesbians from job discrimination.

World's Christian Fundamentals Association Religious group formed in
1919 to provide structure to the fundamentalist religious movement.
The WCFA provided resources for the formation of the anti-evolution
groups of the 1920s. Wilcox, Clude. *Onward Christian Soldiers: The
Religious Right in American Politics*. (Boulder, CO, Westview Press,
1996), Glossary.

P. Boyer, *When Time Shall Be No More: Prophecy Belief in Modern American
Culture*, Cambridge MA, Harvard University Press, 1992; P. Crowley, ed.,
Proceedings of the Forty-Sixth Annual Convention. The Catholic Theoretical
Society of America, Vol. 46, June 12–15, 1991; R. Fowler and A. Hertzke,
Religion and Politics in America: Faith Culture and Strategic Choices, Boulder,
CO, Westview Press, 1995; R. Fuller, *Naming the Antichrist: The History of an
American Obsession*, New York, Oxford University Press, 1995; B. Lawrence,
Defenders of God: The Fundamentalist Revolt Against the Modern Age, San
Francisco, Harper and Row, 1989; M. Moen, *The Transformation of the
Christian Right*, Tuscaloosa, University of Alabama Press, 1992; M. Rozell and
C. Wilcox, *Second Coming: The New Christian Right in Virginia Politics*,
Baltimore, Johns Hopkins University Press, 1996; P. Schaff, *America: A Sketch
of the Political, Social, and Religious Character*, New York, Charles Scribner,
1855; P. van Rooden, "Nineteenth-Century Representations of Missionary
Conversion and the Transformation of Western Christianity," in P. van der
Veer, ed., *Conversion of Modernities: The Globalization of Christianity*, New
York, Routledge, 1996, pp. 65–89; C. Wilcox, *God's Warrior: The Christian
Right in Twentieth Century America*, Baltimore, Johns Hopkins University
Press, 1992.

3. David Stoll, *Is Latin America Turning Protestant? The Politics of Evangelical
Growth*, Berkeley, University of California Press, 1990; David Martin, *Tongues
of Fire: The Explosion of Protestantism in Latin America*, Oxford, Basil
Blackwell, 1990; Pablo A. Deiros, "Protestant Fundamentalism in Latin
America," in Martin E. Marty and R. Scott Appleby, eds., *Fundamentalisms
Observed*, Chicago, University of Chicago Press, 1991, pp. 142–196; Edwin

Eloy Aguilar, Jose Miguel Sandoval, Timothy J. Steigenga, and Kenneth M. Coleman, "Protestantism in El Salvador: Conventional Wisdom versus Survey Evidence," *Latin American Research Review*, 28, 2, 1993, pp. 119–140; John A. Coleman, "The Puritan Ethic Goes South. Will Latin America become Protestant?," *Commonweal*, January 25, 1991, pp. 59–63; Daniel H. Levine, "Protestants and Catholics in Latin America: A Family Portrait," *Bulletin. The American Academy of Arts and Sciences*, 50, 4, 1997, pp. 10–42; and "Popular Groups, Popular Culture, and Popular Religion," *Comparative Studies in Society and History*, 32, 4, 1990, pp. 718–764; Anne Motley Hallum, "Toward an Understanding of the Protestant Movement in Central America: Missionary Patterns and Political Protestants in Nicaragua," Paper presented at the 91st Annual Meeting of the American Political Science Association, Chicago, August 31–September 3, 1995; Andrew J. Stein, "Religion and Mass Politics in Central America," Preliminary Draft Paper; D. Miller, ed., *Coming of Age. Protestantism in Contemporary Latin America*, New York, University Press of America, 1994; E. Cleary and H. Stewart-Gambino, *Power, Politics, and Pentecostals in Latin America*, Boulder, CO, Westview Press.

4. M. K. Silber, "The Emergence of Ultra-Orthodoxy: The Invention of a Tradition," in Jack Wertheimer, ed., *The Uses of Tradition*, Cambridge, MA, Harvard University Press, 1992.

5. A. Ravitzky, *Messianism, Zionism and Jewish Religious Radicalism*, Chicago, University of Chicago Press, 1993; Samuel Heilman, *Defenders of Faith: Inside Ultra-Orthodox Jewry*, New York, Schocken Books, 1992; David Landau, *Piety and Power: The World of Jewish Fundamentalism*, New York, Hill and Wang, 1993.

6. H. Soloveitchik, "Migration, Acculturation, and the New Role of Texts in the Haredi World," in M. E. Marty and R. S. Appleby, eds., *Accounting for Fundamentalisms*, Chicago, University of Chicago Press, 1994, pp. 197–236; S. Heilman, "Quiescent and Active Fundamentalisms: The Jewish Cases," in Marty and Appleby, eds., *Accounting for Fundamentalisms*, pp. 173–196; and "The Vision from the Madrasa and Bes Medrash: Some Parallels between Islam and Judaism," in M. Marty and R. S. Appleby, eds., *Fundamentalisms Comprehended*, Chicago, University of Chicago Press, 1995, pp. 71–95; J. Harris, "Fundamentalism: Objections from a Modern Jewish Historian," in J. Stratton Hawley, ed., *Fundamentalism and Gender*, New York, Oxford University Press, 1994, pp. 137–174.

7. S. Heilman and M. Friedman, "Religious Fundamentalism and Religious Jews: The Case of the Haredim," in M. Marty and R. S. Appleby, eds., *Fundamentalisms Observed*, Chicago, University of Chicago Press, 1991, pp. 197–264;

8. J. O. Voll "Fundamentalism in Sunni Arab World: Egypt and the Sudan," in Marty and Appelby, eds., *Fundamentalisms Observed*, pp. 345–403.

9. M. Retnani, ed., *Penseurs maghrébins contemporains*, Casablanca, EDDIF, 1997; H. Al-Tourabi, *Islam, avenir du monde*, Paris, J. C. Lattes, 1997; A. Laroui, *Islamisme, modernisme, libéralisme*, Casablanca, Centre Culturel

Arabe, 1997; B. Kodmani-Darwish and M. Chartouni-Dubarry, eds., *Les etats arabes face à la contestation Islamiste*, Paris, Armand Colin, 1997.

10. Mumtaz Ahmad, "Islamic Fundamentalism in South Asia: The Jamaat-i-Islami and the Tablighi Jamaat," in Marty and Appleby, eds., *Fundamentalisms Observed*, pp. 457–530. See also, S. V. R. Nasr, *The Vanguard of the Islamic Revolution: The Jama'at-I Islam of Pakistan*, Berkeley, University of California Press, 1994; S. Mardin, "Culture Change and the Intellectual: A Study of the Effects of Secularization in Modern Turkey," in Mardin, ed., *Cultural Transitions in the Middle East*, Leiden, E. J. Brill, 1994; I. Markoff, "Popular Culture, State Ideology, and National Identity in Turkey: The Arabesk Polemic," in Mardin, ed., *Cultural Transitions in the Middle East*; W. Heitmeyer, J. Müller and H. Schröder, *Verlockender Fundamentalismus. Türkische Jugendische in Deutschland*, Frankfurt am Main, Suhrkamp, 1997; M. Heper and A. Evin, eds., *Politics in the Third Turkish Republic*, Boulder, Westview Press, 1993; M. Heper, A. Öncü, and H. Kramer, eds., *Turkey and the West. Changing Political and Cultural Identities*, London, I. B. Tauris & Co., 1993; N. Göle, "Laïcité, modernisme et islamisme en Turquie," *Cahiers d'études sur la Méditerranée orientale et le monde turco-iranien*, 19, 1995, pp. 85–96; and "Authoritarian Secularism and Islamist Politics: The Case of Turkey," in A. R. Norton, ed., *Civil Society in the Middle East*, Leiden, E. J. Brill, 1996, pp. 17–44; A. Mosely Lesch, "The Destruction of Civil Society in the Sudan," in Norton, ed., *Civil Society in the Middle East*, pp. 153–192; R. S. O'Fahey, "Islamic Hegemonies in the Sudan," in L. Brenner, ed., *Muslim Identities and Social Change in Sub-Saharan Africa*, Bloomington, Indiana University Press, 1993, pp. 21–58; G. Warburg, "Mahdism and Islamism in Sudan," *International Journal of Middle East Studies*, 27, 2, 1995, pp. 219–236; N. Levtzion, "The Eighteenth Century. Background to the Islamic Revolutions in West Africa," in Levtzion and J. Voll, *Eighteenth Century Renewal and Reform in Islam*, Syracuse, Syracuse University Press, 1987, pp. 21–38.

11. See O. Ray, "Le néofundamentalisme islamique on l'imaginaire de l'ummah," *L'Esprit*, April 1996, pp. 80–108.

12. N. R. Keddie, "The New Religious Politics: Where, When and Why Do 'Fundamentalisms' Appear?," *Comparative Studies in History and Society*, forthcoming 1998. See also F. Lechner, "The Case Against Secularization: A Rebuttal," *Social Forces*, 69, 4, 1991, pp. 1103–1119; and "Book Reviews: Religious Challenges," *Sociology of Religion*, 55, 3, 1994, pp. 359–363; and "Against Modernity: Antimodernism in Global Perspective," in P. Colony, ed., *The Dynamics of Social Systems*, London, Sage Publications, 1992, pp. 72–92; and "Fundamentalism Revisited," in T. Robbins and D. Anthony, eds., *In Gods We Trust: New Patterns of Religious Pluralism in America* (2nd. ed.), New Brunswick, Transaction Publishers, 1990, pp. 77–97; and "Global Fundamentalism," in W. Swatos, ed., *A Future for Religion? New Paradigms for Social Analysis*, London, Sage Publications, 1993, pp. 19–36.

13. D. Eickelman, ed., *Russia's Muslim Frontiers: New Directions in Cross-Cultural Analysis*, Bloomington, Indiana University Press, 1993; L. Kolakowski, *Chrétiens sans église*, Paris, Gallimard, 1969.

14. E. Sivan, "In God's Cause," in the Erasmus Ascension Symposium, *The Limits of Pluralism. Neo-Absolutism and Relativism*, Amsterdam, Praemium Erasmianum Foundation, 1994.

15. F. Halliday, "Fundamentalism and the Contemporary World," *Contention*, 4, 2, 1995, pp. 41–58; and *Islam and the Myth of Confrontation. Religion and Politics in the Middle East*, London, I. B. Tauris Publishers, 1995; E. Sprinzak, "When Prophecy Fails: The Crisis of Jewish Fundamentalism in Israel," *Contention*, 4, 2, 1995, pp. 105–120; G. Sick, "The United States and Iran: Truth and Consequences," *Contention*, 5, 2, 1996, pp. 59–106.

16. J. L. Peacock, "Weberian, Southern Baptist, and Indonesian Muslim Conceptions of Belief and Action," Reprint from Carol E. Hill, ed., *Symbols and Society: Essays on Belief Systems in Action*, Southern Anthropological Society Proceedings, 9, pp. 82–92; and "Religion and Life History: An Exploration in Cultural Psychology," in E. Bruner, ed., *Text, Play and Story*, American Ethnological Proceedings, 1983, pp. 94–116; and "Traditionalism and Reform, Constancy and Climax in Java and the South," draft; W. Hugenholtz and K. van Vliet-Leigh, eds., *Islam and Europe in Past and Present*, Wassenaar, NIAS, 1997.

17. R. Grew, "On Seeking the Cultural Context of Fundamentalism," University of Michigan, draft; P. van der Veer, ed., *Conversion to Modernities: The Globalization of Christianity*, New York, Routledge, 1996.

18. G. Almond, E. Sivan and R. S. Appleby, "Fundamentalism: Genus and Species," in Marty and Appleby, eds., *Fundamentalisms Comprehended*, pp. 399–424; and "Explaining Fundamentalisms," pp. 425–444; and "Examining the Cases," in ibid, pp. 445–482; and "Politics, Ethnicity, and Fundamentalism," in ibid, pp. 483–504.

19. H. Munson Jr., "Intolerable Tolerance: Western Academia and Islamic Fundamentalism," *Contention*, 5, 3, 1996, pp. 99–118.

20. M. Riesebrodt, *Fundamentalismus as patriarchalische Protestbewegung*, Tübingen, Mohr, 1990.

21. J. F. Burns, "The West in Afghanistan, Before and After," *New York Times*, Feb. 18, 1996, p. 3; and "Misery is Still Afghanistan's Ruler," *New York Times*, April 23, 1995, p. 4; C. Hedges, "Islam Bent Into Ideology: Vengeful Vision of Hope," *New York Times*, October 23, 1994, p. 2; C. Schmidt-Häuer, "Afghanistan im eigenen Land," *Die Zeit*, December 23, 1994, p. 3; M. Lüders, "Allahs Wahrheit im Computer," *Die Zeit*, September 16, 1994, p. 49; E. Hunziker, "Qom – heilige Stadt der Mullahs," *Neue Zürcher Zeitung*, November 20/21, 1993, pp. 84–86.

22. See for instance, S. A. Arjomand, "Shi'ite Jurisprudence and Constitution Making in the Islamic Republic of Iran," in M. Marty and R. S. Appleby, eds., *Fundamentalisms and the State*, Chicago, University of Chicago Press, 1993, pp. 88–109.

23. Eickelman, ed., *Russia's Muslim Frontiers: New Directions in Cross-Cultural Analysis*; J. P. Piscatori, "Asian Islam: International Linkages and Their Impact on International Relations," in J. Esposito, ed., *Islam in Asia: Religion, Politics and Society*, New York, Oxford University Press, 1987, pp. 230–261.

24. Levine, "Protestants and Catholics in Latin America: A Family Portrait."

25. M. E. Yapp, "Full Mosques, Empty Heads," *Times Literary Supplement*, May 30, 1997, p. 4.

26. Almond, Sivan and Appleby, "Fundamentalism: Genus and Species"; and "Explaining Fundamentalisms"; and "Examining the Cases"; and "Politics, Ethnicity, and Fundamentalism."

27. Lechner, "Against Modernity: Antimodernism in Global Perspective"; and "Global Fundamentalism"; and "The Case Against Secularization: A Rebuttal"; and "Book Reviews: Religious Challenges"; and "Fundamentalism Revisited"; Riesebrodt, *Fundamentalismus as patriarchalische protestbewegung*.

28. F. Khosrokhavar, "L'Universel abstrait, le politique et la construction de l'Islamisme comme forme d'altérité," in M. Wieviorka, ed., *Une société fragmentée?*, Paris, Editions La Découverte, 1996, pp. 113–151; Göle, "Laïcité, modernisme et islamisme en Turquie"; and "Authoritarian Secularism and Islamist Politics: The Case of Turkey."

29. Silber "The Emergence of Ultra-Orthodoxy: The Invention of a Tradition."

30. Ahmad, "Islamic Fundamentalism in South Asia: The Jamaat-i-Islami and the Tablighi Jamaat."

31. A. Al Azmeh, *Islams and Modernities*, London, Verso, 1993, pp. 98–101.

32. Soloveitchik, "Migration, Acculturation, and the New Role of Texts in the Haredi World."

33. Arjomand, "Shi'ite Jurisprudence and Constitution Making in the Islamic Republic of Iran."

34. Heilman and Friedman, "Religious Fundamentalism and Religious Jews: The Case of the Haredim," and G. Aran, "Jewish Zionist Fundamentalism: The Blood of the Faithful in Israel (Gush Emunim)," in Marty and Appleby, eds., *Fundamentalisms Observed*, pp. 265–344.

    See also L. J. Silberstein, ed., *Jewish Fundamentalism in Comparative Perspective: Religion, Ideology, and the Crisis of Modernity*, New York and London, New York University Press, 1993.

35. J. O. Voll, "Fundamentalism in the Sunni Arab World: Egypt and the Sudan," in Marty and Appleby, eds., *Fundamentalisms Observed*, pp. 345–403; and "Islam and the Modern Nation-State: Sudan," draft; A. Sachedina "Activist Shi'ism in Iran, Iraq and Lebanon," in Marty and Appleby, eds., *Fundamentalisms Observed*, pp. 403–456; also Tibi, *The Crisis of Modern Islam*.

36. Burns, "The West in Afghanistan, Before and After"; and "Misery is Still Afghanistan's Ruler"; Hedges, "Islam Bent Into Ideology: Vengeful Vision of Hope"; Schmidt-Häuer, "Afghanistan im eigenen Land"; Lüders, "Allahs Wahrheit im Computer"; E. Hunziker, "Qom – heilige Stadt der Mullahs"; and "Die Muslime und die Menschenrechte," *Neue Zürcher Zeitung*, November 22,

1995, p. 77; E. Sciolino, "The Red Menace is Gone. But Here's Islam," *New York Times*, January 21, 1996, pp. 1–4.

37. N. Göle, "Democracy and Secularism in Turkey: Trends and Perspectives," *MESA*, December 6–10 1995, to be published in *Middle East Journal*, pp. 14–15 and 10–11.

38. M. Malia, "Leninist Endgame," *Daedalus*, 121, 2, 1992, pp. 57–76.

39. See S. N. Eisenstadt, "Center–Periphery in Soviet Russia," in A. Motyl, ed., *Rethinking Theoretically about Soviet Nationalities*, New York, Columbia University Press, 1992, pp. 205–225, and "The Breakdown of Communist Regimes," *Daedalus*, 121, 2, 1992, pp. 21–43.

40. Eickelman, ed., *Russia's Muslim Frontiers: New Directions in Cross-Cultural Analysis*; J. P. Piscatori, *Islam in a World of Nation States*, Cambridge, Cambridge University Press, 1986.

41. E. Gellner, "Fundamentalism as a Comprehensive System: Soviet Marxism and Islamic Fundamentalism Compared," in Marty and Appleby, eds., *Fundamentalisms Comprehended*, pp. 277–288.

42. E. Junger, *Feuer und Blut*, Magdeburg, Stahlhelm Verlag, 1925; and *Der Kampf als inneres Erlebnis*, Berlin, Mittler, 1929; and "Der Arbeiter," in his *Werke*, VI, Stuttgart, E. Klett, 1960; R. de Felice, *Il Fascismo. Le interpretazioni dei contemporanei e degli storici*, Bari, Laterza, 1970; and *Le fascisme, un totalitarisme a l'italienne*, Paris, Presses de la Fondation Nationale des Sciences politiques, 1988.

43. G. Obeyskeyere, "Buddhism, Nationhood, and Cultural Identity: A Question of Fundamentals," in Marty and Appleby, eds., *Fundamentalisms Comprehended*, pp. 231–258.

4 Historical setting and variability of fundamentalist movements

1. E. Hobsbawm, *The Age of Revolution*, London, Weidenfeld & Nicholson, 1964; and *Age of Extremes: The Short Twentieth Century, 1914–1991*, New York, Viking Penguin, 1994; T. Von Laue, *The World Revolution of Westernization. The Twentieth Century in Global Perspective*, New York, Oxford University Press, 1987.

2. S. N. Eisenstadt, *Modernization, Protest and Change*, Englewood Cliffs, Prentice Hall, 1966.

3. For general analysis of social movements, see S. Tarrow, *Power in Movement. Social Movements, Collective Action and Politics*, Cambridge, Cambridge University Press, 1994; H. Bash, *Social Problems and Social Movements: An Exploration into the Sociological Construction of Alternative Realities*, Atlantic Highlands, NJ, Humanity Press, 1995; A. Morris and C. McClurg Mueller, eds., *Frontiers in Social Movement Theory*, New Haven, Yale University Press, 1992; W. Galenson, ed., *Comparative Labor Movements*, Englewood Cliffs, Prentice Hall, 1952; R. Heberle, *Social Movements: An Introduction to Political Sociology*, New York, Appleton, 1951; W. Kornhauser, *The Politics of Mass*

Society, Glencoe, Free Press, 1959; N. Smelser, *Theory of Collective Behavior*, New York, Free Press, 1963; M. Traugott, ed., *Repertoires and Cycles of Collective Action*, Durham, Duke University Press, 1995; W. Gamson, "Political Discourse and Collective Action," *International Social Movements Research*, 1, 1988, pp. 219–247; A. Melucci, "Getting Involved: Identity and Mobilization in Social Movements," *International Social Movements Research*, 1, 1988, pp. 329–348.

On socialism, syndicalism and nationalism see P. Snowden, *Socialism and Syndicalism*, London, Collins' Clear-Type Press, 1953; G. Sorel, *Materiaux d'une théorie du proletariat*, New York, Arno Press, 1975; W. Elliot, *The Pragmatic Revolt in Politics. Syndicalism, Fascism and the Constitutional State*, New York, H. Fertig, 1968; J. Joll, *The Anarchists*, London, Eyre & Spottiswoode, 1964; .

For the history of different movements in some selected societies see:
In Asian countries: B. Kesavanarayana, *Political and Social Factors in Andhra (1900–1956)*, Vijayawada, Navodaya, 1976; D. Apter, *Revolutionary Discourse in Mao's Republic*, Cambridge, MA, Harvard University Press, 1994; G. Bennett, *"Yundong" Mass Campaigns in Chinese Communist Leadership*, Berkeley, University of California Press, 1976; E. Koury, *The Patterns of Mass Movements in Arab Revolutionary-Progressive States*, The Hague, Mouton, 1970; C. Uyehara, *Leftwing Social Movements in Japan. An Annotated Bibliography Published for the Fletcher School of Law and Diplomacy*, Tokyo, Tufts University, C. E. Tuttle, 1959.

In Latin America: D. La Botz, *Democracy in Mexico. Peasant Rebellion and Political Reform*, Boston, South End Press, 1995; S. Stokes, *Cultures in Conflict. Social Movements and the State in Peru*, Berkeley, University of California Press, 1995.

In contemporary Europe: D. Della Porta, *Social Movements, Political Violence and the State. A Comparative Analysis of Italy and Germany*, Cambridge, Cambridge University Press, 1995; S. Sarkar, *Green-Alternative Politics in West Germany*, New Delhi, Promilla and Co., 1993; C. Boggs, *Social Movements and Political Power. Emerging Forms of Radicalism in the West*, Philadelphia, Temple University Press, 1986; C. Landauer, *European Socialism*, Berkeley, University of California Press, 1959; G. Rude, *The Crowd in the French Revolution*, Oxford, Clarendon, 1960; C. Joppke, *East German Dissidents and the Revolution of 1989. Social Movements in a Leninist Regime*, New York, New York University Press, 1995; K. Opp, *Origins of a Spontaneous Revolution, East Germany, 1989*, Ann Arbor, University of Michigan Press, 1995; V. Brovkin, *Behind the Front Lines of the Civil War. Political Parties and Social Movements in Russia 1918–1922*, Princeton, Princeton University Press, 1994; V. Kostunica, *Party Pluralism or Monism. Social Movements and the Political System in Yugoslavia, 1944–1949*, Boulder, East European Monographs, 1985.
In N. America: D. Steigerwald, *The Sixties and the End of Modern America*, New York, St. Martin's Press, 1995; R. Jackson, *The 1960s. An Annotated*

Bibliography of Social and Political Movements in the United States, Westpoint, Greenwood Press, 1992; E. Morgan, *The 60s Experience. Hard Lessons About Modern America*, Philadelphia, Temple University Press, 1991; D. Egbert and S. Persons, eds., *Socialism and American Life*, Princeton, Princeton University Press, 1952; J. Gusfield, *Symbolic Crusade: Status Politics and the American Temperance Movement*, Urbana, University of Illinois Press, 1963; R. Niebhur, *The Social Sources of Denominationalism*, Hamden, Shoe String Press, 1954.

4. Ping-ti Ho and Tang Tsou, eds., *China in Crisis. Vol. 1. China's Heritage and the Communist System*, 2 books, Chicago, Chicago University Press, 1968; A. Woodside, "History, Structure and Revolution in Vietnam," *International Political Science Review*, 10, 2, 1989, pp. 143–159; Nguen, Hyes, and Tu Van Tai, *The Le Code-Law in Traditional Vietnam*, Athens, OH, Ohio University Press, 1982.

5. G. A. Hoston, "A 'Theology' of Liberation? Socialist Revolution and Spiritual Regeneration in Chinese and Japanese Marxism," in P. A. Cohen and M. Goldman, eds., *Ideas Across Cultures – Essays on Chinese Thought in Honor of Benjamin J. Schwartz*, Cambridge, MA, Harvard University Press, 1990, pp. 165–194; B. Schwartz, *China and Other Matters*, Cambridge MA, Harvard University Press, 1996; D. Rothermund, "Nationalism and the Reconstruction of Traditions in Asia," draft.

6. S. N. Eisenstadt, "Socialism and Tradition," in Eisenstadt and Y. Azmon, eds. *Socialism and Tradition*, Jerusalem, The Van Leer Foundation, 1975, pp. 1–20.

7. A. von Schelting, *Russland und Europa im russischen Geschichtsdenken*, Bern, A. Francke AG, 1948.

8. Rothermund, "Nationalism and the Reconstruction of Traditions in Asia."

9. S. N. Eisenstadt, *Revolution and the Transformation of Societies*, New York, Free Press, 1978; and "Frameworks of the Great Revolutions: Culture, Social Structure, History and Human Agency," *International Social Science Journal*, 133, 1992, pp. 385–401; V. G. Nahirny, *The Russian Intelligentsia: From Torment to Silence*, New Jersey: Rutgers, Transaction Publication, 1981. K. Riegel, "Der Marxismus-Leninismus als politische Religion," in H. Maier and M. Schäfer, eds., *"Totalitarismus" und "Politische Religionen,"* Munich, Ferdinand Schoningh, 1997, pp. 75–139; P. Pomper, *The Russian Revolutionary Intelligentsia*, New York, Crowell, 1970; F. Venturi, *Roots of Revolution. A History of the Populist and Socialist Movements in Nineteenth Century Russia*, Chicago, University of Chicago Press, 1983; E. Sarkisyanz, *Russland und der Messianismus der Orients*, Tubingen, Mohr, 1955.

10. P. Van der Veer, *Nation and Migration: The Politics of Space in the South Asian Diaspora*, Philadelphia, University of Pennsylvania Press, 1995; and *Religious Nationalism: Hindus and Muslims in India*, Berkeley, University of California Press, 1994. Y. K. Malik and V. B. Singh, *Hindu Nationalists in India: The Rise of the Bharatiya Janata Party*. Boulder, CO, Westview Press, 1994. L. McKean, *Divine Enterprise: Gurus and the Hindu Nationalist Movement*, Chicago, University of Chicago Press, 1996; A. Varshney, "Three Compromised

Nationalisms: Why Kashmir Has Been a Problem," in R. G. C. Thomas, ed., *Perspectives on Kashmir: The Roots of Conflict in South Asia*, Boulder, CO, Westview Press, 1992; and "India: Liberalism vs. Nationalism," *Journal of Democracy*, Books in Review, 1992; and "Contested Meanings: India's National Identity, Hindu Nationalism, and the Politics of Anxiety," *Daedalus*, 122, 3, 1993; Rothermund, "Nationalism and the Reconstruction of Traditions in Asia"; P. Chatterjee, "History and the Nationalization of Hinduism," *Social Research*, 59, 1, 1992, pp. 111–149.

11. Van der Veer, *Nation and Migration: The Politics of Space in the South Asian Diaspora*; and *Religious Nationalism: Hindus and Muslims in India*; Malik and Singh, *Hindu Nationalists in India: The Rise of the Bharatiya Janata Party*; McKean, *Divine Enterprise: Gurus and the Hindu Nationalist Movement*; Varshney, "Three Compromised Nationalisms: Why Kashmir Has Been a Problem"; and "India: Liberalism vs. Nationalism"; and "Contested Meanings: India's National Identity, Hindu Nationalism, and the Politics of Anxiety"; A. Jalal, *Democracy and Authoritarianism in South Asia. A Comparative and Historical Perspective*, Cambridge, Cambridge University Press, 1995.

12. J. E. Llewellyn, *The Arya Samaj as a Fundamentalist Movement: A Study in Comparative Fundamentalism*, Delhi, Manohar, 1993; see also Hussin Mutalib and Taj ul-Islam Hashmi, eds., *Islam, Muslims and the Modern State. Case-Studies of Muslims in Thirteen Countries*, London, Macmillan Press, 1994, and specially chapter 1: Cyrus Bina, "Towards a New World Order: US Hegemony, Client-States and Islamic Alternative," pp. 3–30.

13. P. Chatterjee, *The Nation and Its Fragments: Colonial and Postcolonial Histories*, Princeton, Princeton University Press, 1993; G. Viswanathan, *Masks of Conquest: Literary Study and British Rule in India*, New York, Columbia University Press, 1989; D. Ludden, ed., *Contesting the Nation*, Philadephia, University of Pennsylvania Press, 1996.

14. F. Khosrokhavar, "L'universel abstrait, le politique et la construction de l'islamisme comme forme d'altérité," in M. Wieviorka, ed., *Une société fragmentée?*, Paris, Editions La Decouverte, 1996, pp. 113–151; Jalal, *Democracy and Authoritarianism in South Asia. A Comparative and Historical Perspective*.

15. See T. Kuran, "The Economic Impact of Islamic Fundamentalism," in M. Marty and R. S. Appleby, eds., *Fundamentalisms and the State: Remaking Polities, Economies and Militance*, Chicago, University of Chicago Press, 1993, pp. 302–341; and "Islam and Underdevelopment: An Old Puzzle Revisited," *Journal of Institutional and Theoretical Economics*, 153, 1, 1997; and "The Genesis of Islamic Economics: A Chapter in the Politics of Muslim Identity," *Social Research*, 64, 2, 1997, pp. 301–338.

16. N. Keddie, "The New Religious Politics: Where, When, and Why Do 'Fundamentalisms' Appear?," *Comparative Studies in Society and History*, forthcoming 1998.

17. F. Fukuyama, *The End of History and the Last Man*, New York, Free Press, 1992.
18. Keddie, "The New Religious Politics: Where, When, and Why Do 'Fundamentalisms' Appear?"
19. S. N. Eisenstadt, "Some Observations on 'Post-Modern' Society," in N. Stehr and R. Ericson, eds., *The Culture and Power of Knowledge. Inquiries into Contemporary Societies*, Berlin, Walter de Gruyter, 1992, pp. 51–59; for more general bibliography see S. Seidman, ed., *The Postmodern Turn. New Perspectives on Social Theory*, Cambridge, Cambridge University Press, 1994.
20. N. Elias, *The Court Society*, Oxford, Blackwell, 1983; and *The Civilizing Process*, New York, Urizen Books, 1978–1982; M. Foucault, *The Birth of the Clinic: An Archaeology of Medical Perception*, New York, Vintage Books, 1973; and *Technologies of the Self: A Seminar with Michel Foucault*, Amherst, University of Massachusetts Press, 1988; and *Surveiller et Punir: Naissance de la prison*, Paris, Gallimard, 1975; and *Madness and Civilization: A History of Insanity in the Age of Reason*, New York, Pantheon Books, 1965; M. Weber, *Die protestantische Ethik: Kritiken und Antikritiken*, Gütersloh Germany, Gütersloher Verlagshaus, 1978; and *Politik als Beruf*, Berlin, Dunker and Humblot, 1968; and *On Charisma and Institution Building: Selected Papers*, Chicago, University of Chicago Press, 1968; and *The Rational and Social Foundations of Music*, Carbondale, Southern Illinois University Press, 1958; W. G. Runciman, ed., *Max Weber: Selections in Translation*, Cambridge, Cambridge University Press, 1978.
21. S. N. Eisenstadt and B. Giesen, "The Construction of Collective Identity," *European Journal of Sociology – Archives Européennes de sociologie*, 36, 1, 1995, pp. 72–102; E. Shils, "Primordial, Personal, Sacred, and Civil Ties," in Shils, ed., *Center and Periphery, Essays in Macrosociology*, Chicago, University of Chicago Press, 1975, pp. 111–126.
22. Keddie, "The New Religious Politics: Where, When, and Why Do 'Fundamentalisms' Appear?"
23. The following excerpts from Dr. Hassan al-Tourabi, "Islamic Fundamentalism in the Sunna and Shia World" [http://www.ibmpcug.co.uk/~whip/trabi.htm]:

> The world is now very close, transport, the media, communications, it's all very close. Subsequently, the challenge is very close and you have to respond to it. Unfortunately, the early immediate reactions to Western imperialism and domination were at first, patriotic. National struggles for independence. But the champions of national struggle after they achieved formal independence, and they raised the flag of their new state, were bankrupt. They had nothing to offer.

> The early Arab nationalists played their role. Unity, Pride and Independence, what else? What do you say of economic development? Of justice? Of political systems? What about Arts? Culture? Knowledge? Nothing. It was just an emotion. About unity and defence. Later on came Socialism. Let us cooperate as more than one state to stand up against

the Western challenge. Arab Muslim countries against the West turned
to the East. They looked to the Soviet Union and there was a wave of
Socialism in almost every Muslim country. But Socialism there fell before
it fell in the Soviet Union. It immediately collapsed. The Socialist governments were as corrupt and inefficient as the post-independence
Nationalist and Liberal governments. So you can understand why there
came to be a vacuum for fundamentalism and Islamism.

The Elites Were the Ones that Were Directly Exposed to the West

The movement of Islamic revival has phases. First, spiritual revival, that's
why they call it the revivalist movement – the revival of Islam – sometimes. An identity and an awakening of the spirit. Then a Renaissance,
intellectual renaissance. Not the old traditional literature but let us
produce new literature and address it to contemporary problems and
challenges. And then a resurgence of new action, not just preserving your
religion defensively, but a resurgence. There were a few intellectuals, pio-
neers of fundamentalism in North Africa, in the Middle East, in India
and later on came movements. Most of them were elitist movements
because the elites were the ones that were exposed to the West. Therefore,
they were the ones who responded first to the challenge. Not the masses.

Later on they became mass movements. The latest movements are
mass movements, e.g. the Iranian revolution, the Algerian FIS. Not the
Jam'aat-e-Islami in Pakistan nor the Brotherhood movements in most of
the Arab world, these are elitist movements of quality and quality
matters more than quantity. As I mentioned, for security first and then
for a beginning. But all Islamic movements at first start by educating
their members in ritual practices and normal conduct. Only very rarely
do they address this message of the re-education of the soul to the
masses. Only a few could overcome our traditional custom of leaving
women behind. This is meant for men who aspire to change, who want
to lead change. But some Islamic movements were responsible for the
movement of women's liberation in Muslim societies, in the name of
religion itself. And the model of the Prophet's wives, they crushed customary conduct of segregating women or ignoring women.

Politics Is Only One Dimension of Religion

In politics, Islamic movements wanted, in principle, to integrate politics
and religion, nothing called State and Church. Politics and religion, religion. Politics is only one dimension of religion, is a whole way of life, in
principle. When they advocate the supremacy of Shari'ah, the higher
values, like the natural law here in Europe in earlier times. Only a few
Islamic movements developed these general slogans towards offering
policies and programmes, economic programmes, political programmes,
foreign policy, how to organise a state, etc. . . . Very few, unfortunately,

yet because most of them are still in the state of persuading the whole society, politics has to be integrated into religion.

The economy, in principle, they are against materialism and all of them say that Islam is an economic way of life and they also pursue the principle of justice. Perhaps Socialism has influenced them to concentrate on that priority, but very few Islamic movements are directly involved, as such, in economic life. What new institutions do you propose? How would you mobilise religious energy for economic development and how would you realise justice exactly? Not only in principle, as a slogan, but as a programme.

Culturally, all fundamentalists believe that culture is one. No separation between scientific culture and religious culture. But unfortunately, very few Islamic movements want to develop a university that is both Islamic and modern. Where there is a faculty of Medicine that is Islamic and a faculty of engineering and agriculture that Islamic. Not only studying the Arabic language and ancient literature about Islam with a typical Islamic university life."

For a fuller development of these points see also, Hassan al-Tourabi, *Islam, avenir du monde*, Paris, J. C. Lattes, 1997.

24. M. Kamali, "The Modern Revolutions of Iran," to appear in *Citizenship Studies*, 1997; F. Khosrokhavar, "Les intellectuels post-islamistes en Iran," *Le trimestre du monde*, 1996, pp. 53–62; and "Le sacré et le politique dans la révolution iranienne," in Patrick Michel, ed., *Religion et démocratie*, Paris, Albin Michel, pp. 86–108; and "Le martyre révolutionnaire en Iran," *Social Compass*, 43, 1, 1996, pp. 83–100; H. Esfandiari, *Reconstructed Lives: Women and Iran's Islamic Revolution*, Baltimore, Johns Hopkins University Press, 1997; H. Shahidian, "The Iranian Left and the 'Woman Question' in the Revolution of 1978–1979," *International Journal of Middle East Studies*, 26, 2, 1994.

25. N. Göle, "Laïcité, modernisme et islamisme en Turquie," *Cahiers d'études sur la Méditerranée orientale et le monde turco-iranien*, 19, 1995, pp. 85–96; and "Authoritarian Secularism and Islamist Politics: The Case of Turkey," in A. R. Norton, ed., *Civil Society in the Middle East*, Leiden, E. J. Brill, 1996, pp. 17–44.

26. M. E. Yapp, "Full Mosques, Empty Hearts," *Times Literary Supplement*, May 30, 1997, p. 6.

27. O. Ray, "Le néofundamentalisme islamique on l'imaginaire de l'ummah," *L'Esprit*, April 1996, pp. 80–108; Van der Veer, *Nation and Migration: The Politics of Space in the South Asian Diaspora*; and *Religious Nationalism: Hindus and Muslims in India*; F. Khosrokhavar, *L'Islam des jeunes*, Paris, Flammarion, 1997; J. Rex, *Ethnic Minorities in the Modern Nation State*, London, Macmillan, 1996; R. Hesse, "Der ganz vernünftige Wahn. Sieben Gegendarstellungen zum Islamischen Fundamentalismus," *Kursbuch*, 134, December 1998, pp. 156–178.

28. N. Göle, "Democracy and Secularism in Turkey: Trends and Perspectives," MESA, December 6–10, 1995, to be published in *Middle East Journal*, pp. 12–16.

29. Malik and Singh, *Hindu Nationalists in India: The Rise of the Bharatiya Janata Party*; see also the review article of this book and of J. E. Llewellyn, *The Arya Samaj as a Fundamentalist Movement* by Douglas R. Spitz, in *Journal of Asian Studies*, 54, 4, 1995, p. 1137.

30. T. B. Edsall, "Mistrust of Government Found Festering in White Middle Class," *Washington Post*, September 20, 1996, p. A13.

31. D. Stoll, *Is Latin America Turning Protestant? The Politics of Evangelical Growth*, Berkeley, University of California Press, 1990; D. Martin, *Tongues of Fire. The Explosion of Protestantism in Latin America*, Oxford, Blackwell, 1990; P. A. Deiros, "Protestant Fundamentalism in Latin America," in M. E. Marty and R. S. Appleby, eds., *Fundamentalisms Observed*, Chicago, University of Chicago Press, 1991, pp. 142–196; E. E. Aguilar, J. M. Sandoval, T. J. Steigenga, and K. M. Coleman, "Protestantism in El Salvador: Conventional Wisdom versus Survey Evidence," *Latin American Research Review*, 28, 2, 1993, pp. 119–140; J. A. Coleman, "The Puritan Ethic Goes South. Will Latin America become Protestant?," *Commonweal*, 25, 1991, pp. 59–63; D. H. Levine, "Protestants and Catholics in Latin America: A Family Portrait," *Bulletin. The American Academy of Arts and Sciences*, 50, 4, 1997, pp. 10–42; and "Popular Groups, Popular Culture, and Popular Religion," *Comparative Studies in Society and History*, 32, 4, 1990, pp. 718–764; A. Motley Hallum, "Toward an Understanding of the Protestant Movement in Central America: Missionary Patterns and Political Protestants in Nicaragua," paper presented at the 91st Annual Meeting of the American Political Science Association, Chicago, August 31–September 3, 1995; A. J. Stein, "Religion and Mass Politics in Central America," preliminary draft paper; C. Wagner, *Latin American Theology. Radical or Evangelical?*, Grand Rapids, MI, William B. Eerdman Publishing Company, 1970.

32. Levine, "Protestants and Catholics in Latin America: A Family Portrait." See also the various articles in D. Miller, ed., *Coming of Age. Protestantism in Contemporary Latin America*, New York, University Press of America, 1994.

33. On elaboration of this concept, see S. N. Eisenstadt, "The Axial Age: The Emergence of Transcendental Visions and Rise of Clerics," *European Journal of Sociology*, 23, 2, 1982, pp. 294–314; Eisenstadt, ed., *The Origins and Diversity of Axial Age Civilizations*, New York, State University of New York Press, 1986.

34. S. V. R. Nasr, *Mawdudi and the Making of Islamic Revivalism*, Oxford, Oxford University Press, 1996; and "Democracy and Islamic Revivalism," *Political Science Quarterly*, 110, 2, 1995, pp. 261–285.

35. S. Brower, P. Gritton and S. D. Rose, *Exporting the American Gospel – Global Christian Fundamentalism*, New York, Routledge, 1996.

36. Martin, *Tongues of Fire*.

37. Ping-ti Ho and Tang Tsou, eds., *China in Crisis. Vol. 1. China's Heritage and the Communist System*; Ishtiaq Ahmed, *State, Nation and Ethnicity in Contemporary SouthAsia*, London, Pinter, 1996; M. Alagappa, ed., *Political Legitimacy in Southeast Asia. The Quest for Moral Authority*, Stanford,

Stanford University Press, 1995; R. E. Frykenberg, "Accounting for Fundamentalisms in South Asia: Ideologies and Institutions in Historical Perspective," in M. Marty and R. S. Appleby, eds., *Accounting for Fundamentalisms. The Dynamic Character of Movements*, Chicago, University of Chicago Press, 1994, pp. 591–616.

38. Ahmed, *State, Nation and Ethnicity in Contemporary South Asia*; Alagappa, ed., *Political Legitimacy in Southeast Asia. The Quest for Moral Authority*; Frykenberg, "Accounting for Fundamentalisms in South Asia: Ideologies and Institutions in Historical Perspective".

39. See Martin, *Tongues of Fire*, especially ch. 8: "Instructive Parallels: South Korea and South Africa," pp. 135–162.

40. G. Pandey, *The Construction of Communalism in Colonial North India*, Oxford, Oxford University Press, 1990; Van der Veer, *Religious Nationalism: Hindus and Muslims in India*; A. Vanaik, *The Furies of Indian Communalism. Religion, Modernity and Secularization*, London, Verso, 1997.

41. Van der Veer, *Religious Nationalism: Hindus and Muslims in India*.

42. Ibid.; P. Brass, ed., *Riots and Pogroms*, London, Macmillan Press, 1996; Chatterjee, "History and the Nationalization of Hinduism"; Khosrokhavar, "L'universel abstrait, le politique et la construction de l'islamisme comme forme d'altérité"; S. Tambiah, *Leveling Crowds. Ethnonationalist Conflicts and Collective Violence in South Asia*, Berkeley, University of California Press, 1996; and *Sri Lanka: Ethnic Fratricide and the Dismantling of Democracy*, Chicago, Chicago University Press, 1986; and *Buddhism Betrayed? Religion, Politics and Violence in Sri Lanka*, Chicago, Chicago University Press, 1992; H. von Stietencron, "Die Suche nach nationaler Identität im Indien des 19. und 20. Jahrhunderts," in W. Reinhard, ed., *Die fundamentalistische Revolution*, Freiburg im Breisgau, Rombach, 1995, pp. 111–132; G. Dharampal-Frick, "Zwischen 'Säkularismus' und 'Kommunalismus' Identitätsprobleme in der indischen Politik und Gesellschaft seit der Unabhängigkeit," in W. Reinhard, ed., *Die fundamentalistische Revolution*, pp. 133–150; E. Pulsfort, *Indien am Scheideweg zwischen Sakularismus und Fundamentalismus*, Würzburg, 1991.

43. H. Bechert and R. Gombrich, eds., *The World of Buddhism. Buddhist Monks and Nuns in Society and Culture*, London, Thames and Hudson, 1991; M. Eder, "Geschichte der Japanischen Religion," *Asian Folklore Studies Monographs*, 7, 1 and 2, 1978; D. and A. Matsunaga, *Foundation of Japanese Buddhism, Vol. 1. The Aristocratic Age*, Tokyo, Buddhist Books International, 1974; D. and A. Matsunaga, *Foundations of Japanese Buddhism, Vol. 2. The Mass Movements, Kamakura and Muromachi Periods*, Tokyo, Buddhist Books International, 1976; E. Saunders, *Buddhism in Japan with an Outline of Its Origins on India*, Philadelphia, University of Pennsylvania Press, 1964; Tamaru Noriyoshi, "Buddhism in Japan," in M. Eliade, ed., *The Encyclopaedia of Religion*, vol. 2, New York, Macmillan Publisher Co., 1987, pp. 426–435.

44. H. Nakamura, *The Ways of Thinking of Eastern People India-China-Tibet-Japan*, Honolulu, HI, East-West Center Press, 1964.

45. Z. J. R. Werblowski, *Beyond Tradition and Modernity*, Atlantic Highlands, NJ, Athlone Press, 1976. See also, C. Blacker, "Two Shinto Myths: The Golden Age and the Chosen People," in S. Kenny and J. P. Lehman, eds., *Themes and Theories in Modern Japanese History*, London, Athlone Press, 1988, pp. 64–78; and "The Shinza or God-seat in the Daijosai: Throne, Bed, or Incubation Couch," *Japanese Journal of Religious Studies*, 17, 2–3, June–September 1990, pp. 179–198.

46. Blacker, "Two Shinto Myths; The Golden Age and the Chosen People"; S. Okada, "The Development of State Ritual in Ancient Japan," *Acta Asiatica*, Tokyo, Institute of Eastern Cultures, 1987.

47. K. Pyle, "The Future of Japanese Nationality. An Essay in Contemporary Study," *The Journal of Japanese Studies*, 8, 2, 1982, pp. 223–265; Kosaku Yoshino, *Cultural Nationalism in Contemporary Japan*, London, Routledge, 1992; H. Befu and Manabe Kafuzumi, *An Empirical Study of Nihonjinron: How Real is the Myth?*

     On some very important dimensions of Japanese collective self in historical times, see E. Ohnuki-Tierney, *Rice as Self*, Princeton, Princeton University Press, 1993.

48. For the most recent presentation of the process of the Restoration, see M. B. Jansen, ed., "The Meiji Restoration," in J. W. Hall et al., eds., *The Cambridge History of Japan*, vol. 5, Cambridge, Cambridge University Press, 1989, pp. 308–367; C. Totman et al., "The Meiji Ishin: Product of Gradual Decay, Abrupt Crisis or Creative Will," in H. Wray and H. Conroy, eds., *Japan Examined: Perspectives on Modern Japanese History*, Honolulu, University of Hawaii Press, 1983, pp. 55–78; W.G. Beasley, *The Meiji Restoration*, Stanford, Stanford University Press, 1972; K. Timbergen, *Revolutions from Above*, New Brunswick, Transactions Publishers, 1978.

49. On the Puritans see: M. Walzer, *The Revolution of the Saints*, Cambridge MA, Harvard University Press, 1966.

     On the Intellectuals in the French Revolution, see: A. Cochin, *La révolution et la libre pensée*, Paris, Plon-Nourrit, 1924; and *L'esprit du Jacobinisme*, Paris, Presses Universitaires de France, 1979; F. Furet, *French Revolution*, New York, Macmillan, 1970; and *Interpreting the French Revolution*, Cambridge, Cambridge University Press, 1981.

     On the Russian Intelligentsia, see: Nahirny, *The Russian Intelligentsia: From Torment to Silence*; Riegel, "Der Marxismus-Leninismus als politische Religion"; Pomper, *The Russian Revolutionary Intelligentsia*; Venturi, *Roots of Revolution. A History of the Populist and Socialist Movements in Nineteenth Century Russia*; Sarkisyanz, *Russland und der Messianismus der Orients*.

50. P. Duus and D. Okimoto, "Fascism and the History of Pre-War Japan: The Failure of the Concept," *Journal of Asian Studies*, 39, 1, 1979, pp. 65–76.

51. R. N. Bellah, "Civil Religion in America," *Daedalus*, 96, 1, Winter, 1967, pp. 1–21; and *The Broken Covenant*, New York, Seabury Press, 1975.

52. S. P. Huntington, *American Politics. The Promise of Disharmony*, Cambridge, MA, Harvard University Press, 1981, pp. 23–25.

53. W. F. Naylor, "Some Thoughts upon Reading Tocqueville's Democracy in America," paper for Prof. Edward Shils' seminar on Ideas on Social Solidarity, University of Chicago, May 1995.

54. C. Adamson, "God's Continent Divided: Politics and Religion in Upper Canada and the Northern and Western United States, 1775 to 1841," *Comparative Studies in Society and History*, 36, 3, 1994, pp. 417–446.

55. Huntington, *American Politics. The Promise of Disharmony*.

56. G. M. Thomas, *Revivalism and Cultural Change: Christianity, National Building, and the Market in the Nineteenth-Century United States*, Chicago, The University of Chicago Press, 1989.

57. Jason Epstein in his review of two books by Lind and Hodgson.

58. Ibid.

59. Ibid.

60. See T. Egan, "Inside the World of the Paranoid," *The New York Times*, April 30, 1995, section 4, pp. 1 & 5; P. Applebome, "An Unlikely Legacy of the '60s: The Violent Right," *New York Times*, May 7, 1995, pp. 1–18; S. Fish, "How the Right Hijacked the Magic Words," *The New York Times*, August 13, 1995, p. 7; M. Henneberger, "A Shaken City, Ever Devout, Turns to God," *The New York Times*, April 30, 1995, p. 1.

61. S. N. Eisenstadt, *Traditionalism, Patrimonialism and Modern Neopatrimonialism*, London, Sage Publications, 1973.

62. S. N. Eisenstadt, *European Civilization in a Comparative Perspective*, Oslo, Norwegian University Press, 1987; M. Oakeshott, *Social and Political Doctrines of Contemporary Europe*, London, Basic Books, 1940; F. Heer, *The Intellectual History of Europe*, Garden City, Doubleday, 1968.

63. S. Rokkan, "Dimensions of State Formation and Nation Building: A Possible Paradigm for Research on Variations within Europe," in C. Tilly, ed., *The Formation of National States in Western Europe*, Princeton NJ, Princeton University Press, 1975, pp. 562–600; R. Grew, ed., *Crisis of Political Development in Europe and the United States*, Princeton, Princeton University Press, 1978.

64. Levine, "Protestants and Catholics in Latin America: A Family Portrait."

65. Levine, "Popular Groups, Popular Culture, and Popular Religion."

66. S. Harrison, *India – The Most Dangerous Decades*, Princeton, Princeton University Press, 1960.

67. Ibid.

68. R. Inden, *Imagining India*, Oxford, Blackwell, 1990, p. 220.

69. S. Pollock, "Ramayama and Political Imagination in India," *The Journal of Asian Studies*, 52, 2, May 1993, pp. 261–297.

70. M. Weiner, *The Indian Paradox. Essays in Indian Politics*, New Delhi, Sage Publications, 1989.

71. A. Lijphart, "The Puzzle of Indian Democracy: A Consociational Interpretation," *American Political Science Review*, 90, 2, 1996, pp. 258–268.

72. A. Kohli, "Conclusion – State-Society Relations in India's Changing Democracy," in Kohli, ed., *India's Democracy. An Analysis of Changing State-Society Relations*, Princeton, Princeton University Press, 1988; Jyotirindra Das

Gupta, "India: Democratic Becoming and Combined Development," *Politics in Developing Countries: Comparing Experiences with Democracy*, ed. L. Diamond, J. J. Linz, S. M. Lipset, London, Lynne Rienner Publishers, 1990.

73. Van der Veer, *Religious Nationalism: Hindus and Muslims in India*; Malik and Singh, *Hindu Nationalists in India: The Rise of the Bharatiya Janata Party*; McKean, *Divine Enterprise: Gurus and the Hindu Nationalist Movement*; Varshney, "Three Compromised Nationalisms: Why Kashmir Has Been a Problem"; and "India: Liberalism vs. Nationalism"; and "Contested Meanings: India's National Identity, Hindu Nationalism, and the Politics of Anxiety"; J. Hawley, "Hinduism and the Fate of India," *Wilson Quarterly*, 1991, pp. 20–52; G. Omvedt, *Reinventing Revolution: New Social Movements and the Socialist Tradition in India*, Armonk NY, M. E. Sharpe, 1993; G. Pandey, *The Construction of Communalism in Colonial North India*; S. Kaviraj, "The Man who Discovered India. On the Poetics of Jawaharlal Nehru's Historical Writings," draft.

74. Malik and Singh, *Hindu Nationalists in India: The Rise of the Bharatiya Janata Party*.

75. D. R. Spitz, review article; T. B. Edsall, *Washington Post*.

76. A. Varshney, "The Self-Correcting Mechanisms of Indian Democracy," in *Seminar*, Annual Number, Delhi, January 1995; and "Self-Limited Empowerment: Democracy, Economic Development and Rural India," *Journal of Development Studies*, 29, 4, 1993; and "Three Compromised Nationalisms: Why Kashmir Has Been a Problem"; and "India: Liberalism vs. Nationalism"; and "Contested Meanings: India's National Identity, Hindu Nationalism, and the Politics of Anxiety"; and "Battling the Past, Forging a Future? Ayodhya and Beyond," in P. Oldenburg, ed., *India Briefing, 1993*, Boulder, CO, Westview Press, 1993. See also the special issue on "Community Conflicts and the State in India: Symposium," of the *Journal of Asian Studies*, 56, 2, 1997.

77. D. Eickelman, ed., *Russia's Muslim Frontiers: New Directions in Cross-Cultural Analysis*, Bloomington, Indiana University Press, 1993.

78. R. Cohen, "Algeria is Burning. A Chance to Try to End an Agony," *The New York Times*, February 2, 1997, p. 3; Ali Dahmane, "Vergessen Sie uns, wir sind schon tot," *Die Zeit*, November 11, 1994, p. 2.

79. Cohen, "Algeria is Burning. A Chance to Try to End an Agony"; Dahmane, "Vergessen Sie uns, wir sind schon tot."

80. Ibid.

81. S. V. R. Nasr, "Democracy and Islamic Revivalism," *Political Science Quarterly*, 110, 2, 1995, pp. 271–273; Abdel Azim Ramadan, "Fundamentalist Influence in Egypt: The Strategies of the Muslim Brotherhood and the Takfir Groups," in M. Marty and R. S. Appleby, eds., *Fundamentalisms and the State*, Chicago, University of Chicago Press, 1993, pp. 152–183. For a survey of the different aspects of Islamization in various countries see Hussin Mutalib and Taj ul-Islam Hashmi, eds., *Islam, Muslims and the Modern State. Case Studies of Muslims in Thirteen Countries*, London, Macmillan, 1996.

82. Ramadan, "Fundamentalist Influence in Egypt: The Strategies of the Muslim Brotherhood and the Takfir Groups."
83. M. Nicholson, *The Financial Times*, May 13, 1996. On the continuity of caste see also A. Ghosh's comment in *New York Herald Tribune*, May 6, 1990.
84. V. S. Naipaul, *The New York Herald Tribune*, May 6, 1990.
85. One of the most interesting attempts to implement social policies in terms of Islam is that of "Islamic banking." See T. Kuran, "The Economic Impact of Islamic Fundamentalism"; and "Islam and Underdevelopment: An Old Puzzle Revisited"; and "The Genesis of Islamic Economics: A Chapter in the Politics of Muslim Identity."
86. S. Heilman and M. Friedman, "Religious Fundamentalism and Religious Jews: The Case of the Haredim," in M. Marty and R. S. Appleby, eds., *Fundamentalisms Observed*, Chicago, Chicago University Press, 1991, pp. 197–264; G. Aran, "Jewish Zionist Fundamentalism: The Bloc of the Faithful in Israel (Gush Emunim)," in Marty and Appleby, eds., *Fundamentalisms Observed*, pp. 265–344; D. Landau, *Piety and Power: The World of Jewish Fundamentalism*, New York, Hill and Wang, 1993; A. Ravitzky, *Messianism, Zionism and Jewish Religious Radicalism*, Chicago, University of Chicago Press, 1993; S. Heilman, *Defenders of the Faith: Inside Ultra-Orthodox Jewry*, New York, Schocken Books, 1992.
87. Göle, "Laïcité, modernisme et islamisme en Turquie"; and "Authoritarian Secularism and Islamist Politics: The Case of Turkey," in A. R. Norton, ed., *Civil Society in the Middle East*, Leiden, E. J. Brill, 1996, pp. 17–44; and "Democracy and Secularism in Turkey: Trends and Perspectives," MESA, December 6–10, 1995, to be published in *Middle East Journal*, pp. 12–16.
88. H. G. Koenigsberger, "Riksdag, Parliament and States General in the Sixteenth and Seventeenth Centuries," *The Swedish Riksdag in an International Perspective: Report from the Stockholm Symposium, April 25–27, 1988*, Stockholm, Riksbankens Jubileumsfond, 1989; Stein Kuhnle, *Patterns of Social and Political Mobilizations. A Historical Analysis of the Nordic Countries*, Beverly Hills, Sage Publications, 1975; M. Alestalo, "Structural Change, Classes and the State. Finland in a Comparative Perspective," *Research Reports*, Research Group for Comparative Sociology, University of Helsinki, No. 33, 1986; E. Lindström, *Fascism in Scandinavia, 1920–1940*, Stockholm, Liber, 1985.

5 Some considerations on modernity

1. S. N. Eisenstadt, *Modernizaton: Protest and Change*, Englewood Cliffs, Prentice Hall, 1966; and *Tradition, Change and Modernity*, New York, John Wiley and Sons, 1973.
2. W. Sombart, *Why Is There No Socialism in the United States?*, New York, M.E. Sharpe, 1976 (1st ed. 1906).

3. A. Tocqueville, *Democracy in America*, New York, Vintage Books, 1954; E. Kamenka, ed., *The Portable Karl Marx*, New York, Viking Press, 1983; M. Weber, *Die protestantische Ethik: Kritiken und Antikritiken*, Gütersloh Germany, Gütersloher Verlagshaus, 1978; and *Politik als Beruf*, Berlin, Dunker and Humblot, 1968; and *On Charisma and Institution Building: Selected Papers*, Chicago, University of Chicago Press, 1968; and, *The Rational and Social Foundations of Music*, Carbondale, Southern Illinois University Press, 1958; W. G. Runciman, ed., *Max Weber: Selections in Translation*, Cambridge, Cambridge University Press, 1978; R. N. Bellah, ed., *Emile Durkheim On Morality and Society. Selected Writings*, Chicago, The University of Chicago Press, 1973; M. Jay, *Adorno*, Cambridge, MA, Harvard University Press, 1984.

4. B. Ackerman, *We The People*, Cambridge, MA, Harvard University Press, 1991.

5. E. Shils, "Primordial, Personal, Sacred and Civil Ties," in Shils, ed., *Center and Periphery, Essays in Macrosiology*, Chicago, University of Chicago Press, 1975, pp. 111–126.

6. J. H. Goldthorpe, "Theories of Industrial Society. Reflections on the Recrudescence on Historicism and the Future of Futurology," in *Archives Européennes de sociologie*, 12, 2, 1971; S. N. Eisenstadt, "Convergence and Divergence in Modern and Modernizing Societies," in *International Journal of Middle East Studies*, 8, 1, 1977.

7. J. Habermas, *The Philosophical Discourse of Modernity*, Cambridge, MA, MIT Press, 1987.

8. A. Appendurai, *Modernity at Large. Cultural Dimensions of Globalization*, Minneapolis, University of Minnesota Press, 1996; U. Hannerz, *Transnational Connections. Culture, People, Places*, London, Routledge, 1996; R. Robertson, *Globalization: Social Theory and Global Culture*, London, Sage, 1992.

Select bibliography

Ackerman, B. *We The People*, Cambridge, MA, Harvard University Press, 1991

Adamson, C. "God's Continent Divided: Politics and Religion in Upper Canada and the Northern and Western United States, 1775 to 1841," *Comparative Studies in Society and History*, 36, 3, 1994, pp. 417–46

Ahmed, A. S. *Millennium and Charisma among Pathans*, London, Routledge and Kegan Paul, 1979

Akhavi, S. "Sayyid Qutb: The Poverty of Philosophy and the Vindication of Islamic Tradition," in Mardin, ed., *Cultural Transitions*, pp. 130–52

Alagappa, M., ed. *Political Legitimacy in Southeast Asia. The Quest for Moral Authority*, Stanford, Stanford University Press, 1995

Alestalo, M. "Structural Change, Classes and the State. Finland in a Comparative Perspective," *Research Reports*, Research Group for Comparative Sociology, University of Helsinki, No. 33, 1986

Allen, D., ed. *Religion and Political Conflict in South Asia: India, Pakistan, and Sri Lanka*, Westport, Greenwood Press, 1992

Almond, G., E. Sivan and R. S. Appleby, "Fundamentalism: Genus and Species," in M. Marty and R. S. Appleby, eds., *Fundamentalisms Comprehended*, pp. 399–424

"Explaining Fundamentalisms", in Marty and Appleby, eds., *Fundamentalisms Comprehended*, pp. 425–44

"Examining the Cases," in Marty and Appleby, eds., *Fundamentalisms Comprehended*, pp. 445–82

"Politics, Ethnicity, and Fundamentalism," in Marty and Appleby, eds., *Fundamentalisms Comprehended*, pp. 483–504

Ankori, Z. *Karaites in Byzantium*, New York, Columbia University Press, 1959

Appendurai, A. *Modernity at Large: Cultural Dimensions of Globalization*, Minneapolis, University of Minnesota Press, 1996

Appleby, R. S. *Spokesmen for the Despised*, Chicago, University of Chicago Press, 1997

Aran, G. "Jewish Zionist Fundamentalism: The Bloc of the Faithful in Israel (Gush Emunim)," in Marty and Appleby, eds., *Fundamentalisms Observed*, pp. 265–344

Arjomand, S. A. "The Consolation of Theology: Absence of the Imam and Transition from Chiliasm to Law in Shi'ism," *Journal of Religion*, 1996, pp. 548–71

"Unity and Diversity in Islamic Fundamentalism," in Marty and Appleby, eds., *Fundamentalisms Comprehended*, pp. 179–98

"Shi'ite Jurisprudence and Constitution Making in the Islamic Republic of Iran," in Marty and Appleby, eds., *Fundamentalisms and the State*, pp. 88–110

"Iran's Islamic Revolution in Comparative Perspective," *World Politics*, 38, 3, 1976

"Constitutions and the Struggle for Political Order: A Study in the Modernization of Political Tradition," in Mardin, ed., *Cultural Transitions*, pp. 1–49

"The Crisis of the Imamate and the Institution of Occultation in Twelver Shi'ism: A Sociohistorical Perspective," *IJMES*, 28, 1996, pp. 491–515

Authority and Political Culture in Shi'ism, New York, State University of New York Press, 1988

Arnason, J. P. "The Theory of Modernity and the Problematic of Democracy," *Thesis Eleven*, 26, 1990, pp. 20–46

Aron, R. *Machiavel et les tyrannies modernes*, Paris, Editions de Fallois, 1993

Aschheim, S. "Nietzsche and the German Radical Right, 1914–1933," in Sternhell, ed., *Intellectual Revolt*, pp. 159–76

Azmeh, A. Al. *Islams and Modernities*, London, Verso, 1993

Baker, K. M. *The French Revolution and the Creation of Modern Political Culture*, Oxford, Pergamon Press, 1987

Ball, T. and J. G. A. Pocock, eds. *Conceptual Change and the Constitution*, Lawrence, University of Kansas Press, 1988

Baron, S. *A Social and Religious History of the Jews*, VI, New York, Columbia University Press, 1952–1953

Bash, H. *Social Problems and Social Movements: An Exploration into the Sociological Construction of Alternative Realities*, Atlantic Highlands, NJ, Humanity Press, 1995

Basham, A. L. "Jainism and Buddhism," in T. W. De Banj, ed., *Sources of Indian Tradition*, New York, Columbia University Press, 1950, pp. 37–93

Beasley, W. G. *The Meiji Restoration*, Stanford, Stanford University Press, 1972

Bechert, H. and R. Gombrich, eds. *The World of Buddhism. Buddhist Monks and Nuns in Society and Culture*, London, Thames and Hudson, 1991

Bellah, R. N. "Civil Religion in America," *Daedalus*, 96, 1, 1967, pp. 1–21
  The Broken Covenant, New York, Seabury Press, 1975

Bellah, R. N. ed. *Emile Durkheim On Morality and Society. Selected Writings*, Chicago, University of Chicago Press, 1973

Ben-Sasson, H. ed. *The Story of the Jewish People*, Cambridge, MA, Harvard University Press, 1972

Ben Shamai, H. "Return to the Scriptures in Ancient and Medieval Jewish Sectarianism and Early Islam," in E. Patlagean and A. Le Boulluec, eds., *Les retours aux écritures fondamentalismes presents et passés*, Paris, Peeters Louvain, 1993, pp. 319–42

Berlin, I. "Two Concepts of Liberty," in *Four Essays on Liberty*, London, Oxford University Press, 1975, pp. 118–72
  Vico and Herder, New York, Hogarth Press, 1976
  Against the Current, New York, Hogarth Press, 1980
  The Crooked Timber of Humanity, New York, J. Murray, 1991

Bigger, C. *Kant's Methodology: An Essay in Philosophical Archaeology*, Athens, Ohio University Press, 1996

Bina, C. "Towards a New World Order: US Hegemony, Client-States and Islamic Alternative," in Hussin Mutalib and Taj ul-Islam Hashmi, eds., *Islam, Muslims and the Modern State: Case-Studies of Muslims in Thirteen Countries*, pp. 3–30

Blacker, C. "Two Shinto Myths: The Golden Age and the Chosen People," in S. Kenny and J. P. Lehman, *Themes and Theories in Modern Japanese History*, London, Athlone Press, 1988, pp. 64–78

Blumenberg, H. *Die Legitimät der Neuzeit*, Frankfurt, Suhrkamp, 1987

Bobbio, N. *Il futuro della democrazzia*, Turin: Giulio Einaudi, 1984
  "Postfazione," in N. Bobbio, *Profilo ideologico del Novecento Italiano*, Turin, Giulio Einaudi, 1986, pp. 177–85
  L'eta dei diritti, Turin, Giulio Einandi, 1990

Boggs, C. *Social Movements and Political Power. Emerging Forms of Radicalism in the West*, Philadelphia, Temple University Press, 1986

Bowes, P. *The Hindu Religious Tradition. A Philosophical Approach*, London, Routledge and Kegan Paul, 1978

Boyer, P. *When Time Shall Be No More: Prophecy Belief in Modern American Culture*, Cambridge MA, Harvard University Press, 1992

Brass, P., ed. *Riots and Pogroms*, London, Macmillan Press, 1996

Brower, S., P. Gritton and S. D. Rose, *Exporting the American Gospel: Global Christian Fundamentalism*, New York, Routledge, 1996

Cam, H. *The Hundred and the Hundred Rolls: An Outline of Local Government in Medieval England*, London, Methuen, 1930

Carman, J. B. and F. A. Margolin, eds., *Purity and Auspiciousness in Indian Society*, Leiden, E. J. Brill, 1985

Castoriadis, C. *Philosophy, Politics, Autonomy*, Oxford, Oxford University Press, 1991

Chatterjee, P. *Nationalist Thought and the Colonial World: A Derivative Discourse?*, Zed Books, United Nations University, 1986
"History and the Nationalization of Hinduism," *Social Research*, 59, 1, 1992, pp. 111–149
The Nation and its Fragments: Colonial and Postcolonial Histories, Princeton, Princeton University Press, 1993

Cleary, E. and H. Stewart-Gambino. *Power, Politics, and Pentecostals in Latin America*, Boulder, Westview Press, 1997

Cochin, A. *La révolution et la libre pensée*, Paris, Plon-Nourrit, 1924
L'esprit du Jacobinisme, Paris, Presses Universitaires de France, 1979

Cohen, E. "Christianity and Buddhism in Thailand: The 'Battle of the Axes' and the 'Contest of Power'," *Social Compass*, 38, 2, 1991, pp. 115–40

Cohen, J. and A. Arato, *Civil Society and Political Theory*, Cambridge MA, MIT Press, 1992

Cohn, N. *In the Pursuit of the Millennium*, New York, Harper, 1961

Gupta, J. D. "India: Democratic Becoming and Combined Development," in L. Diamond, J. J. Linz, S. M. Lipset, eds., *Politics in Developing Countries: Comparing Experiences with Democracy*, London, Lynne Rienner Publishers, 1990.

DeBary, W. T., "Some Common Tendencies in Neo-Confucianism," in Nivison and Wright, eds., *Confucianism in Action*

DeBary, W. T., ed. *The Buddhist Tradition in India, China and Japan*, New York, Modern Library, 1972

Della Porta, D. *Social Movements, Political Violence and the State. A Comparative Analysis of Italy and Germany*, Cambridge, Cambridge University Press, 1995

Dharampal-Frick, G. "Zwischen 'Sakularismus' und 'Kommunalismus' Identitätsprobleme in der indischen Politik und Gesellschaft seit der Unabhangigkeit," in W. Reinhard, ed. *Die Fundamentalistische Revolution*

Dirks, N. B. "The Conversion of Caste: Location, Translation, and Appropriation," in van der Veer, ed., *Conversion to Modernities*, pp. 115–36

"Political Authority and Structural Change in Early South Indian History," *Indian Economic and Social History Review*, 13, 2, 1976, pp. 125–57

Douglas, M. *Purity and Danger*, London, Routledge and Kegan Paul, 1966

Downing, B. "Constitutionalism, Warfare, and Political Change in Early Modern Europe," *Theory and Society*, 17, 1988, pp. 7–56

Dryzek, J. "Political Inclusion and the Dynamics of Democratization," *American Political Science Review*, 90, 3, 1996, pp. 475–87

Dunn, J. *Rethinking Modern Political Theory*, Cambridge, Cambridge University Press, 1978

Locke, Oxford, Oxford University Press, 1984

The History of Political Theory and Other Essays, Cambridge, Cambridge University Press, 1996

Duus, P. and D. Okimoto. "Fascism and the History of Pre-War Japan: The Failure of the Concept," *Journal of Asian Studies*, 39, 1, 1979, pp. 65–76

Edsall, T. B. "Mistrust of Government Found Festering in White Middle Class," *Washington Post*, October 20, 1996, p. A13

Egan, T. "Inside the World of the Paranoid," *The New York Times*, 30 April, 1995, section 4, pp. 1 and 5

Eichinger Ferro-Luzzi, G. "The Polythetic-Prototype Approach to Hinduism," in G. Sontheimer and H. Kulke, eds., *Hinduism Reconsidered*, New Delhi, Manohar, 1989, pp. 187–96

Eickelman, D., ed., *Russia's Muslim Frontiers: New Directions in Cross-Cultural Analysis*, Bloomington, Indiana University Press, 1993

Eickelman, D. and J. Piscatori. *Muslim Politics*, Princeton, Princeton University Press, 1996

Eisenstadt, S. N. *Modernization, Protest and Change*, Englewood Cliffs NJ, Prentice Hall, 1966

Tradition, Change and Modernity, New York, John Wiley and Sons, 1973

Traditional Patrimonialism and Modern Neopatrimonialism, London, Sage Publications, 1973

Revolution and the Transformation of Societies, New York, Free Press, 1978

"Transcendental Vision, Center Formation and the Role of Intellectuals," in L. Greenfeld and M. Martin, eds., *Center, and Ideas and Institutions*, Chicago, University of Chicago Press, 1980, pp. 96–109

"Cultural Traditions and Political Dynamics, the Origins and Modes of Ideological Politics," *British Journal of Sociology*, 32, 2, 1981, pp. 155–81

"The Axial Age: The Emergence of Transcendental Visions and Rise of Clerics," *European Journal of Sociology*, 23, 2, 1982, pp. 294–314

"Innerweltliche Transzenden und die Strukturierung der Welt. Max Weber Studie über China und die Gestalt der Chinesischen Zivilisation," in W. Schluchter, ed., *Max Webers Studie über Konfuzianismus und Taoism. Interpretation und Kritik*, Frankfurt, Suhrkamp, 1983, pp. 363–411

"Comparative Liminality: Liminality and Dynamics of Civilization," *Religion*, 15, 1985, pp. 315–38

European Civilization in a Comparative Perspective, Oslo, Norwegian University Press, 1987

"Origins of the West. The Origins of the West in Recent Macrosociological Theory. The Protestant Ethic Reconsidered," *Cultural Dynamics*, Leiden, E. J. Brill, 1991, pp. 113–47

Civilta Comparata, Naples, Liguori, 1991

"Frameworks of the Great Revolutions: Culture, Social Structure, History and Human Agency," *International Social Science Journal*, 133, 1992, pp. 385–401

"Historical Sociology Revolutions," *International Social Science Journal*, 1992

"Some Observations on 'Post-Modern' Society," in N. Stehr and R. Ericson, eds., *The Culture and Power of Knowledge. Inquiries into Contemporary Societies*, Berlin, Walter de Gruyter, 1992, pp. 51–9

Jewish Civilization: The Jewish Historical Experience in a Comparative Perspective, New York, State University of New York Press, 1992

"The Disintegration of the Medieval Jewish Civilizational Framework in the Modern Period and the Integration of Jews in European Societies," in Eisenstadt, *Jewish Civilization*, pp. 85–108

Power, Trust and Meaning, Chicago, University of Chicago Press, 1995

Eisenstadt, S. N., ed. *Post-Traditional Societies*, New York, Norton, 1972

The Origins and Diversity of Axial Age Civilizations, New York, State University of New York Press, 1986

Kulturen der Achsenzeit, 3 vols., Frankfurt, Suhrkamp, 1992

Eisenstadt, S. N. and Y. Azmon, eds. *Socialism and Tradition*, Jerusalem, The Van Leer Foundation, 1975, pp. 1–20

Eisenstadt, S. N. and B. Giesen, "The Construction of Collective Identity," *European Journal of Sociology – Archives européennes de sociologie*, 36, 1, 1995, pp.72–102

Eisenstadt, S. N., R. Kahane, and D. Schuman, eds. *Orthodoxy, Heterodoxy and Dissent in India*, New York, Mouton, 1984

Elias, N. *The Civilizing Process*, New York, Urizen Books, 1978–1982

The Court Society, Oxford, Basil Blackwell, 1983

The Encyclopedia of Religion, New York, Macmillan and Free Press, 1987

Erder, Y. "Mercaziuta shel Eretz Israel beHugei Ha-Karaut Ha'Kduma le-Or Hilchotav shel Mishwaya Al'Aukbari" [The centrality of Israel among ancient Karaism according to Mishwaya Al'Aukbari], *Zion*, 1955, pp. 37–67

"The First Date in 'Megillat Ta'anit' in the Light of the Karaite Commentary on the Tabernacle Dedication," *The Jewish Quarterly Review*, 82, 3–4, January–April, 1992, pp. 263–83

"The Karaite–Sadducee Dilemma," *Israel Oriental Studies*, 14, 1994, pp. 195–215

Esposito, J., ed. *Islam in Asia: Religion, Politics and Society*, New York, Oxford University Press, 1987

Esfandiari, H. *Reconstructed Lives: Women and Iran's Islamic Revolution*, Baltimore, Johns Hopkins University Press, 1997

Fairbank, J. K., ed. *Chinese Thought and Institutions*, Chicago, University of Chicago Press, 1957

de Felice, R. *Il fascismo. Le interpretazioni dei contemporanei e degli storici*, Bari, Laterza, 1970

Le fascisme, un totalitarisme à l'italienne, Paris, Presses de la Fondation Nationale des Sciences Politiques, 1988

Fingarrette, H. "Human Community as Holy Rite. An Interpretation of Confucius' Analects," in *Harvard Theological Review*, 59, 1, 1968, pp. 53–67

Confucius, the Secular as Sacred, New York, Harper and Row, 1972

Fontana, B., ed. *The Invention of the Modern Republic*, Cambridge, Cambridge University Press, 1994.

Foucault, M. *Madness and Civilization: A History of Insanity in the Age of Reason*, New York, Pantheon Books, 1965

The Birth of the Clinic: An Archaeology of Medical Perception, New York, Vintage Books, 1973

Surveiller et punir: Naissance de la prison, Paris, Gallimard, 1975

Technologies of the Self: A Seminar with Michel Foucault, Amherst, University of Massachusetts Press, 1988

Fowler, R. and A. Hertzke. *Religion and Politics in America: Faith Culture and Strategic Choices*, Boulder, Westview Press, 1995

Fox, R. *Kin, Clan, Raja and Rule: State–Hinterland Relations in Preindustrial India*, Berkeley, University of California Press, 1971

Franke, H. "The Role of the State as a Structural Element in Polyethnic Societies," in Sichram, ed., *Foundations and Limits*, pp. 87–112

Frankel, E. *Deutschland und die westlichen Demokratien*, Frankfurt am Main, Suhrkamp, 1990 (incl. "Strukturdefelite der Demokratie und derein pp. 68–95
"Ratenmythos und Soziale Selbstbestimmung," pp. 95–137

Freyer, H. *Theorie Des objektiven geistes: Eine Einleitung in die Kulturphilosophie*, Leipzig, B. G. Teubner, 1923
Die Industriegesellschaft in Ost und West: Konvergenzen und Divergenzen, Mainz, V. Hase and Koehler, 1966

Frykenberg, R. E. "Accounting for Fundamentalisms in South Asia: Ideologies and Institutions in Historical Perspective," in M. Marty and R. S. Appleby, eds., *Accounting for Fundamentalisms: The Dynamic Character of Movements*, Chicago, University of Chicago Press, 1994, pp. 591–616

Fukuyama, F. *The End of History and the Last Man*, New York, Free Press, 1992

Fuller, R. *Naming the Antichrist: The History of an American Obsession*, New York, Oxford University Press, 1995

Furet, F. *The French Revolution*, New York, Macmillan, 1970
Interpreting the French Revolution, Cambridge, Cambridge University Press, 1981
Rethinking the French Revolution, Chicago, University of Chicago Press, 1982
"Jacobinisme," in F. Furet and M. Ozouf, eds., *Dictionnaire critique de la révolution française*, Paris, Flammarion, 1988, pp. 751–62

Gaillat, C. "Jainism," in *The Encyclopedia of Religion*, New York, Mcmillan and Free Press, 1987, 7, pp. 507–14

Gamson, W. "Political Discourse and Collective Action," *International Social Movements Research*, 1, 1988, pp. 219–47

Gellner, E. "Fundamentalism as a Comprehensive System: Soviet Marxism and Islamic Fundamentalism Compared," in M. E. Marty and R. S. Appleby, eds., *Fundamentalisms Comprehended*, pp. 277–88
Muslim Society, Cambridge, Cambridge University Press, 1981

Gibb, H. A. R. *Studies in the Civilization of Islam*, Boston, Beacon Press, 1962

Goldstone, J. A. "Révolutions dans l'histoire et histoire de la révolution," *Revue française de sociologie*, 3, 4, 1983, pp. 405–30
Revolution and Rebellion in the Early Modern World, Berkeley and Los Angeles, University of California Press, 1991

Goldthorpe, J. H. "Theories of Industrial Society. Reflections on the Recrudescence on Historicism and the Future of Futurology," in *Archives européennes de sociologie*, 12, 2, 1971

Göle, N. "Laïcité, modernisme et islamisme en Turquie," *Cahiers d'Etudes sur la Mediterranée orientale et le monde turco-iranien*, 19, 1995, pp. 85–96

"Democracy and Secularism in Turkey: Trends and Perspectives," MESA, Dec. 6–10, 1995, to be published in *Middle East Journal*, pp. 12–16

"Authoritarian Secularism and Islamist Politics: The Case of Turkey," in A. R. Norton, ed., *Civil Society in the Middle East*, Leiden, E. J. Brill, 1996, pp. 17–44

Gonda, J. *Visnuism and Sivaism*, London, The Athlone Press, 1970

Goodwin, G. "Portrayal of India, Caste Kingships and Dominance Reconsidered," *Annual Review of Anthropology*, 17, 1988, pp. 497–552

Grew, R. "On Seeking the Cultural Context of Fundamentalism," University of Michigan, draft, 1997

Grew, R., ed. *Crisis of Political Development in Europe and the United States*, Princeton, Princeton University Press, 1978

Gusfield, J. *Symbolic Crusade: Status Politics and the American Temperance Movement*, Urbana, University of Illinois Press, 1963

Habermas, J. *The Philosophical Discourse of Modernity*, Cambridge MA, MIT Press, 1987

Halliday, F. "Fundamentalism and the Contemporary World," *Contention*, 4, 2, 1995, pp. 41–58

Islam and the Myth of Confrontation. Religion and Politics in the Middle East, London, I. B. Tauris, 1995

Hannerz, U. *Transnational Connections: Culture, People, Places*, London, Routledge, 1996

Hardy, F. *Virama Bhakti: Early Development of Krsna Devotion in South India*, Oxford, Oxford University Press, 1981

Harrison, S. *India – The Most Dangerous Decades*, Princeton, Princeton University Press, 1960

Heberle, R. *Social Movements: An Introduction to Political Sociology*, New York, Appleton, 1951

Heer, F. *The Intellectual History of Europe*, Garden City NY, Doubleday, 1968

Heesterman, J. C. *The Ancient Indian Royal Consecration*, The Hague, Mouton and Co., 1957

The Inner Conflict of Tradition: Essays in Indian Ritual, Kinship and Society, Chicago and London, University of Chicago Press, 1985

"Brahmin, Ritual and Renouncer," in Heesterman, *The Inner Conflict of Tradition: Essays in Indian Ritual, Kinship and Society*, pp. 26–44

The Broken World of Sacrifice: An Essay in Ancient Indian Ritual, Chicago, University of Chicago Press, 1993

M. Heidegger, *German Existentialism*, New York, Philosophical Library, 1965

Hegel's Phenomenology of Spirit, Bloomington, Indiana University Press, 1988

The Fundamental Concepts of Metaphysics, Bloomington, Indiana University Press, 1995

Heilman, S. *Defenders of the Faith: Inside Ultra-Orthodox Jewry*, New York, Schocken Books, 1992

"Quiescent and Active Fundamentalisms: The Jewish Cases," in M. E. Marty and R. S. Appleby, eds., *Accounting for Fundamentalisms*, pp. 173–196

Heilman, S. and M. Friedman. "Religious Fundamentalism and Religious Jews: The Case of the Haredim," M. Marty and R. S. Appleby, eds., *Fundamentalisms Observed*, Chicago, Chicago University Press, 1991, pp. 197–264

Heitmeyer, W., J. Müller and H. Schröder, *Verlockender Fundamentalismus. Turkische Jugendische in Deutschland*, Frankfurt, Suhrkamp, 1997

Heper, M. and A. Evin, eds., *Politics in the Third Turkish Republic*, Boulder, Westview Press, 1993

Heper, M., A. Öncü, and H. Kramer, eds. *Turkey and the West: Changing Political and Cultural Identities*, London, I. B. Tauris, 1993

Herder, J. J. G. *Herder on Social and Political Culture*, Cambridge, Cambridge University Press, 1969

Herf, J. "Reactionary Modernism Reconsidered: Modernity, the West and the Nazis," in Sternhell, ed., *Intellectual Revolt*, pp. 131–58

Hill, C. *The Origins of the English Intellectual Revolution Reconsidered*, Oxford, Oxford University Press, 1997

Hobsbawm, E. *The Age of Revolution*, London, Weidenfeld & Nicolson, 1964

Age of Extremes: The Short Twentieth Century, 1914–1991, New York, Viking Penguin, 1994

Hoston, G. A. "A 'Theology' of Liberation? Socialist Revolution and Spiritual Regeneration in Chinese and Japanese Marxism," in P. A. Cohen and M. Goldman, eds., *Ideas Across Cultures: Essays on Chinese Thought in Honor of Benjamin J. Schwartz*, Cambridge, MA, Harvard University Press, 1990, pp. 165–94

Hucker, C. O., ed. *Chinese Government in Ming Times: Seven Studies*, New York, Columbia University Press, 1969

Hugenholtz, W. and K. van Vliet-Leigh, eds. *Islam and Europe in Past and Present*, Wassenaar, NIAS, 1997

Hulsewe, A. "Law as One of the Foundations of State Power in Early Imperial China," in Schram, ed., *Foundations and Limits*, pp. 11–32

Hunter, S. T., ed. *The Politics of Islamic Revivalism: Diversity and Unity*, Bloomington, Indiana University Press, 1988

Huntington, S. P. *American Politics: The Promise of Disharmony*, Cambridge MA, Harvard University Press, 1981

Khaldun, I. *The Muqadimma*, London, Routledge and Kegan Paul, 1988

Inden, R. *Imagining India*, Oxford, Blackwell, 1990

Ishtiaq, Ahmed. *State, Nation and Ethnicity in Contemporary South Asia*, London, Pinter, 1996

Ishwaran, K., ed. *Change and Continuity in India's Villages*, New York, Columbia University Press, 1970

Jacobson, G. *Apple of Gold: Constitutionalism in Israel and the United States*, Princeton, Princeton University Press, 1993

Jalal, A. *Democracy and Authoritarianism in South Asia: A Comparative and Historical Perspective*, Cambridge, Cambridge University Press, 1995

Jaspers, K. *The Origin and Goal of History*, New Haven, Yale University Press, 1965

Joll, J. *The Anarchists*, London, Eyre and Spottiswoode, 1964

Journal of Asian Studies, 56, 2, 1997, special issue on "Community Conflicts and the State in India: Symposium"

Jungensmeyer, M. *The New Cold War? Religious Nationalism Confronts the Secular State*, Berkeley, University of California Press, 1993

Junger, E. *Feuer und Blut*, Magdeburg, Stahlhelm Verlag, 1925
 Der Kampf also inneres Erlebnis, Berlin, Mittler, 1929
 "Der Arbeiter," in E. Junger, *Werke*, VI, Stuttgart, E. Klett, 1964

Kaltenmark, M. *Lao Tzu and Taoism*, Stanford, Stanford University Press, 1969

Kamali, M. "The Modern Revolutions of Iran," *Citizenship Studies*, 1997

Kamenka, E., ed. *The Portable Karl Marx*, New York, Viking Press, 1983

Kaufmann, W., ed. *The Portable Nietzsche: Selected and Translated*, New York, Viking Press, 1965

Keddie, N. "The New Religious Politics: Where, When, and Why Do 'Fundamentalisms' Appear?" *Comparative Studies in Society and History*, forthcoming 1998

Keddie, N. R., ed. *Debating Revolutions*, New York, New York University Press, 1995

Kepel, G. *The Revenge of God: The Resurgence of Islam, Christianity and Judaism in the Modern World*, Philadelphia, Pennsylvania State University Press, 1994

Kesavanarayana, B. *Political and Social Factors in Andhra (1900–1956)*, Vijayawada, Navodaya, 1976

Keyes, C. F., L. Kendall, and H. Hardacre, eds. *Asian Visions of Authority: Religion and the Modern States of East and Southeast Asia*, Honolulu, University of Hawaii Press, 1994

Khosrokhavar, F. "Les intellectuels post-islamistes en Iran," *Le trimestre du monde*, 1996, pp. 53–62

"Le Sacre et le politique dans la revolution iranienne," in Patrick Michel, *Religion et Democratie*, Paris, Albin Michel, pp. 86–108

"L'universel abstrait, le politique et la construction de l'islamisme comme forme d'altérité," in M. Wieviorka, ed., *Une société fragmentee?*, Paris, Editions La Decouverte, 1996, pp. 113–51

L'Islam des jeunes, Paris, Flammarion, 1997

Kierkegaard, S. A. *Fear and Trembling and the Sickness unto Death*, Princeton, Princeton University Press, 1974

Two Ages: The Age of Revolution and the Present Age, Princeton, Princeton University Press, 1977

Kodmani-Darwish, B. and M. Chartouni-Dubarry, eds. *Les états arabes face a la contestation islamiste*, Paris, Armand Colin, 1997

Koenigsberger, H. G. "Riksdag, Parliament and States General in the Sixteenth and Seventeenth Centuries," *The Swedish Riksdag in an International Perspective: Report from the Stockholm Symposium, April 25–27, 1988*, Stockholm, Riksbankens Jubileumsfond, 1989

Kohli, A., ed. *India's Democracy: An Analysis of Changing State-Society Relations*, Princeton, Princeton University Press, 1988

Kolberg, E. "Authoritative Scriptures in Early Imami Shi'ism," in Patlagean and Le Boulluec, eds., *Les retours aux écritures* pp. 295–312

Kolakowski, L. *Chrétiens sans église*, Paris, Gallimard, 1969

Modernity on Endless Trial, Chicago, University of Chicago Press, 1990

Kornhauser, W. *The Politics of Mass Society*, Glencoe, Free Press, 1959

Kosaku, Yoshino. *Cultural Nationalism in Contemporary Japan*, London, Routledge, 1992

Koury, E. *The Patterns of Mass Movements in Arab Revolutionary-Progressive States*, The Hague, Mouton, 1970

Kuhnle, S. *Patterns of Social and Political Mobilizations. A Historical Analysis of the Nordic Countries*, Beverly Hills, Sage Publications, 1975

Kuran, T. "The Economic Impact of Islamic Fundamentalism," in Marty and Appleby, eds., *Fundamentalisms and the State*, pp. 302–41

"The Genesis of Islamic Economics: A Chapter in the Politics of Muslim Identity," *Social Research*, 64, 2, 1997, pp. 301–38

Lacey, M. and K. Haakonssen, eds. *A Culture of Rights: The Bill of Rights in Philosophy, Politics, and Law, 1791 and 1991*, Cambridge, Cambridge University Press, 1991

Landau, D. *Piety and Power: The World of Jewish Fundamentalism*, New York, Hill and Wang, 1993

Landau-Tasseron, E. "The 'Cyclical Reform': A Study of the Mujaddid Tradition," *Studia Islamica*, 70, 1989, pp. 79–118

Langlois, J. A. Tr., ed. *China under Mongol Rule*, Princeton, Princeton University Press, 1981

Laoust, H. *Les schismes dans l'Islam*, Paris, Payot, 1965

Lapidus, I. M. *A History of Islamic Societies*, Cambridge, Cambridge University Press, 1987

"State and Religion in Islamic Societies," *Past and Present*, 151, 1996, pp. 3–27

Laroui, A. *Islamisme, modernisme, liberalisme*, Casablanca, Centre Culturel Arabe, 1997

Lasky, M. "The Birth of a Metaphor: On the Origins of Utopia and Revolution," *Encounter*, 34, 2, 1970, pp. 35–45 and 3, 1970, pp. 30–42

Utopia and Revolution, Chicago, University of Chicago Press, 1976

Von Laue, T. *The World Revolution of Westernization: The Twentieth Century in Global Perspective*, New York, Oxford University Press, 1987

Lawrence, B. *Defenders of God: The Fundamentalist Revolt Against the Modern Age*, San Francisco, Harper and Row, 1989

Lazarus-Yafeh, H. "Muslim Medieval Attitudes towards the Qur'an and the Bible," in Patlagean and Le Boulluec, eds., *Les retours aux écritures*, pp. 253–68

" 'Tajdid al-Din': A Reconsideration of its Meaning, Roots and Influence in Islam," *The New East*, 31, 1986, pp. 1–10

Lechner, F. "The Case Against Secularization: A Rebuttal," *Social Forces*, 69, 4, 1991, pp. 1103–19

"Fundamentalism Revisited," in T. Robbins and D. Anthony, eds., *In Gods We Trust: New Patterns of Religious Pluralism in America*, 2nd edn, New Brunswick, Transaction Publishers, 1990, pp. 77–97

"Against Modernity: Antimodernism in Global Perspective," in P. Colony, ed., *The Dynamics of Social Systems*, London, Sage Publications, 1992, pp. 72–92

Lefort, C. *Democracy and Political Theory*, Minneapolis, University of Minnesota Press, 1988

LeGoff, J. *Hérésies et sociétés dans l'Europe pre-industrielle*, Paris, Mouton, 1968

Lele, J., ed., *Tradition and Modernity in Bhakti Movements*, Leiden, E. J. Brill, 1981

Levine, D. H. "Popular Groups, Popular Culture, and Popular Religion," *Comparative Studies in Society and History*, 32, 4, 1990, pp. 718–64

"Protestants and Catholics in Latin America: A Family Portrait," *Bulletin. The American Academy of Arts and Sciences*, 50, 4, 1997, pp. 10–42

Levtzion, N. "Eighteenth Century Renewal and Reform Movements in Islam," *The New East*, 31, 1986, pp. 48–70

"The Eighteenth Century, Background to the Islamic Revolutions in West Africa," in N. Levtzion and J. Voll, *Eighteenth Century Renewal and Reform in Islam*, Syracuse, Syracuse University Press, 1987 pp. 21–38

Levtzion, N. and J. O. Voll, eds. *Eighteenth Century Renewal and Reform in Islam*, Syracuse, Syracuse University Press, 1987

Levtzion, N. and G. Weigert. "Religious Reform in Eighteenth-Century Morocco," *Jerusalem Studies in Arabic and Islam*, 19, 1995

Levy, P. *Buddhism: A Mystery Religion?*, New York, Schocken, 1968

Lewis, B. "Islamic Concepts of Revolution," in B. Lewis, *Islam in History*, London, Alcove Press, 1975, pp. 253–66

Lewy, G. *Religion and Revolution*, New York, Oxford University Press, 1974

Lijphart, A. "The Puzzle of Indian Democracy: A Consociational Interpretation," *American Political Science Review*, 90, 2, 1996, pp. 258–68

Lilla, M. "Was ist Gegenaufklärung?" *Merkur*, 566, 1966, pp. 400–11

Making of an Anti-Modern, Cambridge, MA, Harvard UP, 1993

Lindholm, C. "Despotism and Democracy: State and Society in the Premodern Middle East," in J. A. Hall and I. Jarvie, eds., *The Social Philosophy of Ernest Gellner*, Amsterdam, Rodopi, 1996, pp. 329–55

Lindström, E. *Fascism in Scandinavia, 1920–1940*, Stockholm, Liber, 1985

Liu, J. "An Early Sung Reformer, Fan Chun-yiu," in Fairbank, ed., *Chinese Thought*, pp. 105–32

Reform in Sung China, Wang An-Shih, 1021–1086 and his New Policies, Cambridge, Cambridge University Press, 1959

"An Administration Cycle in Chinese History," in J. A. Harrison, ed., *China: Enduring Scholarship*, Tucson, University of Arizona Press, 1972, I, pp. 75–90

Llewellyn, J. E. *The Arya Samaj as a Fundamentalist Movement: A Study in Comparative Fundamentalism*, Delhi, Manohar, 1993

Loewe, M. "Imperial Sovereignty: Dong Zhongslim's Contribution and his Predecessors," in Schram, ed., *Foundations and Limits*, pp. 33–58

Lübbe, H. *Freiheit statt Emanzipationszwang. Die liberalen Traditionen und das Ende der marxistischen Illusionen*, Zurich, Edition Interfrom, 1991

Ludden, D., ed. *Contesting the Nation*, Philadelphia, University of Pennsylvania Press, 1996

Luders, M. "Allahs Wahrheit im Computer," *Die Zeit*, September 16, 1994, p. 49

Madan, T. N., ed., *Way of Life: King, Householders and Renouncer*, Delhi, Vikas Publishing House, 1982
  "The Double Edged Sword: Fundamentalism and the Sikh Religious Tradition," in Marty and Appleby, eds., *Fundamentalisms Observed*, pp. 594–628

Maier, C. S., ed. *Changing Boundaries of the Political*, Cambridge, Cambridge University Press, 1987

Malia, M. "Leninist Endgame," *Daedalus*, 121, 2, 1992, pp. 57–76

Malik S. C., ed., *Dissent, Protest and Reform in Indian Civilization*, Simla, Indian Institute for Advanced Study, 1973

Malik, Y. K. and V. B. Singh, *Hindu Nationalists in India: The Rise of the Bharatiya Janata Party*. Boulder, Westview Press, 1994

Mandelbaum, D. G. *Society in India*, Berkeley, University of California Press, 1970

Mardin, S. "Culture Change and the Intellectual: A Study of the Effects of Secularization in Modern Turkey," in Mardin, ed., *Cultural Transitions in the Middle East*

Mardin, S., ed. *Cultural Transitions in the Middle East*, Leiden, E. J. Brill, 1994

Markoff, I. "Popular Culture, State Ideology, and National Identity in Turkey: The Arabesk Polemic," in S. Mardin, ed., *Cultural Transitions in the Middle East*

Marsden, G. *Fundamentalism and American Culture*, New York, Oxford University Press, 1980

Martin, D. *Tongues of Fire: The Explosion of Protestantism in Latin America*, Oxford, Basil Blackwell, 1990

Marty, M. E. and R. S. Appleby, eds. *Fundamentalisms Observed*, Chicago, University of Chicago Press, 1991
  Fundamentalism and Society, Chicago, University of Chicago Press, 1993
  Fundamentalisms and the State: Remaking Politics, Economies and Militance, Chicago, University of Chicago Press, 1993
  Accounting for Fundamentalisms: The Dynamic Character of Movements, Chicago, University of Chicago Press, 1994
  Fundamentalisms Comprehended, Chicago, University of Chicago Press, 1995

Matteucci, N. "Democrazia e autocrazia nel pensiero; Norberto Bobbio," in *Per una teoria generale della politica: Scritti dedicatti Norberto Bobbio*, Florence, Passiguli Editori, 1983, pp. 149–79

McIlwain, C. *The Growth of Political Thought in the West*, New York, Macmillan, 1932
  Constitutionalism and the Changing World: Collected Papers, London, Cambridge University Press, 1939
  Constitutionalism, rev. ed., Ithaca, Cornell University Press, 1947
McKean, L. *Divine Enterprise: Gurus and the Hindu Nationalist Movement*, Chicago, University of Chicago Press, 1996
McMullen, D. "View of the State in Du You and Liu Zonngyan," in Schram, ed., *Foundations and Limits*, pp. 59–86
Melucci, A. "Getting Involved: Identity and Mobilization in Social Movements," *International Social Movements Research*, 1, 1988, pp. 329–48
Merleau-Ponty, M. *Humanism and Terror*, Boston, Beacon Press, 1969
Metzger, T. *Escape from Predicament – Neo-Confucianism and China's Evolving Political Culture*
Miller, D., ed. *Coming of Age. Protestantism in Contemporary Latin America*, New York, University Press of America, 1994
Moen, M. *The Transformation of the Christian Right*, Tuscaloosa, University of Alabama Press, 1992
Morgan, E. *The 60s Experience. Hard Lessons About Modern America*, Philadelphia, Temple University Press, 1991
Morris, A. and C. McClurg Mueller, eds. *Frontiers in Social Movement Theory*, New Haven, Yale University Press, 1992
Muller, J. "The Radical Conservative Critique of Liberal Democracy in Weimar Germany: Hans Freyer and Carl Schmitt," in Sternhell, ed., *Intellectual Revolt*, pp. 190–218
Mumtaz, A. "Islamic Fundamentalism in South Asia: The Jamaat-i-Islami and the Tablighi Jamaat," in Marty and Appleby, eds., *Fundamentalisms Observed*, pp. 457–530
Munson, H., Jr. *Islam and the Revolution in the Middle East*, New Haven, Yale University Press, 1988
  Review of Mark Jungensmeyer's, "The New Cold War?: Religious Nationalism Confronts the Secular State," in the *International Journal of Middle East Studies*, 27, 3, 1995, pp. 341–401
  "Intolerable Tolerance: Western Academia and Islamic Fundamentalism," *Contention*, 5, 3, 1996, pp. 99–118
Mus, P. "La sociologie de Georges Burvitch et l'Asia," *Cahiers internationaux de sociologie*, 43, 1967, pp. 1–21
Mutalib, H. and Taj ul-Islam Hashmi, eds. *Islam, Muslims and the Modern State: Case Studies of Muslims in Thirteen Countries*, Macmillan, London, 1996

Nahirny, V. C. *The Russian Intelligentsia: From Torment to Silence*, Brunswick NJ: Transaction Publications, 1981

Naipaul, V. S. article in *The New York Herald Tribune*, May 6, 1990

Nasr, S. V. R. *The Vanguard of the Islamic Revolution: The Jama'at-I Islam of Pakistan*, Berkeley, University of California Press, 1994
  "Democracy and Islamic Revivalism," *Political Science Quarterly*, 110, 2, 1995, pp. 271–3
  Mawdudi and the Making of Islamic Revivalism, Oxford, Oxford University Press, 1996

Naylor, W. F. "Some Thoughts upon Reading Tocqueville's Democracy in America," paper for Prof. Edward Shils' seminar on Ideas on Social Solidarity, University of Chicago, May 1995

Nedelski, J. *Private Property and the Limits of American Constitutionalism*, Chicago, University of Chicago Press, 1990

Nemoy, R. ed. *Karaite Anthology – Excerpts from Early Anthology.*

Niebhur, R. *The Social Sources of Denominationalism*, Hamden, Shoe String Press, 1954

Nietzsche, F. W. *Beyond Good and Evil*, Chicago, Gateway, 1955
  The Living Thoughts of Nietzsche, London, Cassell, 1942
  On the Genealogy of Morality, Cambridge, Cambridge University Press, 1994
  The Will to Power, New York, Vintage Books, 1967

Nivison, D. S. and A. F. Wright, eds., *Confucianism in Action*, Stanford, Stanford University Press, 1959

Oberman, H. *The Dawn of the Reformation: Essays in the Late Medieval and Early Reformation Thought*, Edinburgh, T. and T. Clark, 1986
  The Impact of the Reformation: Essays, Grand Rapids, William B. Eerdmans, 1994
  The Reformation: Roots and Ramifications, Edinburgh, T. and T. Clark, 1994

Obeyskeyere, G. "Buddhism, Nationhood, and Cultural Identity: A Question of Fundamentals," in Marty and Appleby, eds., *Fundamentalisms Comprehended*, pp. 231–58

O'Fahey, R. S. "Islamic Hegemonies in the Sudan," in L. Brenner, ed., *Muslim Identities and Social Change in Sub-Saharan Africa*, Bloomington, Indiana University Press, 1993, pp. 21–58

Okada, S. "The Development of State Ritual in Ancient Japan," *Acta Asiatica*, Tokyo, Institute of Eastern Cultures, 1987

Outram, D. *The Enlightenment*, Cambridge, Cambridge University Press, 1995

Ozouf, M. *La fite revolutionnaire*, Paris, Gallimard, 1982

Pandey, G. *The Construction of Communalism in Colonial North India*, Oxford, Oxford University Press, 1990

Pardne, P. A. *Buddhism: A Historical Introduction to Buddhist Values and the Social and Political Forms they Have Assumed in Asia*, New York, Macmillan, 1971

Patlagean, E. and A. Le Boulluec, eds. *Les retours aux écritures fondamentalismes présents et passés*, Paris, Peeters Louvain, 1993

Peacock, J. L. "Weberian, Southern Baptist, and Indonesian Muslim Conceptions of Belief and Action," in Carol E. Hill, ed., *Symbols and Society: Essays on Belief Systems in Action*, Southern Anthropological Society Proceedings, 9, pp. 82–92

"Religion and Life History: An Exploration in Cultural Psychology," in E. Bruner, ed., *Text, Play and Story*, American Ethnological Proceedings, 1983, pp. 94–116

Perez Diaz, V. *The Return of Civil Society: The Emergence of Democratic Spain*, Cambridge MA, Harvard University Press, 1993

Ping-ti Ho and Tang Tsou, eds. *China in Crisis*, vol. 1, *China's Heritage and the Communist System*, Chicago, University of Chicago Press, 1968

Piscatori, J. P. *Islam in a World of Nation States*, Cambridge, Cambridge University Press, 1986

"Asian Islam: International Linkages and Their Impact on International Relations," in J. Esposito, ed., *Islam in Asia: Religion, Politics and Society*, New York, Oxford University Press, 1987, pp. 230–61

Pocock, J. G. A. "Ritual, Language, Power: An Essay on the Apparent Political Meanings of Ancient Chinese Philosophy," in J. G. A. Pocock, *Politics, Language and Time, Essays on Political Thought and History*, New York, Atheneum, 1973, pp. 42–80

The Machiavellian Moment, Princeton, Princeton University Press, 1975

Virtue, Commerce, and History, Cambridge, Cambridge University Press, 1985

Pollock, S. "Ramayama and Political Imagination in India," in *The Journal of Asian Studies*, 52, 2, May 1993, pp. 261–97

Pomper, P. *The Russian Revolutionary Intelligentsia*, New York, Crowell, 1970

Przeworski, A. *Capitalism and Social Democracy*, Cambridge, Cambridge University Press, 1985

Pulsfort, E. *Indien am Scheideweg zwischen Sakularismus und Fundamentalismus*, Würzburg, 1991

Ramadan, A. A. "Fundamentalist Influence in Egypt: The Strategies of the Muslim Brotherhood and the Takfir Groups," in Marty and Appleby, eds., *Fundamentalisms and the State*, pp. 152–83

Ravitzky, A. *Messianism, Zionism and Jewish Religious Radicalism*, Chicago, University of Chicago Press, 1993

Ray, O. "Le néofondamentalisme islamique on l'imaginaire de l'ummah," *L'esprit*, April 1996, pp. 80–108

Reddy, W. *The Rise of Market Culture: The Textile Trade and French Society*, Chicago, University of Chicago Press, 1984

Redfield, R. *Human Nature and the Study of Society*, Chicago, University of Chicago Press, 1962

Reinhard, W., ed. *Die Fundamentalistische Revolution*, Freiburg, Rombach, 1995

Reischauer, E. D. and J.K. Fairbank, *A History of East Asian Civilization*, Vol. 1, *East Asia: The Great Tradition*, Boston, Houghton Mifflin, ·1960

Retnani, M., ed. *Penseurs maghrebins contemporains*, Casablanca, EDDIF, 1997

Rex, J. *Ethnic Minorities in the Modern Nation State*, London, Macmillan, 1996

Riegel, K. "Der Marxismus-Leninismus als politische Religion," in H. Maier and M. Schafer, eds., *"Totalitarismus" und "Politische Religionen,"* Munich, Ferdinand Schoningh, 1997, pp. 75–139

Riesebrodt, M. *Fundamentalismus as patriarchalische protestbewegung*, Tübingen, Mohr, 1990

Robertson, R. *Globalization: Social Theory and Global Culture*, London, Sage, 1992

Rodinson, M. "Terrorisme et Politique dans l'Islam Médiéval" (trans. from English by Annick Pelissier), in B. Lewis, ed., *Les Assassins*, Paris, Berger-Levrault, 1982

Rokkan, S. "Dimensions of State Formation and Nation Building: A Possible Paradigm for Research on Variations within Europe," in C. Tilly, ed., *The Formation of National States in Western Europe*, Princeton, NJ, Princeton University Press, 1975, pp. 562–600

Rosanvallon, P. *Le sacré du citoyen. Histoire du suffrage universel*, Paris, Editions Gallimard, 1992.

Roth, G. and W. Schluchter. *Max Weber's Vision of History, Ethics and Methods*, Berkeley, University of California Press, 1979

Rousseau, J. *The Social Contract and Discourses*, ed. and introd. G. D. H. Cole, New York: Dutton Everyman's Library, 1968

Rozell, M. and C. Wilcox. *Second Coming: The New Christian Right in Virginia Politics*, Baltimore, Johns Hopkins University Press, 1996

Rude, G. *The Crowd in the French Revolution*, Oxford, Clarendon, 1960

Runciman, W. G., ed. *Max Weber: Selections in Translation*, Cambridge, Cambridge University Press, 1978

Salomon, A. *The Tyranny of Progress: Reflections on the Origins of Sociology*, New York, Noonday Press, 1955

In Praise of Enlightenment, Cleveland, World Publishing Company, 1963

Salvador, M. *Europe, America, Marxismo*, Turin, Einaudi, 1990

Salvadori, J. L. and N. Tranfaghia, eds. *Il Modelo politico giacobino e le rivoluzione*, Florence, La Nova Italia, 1984

Sarkisyanz, E. *Russland und der Messianismus der Orients*, Tübingen, Mohr, 1955

Saunders, E. *Buddhism in Japan with an Outline of Its Origins in India*, Philadelphia, University of Pennsylvania Press, 1964

Schaff, P. *America: A Sketch of the Political, Social, and Religious Character*, New York, Charles Scribner, 1855

von Schelting, A. *Russland und Europa im russischen Geschichtsdenken*, Bern, A. Francke AG, 1948

Schmidt, J. "Civil Society and Social Things: Setting the Boundaries of the Social Sciences," *Social Research*, 62, 4, 1995, pp. 899–932

Schmitt, C. *Politische Theologie: Vier Kapitel zur Lehre von der Souveränität*, Munich, Duncker and Humbolt, 1922

The Concept of the Political, New Brunswick, Rutgers University Press, 1976

Political Romanticism, Cambridge, MA, MIT Press, 1986

The Crisis of Parliamentary Democracy, Cambridge MA, MIT Press, 1988

Die Diktatur: Von den anfängen des modernen Souveränitätsgedankens bis zum proletarischen Klassenkampf, Berlin, Duncker and Humbolt, 1989

Scholem, G. *The Messianic Idea in Judaism*, New York, Schocken Books, 1971

Schopenhauer, A. *On the Basis of Morality*, Providence, Berghahn Books, 1995

The World as Will and Representation, New York, Dover Publications, 1966

Essay on the Freedom of the Will, Indianapolis, Bobbs-Merrill, 1960

Schormer, K. and W. H. McLeod, eds. *The Saints: Studies in a Devotional Tradition of India*, Berkeley, University of California Press, 1985

Schram, S. R., ed. *Foundations and Limits of State Power in China*, London, University of London, School of Oriental and African Studies, 1987

Schwartz, B. L. "The Primacy of the Political Order in East Asian Societies: Some Preliminary Generalizations," in Schram, ed., *Foundations and Limits*, pp. 1–10

China and Other Matters, Cambridge MA, Harvard University Press, 1996

Sciolino, E. "The Red Menace is Gone. But Here's Islam," *New York Times*, January 21, 1996, pp. 1–4

Seidman, S., ed. *The Postmodern Turn: New Perspectives on Social Theory*, Cambridge, Cambridge University Press, 1994

Seligman, A. ed. *Order and Transcendence*, Leiden, E.J. Brill, 1989

Shaban, M. A. *The Abbasid Revolution*, Cambridge, Cambridge University Press, 1970

Shahidian, H. "The Iranian Left and the 'Woman Question' in the Revolution of 1978–1979," *International Journal of Middle East Studies*, 26, 2, 1994

Sharon, M. *Black Banners from the East*, Jerusalem, Magnes Press, 1983

Shea, W. "The Catholic Tribe and Fundamentalism as a Stranger," in F. Nichols, ed., *Christianity and the Stranger: Historical Essays*, Atlanta, Scholars Press, 1995, pp. 221–86

Shils, E. "Primordial, Personal, Sacred and Civil Ties," in Shils, ed., *Center and Periphery*, pp. 111–26

"Center and Periphery; and Society and Societies – The Macrosociological View," in Shils, ed., *Center and Periphery*, pp. 3–11

Shils, E., ed. *Center and Periphery: Essays in Macrosociology*, Chicago, University of Chicago Press, 1975

Silber, M. K. "The Emergence of Ultra-Orthodoxy: The Invention of a Tradition," in Jack Wertheimer, ed., *The Uses of Tradition*, Cambridge, MA, Harvard University Press, 1992

Silberstein, L. J., ed. *Jewish Fundamentalism in Comparative Perspective: Religion, Ideology, and the Crisis of Modernity*, New York and London, New York University Press, 1993

Singer, B. *Society, Theory, and the French Revolution: Studies in the Revolutionary Imaginary*, New York, St Martin's Press, 1986

Singer, M. and B. S. Cohn, eds. *Structure and Change in Indian Society*, Chicago, Aldine, 1968

Sivan, E. *Interpretations of Islam: Past and Present*, Princeton, Darwin Press, 1985

"In God's Cause," in the Erasmus Ascension Symposium, *The Limits of Pluralism. Neo-Absolutism and Relativism*, Amsterdam, Praemium Erasmianum Foundation, 1994

"Jihad, Text, Myth, Historical Realities," in Patlagean and Le Boulluec, eds., *Les retours aux écritures*, pp. 83–100

Radical Islam: Medieval Theology and Modern Politics, New Haven, Yale University Press, 1990

Social Research, special issue on the French Revolution and the Birth of Modernity, 1989

Soloveitchik, H. "Migration, Acculturation, and the New Role of Texts in the Haredi World," in Marty and Appleby, eds., *Accounting for Fundamentalisms,* pp. 197–236

Sombart, W. *Why Is There No Socialism in the United States?*, New York, M.E. Sharpe, 1976 (1st edn 1906)

Sorel, G. *Materiaux d'une theorie du proletariat*, New York, Arno Press, 1975

Spence, J. D. and J.E. Wills, eds. *From Ming to Ching*, New Haven, Yale University Press, 1979

Spitz, D. R. review of Y. K. Malik and V. B. Singh, *Hindu Nationalists in India: The Rise of the Bharatiya Janata Party* and of J. E. Llewellyn, *The Arya Samaj as a Fundamentalist Movement* in *Journal of Asian Studies*, 54, 4, 1995, p. 1137

Sprinzak, E. "When Prophecy Fails: The Crisis of Jewish Fundamentalism in Israel," *Contention*, 4, 2, 1995, pp. 105–20

Steigerwald, D. *The Sixties and the End of Modern America*, New York, St Martin's Press, 1995

Steiner, G. *Martin Heidegger*, New York, Viking Press, 1979

Sternhell, Z., ed. *The Intellectual Revolt against Liberal Democracy 1870–1945*, Jerusalem, Israel Academy of Sciences and Humanities, 1996

Stewart, C. and R. Shaw, eds. *Syncretism/Anti-Syncretism: The Politics of Religious Synthesis*, London, Routledge, 1994

Stoll, D. *Is Latin America Turning Protestant? The Politics of Evangelical Growth*, Berkeley, University of California Press, 1990

Stratton Hawley, J., ed. *Fundamentalism and Gender*, New York, Oxford University Press, 1994, pp. 137–74

Strauss, L. *What is Political Philosophy? And Other Studies*, Glencoe, Free Press, 1959

  Thoughts on Machiavelli, Seattle, University of Washington Press, 1969

  The Political Thought of Hobbes: Its Basis and its Genesis, Chicago, University of Chicago Press, 1973

  The Concept of the Political, New Brunswick, Rutgers University Press, 1976

  The City and Man, Chicago, University of Chicago Press, 1978

  The Rebirth of Classical Political Rationalism: An Introduction to the Thought of Leo Strauss, Chicago, University of Chicago Press, 1989

Stutley, M. and J. Stutley. *A Dictionary of Hinduism, Its Mythology, Folklore and Development, 1500BC-AD1500*, Bombay, Allied Publishers, 1977

Swearer, D. K. "Fundamentalistic Movements in Theravada Buddhism," in Marty and Appleby, eds., *Fundamentalisms Observed*, pp. 628–91

Talmon, J. L. *The Origins of Totalitarianism Democracy*, New York, Praeger, 1960

Tamaru, N. "Buddhism in Japan," in M. Eliade, ed., *The Encyclopaedia of Religion*, II, New York, Macmillan, 1987, pp. 426–35.

Tambiah, S. T. *Sri Lanka: Ethnic Fratricide and the Dismantling of Democracy*, Chicago, University of Chicago Press, 1986

Buddhism Betrayed? Religion, Politics and Violence in Sri Lanka, Chicago, University of Chicago Press, 1992

Leveling Crowds. Ethnonationalist Conflicts and Collective Violence in South Asia, Berkeley, University of California Press, 1996

Tarrow, S. *Power in Movement. Social Movements, Collective Action and Politics*, Cambridge, Cambridge University Press, 1994

Taylor, C. *Sources of the Self: The Making of the Modern Identity*, Cambridge MA, Harvard University Press, 1989

Hegel and the Modern Society, Cambridge, Cambridge University Press, 1989

Thapar, R. "Householders and Renouncers in the Brahmanical and Buddhist Traditions," in Madan, ed., *Way of Life*, pp. 273–98

Thomas, G. M. *Revivalism and Cultural Change: Christianity, National Building, and the Market in the Nineteenth-Century United States*, Chicago, University of Chicago Press, 1989

Tibi, B. *The Crisis of Modern Islam*, Utah, University of Utah Press, 1988

Krieg der Zivilisationen: Politik und Religion zwischen Vernunft und Fundamentalismus, Hamburg, Hoffmann and Campe, 1995

Tilly, C. "Does Modernization Breed Revolution?" *Comparative Politics*, 5, 3, 1973, pp. 425–47

Coercion, Capital, and European States, AD 990–1990, Oxford, Basil Blackwell, 1990

Timbergen, K. *Revolutions from Above*, New Brunswick, Transactions Publishers, 1978

Tiryakian, E. "Three Meta Cultures of Modernity: Christian, Gnostic, Chthonic," *Theory, Culture and Society*, Vol. 13, No. 1, 1996, pp. 99–118

Tocqueville, A. *Democracy in America*, New York, Vintage Books, 1954

Todorov, T. *The Conquest of America: The Question of the Other*, New York, Harper and Row, 1984

The Morals of History, Minneapolis, University of Minnesota Press, 1995

Totalitarian Democracy and After: International Colloquium in Memory of Jacob L. Talmon, 21–24 June 1982, Jerusalem, The Hebrew University, 1984, pp. 37–56

Toulmin, S. *Cosmopolis, the Hidden Agenda of Modernity*, New York, Free Press, 1990

Traugott, M., ed. *Repertoires and Cycles of Collective Action*, Durham, Duke University Press, 1995

Al-Turabi, H. "Islamic Fundamentalism in the Sunna and Shia World," [http://www.ibmpcug.co.uk/~whip/trabi.htm]
Islam, avenir du monde, Paris, J. C. Lattes, 1997

Vanaik, A. *The Furies of Indian Communalism. Religion, Modernity and Secularization*, London, Verso, 1997

Van der Veer, P. *Nation and Migration: The Politics of Space in the South Asian Diaspora*, Philadelphia, University of Pennsylvania Press, 1995
Religious Nationalism: Hindus and Muslims in India, Berkeley, University of California Press, 1994

Van der Veer, P. ed. *Conversion to Modernities: The Globalization of Christianity*, New York, Routledge, 1996

A. Varshney, "Three Compromised Nationalisms: Why Kashmir Has Been a Problem," in R. G. C. Thomas, ed., *Perspectives on Kashmir: The Roots of Conflict in South Asia*, Boulder, Westview Press, 1992
"India: Liberalism vs. Nationalism," *Journal of Democracy*, Books in Review, 1992
"Contested Meanings: India's National Identity, Hindu Nationalism, and the Politics of Anxiety," *Daedalus*, 122, 3, 1993
"The Self-Correcting Mechanisms of Indian Democracy," in *Seminar*, Annual Number, Delhi, January 1995

Venturi, F. *Roots of Revolution. A History of the Populist and Socialist Movements in Nineteenth Century Russia*, Chicago, University of Chicago Press, 1983

Vico, G. *The New Science of Giambattista Vico*, Abridged and rev. edn., Garden City NY, Anchor Books, 1961

Viswanathan, G. *Masks of Conquest: Literary Study and British Rule in India*, New York, Columbia University Press, 1989

Voegelin, E. *Order and History*, Baton Rouge, Louisiana State University, 1954
Enlightenment and Revolution, ed. John H. Hallowell, Durham NC, Duke University Press, 1975
The New Science of Politics, Chicago, University of Chicago Press, 1952
Das Volk Gottes, Munich, Wilhelm Fink Verlag, 1994
Die politischen Religionen, Munich, Wilhelm Fink Verlag, 1996

Voll, J. "Fundamentalism in the Sunni Arab World: Egypt and the Sudan," in Marty and Appleby, eds., *Fundamentalisms Observed*, pp. 345–403

Wagner, C. *Latin American Theology: Radical or Evangelical?*, Grand Rapids, William B. Eerdman Publishing Company, 1970

Wagner, P. *A Sociology of Modernity: Liberty and Discipline*, London, Routledge, 1994

Wakeman, F., Jr. *The Great Enterprise: The Manchu Reconstruction of the Imperial Order in Seventeenth-Century China*, Berkeley and Los Angeles, University of California Press, 1986

Walzer, M. "Puritanism as a Revolutionary Ideology," in B. Laughlin, ed., *Studies in Social Movements*, New York, Free Press, 1959

    The Revolution of the Saints, Cambridge MA, Harvard University Press, 1966

Walzer, M., ed. *Regicide and Revolution: Speeches at the Trial of Louis XVI*, London, Cambridge University Press, 1974

Warburg, G. "Mahdism and Islamism in Sudan," *International Journal of Middle East Studies*, 27, 2, 1995, pp. 219–36

Watt, W. *Islamic Fundamentalism and Modernity*, London, Routledge, 1988

Weber, M. *Ancient Judaism*, Glencoe, Free Press, 1952

    The Rational and Social Foundations of Music, Carbondale, Southern Illinois University Press, 1958

    The Religion of China: Confucianism and Taoism, trans. H. Gerth, New York, Free Press, 1964

    On Charisma and Institution Building: Selected Papers, Chicago, University of Chicago Press, 1968

    Politik als Beruf, Berlin, Duncker and Humblot, 1968

    Die protestantische Ethik: Kritiken und Antikritiken, Gütersloh, Gütersloher Verlagshaus, 1978

    Gesammelte Aufsätze zur Religionssoziologie, Tübingen, J. C. B. Mohr, 1922, 1978

Weiner, M. *The Indian Paradox: Essays in Indian Politics*, New Delhi, Sage Publications, 1989

Werblowski, Z. J. R. *Beyond Tradition and Modernity*, Atlantic Highlands NJ, Athlone Press, 1976

Wilcox, C. *God's Warrior: The Christian Right in Twentieth Century America*, Baltimore, Johns Hopkins University Press, 1992

    Onward Christian Soldiers: The Religious Right in American Politics, Boulder, Westview Press, 1996

Woodside, A. "History, Structure and Revolution in Vietnam," *International Political Science Review*, 10, 2, 1989, pp. 143–59

Wright, A. F. *Buddhism in Chinese History*, Stanford, Stanford University Press, 1959

    The Confucian Persuasion, Stanford: Stanford University Press, 1960

Wright, A. F., ed. *Studies in Chinese Thought*, Chicago, University of Chicago Press, 1953

Wright, A. F. and D. Twitchett, eds. *Perspectives on the Tang*, New Haven, Yale University Press, 1973

Yang, C. K. "The Functional Relationship between Confucian Thought and Chinese Religion," in Fairbank, ed., *Chinese Thought,* pp. 269–91

Yapp, M. E. "Full Mosques, Empty Hearts," *Times Literary Supplement*, May 30, 1997

Index

Abbasid revolution 41
absolutism
  in France 61
  and revolutionary movements 127
accountability of rulers
  in Axial-Age Civilizations 6, 13
    Islamic 21, 22–3
  in Communist regimes 108
  in fundamentalist regimes 108, 150
  and Great Revolutions 41
  in Japan 157
  in modern states 60–1, 122
Ackerman, Bruce 199
Adamson, Christopher 167–8
Advani, L. K. 147
Afghanistan, Taliban movement 88, 96,
    103
Africa
  changes of regime 121
  and Islam 87, 88, 89, 132, 185–6
Agudat Israel 85
Algeria 186
Almond, G. 94
alternative visions
  in Axial-Age Civilizations 7–9, 10–16
  see also transcendental and mundane
    orders
American Revolution 25, 39, 116
  declarations 43
  and the Meiji Restoration in Japan
    161
  and the pluralistic concept of democracy
    72
  and political groups 45
  utopian visions 42
Anabaptists 35, 83
anarchist movements 77
Appendurai, Arjun 207

Appleby, R. S. 94
Arabian utopianism 101
Arjomand, Said 41
Arnason, Johann 68
Artasharta of Katulya 10
Asian civilizations
  and modernity 121, 123
  social contract in 10
  see also South/Southeast Asia
Augustine, St. 9, 24, 40
Australia 121
authenticity, and Islamic fundamentalism
    144
autonomous intellectuals, in Axial-Age
    Civilizations 6, 7
autonomy
  and the cultural program of modernity
    56, 57–8, 62, 63, 64–6
  of human will, and modern
    fundamentalist movements 91–2,
    112, 117
  in India 181
  and the political program of modernity
    68
Axial-Age Civilizations 3–38
  basic antinomies in the cultural programs
    of 7–13
  and Great Revolutions 93
  heterodoxies and utopianism in 3–7
  and Japan 155–6, 157, 163
  and modernity 118, 120, 126, 201
    cultural program of 62, 66, 67
    political program of 73
  monotheistic 19–25
  other-worldly 13–16
  patrimonial regimes 174
  proto-fundamentalist movements in
    25–38, 39, 40, 90, 105

rulers in 5–6, 10, 60
this-worldly, Confucianism 16–18
Aziz Al Azmeh 20, 34, 100–1

Ba'ath movement 129, 131
Bellah, Robert N. 165
Berlin, Isaiah 71
Bhakti 14
Bible, Old and New Testaments 31–2
BJP (Bharatiya Janata Party) 146–7, 188, 189
Bobbio, Norberto 73
"bourgeois" culture, decline of 139
Bowman, Carol 148
Buckley, William F. 171
Buddhism
    alternative visions in 14, 15–16
    and Axial-Age civilization 4, 6, 8
    Buddhist countries 1, 93, 114
    and communal–religious movements 154
    and Hinduism 11
    in Japan 155, 156–9
    and neo-Confucianism 18
    and primordial orientations 93
    and proto-fundamentalist movements 27, 28, 29–30
    Sangha 6
    Theravada 114
Burma 122, 125, 129, 130, 132

Calvinism 25, 49, 83
Canada 121
capitalism
    and modernity 52, 54–5, 79
    and proto-fundamentalism 36
    and socialist and nationalistic movements 117–18
Castoriadis, Cornelius 65
Catholicism
    and fundamentalism 30, 150, 176–7, 178
    in Latin America 179
    medieval 23–4, 35
    and modern dislocation processes 149
    and the New Testament 31
center formation, in Axial-Age Civilizations 5
center-oriented movements
    and Great Revolutions 49, 52
    modern fundamentalist movements 77
    social movements 76–7, 80, 81
center–periphery relations
    in fundamentalist and Communist regimes 107
    and modernity 58, 59, 61–2, 73
    and proto-fundamentalist movements 37, 92

China
    Axial-Age Civilization 15
    classical Chinese belief systems 27
    and collectivities 16–18
    conception of the Mandate of Heaven 6
    construction of new state in 122, 123
    early imperial 4
    fundamentalism in 153
    literati in 6
    and modernity 191
    post-Mao period 126
Chinese Revolution 39, 116, 125
    and political groups 45
    and the political program of modernity 74
    and socialist symbols 131
    and utopian visions 42
Christian Coalition 83
Christian meta-narrative of modernity 51, 62
Christianity
    and Axial-Age Civilizations
        crystallization of 4
        heterodoxy and orthodoxy in 29, 30
    Calvinism 25
    and Judaism 11
    Lutheranism 24–5
    medieval Catholicism 23–4, 35
    and patrimonial regimes 174
    proto-fundamentalist components in 35–6
    and sacred text 26
    sectarianism 22, 23–5
    in the United States 147–9, 171–2
    utopian fundamentalism in 150
    see also Catholicism; Protestantism
church and state, separation of 166
citizenship
    and the development of communal-religious movements 176
    and revolutionary movements 127
    in the Roman Empire 165
    transformation of, and modernity 60, 61, 70, 71, 139
City of God and City of Man 9, 24, 40, 49, 56
city states of antiquity 78
civil society
    and the development of communal-religious movements 176
    and Jacobin tendencies 92
    in Japan 161–2, 163
    and the political program of modernity 52, 54, 62, 69, 73
class
    and the capitalist political economy 54
    and composition of Great Revolutions 46
    and the modern political process 78

Cochin, Albert 45
Cold War 80, 120, 121, 136
collective identity
    in European Protestant countries 177–8
    in India 179–82
    and modernity 53, 111
    Muslim 191
    primordial 64
        and modern fundamentalist
            movements 93, 113
    in the United States 165–9, 170, 173
collectivities, reconstruction of, in
            Axial-Age Civilizations 4–5
common good
    different conceptions of the 79
    and pluralistic conceptions of democracy
            71–2
common will, and the political program of
        modernity 69, 70–1
communal-nationalist-religious movements
    challenge to modern pluralistic regimes
        184–95
    development of, compared with
        fundamentalist movements 149–55,
        175–6
    and dislocation processes 141–3
    in India 184
    and modernity 119–20, 135–6, 206
    in Southeast Asia 93, 107, 113–15,
        116–17, 175
Communist movements and regimes
    challenges to Western hegemony 121
    and communal–religious national groups
        153
    compared with modern fundamentalist
        movements 106–12, 114–15, 117–18
    and dislocation processes 145–6
    and modernity 125–6, 128, 135
Confucianism 8, 16–18, 27, 29, 56, 153
    in Japan 155, 156–9
Counter Reformation 24, 51
counter-cultures 139
Counter-Reformation, and man, cosmos
        and nature 56–7
cultural homogenization 122, 138

democracy
    and modernity 61
    and the political program of modernity
        61, 71–2, 74–5
democratization, and modern
        fundamentalist movements 194
Descartes, R. 63
diasporas
    emergence of new 138, 140
    Muslim 88, 98, 107, 138, 142

dislocation processes
    in India 183–4
    and modern fundamentalist movements
        141–5
    and national, socialist and Communist
        movements 145–7
    in the United States 147–9
Dunn, John 70
Durkheim, E. 70, 197, 199

Eastern Europe 120, 123, 201, 202
    and fascism 133
    and nationalist movements 140
economic decline
    global 137–8
    in the United States 172
economic development, and revolutionary
        movements 127
economic dislocation, and modern
        fundamentalist movements 141–2
economic globalization 136, 137
economic policies, "Islamic economics"
        191
Edsall, Thomas B. 147
Edsell, I. 184
educated groups
    and the American Christian right 148
    and modern fundamentalist movements
        142, 143–4
Egypt 1, 129, 187
Elias, Norbert 65, 139
elites
    in Axial-Age Civilizations 6, 7, 11, 12
    in China, and Confucianism 18
    and Great Revolutions 47–8
    and modern fundamentalist movements
        119
    and proto-fundamentalist movements
        36–7, 38
    see also intellectuals
enemies
    of modern fundamentalism 90
    and Communist regimes 108–9
English Puritans 42
English Revolution (Civil War) 25, 39
    and accountability of rulers 60
    components of 46
    and historical background 42
    and the Meiji Restoration in Japan 161
    political processes 44–5
    primordial themes 43
Enlightenment
    and communal religious movements
        135–6
    and the cultural and political programs of
        modernity 57, 65, 68, 134, 193

and fascist/national-socialist movements
113, 124–5
and Judaism 33, 84
and modern fundamentalism 39, 89, 91
compared with Communist regimes
109, 111, 115
and proto-fundamentalism 36, 40
and the separation of church and state
166
Epstein, Jason 171–2
Erasmus 63

Falwell, Rev. Jerry 83
fascist movements
as challenges to Western hegemony 121,
133
Jacobin components of 73, 80, 110
and modernity 112–13, 114, 116, 118,
193, 194
Ferro-Luzzi, Gabriella Eichinger 14
Foucault, Michel 65, 139
France, absolutism in 61
Frankfurt school 199
French Revolution 25, 39, 116
components of 46
Jacobin clubs 50
and the Meiji Restoration in Japan 161
and political groups 45
and the political program of modernity
74
primordial themes 43
sanctification of violence 50
utopian visions 42
Freyer, Hans 67
fundamentalism
use of term 83, 95
see also modern fundamentalist
movements; proto-fundamentalist
movements
Furet, François 45

Gandhi, Indira 130, 180, 183
Gandhi, M. 130, 183, 184
Gellner, Ernest 22, 109
German romanticism 64
globalization
and dislocation processes 145, 149
of the economy 136, 137
gnostic meta-narrative of modernity 51, 62
gnostic orientations
in Christianity 24
in Great Revolutions 43
in modern fundamentalist movements
93
and modernity 56
and proto-fundamentalist movements 40

Göle, Nulifer 104, 143–5, 191
Gonder, M.D. Deve 188
Great Revolutions 39–50
and Christianity 25
Communist 126
components of 45–6
and "counter-revolutionary" forces 46
historical roots of 40–3
and Jacobin ideology 72, 105
liminal dimensions of 49–50
and the Meiji Ishin in Japan 160–1
and modern fundamentalist movements
93, 116, 192
and modernity 2, 3, 39, 40
participation by intellectuals in 47–8
and political processes 43–5
and the political program of modernity
68, 74, 75
and proto-fundamentalism 36
and socialist and communist movements
115
and utopian visions 42, 52
Great Tradition
in Axial-Age Civilizations 5
and Islam 132
Greece, ancient 6, 28
and monotheistic civilizations 29
Grew, Raymond 91, 92, 110
Guinea 185
Gush Emunim (Block of the Faithful) 84,
85, 86, 103

Habermas, Jürgen 206
Hannerz, Ulf 207
Haredim Jews 89, 90, 92
Harrison, Selig 180
hegemony *see* Western hegemony
Heidegger, Martin 67
Heilman, S. 86
Herder, J.G. 63–4
heterodox sectarian movements 1
and Axial-Age Civilizations 3–7, 13–14,
105
in Judaism 20
and modern social movements 76
heterodoxy
in China 18
in modern fundamentalist movements
102
and orthodoxy, in proto-fundamentalist
movements 28–30
Hindu nationalism 146–7
Hinduism 56
alternative visions in 14, 15–16
and Axial-Age Civilization 4, 6, 8
Brahmins 6

Hinduism (*cont.*)
  Buddhist reformulation of the premises
      of 11
  fundamentalist movements in 114
  nationalist movements in India 146–7,
      183, 184
  and proto-fundamentalist movements 27,
      28, 29–30
  religious communal movements in 154
  and sectarianism 22
history, totalizing and pluralistic visions of
      63–4
Hobbes, Thomas 69
Hobsbawm, Eric 44
Hodgson, Godfrey 171–2
holy men of antiquity 11
homosexuality, views of the American
      Christian right 148–9
Hsunt-su 10
Hungary, Judaism in 84
Hunter, James Davison 147–9
Huntington, Samuel P. 165–6, 169, 206–7

Ibn Khaldoun 10, 22, 23, 37, 100
Imperial regimes, and revolutionary
      movements 127
Inden, R. 181
India 175, 179–84, 188–90
  collective identity 179–82
  dislocation processes in 183–4
  Hindu nationalist movements 146–7, 183,
      184, 188–9
  modern fundamentalist movements 1, 87,
      88, 89, 93
  politics 122, 125, 128, 130, 182–3, 188–90
  and socialism 131
individual responsibility, and Confucianism
      17
individual rights, and the political program
      of modernity 69–70, 71
individualism, and modernity 51
Indonesia 122
industrialization, and modernity 79
instrumental rationality
  and Communist regimes 111
  and the cultural program of modernity
      63, 64
intellectuals
  in Axial-Age Civilizations 6, 7
  as leaders of modern fundamentalist
      movements 102
  participation in Great Revolutions 47–8
  in Turkey 104
  see also elites
interest groups, and the modern political
      process 78

Iran
  Islamic fundamentalism 88, 96–7, 108,
      111, 185, 191
  Zoroastrianism 4
Iraq
  Ba'ath movement 129, 131
  Islamic fundamentalism in 88
Islam
  and Axial-Age Civilizations
      crystallization of 4
      proto-fundamentalist orientations in
          29, 33–5, 37
      tribes converted to 23
  Diaspora communities 88, 98, 107, 142
  and the ideal of the *unmah* 20
  Jacobin components of 96–7
  Mahdist movement 22, 87
  Medinan Caliphate 34
  modern fundamentalism 1, 86–9, 90, 107,
      151, 185, 186–8
      and essentialized tradition 100–1
      in Iran 88, 96–7, 108, 111, 185, 186, 191
      and jihad 94
      and primordial components of
          collective identity 93, 107
      and socialism 136
      in Turkey 88, 89, 96, 98, 143–5, 185,
          186
      and universalism 115
  and modernity 118
  and nationalist movements 128–9
  and patrimonial regimes 174, 175
  political dynamics and sectarianism 20–3
  and sacred text (Koran) 26, 31, 144
  sanctification of violence in 50
  Shi'ite 22, 33–4, 88
  and socialist symbols 131–2
  Sufism 22
  Sunni 22, 23–4, 87
  ulema (religious establishment) 6, 21, 22,
      88
  and the Wahhabites 23, 33, 34–5, 87, 101
Islamic law (sharia) 21
Israel
  ancient 6, 12
  modern fundamentalist movements 84–6,
      89, 103, 190
  and Muslim fundamentalists 90
  State of 20, 84–6
  see also Judaism
Ivory Coast 185

Jacobin clubs 50
Jacobin components
  in communal-national movements 114,
      117

in modern fundamentalist movements 2, 82, 90, 91, 92, 93, 94–7, 115, 150, 196
  and American Protestantism 151–2, 173, 185
  compared with Communism 106–12
  and Islam 151
  power of 105–6
  and Western Europe 177, 178
in the political program of modernity 72–4
in social movements 76, 77, 80
Jainism 14
Japan 12, 120, 122, 125
  civil society in 161–2, 163
  Meiji Ishin 159–61
  and modernity 134
  nationalist movements 128, 129, 130, 155
  politics 140
  and socialism 131
  weak development of fundamentalist movements in 155–63
Jasper, Karl 3
John Birch Society 171
Jordan 186, 187
Judaism
  anti-Zionist ultra-orthodox 84–6
  Christian reformulation of the premises of 11
  and the crystallization of Axial-Age Civilizations 4
  and the Enlightenment 33, 84
  Liberal or Reformed 33, 84
  modern fundamentalist movements 1, 98, 107
    Gush Emunim (Block of the Faithful) 84, 85, 86, 103
    Haredim 89, 90, 92, 103
  and modernity 118
  period of exile 19–20
  and primordial components of collective identity 93, 107
  proto-fundamentalism 26, 29
    Karaite movement 31–2, 32–3
    and the Old Testament 31–2
  Sabbatean movement 20
  and sacred text 26
  sages 6
  Second Commonwealth 4, 19, 32
  transcendental and mundane orders in 19–20
  and utopian sectarianism 90
  Zionist movement 84–6, 90
  see also Israel
Jünger, Ernst 67

Kant, I. 57
Keddie, Nikkie 89, 113, 136, 137

Kenya 185
Khatami, Muhammad 96, 191
Khomeini, Ayatollah Ruholla 108, 142, 186
Kierkegaard, S. 67
Kolakovski, Lessek 67
Korea 16, 153–4
Kuran, Timur 191

Latin America
  Catholicism in 179
  changes of regime, and modernity 121, 123
  evangelistic movement in 94, 149
  and fascism 133
  Protestantism in 84, 149, 152, 178
  resistance movements in 125
law
  development of autonomous spheres of 6
  Islamic (sharia) 21
  rule of, in modern nation states 122
leadership
  and Great Revolutions 45
  and modern fundamentalist movements 119
  see also elites
Lechner, Frank J. 97
Lefort, Claude 68
legitimization
  of Communist regimes 108
  in modern nation states 122
  and the political program of modernity 59, 71
  of the political regime in India 188–9
  of the postwar regime in Korea 153–4
  of rulers
    and Great Revolutions 41
    Islamic 21–2
    and sovereignty 53
  and social movements 76, 77
Levine, D.H. 149
Lewis, Bernard 22
Lijphart, Arend 182
Lilla, Mark 67
Little Traditions, in Axial-Age Civilizations 5
lobby groups 78
Locke, John 69, 70
Luebe, H. 71
Lutheranism 24–5, 49

McCarthy, Joe 171
Mahdist movement (Islamic) 22, 87
Malaysia 187
  fundamentalist movements 87, 88, 93, 102, 103

Mali 185
Malia, Martin 108
Marsden, George 83
Marx, Karl 197, 199
materialism, and the cultural program of
modernity 67
Mawdudi 151
medieval Catholicism 23–4
Merleau-Ponty, M. 50
messianic movements, in Judaism 20
Middle East
patrimonial regimes 174
and socialist symbols 131–2
see also Islam
migration 138
Mill, J.S. 70
missionary orientations
in Great Revolutions 42, 43
in modern fundamentalist movements 91,
93
modern fundamentalist movements 82–118
challenge to modern pluralistic regimes
184–95
and communal religious movements
149–55
and communal-national movements
135–6
and dislocation processes 141–7
distinct sectarian utopian characteristics
89–94
historical settings of 82–9
intercivilizational setting of 119–25
and internal "Western" cultural discourse
141
Jacobin components of 2, 82, 90, 91, 92,
93, 94–7, 116, 150, 196
compared with Communism 106–12,
114–15
power of 105–6
Japan, weak development of 155–63
in Jewish communities 84–6
and modernity 1–3, 39, 40, 82, 91–2, 97,
103
compared with Communism 109,
111–12, 115, 117–18
in Turkey 104–5
Muslim 1, 86–9
and proto-fundamentalism 82, 83, 90,
90–1, 93, 96, 105–6, 115–16, 142, 150
and tradition 98–105
in the United States 170–3, 185
and Western discourse 82
modernity 196–207
civilization of 198–9
and communal-religious movements
119–20, 135–6, 206

crystallization of 35–6, 39, 52, 62, 65
and national and Communist
movements and regimes 125–35
role of elites in 48
cultural and political programs of 51–81,
193
and accountability of rulers 58, 60–1
antimonies, tensions and criticisms
62–7
and capitalist political economies 52,
54–5
and center–periphery relations 58, 59,
61–2
challenges to 205–6
constructivist approach to 68
differences between 202–3
factors shaping 203–5
Jacobin component in 72–3
and Japan 161–3
and social contract 69–71
and social movements 61–2, 74, 75–8,
121
and socialist and nationalist
movements/regimes 133–5
and transcendental and mundane
orders 56–8, 59, 62
and utopian visions 51–2, 59, 61, 68
cultural and structural dimensions of 198
development of modern states and
collectivities 52–3
fascist/national-socialist attitudes to
112–15
global transposition of themes of 201–2
meta-narratives of 51, 62, 66–7
and modern fundamentalism 1–3, 39, 40,
82, 91–2, 97, 103
compared with Communism 109,
111–12, 115, 117–18
in Iran 96–7
in Turkey 104–5
"original" 197
pluralistic and totalistic programs of 191
reappraisal of 196
tensions and antinomies in 199–200, 207
and Western hegemony 120–1, 123–5
and Western societies, changing
conceptions of 138–41
modernization, "classical theories" of 197–8
monasteries 48
Mongols, conversion to Islam 23
monotheistic civilizations, development of
fundamentalist movements in 150,
152–4
monotheistic religions
in Axial-Age civilizations 9, 19–25, 27,
29, 116

orthodoxy and heterodoxy in 29, 30
see also Christianity; Islam; Judaism
Montaigne, M. de 63
moral autonomy, and modernity 58, 64
moral choice, and modern fundamentalist
    movements 3, 91–2
Moral Majority 83
moral-rational vision, and modernity 58, 59
Morocco, modern fundamentalist
    movements 102
Motzu 10
Mowlay Suleiman, Sultan of Morocco 21
Muhammad Ahmad (Sudanese leader) 87
Muhammad (prophet) 20
multiculturalism, growth of 136, 138, 140
Mumtaz Ahmad 99
Munson, Henry Jr 20
Muslims *see* Islam

Naipaul, V.S. 188–9
Nasr, S.V.R. 186–7
national-socialist movements
    Jacobin components of 73, 110
    and modernity 112–13, 114, 116, 118,
        123–5
nationalistic movements
    communal, in Southeast Asia 93, 107,
        113–15, 116–17
    and dislocation processes 145–7
    Jacobin components of 73, 80
    and modernity 112–15, 125–35
    and primordial components of collective
        identity 93
    and socialist symbols 130–2, 135
    see also communal-nationalist-religious
        movements
natural rights, and the political program of
    modernity 69
nature, and the cultural program of
    modernity 56–8, 64
Naylor, Wendy F. 166
Nehru, J. 130, 183, 184, 189
neo-Confucianism 16–17, 18
Netherlands, Revolt of the 25, 39–40, 42
New Zealand 121
Nietzsche, F. 66, 67
North Africa, Islamic fundamentalism in 88

Obeyskeyere, G. 114
Old Testament 31–2
Oral Law (Jewish) 31–2, 33
other-worldly civilizations
    and communal–religious movements 154
    modern regimes in 175
    proto-fundamentalism in 30–1
    sectarianism and utopianism in 13–16

other-worldly visions, in Iranian
    fundamentalism 109
Ozouf, Mona 45

pagan meta-narrative of modernity 51, 62
Pakistan 182
    fundamentalist movements 87, 88, 93,
        102, 103
    Jama'at Islam 99, 186, 187
Pathans, conversion to Islam 23
patrimonial regimes 174–5
patriotic themes, and Great Revolutions 42,
    43
Perot, Ross 168
Plato 100
pluralistic regimes, fundamentalist
    challenge to 184–95
pluralistic visions
    denial of, by fundamentalist and
        Communist regimes 109
    of history 63–4
    of human society 63
    of the political program of modernity 68,
        68–9, 71–2, 74, 75
political parties, and the modern political
    process 78
political processes
    and Great Revolutions 43–5
    and modern fundamentalist movements
        93–4, 112
    in Iran 96–7
    and social movements 78–81
politics
    changes in modern 140
    and Confucianism 17, 18
Pollock, Sheldon 181
popular cultures, and modern
    fundamentalist movements 94
post-modernism 66, 136, 137–8
primordial collectivities/themes
    and the cultural program of modernity 64
    in European collective identity 178
    in Great Revolutions 43
    in Jewish collective identity 85
    and modern fundamentalist movements
        93, 113, 116, 117
    and national-fascist movements 118
    and nationalist movements 128
    and the political program of modernity 71
    and social movements 77, 80
pristine transcendental visions
    in Axial-Age Civilizations 10, 14
    in Islam 21, 23
    and modern fundamentalism 100, 103, 116
    and proto-fundamentalist movements 26,
        31–2, 37

property rights, and the political program of
    modernity 69
protest
    and Great Revolutions 41–2
    and modern fundamentalism 39
        and Communism 106
    and modernity 59, 61
    shift in nature of protest movements 140
    and social movements 75, 76
    themes of
        in modern nation states 122, 123–5
        in the United States 169–70
Protestantism
    Anabaptists 35, 83
    Calvinism 25, 49, 83
    in Europe 177–8
    in Latin America 84, 149, 152, 178
    Lutheranism 24–5, 49
    and modern dislocation processes 149
    proto-fundamentalism in 30, 31, 35–6
    Puritans 42, 45, 74
    and sacred text 26
    in the United States 1, 31, 45, 82–3, 93,
        151–2
    utopian fundamentalism in 150
proto-fundamentalist movements
    in different Axial-Age Civilizations
        25–38, 39
    and modern fundamentalism 82, 83, 90,
        90–1, 93, 96, 105–6, 115–16, 142, 150
    in monotheistic civilizations 152–3
public opinion
    and modernity 61
    in the United States 147–9

rationality
    decline of 203
    fundamentalism and Western discourse
        82
    and modernity 139
reason
    and Axial-Age Civilizations 8–9
    and the cultural program of modernity
        62–3, 64
    fundamentalism and Western discourse 82
Reed, Ralph 83
reflexivity
    and alternative visions, in Axial-Age
        Civilizations 8, 9
    and Confucianism 17
    and the cultural program of modernity
        57, 62, 64
Reformation 40
    and the cultural program of modernity
        51, 56–7, 65
    and the development of Great
        Revolutions 49

and the political program of modernity
    75
and sectarianism 24–5
Renaissance 40
    and the cultural program of modernity
        51, 65
    and the political program of modernity
        75
representation/representative institutions,
    and modernity 51, 53, 60, 61, 70
revolutionary movements and politics
    Jacobin components of 73, 74
    and modernity 68, 71, 123–35
    see also Great Revolutions
Riesebrodt, Martin 96, 97
rights
    development of conception of 6
    and the political program of modernity
        69–70
Robertson, Pat 83
Robertson, Roland 207
Robespierre, M. 50
Roman Empire 165
Romanticism
    and the cultural program of modernity
        64, 67, 69, 135
    and national–socialist movements 124,
        125, 128
Rome, ancient 28
Rousseau, Jean-Jacques 70–1, 100
rulers
    in Axial-Age Civilizations 5–6, 10, 60
    in India, and dharma 181
    Islamic 21–2
    political, and modern fundamentalist
        movements 102–3
    selection of, and the modern political
        process 78
    and the transformation of the concept of
        sovereignty 53
    see also accountability of rulers;
        legitimization of rulers
Russia
    and patrimonial regimes 174
    Slavophiles 124, 126
Russian Revolution 39, 116, 125
    and political groups 45
    and the political program of modernity 74
    and socialist symbols 130
    utopian visions 42

Sadiq al-Mahdi (prime minister of Sudan)
    87
salvationist visions
    in Axial-Age Civilizations 4, 5
    in Communist and fundamentalist
        regimes 106–9, 111, 126

Saudi Arabia 96
Schmitt, Carl 67
Schopenhauer, A. 67
sectarianism
    in Axial civilizations
        otherworldly 13–16
        proto-fundamentalist movements
            25–38, 40
        Christian 22, 23–5
    and Islam 22
    political, and Great Revolutions 46
    see also heterodox sectarian movements;
        utopian sectarianism
Senegal 185
Shils, Edward 71, 199
Sidi Muhammed, Sultan of Morocco 21
Sikhism 28
Silvan, Emmanuel 90
Singapore 153
Sivan, E. 33–4, 94
Slavophiles 124, 126
social change, and modern nation states
    121–3
social contract
    concept of
        in Axial-Age Civilizations 10
    and the political program of modernity
        69–71
social movements
    and the cultural and political programs of
        modernity 61–2, 74, 75–8, 121
    Jacobin components of 74
    and the modern political process 78–81
socialist movements and regimes
    compared with modern fundamentalist
        movements 106–12, 114–15, 117–18
    and dislocation processes 145–6
    and socialist symbols 130–2, 135
    see also Communist movements and
        regimes
socialist symbols, in nationalistic regimes
    130–2
Sofer, Hatam 84, 98
Soloveitchik, Haim 86
South/Southeast Asia
    Buddhist societies 1, 93, 114
    communal-national religious movements
        93, 107, 113–15, 116–17, 175
    Islamic fundamentalist movements 88–9
    patrimonial regimes 174
    resistance movements 125
sovereignty, transformation of, and
    modernity 53, 60–1
Soviet Union, demise of the 136, 137, 140
Spanish Civil War 121
Spitz, D. R. 146, 183
Sri Lanka 89, 114, 179

Straus, Leo 67
Sudan
    fundamentalist regime 185, 186
    Madhist movement 87, 88
Syria, Ba'ath movement 129, 131

Taiwan 153
Tanzania 129, 130
Taoism
    in Japan 155
    and neo-Confucianism 18
technocratic direction/rationality
    and fascist/national-socialist movements
        112–13
    and modernity 58, 59, 63, 64, 65, 67, 74,
        111, 138
territorial boundaries, and the modern state
    52–3
terror
    sanctification of
        and Great Revolutions 50
        and Jacobin tendencies 92
Thailand 122, 125, 128, 129, 130
Theravada Buddhism 114
this-worldly orientation
    in Christianity 23–5
    in Communist regimes 109
    in Confucianism 16–18
    and proto-fundamentalist movements 28
Thurmond, Strom 171
Tilly, Charles 44
Tiryakian, E. 51
Tocqueville, A. de 199
totalistic visions
    of Hindu movements 114
    of history 63–4
    of human society 63
    of modern fundamentalist movements 83,
        91, 93, 150, 151
    and Communism 106–9
    and essentialized tradition 98–105
    of the political program of modernity 68,
        69, 71, 72–4
"totalitarian democracy" 72
totalitarian regimes, and semi-subterranean
    cults 153
Toulmin, Stephen 63
tradition, and modern fundamentalist
    movements 98–105
transcendental and mundane orders
    in Axial-Age Civilizations 4, 5–6, 8, 9,
        10–12, 13
    and proto-fundamentalist movements
        25–6, 27, 40
    and the cultural program of modernity
        56–8, 59, 62, 63
    and Judaism 19

transcendental visions
  in Axial-Age Civilizations 13, 28
  in monotheistic civilizations 19, 153
  see also pristine transcendental visions
Tunisia 187
Turkey
  Islamic fundamentalism 88, 89, 96, 98,
    143–5, 185, 186, 190
  and modernity 104–5
  Kemalist revolution 190

Uganda 185
underclass 139
United States 163–73
  changes in the understanding of
    modernity 138–9
  collective identity 165–9, 170, 173
  fundamentalist movements 170–3, 185
    Christian right 147–9, 171–2
    and modernity 118
    Muslim 90
    Protestant 1, 31, 45, 82–3, 93, 151–2
  India compared with 183–4
  Jewish communities 84, 86
  protest themes 169–70
  and the separation of church and state
    166
universalistic visions
  in American Protestantism 152
  in fundamentalist and Communist
    regimes 108–9, 114–15, 116, 117
  and Great Revolutions 42–3
  and modern fundamentalist movements
    141
utopian sectarianism
  and criticisms of modernity 111–12, 115
  and modern fundamentalist movements
    89–94, 95
  and proto-fundamentalist movements
    116
utopian visions
  of the American community 168, 170
  and Great Revolutions 42
  in Islam 101
  and modern fundamentalist movements
    150
  and modernity 51–2, 59, 61, 68

Veer, Peter van der 92
Vejpayee, Atal Behais 188
Vico, G.B. 63–4
Vietnam 16, 123
Vietnamese Revolution 39, 125
  and political groups 45
  and the political program of modernity
    74
  utopian visions 42

violence
  ritualization of, and modern
    fundamentalist movements 89, 92
  sanctification of, and Great Revolutions
    50
Voegelin, Eric 24, 40, 52, 67
Voll, John 34–5, 87

Wagner, Peter 65
Wahhabi movement (Islamic) 23, 33, 34–5,
    87, 101
Wallace, George 171
Walzer, Michael 60
Weber, Max 12, 36, 65, 139, 197, 199
welfare state 79
Werblowski, Z.J.R. 157
Western discourse, and modern
    fundamentalist movements 82
Western Europe
  and "transnational" Europeanization 140
  weakness of modern fundamentalist
    movements in 176–8
Western hegemony
  and confrontation with other civilizations
    79, 120–1, 123–5, 135–6
  and modernity 201
  weakening of 136, 137
Western societies, changes in the
    understanding of modernity in
    138–41
"white dominions" 121
Wiebe, Robert 170–1
will
  autonomy of human, and modern
    fundamentalist movements 91–2,
    112, 117
  common will, and the political program
    of modernity 69, 70–1
Wittrock, Bjorn 110
women
  greater choice for 138
  and Islamic fundamentalism 96, 97,
    144–5
  in Turkey 105
World's Christian Fundamentals
    Association 83
World Conqueror 94
World Creator 94
World Renouncer 94
World Transformer 94

Yapp, M.E. 97, 143
young people, and modern fundamentalist
    movements 143

Zionist movement 84–5, 90
Zoroastrianism 4